Complete Turkish

The Absolute Course for Beginners

Ahmet Murat TAŞER, PhD

2021

Complete Turkish
The Absolute Course for Beginners

Ahmet Murat TAŞER, PhD

1. Edition / 2021

ISBN

9798535929897

PAGE & COVER DESIGN by

Şeref Ali TAŞER

IMPRINT: INDEPENDENTLY PUBLISHED

THANKS TO

My family, standing by me at every step ... (And this includes the design and the occasional cups of coffee for encouragement)

And especially my daughter for allowing me to include some excerpts from her published novel of İpin Ucunu Kaçıran İnsanlar, ISBN: 978-605-7610-24-9 in this book.

BEFORE STARTING

This book has been prepared in order to meet the resource material need in Turkish learning. For this reason, I hope this book would be a reference to all who need.

Ahmet Murat TAŞER, PhD

With this new edition, this book is restructured in order to present a more pleasant studying experience to Turkish learners. In addition, all dialogues at the beginning of the lessons and all following vocabulary are recorded by local speakers to aid the learning experience and develop your listening and pronunciation skills. Students will be guided for the audio material throughout the book.

To access the audio please click on the link below:

https://drive.google.com/drive/folders/1r-sumHOh_8VWxhhxvGlb8vEDck__Hlvw?usp=drive_link

or visit through the Qr code below:

Contents

Contents

In this unit you will find:

An authentic text from a published Turkish novel

With this unit, you will be able to:
Capture meaning from context with / without using a dictionary

Use the reported speech

Verb conjugations, declension tables for prepositions

INTRODUCTION

With this new edition, this book is restructured in order to present a more pleasant studying experience to Turkish learners. In addition, all dialogues at the beginning of the lessons and all following vocabulary are recorded by local speakers to aid the learning experience and develop your listening and pronunciation skills. Students will be guided for the audio material throughout the book.

To access the audio please click on the link below:

https://drive.google.com/drive/folders/1r-sumHOh_8VWxhhxvGlb8vEDck__Hlvw?usp=drive_link

or visit through the Qr code below:

This book is prepared for Turkish learners at the beginner level. This book not only teaches the general principles of the Turkish language, but also provides the students with the most common uses of the language. The grammar and vocabulary are carefully utilized to serve the students in participating in daily conversations of various contexts.

This book contains 15 regular units, an answer key, and glossaries for both Turkish and English. The units consist of Dialogues, Vocabulary, Grammar, and Exercise sections.

In the Dialogue part, which is the main section in each unit, learners will find a dialogue covering the chapter's grammar and vocabulary. The dialogues are constructed specifically to highlight the most general aspects of daily communication, ranging from greeting to shopping, and from travelling to visiting a doctor. In addition, the Turkish translation of the dialogues is given for the early units (the first 5 units).

All the dialogues are recorded by native speakers, which is crucial for improving listening and speaking skills with correct pronunciation.

Learners are expected to participate actively in the dialogues as characters and improve their reading and speaking skills.

The grammar sections detail the grammar presented in the dialogues and the vocabulary sections compile the words and expressions read in the dialogues. Learners will also enjoy a number of exercises through each unit, with an answer key at the end of the book.

The 16th ‑ 20th units, which have authentic reading texts from a published novel, are also added to the book to give the learner a glimpse of authentic Turkish reading. Here, guessing the meanings of unknown words from context is intended. This section also includes additional grammar points.

The Grammar Summary and Key to the Exercises are given at the end of the book

The book also has Turkish-English and English-Turkish glossaries containing all the words and expressions mentioned in the book.

Enjoy!

THE TURKISH LANGUAGE

The sentence order in Turkish is the opposite of English. This, at the beginning may be challenging to English speakers. In Turkish, the verb of the sentence goes to the end of the sentence. The verb also carries the tense information. In addition to that, both in written and spoken Turkish, the subject may not be used on many occasions. Regardless of the subject is used or not, the subject information is also carried by the verb of the sentence.

One uniqueness of Turkish is that there is no gender information for the nouns and pronouns. The gender is understood from the context.

ABBREVIATIONS

Abbreviations	Meaning
pl.	Plural
lit.	Literally
inf.	Infinitive form
m	Masculine
f	Feminine
e.g.	for example
i.e.	that is
etc.	and so on
NB	nota bene, mark well

THE TURKISH ALPHABET AND THE PRONOUNCIATION KEY

The Turkish letters, their names, and sounds are given in the following table:

Letter	Name	Sound	Letter	Name	Sound
a	a	as in "but"	m	me	as in "man"
b	be	as in "back"	n	ne	as in "name"
c	ce	as in "jump"	o	o	as in "toe"
ç	çe	as in "cheap"	ö	ö	as in "burst"
d	de	as in "dumb"	p	pe	as in "pen"
e	e	as in "end"	r	re	as in "rock"
f	fe	as in "fat"	s	se	as in "sweet"
g	ge	as in "girl"	ş	şe	as in "sheep"
ğ	yumuşak g*	as in "drought"	t	te	as in "ten"
h	he	as in "high"	u	u	as in "you"
ı	ı	as in "tablet"	ü	ü	as in "cute"
i	i	as in "in"	v	ve	as in "vise"
j	je	as in "treasure"	y	ye	as in "you"
k	ke	as in "key"	z	ze	as in "zero"
l	le	as in "long"			

Note: The letter "ğ" has no sound by itself. It is used to lenghten and soften the sound of the previous letter. So, it cannot be placed in front of a word.

In addition, the symbol "^" is also put over the vowels to lenghten and soften the sound of the vowel, e.g. "â".

Türk Alfabesi –the Turkish Alphabet

Repeat the letters you hear.

Türkçe sesleri tanıma – familiarization to the Turkish sounds

Repeat the words you hear.

arı	masa
bisiklet	nazik
cüzdan	oyuncak
çay	öğretmen
dondurma	pamuk
ekmek	reçel
fener	saat
gümüş	şehir
yağmur	tavşan
hafta	ucuz
ıhlamur	ütü
ipek	vergi
Jale	yaprak
kaşık	zengin
leylek	

Unit One: Hoşgeldiniz!

Welcome!

With this unit, you will be able to:
• Identify yourself – your name, nationality, and occupation • Introduce someone • Greet people • Ask simple questions • Give affirmative and negative answers • Use the sentence order and vowel harmony

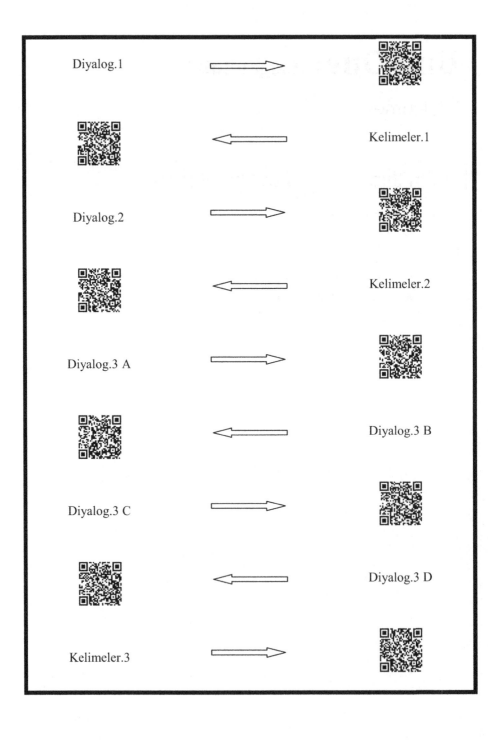

Bölüm 1
Part 1

Dialogue 1

Esenboğa Havaalanı'nda At the Esenboğa Airport

İbrahim and Michelle Korkmaz wanted to visit Türkiye for vacation. They live in London and work in the same high school. They are both teachers. They planned to travel all around Türkiye during their visit. They wanted to start their travel from Ankara, the capital.

They have just arrived at the Esenboğa Airport in Ankara. They knew that someone would wait for them to take them to the hotel, but no one was waiting for them at the arrivals. After a short while, a young lady approached.

Serra:	Affedersiniz! Siz Bay ve Bayan Korkmaz mısınız? *Excuse me! Are you Mr. and Mrs. Korkmaz?*
İbrahim:	Evet. Ben İbrahim Korkmaz'ım. Ve bu eşim Michelle. *Yes. I'm İbrahim Korkmaz. And, this is my wife, Michelle.*
Serra:	Merhaba, Bay ve Bayan Korkmaz. Türkiye'ye hoş geldiniz! *Hello, Mr. and Mrs. Korkmaz. Welcome to Türkiye!*
Michelle:	Çok teşekkürler! *Thanks a lot!*
Serra:	Benim ismim Serra. Oteldenim. *My name is Serra. I'm from the hotel.*
İbrahim:	Tanıştığımıza memnun oldum, Serra! *Nice to meet you, Serra!*
Serra:	Ben de memnun oldum! *Nice to meet you, too!*

Vocabulary

bay	*Mr.*	**çok**	*a lot, very*
adam	*man*	**eşim**	*my spouse*
bayan	*Mrs., Ms.*	**evet**	*yes*
ben	*I*	**kadın**	*woman*
bu	*this (is)*	**otel**	*hotel*
çocuk	*child, boy or girl*	**ve**	*and*

Affedersiniz!	*Excuse me!*
Merhaba!	*Hello!*
Türkiye'ye hoş geldiniz!	*Welcome to Türkiye!*
Çok teşekkürler!	*Thanks a lot!*
Tanıştığımıza memnun oldum!	*Nice to meet you!*
Ben de memnun oldum!	*Nice to meet you, too!*
Benim ismim ...	*My name is ...*
Oteldenim.	*I'm from the hotel.*

In the dialogue above, Serra approches İbrahim and Michelle at the airport. She starts the conversation by **Affedersiniz!**, *Excuse me!* and asks them whether they are the people she was to meet. İbrahim introduces his *wife Michelle* as **Bu eşim Michelle,** *This is my wife, Michelle.* Please note that **eş** actually means *spouse*, both *husband* and *wife,* but it is more preferred than **kocam**, *my husband* or **karım**, *my wife.* After confirmation, she introduces herself first, then greets and welcomes them.

Dialogue 2

In a minute, a young man comes running.

Talha: Merhaba! Günaydın!
Hello! Good morning!

İbrahim: Günaydın! Buyurun! Kimsiniz?
Good morning! Please! Who are you?

Talha: Adım Talha İlkbahar. Ben şoförüm. İlkbahar Otel'denim. Siz neredensiniz? Birleşik Krallık'tan mısınız?
My name is Talha İlkbahar. I'm the driver. I'm from the Hotel İlkbahar. Where are you from? Are you from the United Kingdom?

İbrahim: Evet. Birleşik Krallık'tanız. Eşim İngiliz, ama ben Türküm.
Yes. We're from the United Kingdom. My wife is English, but I'm Turkish.

Talha: Tamam! Siz de İbrahim Korkmaz Bey ve Michelle Korkmaz Hanım'sınız.
Alright! And, you are Mr. İbrahim Korkmaz and Mrs. Michelle Korkmaz.

İbrahim: Doğru. Ben İbrahim Korkmaz'ım. Ve bu da eşim Michelle.
Right! I'm İbrahim Korkmaz. And, this is my wife Michelle.

Talha: Memnun oldum, İbrahim Bey ve Michelle Hanım. Hoş geldiniz!
Nice to meet you, Mr. and Mrs. Korkmaz. Welcome.

İbrahim: Hoş bulduk! Pekâlâ! Erkenci miyiz?
Thanks! Alright! Are we early?

Talha:	Hayır. Erkenci değilsiniz.
	No. You are not early.
Serra:	Evet, onlar tam zamanında, fakat sen geç kaldın.
	Yes, they are just on time, but you are late!
Talha:	Bu Serra. Benim kız kardeşim, ve o da otelden. Üzgünüm, ben geç kaldım.
	This is (She's) Serra. She is my sister, and she's from the hotel, too. I'm sorry, I'm late.
Serra:	Evet, lütfen kusura bakmayın, biz geç kaldık!
	Yes, please excuse us, we are late!
İbrahim:	Sorun değil.
	No problem.

1. Were Serra and Talha on time?
2. Did Talha know Serra before?

~im; possessive marker

Vocabulary

ama	*but*	**hayır**	*no*
benim	*my*	**kız kardeş**	*sister*
bey	*Mr.*	**o**	*he or she*
biz	*we*	**onlar**	*they*
de /da	*also, too*	**sen**	*you*
erkenci	*early*	**siz**	*you (pl)*
fakat	*but*	**şoför**	*driver*
geç	*late*	**zamanında**	*on time*
hanım	*Mrs., Ms.*		

(Benim) Adım ...	*My name is ...*
(Sen) Kimsin?	*Who are you?*
(Siz) Kimsiniz?	*Who are you (pl)?*
Birleşik Krallık'tan mısınız?	*Are you from the United Kingdom?*
Birleşik Krallık'tanım.	*I'm from the United Kingdom.*
Bu kim?	*Who is he/she?*
Buyurun!	*Welcome!, Please!, Come in!, Tell me!, Go on, I'm up to you!, or After you!*
Doğru!	*Right!, Correct!*
Erkenci miyiz?	*Are we early?*

Eşim İngiliz.	*My wife / husband is English.*
Geç kaldık.	*We're late?*
Günaydın!	*Good morning!*
Hoş bulduk!	*Thank you! (In response to Hoş geldiniz!)*
Kusura bakmayın!	*Excuse me!, Excuse us!*
Lütfen!	*Please!*
Memnun oldum!	*Nice to meet you!*
Neredensiniz?	*Where are you from?*
Pekâlâ!	*Well!*
Sorun değil!	*No problem!*
tam zamanında	*just in time*
Tamam!	*Alright!, Okay!*
Üzgünüm!	*I'm sorry*

In the second dialogue, Talha enters the conversation, introduces himself and welcomes them. He also introduces his sister, Serra. While he introduces himself and Serra, he first tells the names, and then mentions that they are from the hotel. He says **Oteldenim**, *I'm from the hotel*, and **O da otelden**, *She's from the hotel, too*. We see the same word **da**, *too, also*, in **Bu da eşim Michelle**, *And this is my wife Michelle*. We also see **de**, in the same meaning in **Ben de memnun oldum**, *Nice to meet you, too*. Here, the spelling changes depending on the preceding vowel. It's called the vowel harmony and it has many different types and usages in Turkish. Each vowel harmony will be studied in detail when necessary. Here, let's make a start with it.

When the preceding vowel is one of **a**, **o**, **u**, or, **ı**, the word is spelled as **da**. In case that the preceding vowel is one of **e**, **ö**, **ü**, or, **i**, it is spelled as **de**. In other words,

Last vowel of the preceding word	a,ı, o, u	e,i, ö, ü
the ending (suffix) da / de	da	de

Examples:

Ben de	*I also*
Bu da	*He / She also*
İbrahim de	*İbrahim also*
Serra da	*Serra also*

Bölüm 2
Part 2

addressing and introducing people

In Turkish addressing people is possible by following two ways: By using the last or by using the first names.

First, when using the last names, **Bay** and **Bayan** can be used in place of Mr. and Mrs. in English. e.g. **Bay Korkmaz** for *Mr. Korkmaz* and **Bayan Korkmaz** for *Mrs. Korkmaz*.

Unlike English, in Turkish introductions are done by using the first names with the titles according to the genders, e.g. **İbrahim Bey** instead of *Mr. Korkmaz* and **Michelle Hanım** instead of *Mrs. Korkmaz*.

This is the second way. Even though the both are accepted, second way, using the first names, is a lot more common in daily language.

While introducing someone, simply **bu**, *this is,* and the name is enough, e.g. **Bu Michelle**, *This is Michelle*, or **Bu şoför**, *This is the driver*. Or, **Bu adam şoför**, *This man is the driver, and* **Bu kadın şoför**, *This woman is the driver*. However when possession is explained, then the ending (suffix) of possession is necessary at the end, e.g. **Bu eşim**, *This is my wife*, **Bu şoförüm**, *This is my driver*, or **Bu kız kardeşim**, *This is my sister*. Here the ending -**m** is for possession meaning *my* and goes to the end of the word. Note that **benim** can also be used in the following forms, e.g. **Bu benim eşim**, *This is my wife*, **Bu benim şoförüm**, *This is my driver*, or **Bu benim kız kardeşim**, *This is my sister*.

The vowel preceding the letter **m** can be **i, ı, u,** or **ü** depending on the last vowel of the modified (preceding) noun, which is called the vowel harmony. (Expressing possession will be studied in detail in Unit 2.)

The ending **–m** is also used while introducing oneself, but in this context, comes to mean *I'm*, e.g. **Ben İbrahim Korkmaz'ım**, *I'm İbrahim Korkmaz,* **Ben şoförüm**, *I'm the driver,* or **Ben Türküm**, *I'm Turkish*. Here again, the vowel preceding the ending **–m** depends on the preceding vowel. (The details for the vowel change and personal pronouns and endings will be studied in detail in this unit.)

Note that, while using proper names, an apostrophe is necessary before the ending, e.g. **Ben İbrahim Korkmaz'ım**, *I'm İbrahim Korkmaz*, but not necessary with others, e.g. **Ben şoförüm**, *I'm the driver*.

When talking to someone about himself/herself, or asking a question to someone, **Siz .....-misiniz?**, *Are you .....?* or **Siz ....-siniz.**, *You are .....* is used. Here the pronoun **Siz** means *plural You*, and the ending at the end -**siniz** means *you are (pl)*. The other ending **–mi?** is used to form a question just like *are you?*. Please note that, using the pronoun **Siz,** *you (pl)* at the beginning of the sentence is optional since the ending **–siniz** already bears the meaning, e.g. **(Siz) İngilizsiniz.**, *You are English*, or **(Siz) İngiliz misiniz?**, *Are you English?*

NB When Turks talk to someone, they prefer using the second plural pronouns or endings even if there is only one person. It is regarded as a way of expressing respect and it is therefore used in formal situations. For example, İbrahim asks Talha who he is, but in the plural form. He asks **(Siz) Kimsiniz?**, *Who are you (pl)?*, instead of asking **(Sen) Kimsin?**, *Who are you (singular)?*, even if he knows that he is alone. Here **sen** and the ending **–sin** are used for the second singular person. (The personal pronouns and endings will be studied in detail in this unit.)

In Türkiye, conversations with strangers start with plurals, however as the conversation (and the relationship) develops, either one side of the conversation may propose the other to address him or herself by using singular pronoun. So, when you are introduced to someone, first address him or her with plurals. As the time passes either one of you may propose to use the singular form..

Finally, the words **adım** and **ismim** mean the same, *my name*. For example, **(Benim) Adım Talha** or **(Benim) İsmim Talha**, *My name is Talha*. Here, the word **benim** means *my* but it's optional to use it in the sentence since the ending **-m** carries the meaning of the person **ben**, *I*.

exercise 1

Answer the question according to the given clues below. Make four sentences for each question.

Example:

Siz kimsiniz? *(Who are you?)*   **Ben Talha'yım.** *(I'm Talha.)*

Bu kim? *(Who is he / she?)*   **Bu Talha.** *(He's Talha.)*

Siz kimsiniz?   **Ben**

1. İbrahim Korkmaz.....................   3. otelden ....

2. şoför..................................   4. Türk..................................

Bu kim?   **Bu**

1. Michelle.............................   3. Serra................................

2. şoför.................................   4. İbrahim Korkmaz.................

greetings

Several greeting phrases are given in the dialogues above. The first one is **Merhaba!**, *Hello!* which can be used in formal and informal situations regardless of the time of the day. The second is **Günaydın!** meaning *Good morning!* You can also use **İyi akşamlar!** for *Good evening!*, **İyi geceler!** for *Good night!*, and **İyi günler!** for *Have a good day!* when starting a conversation according to the time of the day.

The response should be the same for the greeting phrases given above. However, in response to **Hoş geldiniz!**, *Welcome!* **Hoş bulduk!**, lit. *We found you well!* should be said, or simply thanking is possible. But replying **Hoş geldiniz!** with **Hoş geldiniz!** is not appropriate.

And the phrase **Buyurun!** or **Buyur!** which can be translated into English to have a number of meanings such as *Welcome!, Please!, Come in!, Tell me!, Go on, I'm up to you!*, or *After you!*, is another unique greeting phrase in Turkish. The better is to understand the meaning from the context.

When introduced, it's possible to respond by saying **Tanıştığımıza memnun oldum!**, or simply **Memnun oldum!**. Both phrases means *Nice to meet you!* In response, **Ben de memnun oldum!**, *Nice to meet you, too!* is used commonly. However, it's also possible to say the same greeting sentence back.

apologizing

Both Serra and Talha apologize for being late. Serra uses the structure of **Kusura bakmayın!**, *Excuse me!*, or *Excuse us!*, and Talha says **Üzgünüm!**, *I'm sorry!* Both of the apologies mean the same and can be used in the same way in daily language.

Bölüm 3
Part 3

Dialogue 3

Kısa konuşmalar Short dialogues

Practice these short dialogues about greeting and introducing people.

A.

Yasemin:	Günaydın! *Good morning!*
Okan:	Günaydın! *Good morning!*
Yasemin:	Benim adım Yasemin. Senin adın ne? *My name is Yasemin. What's your name?*
Okan:	Memnun oldum, Yasemin. Benim adım Okan. *Nice to meet you, Yasemin. My name is Okan.*
Yasemin:	Memnun oldum, Okan. *Nice to meet you, Okan.*
Okan:	Sen Kanadalı mısın? *Are you Canadian?*
Yasemin:	Evet, ben Kanadalıyım. *Yes, I'm Canadian.*
Okan:	Ne iş yapıyorsun? *What job do you do?*
Yasemin:	Ben bir mühendisim. *I'm an engineer.*

B.

Serra:	Merhaba! Ben Serra! Ya sen? *Hello! I'm Serra! You?*
Jake:	Merhaba, Serra! Ben Jake. *Hello Serra! I'm Jack.*
Serra:	Memnun oldum. *Nice to meet you.*
Jake:	Ben de memnun oldum. *Nice to meet you, too.*
Serra:	Nerelisin? *Where are you from?*
Jake:	Ben Amerikalıyım. Sen? *I'm American. You?*

Serra:	Türküm. Ben burada öğrenciyim. Ya sen? *I'm Turkish. I'm a student here. What about you?*
Jake:	Ben de burada öğrenciyim. *I'm a student here, too.*

C.

John:	İyi günler Michelle! Bu Jake. *Good day Michelle! This is Jake.*
Michelle:	Merhaba, Jake! Memnun oldum. Ben İngilizim. Ben burada bir öğretmenim. *Hello Jake! Nice to meet you. I'm English. I'm a teacher here.*
Jake:	Ben de memnun oldum. *Nice to meet you, too.*
Michelle:	Sen nerelisin? *Where are you from?*
Jake:	Ben Almanım. *I'm German.*
Michelle:	Sen de öğretmen misin? *Are you a teacher, too?*
Jake:	Hayır, değilim. *No, I'm not.*

D.

Eymen:	İyi günler, kardeşim! Onun adı ne? *Good day, brother! What's her name?*
Talha:	Onun adı Michelle. *Her name is Michelle.*
Michelle:	Ben Michelle. Senin adın ne? *I'm Michelle. What's your name?*
Eymen:	Ben de Eymen. *And my name is Eymen.*
Michelle:	Memnun oldum, Eymen. *Nice to meet you, Eymen.*
Eymen:	Ben de memnun oldum, Michelle. *Nice to meet you, too, Michelle.*
Michelle:	Peki, nasılsın Eymen? *Well, how are you Eymen?*
Eymen:	İyiyim. Sen nasılsın? *I'm fine. How are you?*
Michelle:	Ben de iyiyim. Teşekkürler. *I'm fine, too. Thanks.*

Vocabulary

Alman	German	lezzetli	delicious
Amerikalı	American	mühendis	engineer
bir	a, one	muhasebeci	accountant
bugün	today	ne?	what?
burada	here	öğrenci	student
erkek kardeş	brother	öğretmen	teacher
ev hanımı	housewife	onun	his/her
İngiliz	English	oyuncu	actor/actress
iş	job, work	Rus	Russian
iş insanı	businessman/ businesswoman	yemek	food, meal
iyi	fine	yemek	to eat
Kanadalı	Canadian		

İyiyim.	I'm fine.
Nasılsın?	How are you?
Ne iş yapıyorsun?	What do you do (for a living)? (lit. What job do you do?)
Nerelisin?	Where are you from?
Onun adı ...	His/her name is ...
Onun adı ne?	What's his/her name?
Peki!	Well, alright!
Sen?	You? / What about you?
Senin adın ne?	What's your name?
Ya sen?	And you? / What about you?

More Professions

aşçı	cook
doktor	doctor
garson	waiter
hemşire	nurse
hostes	hostess
iş insanı	businessman or businesswoman
kasap	butcher

manav	green grocer
mühendis	engineer
öğretmen	teacher
pilot	pilot
satıcı	seller
sekreter	secretary
şarkıcı	singer
şef	chef
temizlikçi	cleaner
terzi	tailor
tezgâhtar	cashier
türkücü	singer (folkloric)
yönetici	manager

In these short dialogues given above, we see more of the ways of greeting and introduction. Apart from that, there are some question words such as **Ne?**, *What?* and **Nasıl?**, *How?*, We also encounter another question in the present tense, **Ne iş yapıyorsun?**, *What job do you do?*, for asking the occupation of others. For now, we will not get into detail but use these structures just to get more into the first conversations right after the introduction.

Also note that **yemek** means *food* or *meal*. But, it is a verb, too. Then the meaning is *to eat*.

Bölüm 4
Part 4

dilbilgisi grammar

sentence order

The sentence order in Turkish is opposite of that in English, starting with a subject and ending with a verb.

absence of 'to be'

In Turkish, the verb "to be" is not used in present tense. Instead it is substituted by a personal suffix or ending at the end. There's a special ending for each person.

NB In Turkish, there is no gender information in the personal pronouns, which means there is no diffrerence between he, she, or it. And the third singular person **o**, *he, she, it*, has no ending or suffix.

Michelle İngiliz.	=	**O İngiliz.**	
Michelle is English.	=	*She is English.*	
Michael İngiliz.	=	**O İngiliz.**	
Michael is English.	=	*He is English.*	

Below are given the special endings for each person:

(Ben)	-im	*I am*
(Sen)	-sin	*You are*
(O)	-	*He/She is*
(Biz)	-iz	*We are*
(Siz)	-siniz	*You are*
(Onlar)	-ler/lar	*They are*

NB In Turkish, personal pronouns (**ben, sen, o, biz, siz, onlar**) do not have to be used in the sentences. So, either to use them or not is optional. (It's why they're in brackets.) However, it is important to use them when we want to clear vagueness.

Examples:

Ben İngilizim.	=	**İngilizim.**	*I'm English.*
Sen İngilizsin.	=	**İngilizsin.**	*You're English.*
O İngiliz.	=	**İngiliz.**	*He/She's English.*
Biz İngiliziz.	=	**İngiliziz.**	*We're English.*

Siz İngilizsiniz.	=	**İngilizsiniz.**	*You're English.*
Onlar İngilizler.	=	**İngilizler.**	*They're English.*

Please note that there are two ending possibilities with **onlar,** *they.* It's also possible to use it without **-ler/lar** as in **Onlar İngiliz,** *They're English.* But in this case, the personal pronoun **onlar** must be used in the sentence. It's not optional.

In other words;

(Onlar) İngilizler.	*They're English.*
Onlar İngiliz.	*They're English.*

Examples:

Ben İbrahim Korkmaz'ım.	*I'm İbrahim Korkmaz.*
Michelle İngiliz.	*Michelle is British.*
İbrahim Türk.	*İbrahim is Turkish.*
Talha erkenci.	*Talha is early.*
Üzgünüm.	*I'm sorry.*
Serra otelden.	*Serra is from the hotel.*

vowel harmony

The vowels in the previous special endings table may change according to the last vowel in the preceding word. Here, there's another usage of vowel harmony. The details given below apply the previous special endings table.

1. The vowel "i" in the ending depends on the preceding vowel.

the preceding vowel	the suffix or ending
a, ı	**-ım, sın, ız, sınız** *I'm, You're, We're, You're*
e, i	**-im, sin, iz, siniz** *I'm, You're, We're, You're*
o, u	**-um, sun, uz, sunuz** *I'm, You're, We're, You're*
ö, ü	**-üm, sün, üz, sünüz** *I'm, You're, We're, You're*

The vowels in the special endings and the preceding vowels are underlined. Notice the vowel change in the endings depending on the last vowel in the preceding word.

Examples:

İngiliz̲im, İngiliz̲sin, İngiliz̲iz, İngiliz̲siniz
I'm English, You're English, We're English, You're English

Türküm, Türksün, Türküz, Türksünüz
I'm Turkish, You're Turkish, We're Turkish, You're Turkish

Almanım, Almansın, Almanız, Almansınız
I'm German, You're German, We're German, You're German

Rusum, Russun, Rusuz, Russunuz
I'm Russian, You're Russian, We're Russian, You're Russian

2. The endings '-ler' or 'lar' in the table given above, depend on the preceding vowel.

Last vowel of the preceding word	a, ı, o, u	e, i, ö, ü
the ending –ler -lar	**-lar**	**-ler**

The vowels in the special endings and the preceding vowels are underlined. Notice the vowel change in the endings depending on the last vowel in the preceding word.

Examples:

İngiliz + ler	**İngilizler**	*English people*
Türk + ler	**Türkler**	*Turkish people*
Öğrenci + ler	**Öğrenciler**	*Students*
Alman + lar	**Almanlar**	*German people*
Kanadalı + lar	**Kanadalılar**	*Canadian people*
Oyuncu + lar	**Oyuncular**	*Actors or actresses*

exercise 2

Add the correct ending to the given word according to persons.

Pay attention to the last vowel in the word and change the vowel in the ending accordingly. The last vowel of the word and the vowel in the ending are underlined for the example.

Example: **mühendis** *(engineer)*

Ben mühendisim.	*I'm an engineer.*
Sen mühendissin.	*You're an engineer.*
O mühendis.	*He/She's an engineer.*
Biz mühendisiz.	*We're engineers.*
Siz mühendissiniz.	*You're engineers.*
Onlar mühendis/Mühendisler.	*They're engineers.*

şoför, Türk, öğretmen, Alman, Rus

Ben .... Biz ....

Sen .... Siz ....

O .... Onlar ....

the ending (suffix) connector 'y'

The letter "y" is necessary only with **Ben**, *I'm* and **Biz**, *We're* <u>when the preceding word ends with a vowel</u>. Again pay attention to the vowel change as mentioned above.

(Ben)	-(y)im	I am
(Biz)	-(y)iz	We are

Examples:

Ben muhasebeciyim.   **Biz muhasebeciyiz.**
I'm an accountant.   *We're accountants.*

Ben erkenciyim.   **Biz erkenciyiz.**
I'm early.   *We're early.*

exercise 3

Add the correct ending to the given word according to persons.

Example: **öğrenci** *(student)*

Ben öğrenciyim.   *I'm a student.*
Biz öğrenciyiz.   *We're students.*

muhasebeci, öğrenci, oyuncu, iş insanı, ev hanımı, Kanadalı

Ben .... Biz ....

endings with proper names

As mentioned earlier, when it is necessary to add endings to proper names, it's required to put an apostrophe before the ending.

Examples:

Ben Serra'yım.	*I'm Serra.*
Ben Michelle'im.	*I'm Michelle.*
Ben İbrahim Korkmaz'ım.	*I'm İbrahim Korkmaz.*

questions

As seen in the dialogues above, the ending (suffix) **mi?** is put at the end of a sentence separately. Then the personal endings are added accordingly. The question ending **mi?** is a 4 way vowel harmony, meaning **mi?** can change to: **mi? / mı? / mu? / mü?**, depending on the preceding vowel.

Last vowel of the preceding word	a,ı	e,i	o,u	ö,ü
the ending mi? (x4)	mı?	mi?	mu?	mü?

To put it differently, it's possible to change a positive sentence to a question in three steps:

Example sentence:

Siz İngilizsiniz.	*You're English.*

1. First, separate the ending you put at the end to form a sentence.

Siz İngiliz **siniz.**	*You're English.*

2. Then, put the question ending mi? right before the personal ending. Remember that the vowel may change depending on the preceding vowel. (It's underlined in the example.)

Siz İngiliz <u>**mi**</u>**siniz.**	*Are you English.*

3. Finally, put a question mark "?" at the end.

Siz İngiliz misiniz<u>?</u>	*Are you English?*

Examples:

Ben muhasebeci miyim?	*Am I an accountant?*
Sen oyuncu musun?	*Are you an actor/actress?*
Serra öğrenci mi?	*Is Serra a student?*
Biz şoför müyüz?	*Are we drivers?*
Siz İngiliz misiniz?	*Are you English?*
Onlar Rus mu?	*Are they Russian?*

Please note that even if there are two ending possibilities with **onlar**, *they* in positive sentences, only one is accepted in the questions.

In other words;

(Correct)	**Onlar Rus mu?**	*Are they Russian?*
(Incorrect)	**Onlar Ruslar mı?**	

değil

Değil is used to make negative "to be" sentences. It's placed at the end of a sentence. Personal endings are also added to **Değil**.

Below are given the special endings for each person:

(Ben)	değilim	*I'm not*
(Sen)	değilsin	*You're not*
(O)	değil	*He/She is not*
(Biz)	değiliz	*We're not*
(Siz)	değilsiniz	*You're not*
(Onlar)	değiller	*They're not*

NB In Turkish, personal pronouns (**ben, sen, o, biz, siz, onlar**) do not have to be used in the sentences. So, either to use them or not is optional. (It's why they're in brackets.) However, it is important to use them when we want to clear vagueness.

Examples:

Ben oteldenim.
I'm from the hotel.

Ben otelden değilim.
I'm not from the hotel.

Serra otelden.
Serra is from the hotel.

Serra otelden değil.
Serra isn't from the hotel.

Bugün yemek lezzetli.
The food is delicious today.

Bugün yemek lezzetli değil.
The food isn't delicious today.

Michelle İngiltere'den.
Michelle's from England.

Michelle İngiltere'den değil.
Michelle's not from England.

Siz erkencisiniz.
You're early. (pl)

Siz erkenci değilsiniz.
You're not early. (pl)

Sen İngilizsin.
You're English.

Sen İngiliz değilsin.
You're not English.

Onlar Türk.
They're Turkish

Onlar Türk değiller / değil.
They're not Turkish.

Please note that there are two ending possibilities with **onlar,** *they* as mentioned above. Here, it's possible to use both **değil** and **değiller.**

But when using with **değil**, the personal pronoun **onlar** must be used in the sentence. It's not optional.

In other words;

Onlar Türk./ (Onlar) Türkler.   *They're Turkish.*
Onlar Türk değil.   *They're not Turkish.*
(Onlar) Türk değiller.   *They're not Turkish.*

Additionally, it's possible to make short answers by using only the **değil** + ending.

Sen otelden misin?
Are you from the hotel?

Değil<u>im</u>.
I'm not.

Serra otelden mi?
Is Serra from the hotel?

Değil.
She's not.

Michelle İngiltere'den mi?
Is Michelle from England?

Değil.
She's not.

Siz erkenci misiniz?
Are you early? (pl)

Değil<u>iz</u>.
We're not.

Sen İngiliz misin?
Are you English?

Değil<u>im</u>.
I'm not.

Note that for **onlar,** *they*, the short answer is only possible with **değiller.**

Examples:

Onlar Türk mü?
Are they Turkish?

Değil<u>ler</u>. (not "değil")
They're not.

Onlar erkenci mi?
Are they early?

Değil<u>ler</u>. (not "değil")
They're not.

exercise 4

Give negative answers to the questions given. Use **değil + ending** in your answers. Answer the questions as if in a conversation.

Example: **Sen Talha mısın?**   *Are you Talha?*
Hayır, Ben Talha değilim.   *No, I'm not.*

Siz şoför müsünüz?   **Hayır,** ....

Sen öğrenci misin?   **Hayır,** ....

Biz erkenci miyiz?   **Hayır,** ....

İbrahim Rus mu?   **Hayır,** ....

Ben öğretmen miyim?   **Hayır,** ....

Onlar Alman mı?   **Hayır,** ....

questions with "değil"

It's also possible to make questions with **Değil**.

To form a question with **değil**, the question word **mi?** is used. It's again placed separately. Then the personal endings are added accordingly. In this case, the question ending **mi?** remains the same for each person, since the preceding word **değil** remains the same for each person.

Below are given the special endings for each person:

(Ben)	değil miyim?	*Aren't I?*
(Sen)	değil misin?	*Are you not?*
(O)	değil mi?	*Is he/she not?*
(Biz)	değil miyiz?	*Are we not?*
(Siz)	değil misiniz?	*Are you not?*
(Onlar)	değiller mi?	*Are they not?*

Examples:

Ben muhasebeci değil miyim?   *Aren't I an accountant?*

Sen oyuncu değil misin?   *Aren't you an actor/actress?*

Serra öğrenci değil mi?   *Isn't Serra a student?*

Siz İngiliz değil misiniz?   *Aren't you English?*

Biz şoför değil miyiz?   *Aren't we drivers?*

Onlar Rus değil mi / değiller mi?   *Aren't they Russian?*

Please note that there are two ending possibilities with **onlar,** *they* as mentioned above. Here, it's possible to use both **değil mi?** and **değiller mi?**

But when using with **değil mi?**, the word **onlar** must be used in the sentence. It's not optional.

In other words;

(Onlar) Rus değiller mi? *Aren't they Russian?*

Onlar Rus değil mi? *Aren't they Russian?*

exercise 5

Change the questions to negative questions. Use **değil mi + ending?** in your answers. Remember there are two options for the last question with **onlar.**

Example:

Sen Talha mısın? *Are you Talha?* Sen Talha değil *t mısın?*

Sen Talha değil misin? *Aren't you Talha?*

Siz şoför müsünüz? Siz şoför değil misiniz?

Sen öğrenci misin? Sen öğrenci değil misin?

Biz erkenci miyiz? Biz erkenci değil miyiz?

İbrahim Rus mu? İbrahim Rus değil mi?

Ben öğretmen miyim? Ben öğretmen değil miyim?

Onlar Alman mı? Onlar Alman değil mi?

Unit Two: Otelimiz merkezde!

Our hotel is at the centre!

With this unit, you will be able to:

- Talk about people and places
- Express ideas and plans
- Use a, an
- Use defining adjectives
- Use plurals
- Express possession
- Use "there is / are", "there isn't / there aren't", and "is there? / are there?"

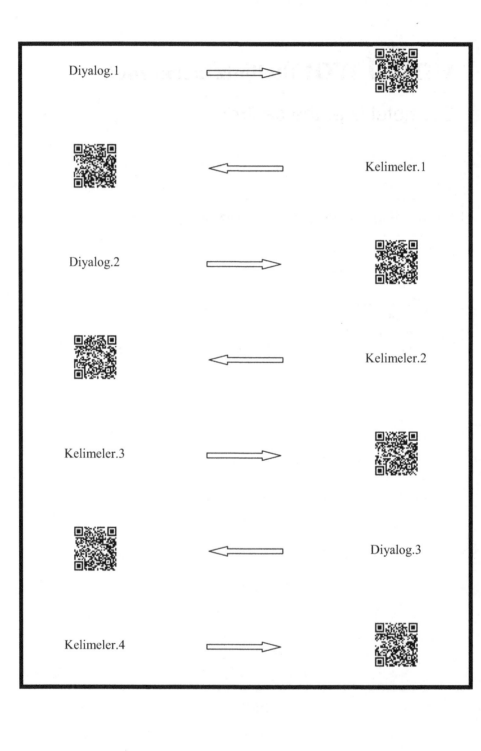

Bölüm 1
Part 1

Dialogue 1

otel nerede? where is the hotel?

Talha and Serra pick İbrahim and Michelle Korkmaz up from the arrivals. While they are leaving the airport, İbrahim starts a conversation about the hotel's location.

İbrahim: **Talha, sen ve Serra birliktesiniz. Başka biri var mı?**
Talha, you and Serra are together. Is there someone else?

Talha: **Hayır, sadece Serra ve ben. Başka biri yok.**
No, only Serra and I. There isn't anyone else.

İbrahim: **Yol uzun mu peki? Otel nerede?**
Well, is the road long? Where is the hotel?

Serra: **Otelimiz merkezde, şehrin merkezinde. Tam Kızılay Meydanı'nda.**
Our hotel is at the centre, in the centre of the city. Right at the Kızılay Square.

İbrahim: **Yani otel merkezî. Şehrin ortasında. Ortada ve her yere yakın.**
So, the hotel is central. In the middle of the city. In the middle and close to everywhere.

Serra: **Evet, otel otobüs ve metro duraklarına da yakın. Aynı zamanda, otelin taksisi de var.**
Yes, the hotel is close to the bus and metro stops, too. At the same time, the hotel also has a taxi.

Michelle: **Çok güzel. Otelin lokantası da var mı?**
Very nice. Does the hotel have a restaurant, too?

,Talha: **Evet, kesinlikle var. Otelin karşısında. Karşıda bir lokanta var.**
Yes,it absolutely does. At the opposite of the hotel. There is a restaurant at the opposite.

1. Is there anyone else apart from Serra and Talha?
2. Where is the hotel?

Vocabulary

başka	other, else	otelimiz	our hotel
biri	someone	otelin karşısında	at the opposite of the hotel
birlikte	together	otelin lokantası	the restaurant of the hotel
duraklarına	to the bus stops	otobüs	bus
güzel	nice, beautiful	sadece	only
her yere	to everywhere	şehrin merkezinde	in the centre of the city
karşıda	at the opposite	şehrin ortasında	in the middle of the city
Kızılay Meydanı	the Kızılay Square	tam	right at the
lokanta	restaurant	uzun	long
merkez	centre	var	there is / are
merkezî	central	yakın	close to
metro	metro, subway	yok	there isn't / aren't
ortada	in the middle	yol	road
Aynı zamanda		At the same time	
Kesinlikle!		Absolutely!	
Nerede?		Where?	
Yani		So	

In the dialogue above, İbrahim knows Serra and Talha are together. He also wants to know if there are any other people from the hotel. He asks **Başka biri var mı?**, Is *there anyone else?* Talha's response to the question is negative **yok**, *there isn't*. Then he asks about the location of the hotel they're going to. And they talk about the possibilities in the vicinity.

In the dialogue, there are several phrases about possession. They're **şehrin merkezi**, *the centre of the city*, **şehrin ortası**, *the middle of the city*, **otelin taksisi**, *the taxi of the hotel*, **otelin lokantası**, *the restaurant of the hotel*, and **otelin karşısı**, *the opposite of the hotel*.

The formation of the possessives will be studied in detail further in this unit.

Note that, there are also endings (suffixes) added to these phrases. They're the endings that show location, **-de / -da**, *at, in, or on*.
Remember **de / da** mentioned in Unit 1. They mean *too* or *also*. Also remember that they were written separately.

But, here the endings are different. They show location. Also note that they are written together with the words. Even if they will be studied in detail in Unit 6, let's make a start with them here.

Remember the vowel change of **de** / **da**, *too* or *also*, depending on the last vowel of the preceding word, mentioned in Unit 1. The same vowel harmony is also necessary for the endings that show location, **-de** / **-da**, *at, in, or on*.

Let's look at the vowel harmony table again.

Last vowel of the preceding word	a, ı, o, u	e, i, ö, ü
the ending -da / -de	-da	-de

In other words, when the preceding vowel is one of **a**, **o**, **u**, or, **ı**, the word is spelled as **-da**. In case that the preceding vowel is one of **e**, **ö**, **ü**, or, **i**, it is spelled as **-de**. Below, the last vowel and the vowel in the ending are underlined. Examples:

şehrin merkez<u>inde</u>	*at the centre of the city*
şehrin ortas<u>ında</u>	*in the middle of the city*
otelin karşıs<u>ında</u>	*at the opposite of the hotel*
Kızılay Meydan<u>ı'nda</u>	*at the Kızılay Square*

Additionally, you may have already noticed the letter **n** between the second words of a phrase and the endings. It's necessary <u>only</u> when the second word of a phrase ends with a vowel. Examples:

şehrin merkezi**nde**	*at the centre of the city*
merkez**de**	*at the centre*
şehrin ortası**nda**	*in the middle of the city*
orta**da**	*in the middle*
otelin karşısı**nda**	*at the opposite of the hotel*
karşı**da**	*at the opposite*

Dialogue 2

arabada in the car

İbrahim inquires about Talha's family.

İbrahim: Talha, başka kardeşin var mı?
                Talha, do you have any other sisters or brothers?

Talha: Evet, Eymen var. Küçük erkek kardeşim.
                Yes, there is Eymen. My little brother.

Michelle: O da otelde mi?
                Is he at the hotel, too?

Talha: Hayır, o ortaokulda öğrenci. Ayrıca, çok yaramaz ve çok
                akıllı.
                *No, he is a student in middle school. In addition, he is very naughty and
                very clever.*

Michelle: Çok genç! Peki çalışkan mı?
                Very young! Is he studious, too?

Serra: Pek değil. Ama başarılı.
                Not much. But he is successful.

Michelle: Ya annen ve baban?
                What about your mother and father?

Talha: Babam otel yöneticisi, ve annem muhasebeci ama aynı
                zamanda ev hanımı. Annem çok çalışkandır.
                *My father is the hotel manager, and my mother is an accountant but at the
                same time, she is a housewife. She is very hardworking.*

Serra: Michelle hanım, bir şey söylemek istiyorum.
                Ms. Michelle, I'd like to say something.

Michelle: Buyur Serra! Ben de cevap vermek isterim.
                Go on Serra. I also want to give an answer.

Serra: Türkçeyi çok akıcı ve güzel konuşuyorsunuz.
                You speak Turkish very fluently and well.

İbrahim: Evet, Michelle Türkçeyi çok güzel konuşuyor ve o aynı
                zamanda Fransızca ve Almancayı da güzel konuşur.
                *Yes, Michelle speaks Turkish very well and at the same time, she speaks
                French and German well, too.*

---

1. How many brothers and sisters does Talha have?
2. How many foreign languages does Michelle speak?

Vocabulary

Almanca	*German*	**isterim**	*I want*
akıllı	*clever*	**istiyorum**	*I want*
anne	*mother*	**kardeş**	*brother or sister*
baba	*father*	**konuşur**	*he/she speaks*
başarılı	*successful*	**konuşuyorsunuz**	*you (pl) speak*
bir şey	*something*	**lisede**	*in high school*
cevap	*answer*	**okul**	*school*
cevap vermek	*to give an answer*	**ortaokulda**	*in middle school*
çalışkan	*studious, hardworking*	**otel yöneticisi**	*hotel manager*
çocuk	*child*	**otelde**	*at the hotel*
Fransızca	*French*	**pek**	*rather*
genç	*young*	**söylemek, anlatmak**	*to say, to tell*
güzel	*well, nice*	**Türkçe**	*Turkish*
ilkokulda	*in elementary school*	**üniversitede**	*in university*
İngilizce	*English*	**yaramaz**	*naughty*

Ayrıca	*In addition*
Buyur!	*Go on!*
istiyorum	*I want*
Pek değil!	*Not much!*
Ya?	*What about?*

In the second dialogue, İbrahim wants to learn more about Talha and his family. Talha and Serra talk about their family members. Here we see **çalışkan** is used for two different meanings, *studious* and *hardworking*.

In the dialogue above, we see several sentences formed with verbs other than the verb "to be". They are; **Bir şey söylemek istiyorum**, *I want to say something,* **Türkçeyi çok akıcı ve güzel konuşuyorsunuz**, *You speak Turkish very fluently and well,* **Michelle Türkçeyi çok güzel konuşuyor**, *Michelle speaks Turkish very well,* and **O aynı zamanda Fransızca ve Almancayı da güzel konuşur**, *At the same time, she speaks French and German well, too.*

As mentioned in Unit 1, the sentence order in Turkish is different from that of English. In Turkish, the verb goes to the end of the sentence.

Another thing is that these sentences are formed in the present tenses. For example, **istiyorum** and **isterim** are translated into English as *I want*. But, the former is in the present progressive tense and the latter is in the present tense. Similarly, the verbs **konuşuyor** and **konuşur**, both are translated the same, *he/she speaks*.

But, of course, there are differences between the tenses. While the present progressive is more suitable to express that an action is taking place at the moment of speech, the present tense is more suitable to express an action takes place repeatedly or regularly.

Even though there are more elements to be examined in the sentences mentioned above, the direct translation is given only for you to get familiar with the present tenses for now. Each element and structure will be studied in detail, step by step in the further units.

Bölüm 2
Part 2

dilbilgisi grammar
the ending (suffix) '-dir'

In the second dialogue, Talha talks about his mother and says **Annem çok çalışkandır**, *My mother is very hardworking*. Remember that in Turkish, the verb "to be" is not used in the present tense. So, it's also possible to say the same sentence as **Annem çok çalışkan**, *My mother is very hardworking*. And note that both sentences mean the same.

Here the ending **–dır**, *is / are* is used to make the sentence more formal, more official. This is necessary when speaking to the higher people, talking about important things, making a prediction, and giving a general idea or your view / opinion about something. And this type of usage is more common in the written language.

vowel harmony

The ending **-dır** is a 4 way vowel harmony, meaning **-dır** can change to **-dir** / **-dır** / **-dur** / **-dür**, depending on the preceding vowel.

Last vowel of the preceding word	a,ı	e,i	o,u	ö,ü
the ending -dır (x4)	-dır	-dir	-dur	-dür

The final vowel in the preceding word and the vowel in the ending are underlined in the examples:

Serra çalışkandır.   *Serra is studious/hardworking.*

Talha erkencidir.   *Talha is early.*

Can oyuncudur.   *Can is an actor.*

Talha şofördür.   *Talha is a driver.*

Onlar Almandır.   *They are German.*

exercise 1

Add the ending **–dir** (x4) to the second words of the sentences to make them more formal. Pay attention to the vowel change in the ending according to the preceding vowel. Note that both sentences mean the same.

Example: **Michelle İngiliz.**   **Michelle İngilizdir**.
              Michelle is English.   *Michelle is English.*

Hans Alman.   ....

Eymen akıllı   ....

Talha çalışkan.   ....

Otel yeni.   ....

İrem güzel.   ....

Serra başarılı.   ....

Otel merkezî.   ....

Ali oyuncu.   ....

the consonant harmony of the ending '-dir'

In Turkish, there is also a consonant harmony which has a number of different aspects and usages. We will be talking about it through the book when necessary. Here, we make a start with the ending '**–dir**'. The first letter of the ending changes into '**t**' when the preceding consonant, which is the last letter of the preceding word ends with one of the letters of '**f**', '**s**', '**t**', '**k**', '**ç**', '**ş**', '**h**', and '**p**'.

To put it differently;

Last letter of the preceding word	f	s	t	k	ç	ş	h	p
the ending –dir / -dır / -dur / -dür change to:	-tir / -tır / -tur / -tür							

Some examples are given below. The final consonants and the first letters of the endings are in bold and underlined. (The words given here were selected only to show the consonant changes. So, please pay attention to the consonant changes rather than the meaning.)

İbrahim Tür<u>kt</u>ür. (~~Türkdür~~)	*İbrahim is Turkish.*
Vladimir Ru<u>st</u>ur. (~~Rusdur~~)	*Vladimir is Russian.*
Bu bir sepe<u>tt</u>ir. (~~sepetdir~~)	*This is a basket.*
Michelle çok a<u>çt</u>ır. (~~açdır~~)	*Michelle is very hungry.*
Kamil kasa<u>pt</u>ır. (~~kasapdır~~)	*Kamil is a butcher.*
Serçe bir ku<u>şt</u>ur. (~~kuşdur~~)	*The sparrow is a bird.*
İbrahim ve Michelle bir çif<u>tt</u>ir. (~~çiftdir~~)	*İbrahim and Michelle are a couple.*
Sevgi bir şe<u>ft</u>ir. (~~şefdir~~)	*Sevgi is a chef.*

the ending '-dir' in questions

As studied in Unit 1, the ending **mi?** is put at the end of a sentence separately to form questions. Then, as mentioned in the first unit, the personal endings are added to the ending **mi?** accordingly. There's only one personal ending here, **-dir**.

So, the question ending and the ending will be **midir?**, *Is he/she/it?* or *Are they?* This ending is also a 4 way vowel harmony, meaning **midir?** can change to: **midir?** / **mıdır?** / **mudur?** / **müdür?**, depending on the preceding vowel.

Last vowel of the preceding word	a,ı	e,i	o,u	ö,ü
the ending midir? (x4)	mıdır?	midir?	mudur?	müdür?

To put it differently, it's possible to change a positive sentence to a question in three steps:

Example sentence:

O İngilizdir.   *He/She is English.*

1. First, separate the ending you put at the end.

İngil<u>i</u>z   d<u>i</u>r.   *He/She is English.*

2. Then, put the question ending **mi?** (x4) right before the ending **–dir** (x4). Remember that the vowel may change depending on the preceding vowel. (It's underlined in the example.)

O İngil<u>i</u>z   <u>mi</u>dir.   *Is he/she English.*

3. Finally, put a question mark "?" at the end.

O İngiliz midir?   *Is he/she English?*

Examples:

Serra çalışkan mıdır?	*Is Serra is studious/hardworking?*
Talha erkenci midir?	*Is Talha early?*
Ali oyuncu mudur?	*Ali is an actor.*
Talha şoför müdür?	*Is Talha a driver?*
Onlar Alman mıdır?	*Are they German?*

the ending '-dir' in negatives

As you learned in Unit 1, "to be" sentences are made negative by adding **değil**, *isn't* or *aren't*. Here the ending **–dir** can also be attached to the negation word **değil** as in **değildir**. When using the ending **–dir** with **değil**, you do not need to consider the vowel harmony for the ending since the preceding vowel is always the same.

Serra çalışkan değildir.	*Serra isn't studious.*
Talha erkenci değildir.	*Talha isn't early.*
Ali oyuncu değildir.	*Ali isn't an actor.*
Talha şoför değildir.	*Talha isn't a driver.*
Onlar Alman değildir.	*They aren't German.*

It is also possible to use **değil** in questions. Again, the question ending **midir?** will not change since the preceding vowel is always the same.

Serra çalışkan değil midir?	*Isn't Serra studious?*
Talha erkenci değil midir?	*Isn't Talha early?*
Ali oyuncu değil midir?	*Isn't Ali an actor?*
Talha şoför değil midir?	*Isn't Talha a driver?*
Onlar Alman değil midir?	*Aren't they German?*

exercise 2

Form questions with the words given. Then give positive and negative answers to the questions. Use **–dir** (x4) in your questions and answers. Pay attention to the vowel and consonant change in the questions and answers.

Example:

Michelle / İngiliz	*Michelle / English*
Michelle İngiliz midir?	*Is Michelle English?*
Evet, Michelle İngilizdir	*Yes, Michelle is English.*
Hayır, Michelle İngiliz değildir.	*No, Michelle isn't English.*

Charles / Kanadalı ....

....

İbrahim / Türk ....

....

John / genç ....

....

Michelle / ev hanımı ....

....

İrem / öğrenci ....

....

Otel / yeni ....

....

Ankara / büyük ....

absence of 'the'

As you may have already noticed, in Turkish, the definite article "the" is not used. Examples:

Şoför çalışkan.	*The driver is hardworking.*
Sen şoförsün.	*You are a driver. / You are the driver.*
Otel yeni.	*The hotel is new.*

Since, the definite article is not used, it is necessary to pay attention to the context to distinguish between the definite and indefinite nouns in this position. Since, for example, **şoför**, *driver* can be translated both as *the driver*, and *a driver*:

Ben şoförüm.	*I'm a driver.*
Ben şoförüm.	*I'm the driver.*

The above situation is not affected by whether the qualifying noun is the subject or object of the sentence. In other words, the situation is the same whether the qualifying noun is the subject or the object.

Serra <u>bir öğretmen</u>.	*Serra is <u>a teacher</u>. (object position)*
<u>Bir öğretmen</u> burada.	*<u>A teacher</u> is here. (subject position)*

'a', 'an'

bir is used instead of the indefinite article *a/an*. But, it's not a requirement as in English.

Examples:

Talha bir şoför.	*Talha is a driver.*
Talha şoför.	*Talha is a driver.*
Bir şoför burada.	*A driver is here.*
Serra bir öğrencidir.	*Serra is a student.*
Serra öğrencidir.	*Serra is a student.*

More on articles

Even though the definite article "**the**" is not used, it is understood and translated as "**the**" <u>when the defined noun is in the subject position</u>, or <u>used in a complement</u>. Read the examples:

Serra <u>bir öğretmen</u>.	*Serra is <u>a teacher</u>. (object position)*
Serra <u>öğretmen</u>.	*Serra is a/<u>the teacher</u>. (object position)*
<u>Bir öğretmen</u> burada.	*<u>A teacher</u> is here. (subject position)*
<u>Öğretmen</u> burada.	*<u>The teacher</u> is here. (subject position)*

adjectives

Adjectives in Turkish are used to modify nouns as in English. They modify nouns in a number of ways such as showing possession, quantity, quality, degree, etc. Below are listed some adjectives with their opposites. Note that you have already learned some of them in the previous dialogues.

Sıfatlar / Adjectives

sonra	*later, after*	X	**önce**	*before*	
biraz	*a little, some*	X	**çok**	*very, a lot*	
büyük	*big*	X	**küçük**	*little, small*	
yeni	*new*	X	**eski**	*old*	
aç	*hungry*	X	**tok**	*full*	
harika	*wonderful*	X	**berbat**	*awful*	
akıcı	*fluent*	X	**tutuk**	*inarticulate*	
çalışkan	*studious / hardworking*	X	**tembel**	*lazy*	
genç	*young*	X	**yaşlı**	*old*	
kolay	*easy*	X	**zor**	*difficult, hard*	
yaramaz	*naughty*	X	**uslu**	*docile*	
başarılı	*successful*	X	**başarısız**	*unsuccessful*	
yok	*there isn't / aren't*	X	**var**	*there is / are*	
uzun	*long*	X	**kısa**	*short*	
merkezde	*in the centre*	X	**kenarda**	*on the sideline*	
yakın	*close to*	X	**uzak**	*far from*	
çok	*very, a lot*	X	**az**	*little, few*	
güzel	*nice, well*	X	**çirkin**	*ugly*	
yakında	*close, near*	X	**uzakta**	*far*	
lezzetli	*delicious*	X	**lezzetsiz**	*unsavory*	
erkenci	*early*	X	**geç**	*late*	
üzgün	*sad*	X	**neşeli**	*joyful*	
mutlu	*happy*	X	**mutsuz**	*sad*	
doğru	*right, correct*	X	**yanlış**	*wrong*	

Examples:

Talha çalışkan.	*Talha is hardworking.*
Serra uslu.	*Serra is docile.*
Eymen yaramaz.	*Eymen is naughty.*
Yol uzun.	*The road is long.*
Öğrenci başarılı.	*The student is successful.*

Bölüm 3
Part 3

Dialogue 3

otelde at the hotel

İbrahim and Michelle arrive at the hotel very tired. They plan to go to their room first to rest and then to go out.

İbrahim:	Otel gayet büyük ve yeni. Bu çok iyi.
	The hotel is very big and new. This is very nice.
Michelle:	Evet, harika. Ama ben çok yorgunum. Hemen odamıza gitmek ve biraz dinlenmek istiyorum.
	Yes, excellent. But, I'm very tired. I want to go to our room and rest a little right away.
İbrahim:	Evet, ben de. Ama sonra bugün biraz da gezmek istiyorum.
	Yes, me too. But later, I also want to take a short trip today.
Michelle:	Tabii. Önce burada güzel bir yemek yeriz.
	Sure! First, we can (let's) eat a nice meal here.
İbrahim:	Evet, ben de önce bir şeyler yemek istiyorum. Biraz açım. Sonra, Anıtkabir'e gideriz.
	Yes, I also want to eat something first. I'm a little hungry. Later on, we can/will (let's) go to Anıtkabir.
Michelle:	Yakında mı?
	Is it close?
İbrahim:	Evet, oldukça yakında.
	Yes, it's rather close.

1. What will they do first?
2. What do they plan to do next?

Vocabulary

Anıtkabir	*Atatürk's Mausoleum*	**hemen**	*right away*
bir şey	*something*	**oda**	*room*
bir şeyler	*something*	**odamıza**	*to our room*
biraz	*a little, some*	**oldukça**	*rather, very*
biraz gezmek	*to take a short trip*	**orada**	*there*
bugün	*today*	**önce**	*before, first*
burada	*here*	**sonra**	*later, after, later on*
büyük	*big*	**yakında**	*near, close*
dinlenmek	*to rest*	**yemek**	*meal, food*
gayet	*rather, very*	**yemek**	*to eat*
gezmek	*to take a trip*	**yeni**	*new*
gitmek	*to go*	**yorgun**	*tired*

Açım.	*I'm hungry.*
Gideriz.	*Let's go./We'll go.*
Harika!	*Excellent!*
Tabii ki!	*Sure!*
Tokum.	*I'm full.*
Yeriz.	*Let's eat./We'll eat.*

In the dialogue above, they talk about places and make plans. They first use the present progressive tense to say what they want to do as in **dinlenmek istiyorum**, *I want to rest*, and **Bir şeyler yemek istiyorum**, *I want to eat something*.

And, they also say **gideriz,** *we (can/will) go* and, **yeriz,** *we (can/will) eat* to express their plans. These sentences are in the present tense. As seen above, apart from talking about actions taking place repeatedly and regularly, it is also suitable to express plans. Again, all the usages will be studied in the next units.

Bölüm 4
Part 4

dilbilgisi grammar
plurals

In Turkish, the ending **-ler** or **–lar**, *-s*, *-es*, or *-ies* is added to nouns to make them plural.

The endings **-ler** or **-lar** depend on the preceding vowel.

Last vowel of the preceding word	a,ı, o, u	e,i, ö, ü
the endings –ler / -lar	-lar	-ler

The vowels in the ending and the preceding vowels are underlined. Notice the vowel change in the endings depending on the last vowel in the preceding word.

Examples:

öğrenci + ler	**öğrenciler**	*students*
oyuncu + lar	**oyuncular**	*actors or actresses*
otel + ler	**oteller**	*hotels*
yol + lar	**yollar**	*roads*
kardeş + ler	**kardeşler**	*brothers or sisters*
çocuk + lar	**çocuklar**	*children*

In Turkish, the uncountable nouns can be plural, too.

Examples:

çay	**çaylar**	*tea*
su	**sular**	*water*
reçel	**reçeller**	*jam*
kahve	**kahveler**	*coffee*

In Turkish, it is also possible to make **bir şey**, *something* plural as **bir şeyler**. But the meaning remains the same.

For example ,in the dialogue above, İbrahim says;

Bir şeyler yemek istiyorum.   *I want to eat something.*

Note that the translation remains the same even without pluralization.

Bir şey yemek istiyorum.   *I want to eat something.*

expressing possession

In Turkish, possession is expressed by using special words for each person. They are listed below:

Benim	*my*
Senin	*your*
Onun	*his / her*
Bizim	*our*
Sizin	*your (pl)*
Onların	*their*

However, using these words isn't enough to express possession. For example,

benim anne   isn't enough to mean   **my mother**

It's also necessary to add special endings to the second words. However, the endings differ depending on the word's final letter.

•   In case the word ends with a vowel, the following endings are added to the word.

(Benim)	**-m**	*my*
(Senin)	**-n**	*your*
(Onun)	**-si**	*his / her*
(Bizim)	**-miz**	*our*
(Sizin)	**-niz**	*your (pl)*
Onların	**-si**	*their*

NB Since the endings added to the words bear the personal information, the first part (word) can be omitted. That's why the first part of the formation is written in brackets. One exception to this is **onların**, *their*. **Onların** cannot be omitted.

Examples:

(benim) annem	*my mother*
(senin) annen	*your mother*
(onun) annesi	*his / her mother*
(bizim) annemiz	*our mother*
(sizin) anneniz	*your mother*
onların annesi	*their mother*

The vowel "**i**" in the endings changes to "**ı**", "**u**", or "**ü**" depending on the last vowel of the preceding word.

Last vowel of the preceding word	a,ı	e,i	o,u	ö,ü
The vowel in the ending	ı	i	u	ü

Examples: (Only **onun**, *his / her*, **bizim**, *our*, **sizin**, y*our*, and **onların**, *their* are given in the examples since only the endings of these include the vowel "i".) The vowel in the ending and the preceding vowel are underlined.

(onun) bab<u>a</u>s<u>ı</u>	*his / her father*
(bizim) ann<u>e</u>m<u>iz</u>	*our mother*
(sizin) piyan<u>o</u>n<u>uz</u>	*your piano*
onların türk<u>üsü</u>	*their song*

* In case the word ends with a consonant, the following endings are added to the word:

(Benim)	**-im**	*my*
(Senin)	**-in**	*your*
(Onun)	**-i**	*his / her*
(Bizim)	**-imiz**	*our*
(Sizin)	**-iniz**	*your (pl)*
Onların	**-i**	*their*

Examples:

(benim) kardeş**im**.	*my sister (or brother)*
(senin) kardeş**in**.	*your sister*
(onun) kardeş**i**.	*her/his sister*
(bizim) kardeş**imiz**.	*our sister*
(sizin) kardeş**iniz**.	*your sister*
onların kardeş**i**.	*their sister*

Again, the vowel "i" in the sufixes changes to "ı", "u", or "ü" depending on the last vowel of the preceding word. The previous vowel harmony table is also applicable here.

Examples: (Only **benim**, *my* is given in the examples to show the vowel change better.) The vowel in the ending and the preceding vowel are underlined.

(benim) öğretm<u>e</u>n<u>im</u>.	*my teacher*
(benim) dokt<u>o</u>r<u>um</u>.	*my doctor*
(benim) şof<u>ö</u>r<u>üm</u>.	*my driver*
(benim) tezgâht<u>a</u>r<u>ım</u>.	*my cashier*

the consonant harmony

In case the word ends with one the consonants "**ç**", "**k**", "**p**", or "**t**", this letter changes accordingly as given in the table below before the endings are added.

Last consonant of the first word	ç	k	p	t
It changes to	c	g / ğ	b	d

Examples: (Only the ending for **benim**, *my* is given in the examples to show the consonant change better.) The changing consonant is underlined.

ağaç	*tree*	**ağacım**	*my tree*
renk	*colour*	**rengim**	*my colour*
çocuk	*child*	**çocuğum**	*my child*
çorap	*sock*	**çorabım**	*my socks*
cilt	*skin*	**cildim**	*my skin*

Note that there are some exceptions with the consonants "**p**" and "**t**".

Examples:

ip	*rope*	**ipim**	*my rope*
at	*horse*	**atım**	*my horse*

•   In case another noun other than the personal pronouns (I, you, he/she, etc.) or a proper name (like John or Mary) is used to form possessives (my, your, his/her, etc.), <u>two steps</u> are necessary to express the possession.

STEP 1.

First, if the first part (word) ends with a vowel, the ending **–nin / -nın / -nun / -nün** "meaning 's" is added depending on the last vowel. The previous vowel harmony table is also applicable here. Remember that an apostrophe is necessary after proper names before attaching the endings.

Examples:

terzinin	*the tailor's*
türkücünün	*the singer's*
hemşirenin	*the nurse's*
oyuncunun	*the actor's*
Talha'nın	*Talha's*
Ali'nin	*Ali's*

If the first part (word) ends with a consonant, the ending **–in / -ın / -un / -ün** is added depending on the last vowel. The previous vowel harmony table is also applicable here.

Examples:

öğretmen<u>in</u>	*the teacher's*
şof<u>ör</u><u>ün</u>	*the driver's*
tezgâht<u>ar</u><u>ın</u>	*the cashier's*
gars<u>on</u><u>un</u>	*the waiter's*
çocukl<u>ar</u><u>ın</u>	*the children's*
kardeş<u>ler</u><u>in</u>	*the sisters'*
Mich<u>elle</u>'<u>in</u>	*Michelle's*
J<u>o</u>hn'<u>un</u>	*John's*

the consonant harmony

In case the first part (word) ends with one the consonants "**ç**", "**k**", "**p**", or "**t**", this letter changes accordingly before the ending **–in / -ın / -un / -ün** is added. The previous consonant harmony table is also applicable here.

Examples:

ağaç	*tree*	**ağacın**	*of the tree / the tree's*
renk	*colour*	**rengin**	*of the colour / the colour's*
çocuk	*child*	**çocuğun**	*of the child / the child's*
çorap	*sock*	**çorabın**	*of the socks / the socks'*
kasap	*butcher*	**kasabın**	*of the butcher / the butcher's*
cilt	*skin*	**cildin**	*of the skin / the skin's*

Note that there are some exceptions with the consonants "**p**" and "**t**".

Examples:

ip	*rope*	**ipin**	*of the rope / the rope's*
at	*horse*	**atın**	*of the horse / the horse's*

NB The consonant harmony is not applied when the word is a proper name.

Examples:

Tunç	**Tunç'un**	*Tunç's*
Irak	**Irak'ın**	*of Iraq / Iraq's*
Mehtap	**Mehtap'ın**	*Mehtap's*
Murat	**Murat'ın**	*Murat's*

STEP 2.

Secondly, the possession ending for **onun**, *his* or *her* or if plural **onların**, *their* is added to <u>the second word</u>. Since, the first word can be considered as **o**, *he* or *she* or **onlar**, *they* if plural. Remember that, the possession ending for **onun** or **onların** is the same.

As mentioned above, the possession ending for **onun**, *his* or *her* or **onların**, *their* is **–si / -sı / -su / -sü** if the word ends with a vowel and **–i / -ı / -u / -ü** if the word ends with a consonant. And, the vowel in the ending changes depending on the last vowel in the word.

Below are two groups of examples. First, the second words that end with a vowel. Pay attention to the vowel change. (The endings for **onun**, *his* or *her* and **onların**, *their* are given in brackets to make the meaning clearer.)

Examples:

öğretmenin / onun ann**esi**	*the teacher's mother / his or her mother*
şoförün / onun bab**ası**	*the driver's father / his or her father*
Michelle'in / onun piyan**osu**	*Michelle's piano / her piano*
Ali'nin / onun türk**üsü**	*Ali's song / his song*
çocukların / onların od**ası**	*the children's room / their room*
kardeşlerin / onların od**ası**	*the sisters' room / their room*

Secondly, the second words that end with a consonant. Pay attention to the vowel change. (The same first words are used in the examples to show the formation better.)

Examples:

öğretmenin / onun kard**eşi**	*the teacher's sister / his or her sister*
şoförün / onun dokt**oru**	*the driver's doctor / his or her doctor*
Michelle'in / onun öğretm**eni**	*Michelle's teacher / her teacher*
Michelle'in / onun öğretmenl**eri**	*Michelle's teachers / her teachers*
Ali'nin / onun ot**eli**	*Ali's hotel / his hotel*
Ali'nin / onun otell**eri**	*Ali's hotels / his hotels*
çocukların / onların ok**ulu**	*the children's school / their school*
kardeşlerin / onların ok**ulu**	*the sisters' school / their school*

exercise 3

Read the pair of words. Express possession by using these words. Pay attention to the <u>vowel</u> and <u>consonant</u> changes. The English translation of the answers are given in advance for your ease.

Example: **otel / oda**   *(the hotel's room/the room of the hotel)*

otel**in** oda**sı**

ben / şoför   ..... *(my driver)*

okul / şoför   ..... *(the driver of the school / the school's driver)*

öğrenci / ad   ..... *(the name of the student / the student's name)*

şoför / baba   ..... *(the father of the driver / the driver's father)*

İbrahim / eş   ..... *(the wife of İbrahim / İbrahim's wife)*

Talha / iş   ..... *(the work of Talha / Talha's work)*

Serra / okul   ..... *(the school of Serra / Serra's school)*

Eymen / cevap   ..... *(the answer of Eymen / Eymen's answer)*

Kasap / çocuk   ..... *(the child of the butcher / the butcher's child)*

exercise 4

Read the group of words. The first two words are from the Exercise 4. The third word is an adjective. Now you will make sentences by using the adjectives and the phrases you formed in Exercise 4. Use the ending **–dir** (x4) in your answers. Pay attention to the <u>vowel</u> and <u>consonant</u> changes. The English translation of the answers are given in advance for your ease.

Example: **otel / oda / küçük**   *(the hotel's room is small.)*

Otel**in** oda**sı** küçük**tür.**

ben / şoför / genç   ..... *(My driver is young.)*

okul / şoför / yaşlı   ..... *(The school's driver is old.)*

öğrenci / ad / zor   ..... *(The student's name is difficult.)*

şoför / baba / çalışkan   ..... *(The driver's father is hardworking.)*

İbrahim / eş / başarılı	..... *(İbrahim's wife is successful.)*
Talha / iş / kolay	..... *(Talha's work is easy.)*
Serra / okul / büyük	..... *(Serra's school is big.)*
Eymen / cevap / doğru	..... *(Eymen's answer is correct.)*
Kasap / çocuk / yaramaz	..... *(The butcher's child is naughty.)*

var there is / there are

In Turkish, "there is / there are" is expressed by using **var**. Note that a place information is also given in the sentences. (The place information sections are underlined.)

Also note that **bir** can be used instead of *a / an*. But remember, it's not always necessary to use **bir** with singulars.

Examples:

<u>Otelde</u> **(bir) taksi var.**	*There's a taxi <u>at the hotel.</u>*
<u>Okulda</u> **öğrenciler var.**	*There are students <u>in the school.</u>*
<u>Burada</u> **bir çocuk var.**	*There's a child <u>here.</u>*
<u>Orada</u> **çocuklar var.**	*There are children <u>over there.</u>*
<u>Şehrin merkezinde</u> **bir otel var.**	*There's a hotel <u>in the centre of the city.</u>*
<u>Otelin karşısında</u> **lokantalar var.**	*There are restaurants <u>at the</u> <u>opposite of the hotel.</u>*

NB It's also possible to use **var**, there is / are, without the place information. But in this case, <u>possessives are used</u>. **Pay attention to the change in the meaning.**

Both the sentences with a place information and with possessives are given in the examples below. (Both the place information and possessive sections are underlined.)

Examples.

<u>Otelde</u> **(bir) taksi var.**	*There's a taxi at <u>the hotel.</u>*
<u>Otelin</u> **(bir) taksi<u>si</u> var.**	*The hotel has a taxi.*
	(Literally, There's a taxi of the hotel.)
<u>Okulda</u> **öğrenciler var.**	*There are students <u>in the school.</u>*
<u>Okulun</u> **öğrenciler<u>i</u> var.**	*The school has students.*
	(Lit., There are the students of the school.)

More examples with the possessives:

Michelle'in (bir) piyanosu var.	*Michelle has a piano.*
Çocukların (bir) odası var.	*The children have a room.*
Ali'nin (bir) oteli var.	*Ali has a hotel.*
Ali'nin otelleri var.	*Ali has hotels.*
Benim (bir) kız kardeşim var.	*I have a sister.*

It's also possible to add the ending of **–dır** to these sentences. Note that there's no vowel change since the preceding word is always the same. See the vowel harmony table.

Examples:

Michelle'in (bir) piyanosu vardır.	*Michelle has a piano.*
Çocukların (bir) odası vardır.	*The children have a room.*
Ali'nin (bir) oteli vardır.	*Ali has a hotel.*
Ali'nin otelleri vardır.	*Ali has hotels.*
Benim (bir) kız kardeşim vardır.	*I have a sister.*
Okulda öğrenciler vardır.	*There are students in the school.*

yok there isn't / there aren't

In Turkish, "there isn't / there aren't" is expressed by using **yok**. Note that a place information is also given in the sentences. (The place information sections are underlined in the examples.)

Also note that **bir**, *a / an* and plurals generally are not used in the sentences with **yok** even it's grammatically correct to use them.

Otelde bir taksi yok.	*There aren't taxis at the hotel.*
Okulda bir öğrenci yok.	*There aren't students in the school.*
Okulda öğrenciler yok.	*There aren't students in the school.*
Burada bir çocuk yok.	*There aren't children here.*
Orada çocuklar yok.	*There aren't children over there.*

Additionally, **hiç,** *any* is usually used in the sentences with **yok**, *there isn't / there aren't*.

Otelde hiç taksi yok.	*There aren't any taxis at the hotel.*

Okulda hiç öğrenci yok.   *There aren't any students in the school.*

Burada hiç çocuk yok.   *There aren't any children here.*

Orada hiç çocuk yok.   *There aren't any children over there.*

NB It's also possible to use **yok**, *there isn't / aren't*, without the place information. But in this case, underline{possessives are used}. **Pay attention to the change in the meaning.**

Both the sentences with a place information and with possessives are given in the examples below. (Both the place information and possessive sections are underlined.) Examples.

Otelde hiç taksi yok.   *There aren't any taxis at the hotel.*

Otelin hiç taksisi yok.   *The hotel doesn't have any taxis.*

                                (Literally, There aren't any taxis of the hotel.)

Okulda hiç öğrenci yok.   *There aren't any students in the school.*

Okulun hiç öğrencisi yok.   *The school doesn't have any students.*

                                (Lit., There aren't any students of the school.)

More examples with the possessives:

Michelle'in (hiç) piyanosu yok.   *Michelle doesn't have any pianos.*

Çocukların (hiç) odası yok.   *The children don't have any rooms.*

Ali'nin (hiç) oteli yok.   *Ali doesn't have any hotels.*

Benim (hiç) kız kardeşim yok.   *I don't have any sisters.*

It's also possible to add the ending of **–dur** to these sentences. Note that there's no vowel change since the preceding word is always the same. However, pay attention to the consonant change. Remember, **-dir / -dır / -dur / -dür** changes to **-tir / -tır / -tur / -tür** because of the last consonant **k** in the preceding word. See the vowel and consonant harmony tables.

Examples:

Michelle'in (hiç) piyanosu yoktur.   *Michelle doesn't have (any) pianos.*

Çocukların (hiç) odası yoktur.   *The children don't have (any) rooms.*

Ali'nin (hiç) oteli yoktur.   *Ali doesn't have (any) hotels.*

Benim (hiç) kız kardeşim yoktur.   *I don't have (any) sisters.*

Okulda (hiç) öğrenci yoktur.   *There aren't (any) students in the school.*

the question form of "var / yok"

The question is formed by placing the question word at the end separately.

- For **var**, the question ending is **var mı?**, *is there? / are there?*

Examples: (The same examples above are used here, too, in order to show the formation better.)

Also note that **bir**, *a / an* and plurals <u>generally</u> are not used in the questions even it's grammatically correct to use them.

Otelde taksi var mı?	*Are there taxis at the hotel?*
Okulda öğrenci var mı?	*Are there students in the school?*
Orada çocuk var mı?	*Are there children over there?*

More examples with the possessives:

Michelle'in piyanosu var mı?	*Does Michelle have a piano?*
Çocukların odası var mı?	*Do the children have a room?*
Ali'nin oteli var mı?	*Does Ali have a hotel?*
Ali'nin otelleri var mı?	*Does Ali have hotels?*
Senin kız kardeşin var mı?	*Do you have a sister?*

It's also possible to add the ending of **–dır** to these sentences. Note that there's no vowel change since the preceding word is always the same. See the vowel harmony table if necessary.

Michelle'in piyanosu var mıdır?	*Does Michelle have a piano?*
Çocukların odası var mıdır?	*Do the children have a room?*
Ali'nin oteli var mıdır?	*Does Ali have a hotel?*
Senin kız kardeşin var mıdır?	*Do you have a sister?*
Okulda öğrenci var mıdır?	*Are there students in the school?*

- For **yok**, the question ending is **yok mu?**, *isn't there? / aren't there?*

Additionally, **hiç,** *any* is <u>usually</u> used in the questions with **yok mu?** Examples:

Otelde (hiç) taksi yok mu?	*Aren't there (any) taxis at the hotel?*
Okulda (hiç) öğrenci yok mu?	*Aren't there (any) students in the school?*
Orada (hiç) çocuk yok mu?	*Aren't there (any) children over there?*

More examples with the possessives:

Michelle'in (hiç) piyanosu yok mu?	*Doesn't Michelle have (any) pianos?*
Çocukların (hiç) odası yok mu?	*Don't the children have (any) rooms?*

Ali'nin (hiç) oteli yok mu?   *Doesn't Ali have (any) hotels?*

Senin (hiç) kız kardeşin yok mu?   *Don't you have (any) sisters?*

Okulda (hiç) öğrenci yok mu?   *Aren't there (any) students in the school?*

It's also possible to add the ending of **–dur** to these sentences. Note that there's no vowel change since the preceding word is always the same. See the vowel and consonant harmony tables if necessary.

Michelle'in (hiç) piyanosu yok mudur?   *Doesn't Michelle have (any) pianos?*

Çocukların (hiç) odası yok mudur?   *Don't the children have (any) rooms?*

Ali'nin (hiç) oteli yok mudur?   *Doesn't Ali have (any) hotels?*

Senin (hiç) kız kardeşin yok mudur?   *Don't you have (any) sisters?*

Okulda (hiç) öğrenci yok mudur?   *Aren't there (any) students in the school?*

exercise 5

Make questions with the words given. Then give positive and negative answers. Use **bir**, *a, an* in the questions and positive answers. And use **hiç**, *any* in the negative answers.

Example: **otel / şoför / ?**   **Otelin bir şoförü var mı?**
                                        (Does the hotel have a driver?)

                                        Evet, otelin bir şoförü var.
                                        (Yes, the hotel has a driver.)

                                        Hayır, otelin hiç şoförü yok.
                                        (No, the hotel doesn't have any drivers.)

sen / eş   ....

otel / lokanta   ....

okul / öğrenci   ....

Michelle / kardeş   ....

biz / iş   ....

otel / yönetici   ....

Unit Three: Önce yemek sonra Anıtkabir'e bir gezi

Eating first, then taking a trip to Anıtkabir

With this unit, you will be able to:

- Talk about food, places
- Order food
- Express wishes and plans
- Learn the numbers, 0-20
- Use sentences in the present and present progressive tenses
- Use infinitives as the Direct Object

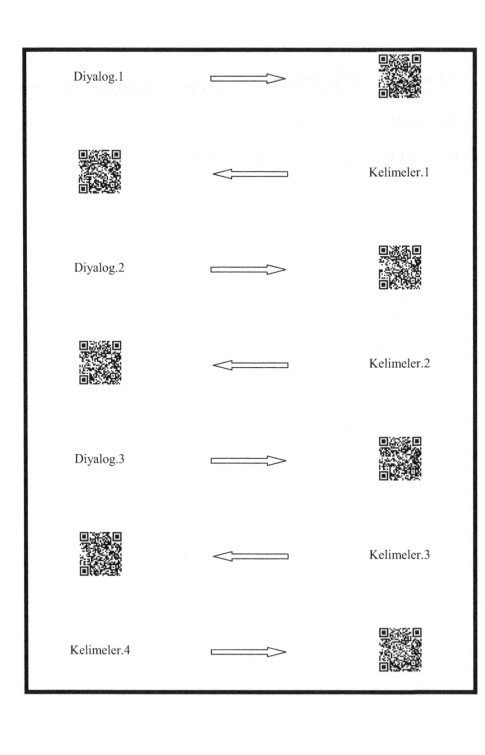

Bölüm 1
Part 1

Dialogue 1

kahvaltı breakfast

After resting a little in their rooms, Michelle and İbrahim gets out of the hotel trying to find a place to have breakfast.

İbrahim:	Bak Michelle, bu kafe müsait. Burada çok fazla insan yok.
	Look, Michelle, this cafe is available (to sit). There aren't many people here.
Michelle:	Evet, biliyorum burası sakin. İçeride boş masalar görüyorum. Burada yer miyiz?
	Yes, I know it's quiet here. I see uncoccupied tables inside. Shall we eat here?
İbrahim:	Tabii ki. Önden buyur lütfen.
	Sure. After you. (Come in.)
Michelle:	Masada mcnü var. Buradan seçeriz.
	There's a menu on the table. We can choose from here.
İbrahim:	Ben hafif birşeyler almak istiyorum. Ya sen?
	I want to take something light. What about you?
Michelle:	Önce menüye bir bakmak istiyorum. İşte, garson da geliyor.
	I'd like to look at the menu first. Look, here comes the waiter.

1. Is the cafe crowded?
2. Where is the menu?

Vocabulary

almak	*to take*	**içeride**	*inside*
bakmak	*to look*	**istemek**	*to want*
bilmek	*to know*	**masa**	*table*
boş	*empty, unoccupied*	**menü**	*menu*
etmek	*to do, to perform*	**müsait**	*available*

fazla	*too many, too much*	sakin	*quiet*
garson	*waiter*	seçmek	*to choose*
gelmek	*to come*	yapmak	*to do*
görmek	*to see*	yemek	*to eat*
hafif	*light*	yemek	*food*

Bak!	*Look!*
İşte garson da geliyor.	*Here comes the waiter.*
Önden buyur lütfen!	*After you!*
Tabii ki!	*Sure!*

In the dialogue above, İbrahim wants to find a good location to have breakfast with his wife. They see a cafe with few people. He says, **Burada çok fazla insan yok**, *There are not many people here*.

Michelle says, **Burası sakin**, *Here's quiet*. Note the difference between **Burası** and **Burada**. The former can be translated as *here* while the latter as *in here*.

İbrahim responds to **tabii ki**, *sure* to Michelle's question of **Burada yer miyiz?**, *Can/shall we eat here?* In fact, **tabii ki** is the short form of the answer. The long form should be **Tabii ki burada yeriz**, *it's sure that we can/shall eat here*.

Also note that **yapmak** and **etmek** have similar meanings. They are both used alone and in phrasal verb form such as **kahvaltı yapmak**, *to have breakfast*, kahvaltı etmek, *to have breakfast,* **banyo yapmak**, *to take a bath*, **ziyaret etmek**, to *visit*, etc.

exercise 1

Which is the odd one out in each row?

yemek	istemek	içmek	içeride
garson	fazla	boş	hafif
masa	insan	yemek	önden
müsait	sakin	boş	bak

Dialogue 2

Ne yeriz? What shall we eat?

The waiter takes their order.

Garson:	Efendim, hoş geldiniz. Ne sipariş etmek istersiniz? *Sir and madam, welcome. What would you like to order?*
Michelle:	Ben sahanda yumurta, beyaz peynir, biraz zeytin ve tereyağı istiyorum. Bir de yanında iki dilim ekmek istiyorum. *I'd like fried egg, white cheese, some olives and butter. And, I want two slices of bread along with them.*
İbrahim:	Ben peynirli bir poğaça ve biraz reçel alırım. *I'll take a pastry with cheese and (I'll take) some jam.*
Garson:	Efendim, kafemizde bugüne özel menemen var. Denemek ister misiniz? *Sir and madam, we have menemen special for today. Would you like to try it out?*
Michelle:	Evet, ben menemen de alırım. *Yes, I'll take menemen, too.*
Garson:	Kahvaltının yanında içecek bir şey ister misiniz? *Would you like anything to drink with the breakfast?*
Michelle:	Ben kahvaltı ile birlikte şekerli ve sütlü bir (bardak) çay istiyorum. Kahvaltı sonrasında ise sade bir (fincan) kahve. *I want a cup of tea with milk and with sugar with the breakfast. And after the breakfast, a cup of coffee without milk and without sugar.*
İbrahim:	Ben şekersiz bir çay alırım. *I'll take a cup of tea without sugar.*
Garson:	Başka bir istediğiniz var mı? *Anything else?*
İbrahim:	Şimdilik yeterli, teşekkürler. Hesabı alabilir miyim lütfen? *Enough for now, thanks. Can I take the account/bill please?*

1. Did they order the same thing for the breakfast?
2. Will both take menemen?

Vocabulary

akşam yemeği	*dinner*	**öğün**	*meal*
başka	*else*	**özel**	*special*
beyaz peynir	*white cheese*	**poğaça**	*pastry*
bir de	*and, too*	**peynirli bir poğaça**	*a piece of pastry with cheese*
birlikte	*to getter*	**reçel**	*jam*
denemek	*to try*	**sade**	*without sugar and milk*
dilim	*slice*	**sahanda yumurta**	*scrambled eggs*
ekmek	*bread*	**sipariş etmek**	*to order food*
içecek	*drink*	**şekerli**	*with sugar*
içmek	*to drink*	**şekersiz**	*wthout sugar*
iki	*two*	**şimdilik**	*for now*
ile	*with*	**tereyağı**	*butter*
kahvaltı	*breakfast*	**yanında**	*with this*
menemen	*eggs cooked with with tomatoes and peppers*	**yeterli**	*enough*
öğle yemeği	*lunch*	**zeytin**	*olives*
bugüne özel		*special for today*	
Hesabı alabilir miyim lütfen?		*Can I take the account/bill please?*	

In the second dialogue, we see two different phrases with the same meaning. They are; **kahvaltının yanında** and **kahvaltı ile birlikte**, *with the breakfast*.

In Turkish, countable and uncountable nouns can be used in singular form, e.g. **peynir**, *cheese*, **zeytin**, *olives*, **ekmek**, *bread* and **yumurta**, *eggs*. Even when with quantifiers, they remain singular, e.g. **iki dilim ekmek**, *two slices of bread* and **iki yumurta**, *two eggs*. In addition, note that **biraz** ,may be used with both countables and uncountables similar to *some* in English, e.g. **biraz zeytin**, *some olives* and **biraz reçel**, some jam.

In addition, in Turkish, it is possible to say **bir çay**, *a tea* directly instead of **bir bardak çay**, *a cup of tea* or to say **bir kahve**, *a coffee* directly instead of **bir fincan kahve**, *a cup of coffee.*

Bölüm 2
Part 2

dilbilgisi grammar

fiillerin yalın hali the bare form of the verbs

In Turkish, all the verbs end with **–mek** or **–mak**, *to* when they are in the infinitive form. The verbs are listed in the infinitive form (with **–mek** or **–mak**) in dictionaries, too. For example, **ye**, *eat* and **yemek**, *to eat* or **al**, *take* and **almak**, to take.

The verb form without the ending **–mek** or **–mak**, *to,* is called **the bare form of the verb** or **the bare infinitive**.

the vowel harmony

The ending **–mek** or **–mak** depends on the last vowel of the bare form of the verb.

Last vowel of the bare form of the verb	a,ı, o, u	e,i, ö, ü
the endings –mek / -mak	-mak	-mek

The vowel in the bare form of the verbs and the vowel in the ending are underlined. Notice the vowel change in the endings depending on the last vowel in the bare infinitive.

Examples:

gel + mek	gelmek	*to come*
iç + mek	içmek	*to drink*
konuş + mak	konuşmak	*to speak*
al + mak	almak	*to take*

The bare forms of the verbs are used when we want to conjugate the verbs for various tenses.

şimdiki zaman the present progressive tense

The present progressive tense is usually used to express an action on progress at the time of the speech. It is possible to use the present progressive in place of the general present tense, too. For the conjugation of the verbs, special personal endings are added to the bare form of the verbs.

However, the endings depend on the final letter of the verb. The endings following a consonant or a vowel differ. These differences will be studied step by step in the following pages.

* In case the verb ends with a consonant, the following endings are added:

(Ben)	-iyorum	*I'm ...-ing*
(Sen)	-iyorsun	*You are ...-ing*
(O)	-iyor	*He / She It is ...-ing*
(Biz)	-iyoruz	*We are ...-ing*
(Siz)	-iyorsunuz	*You (pl) are ...-ing*
Onlar	-iyor / -iyorlar	*They are ...-ing*

Examples: **gel mek** *(to come)*

Ben geliyorum.	*I'm coming.*
Sen geliyorsun.	*You're coming.*
O geliyor.	*He/She is coming.*
Biz geliyoruz.	*We're coming.*
Siz geliyorsunuz.	*You're (pl) coming.*
Çocuklar geliyor / geliyorlar.	*The children are coming.*
Arabalar geliyor.	*The cars are coming.*

NB Since the endings added to the verbs bear the personal information, the subjects can be omitted. That's why the subjects are written in brackets in the table. One exception to this is **onlar**, *they*. **Onlar** cannot be omitted.
In addition, note that there are two ending options for the 3rd plural person, **onlar**, *they*, singular (**-iyor**) and plural (**-iyorlar**). However, for the nonhumans in the subject position, plural ending cannot be preferred.

Examples:

Çocuklar *(human)* **geliyor / geliyorlar.**   *The children are coming.*
Arabalar *(nonhuman)* **geliyor / ~~geliyorlar~~.**   *The cars are coming.*

the vowel harmony

The letter "i" in the present progressive tense endings may change to "ı", "u", or "ü" depending on the last vowel of the verb.

Last vowel of the verb	a,ı	e,i	o,u	ö,ü
The vowel in the ending	ı	i	u	ü

Examples:

iç mek	**Ben içiyorum.**	*I'm drinking.*
bak mak	**Sen bakıyorsun.**	*You're looking.*
gör mek	**Biz görüyoruz.**	*We're seeing.*
uç mak	**Onlar uçuyorlar.**	*They're flying.*

• In case the verb ends with a vowel, two steps are needed for the conjugation.

STEP 1

First, the last vowel is changed according to the table below.

The preceding vowel of the last vowel	a,ı	e,i	o,u	ö,ü
The last vowel changes into	a, ı	e, i	a, u	e, ü

In the examples below, see the last vowel and the preceding vowel and notice that the last vowel changes depending on the preceding one.

Examples:

iste mek	*(to want)*	**isti**
söyle mek	*(to say)*	**söylü**
atla mak	*(to jump)*	**atlı**
kirala mak	*(to rent)*	**kiralı**
kurula mak	*(to dry something)*	**kurulu**
özle mek	*(to miss)*	**özlü**
uyu mak	*(to sleep)*	**uyu**
harca mak	*(to spend)*	**harcı**
yürü mek	*(to walk)*	**yürü**

STEP 2

Second, the following personal endings are added to the verbs.

(Ben)	-yorum	*I'm ...-ing*
(Sen)	-yorsun	*You are ...-ing*
(O)	-yor	*He / She It is ...-ing*
(Biz)	-yoruz	*We are ...-ing*
(Siz)	-yorsunuz	*You (pl) are ...-ing*
Onlar	-yor / -yorlar	*They are ...-ing*

(Only the ending for **ben**, *I* is given in the examples to show the vowel change better. Additionally, the words given here were selected only to show the vowel changes. So, please pay attention to the vowel changes rather than the meaning.)

Examples:

iste mek	Ben istiyorum.	*I want. (Lit. I'm wanting.)*
söyle mek	Ben söylüyorum.	*I'm telling.*
atla mak	Ben atlıyorum.	*I'm jumping.*
kirala mak	Ben kiralıyorum.	*I'm renting.*
kurula mak	Ben kuruluyorum.	*I'm drying (something.).*
özle mek	Ben özlüyorum.	*I'm missing (someone).*
uyu mak	Ben uyuyorum.	*I'm sleeping.*
harca mak	Ben harcıyorum.	*I'm spending.*

The verbs **gitmek**, *to go*, **etmek**, *to do or to perform*, **demek**, *to say*, and **yemek**, *to eat* have a special spelling in the present progressive tense.

Examples:

git mek	*(to go)*
Gidiyorum.	*I'm going.*
Gidiyorsun.	*You're going.*
Gidiyor.	*He / She / It is going.*
Gidiyoruz.	*We're going.*
Gidiyorsunuz.	*You're (pl) going.*
Onlar gidiyorlar.	*They're going.*

etmek	*(to do or to perform)*
Ediyorum.	*I'm doing.*
Ediyorsun.	*You're doing.*
Ediyor.	*He / She / It is doing.*
Ediyoruz.	*We're doing.*
Ediyorsunuz.	*You're (pl) doing.*
Onlar ediyorlar.	*They're doing.*

y**e** mek	*(to eat)*
Yiyorum.	*I'm eating.*
Yiyorsun.	*You're eating.*
Yiyor.	*He / She / It is eating.*
Yiyoruz.	*We're eating.*
Yiyorsunuz.	*You're (pl) eating.*
Onlar yiyorlar.	*They're eating.*

d**e** mek	*(to say)*
Diyorum.	*I'm saying.*
Diyorsun.	*You're saying.*
Diyor.	*He / She is saying.*
Diyoruz.	*We're saying.*
Diyorsunuz.	*You're (pl) saying.*
Onlar diyorlar.	*They're saying.*

exercise 2

Form positive sentences in the present progressive tense with the given clues. Pay attention to the vowel change before adding the ending. Also note that numbers 4 and 5 have two conjugations since there are two ending options for **onlar**, *they*.

Example:

Ben / çay / içmek   **Ben çay içiyorum.**
I / tea / to drink   *I'm drinking tea.*

1. **sen/beni/bilmek** ....

2. **biz/dinlenmek** ....

3. **o/otele/gitmek** ....

4. **onlar/sahanda yumurta/yemek** ....

5. **insanlar/menüye/bakmak** ....

6. **siz/kafede menüden yemek/seçmek** ....

7. **ben/seni/görmek** ....

8. **sen/ gezmek / istemek** ....

9. **biz/ uyumak** ....

the negative form

To form negative sentences in the present progressive tense, the negative ending **–mi** is added <u>right before</u> the personal ending.

The negative ending **–mi** added right before the personal endings are given in the table below:

(Ben)	-miyorum	*I'm not ...-ing*
(Sen)	-miyorsun	*You aren't ...-ing*
(O)	-miyor	*He / She It isn't ...-ing*
(Biz)	-miyoruz	*We aren't ...-ing*
(Siz)	-miyorsunuz	*You (pl) aren't ...-ing*
Onlar	-miyor / -miyorlar	*They aren't ...-ing*

Examples: **gel mek** *(to come)*

Ben gelmiyorum.	*I'm not coming.*
Sen gelmiyorsun.	*You're not coming.*
O gelmiyor.	*He/She is not coming.*
Biz gelmiyoruz.	*We're not coming.*
Siz gelmiyorsunuz.	*You're (pl) not coming.*
Çocuklar gelmiyor/gelmiyorlar.	*The children are not coming.*
Arabalar gelmiyor.	*The cars are not coming.*

Note that the negative ending **–mi** is a 4 way vowel harmony meaning it changes to "**-mı**", "**-mu**", or "**-mü**" depending on the preceding vowel.

Last vowel of the preceding verb	a,ı	e,i	o,u	ö,ü
The negative ending –mi (x4)	-mı	-mi	-mu	-mü

Examples:

Ben içmiyorum.	*I'm not drinking.*
Sen bakmıyorsun.	*You're not looking.*
O uyumuyor.	*He/She is not sleeping.*
Biz görmüyoruz.	*We're not seeing.*

NB The final letters of the verbs (consonant or vowel) don't make any difference in the negative conjugation.

exercise 3

Form negative sentences in the present progressive tense with the given clues. Pay attention to the vowel change before adding the ending. Also note that numbers 4 and 5 have two conjugations since there are two ending options for **onlar**, *they*.

Example:

Ben / çay / içmek   **Ben çay içmiyorum.**
I / tea / to drink   *I'm not drinking tea.*

1. **sen/beni/bilmek**   ....
2. **biz/dinlenmek**   ....
3. **o/otele/gitmek**   ....
4. **onlar/sahanda yumurta/yemek**   ....
5. **insanlar/menüye/bakmak**   ....
6. **siz/kafede menüden yemek/seçmek** ....
7. **ben/seni/görmek**   ....
8. **sen/ gezmek / istemek**   ....
9. **biz/ uyumak**   ....

the question form

To form a question in the present progressive tense, two steps are needed.

STEP 1

First, the verb is conjugated for the 3rd singular person (**o**, *he / she / it*). Remember that for the 3rd singular person (**o**, *he / she / it*) the ending is either **–iyor** or **–yor**. See the present progressive tense verb conjugations. Also remember the vowel change.

Examples:
The verb is conjugated for the 3rd <u>singular person (**o**, *he / she / it*)</u>.

söylemek	*(to say)*	**söylüyor**	*(He / she is saying)*
gelmek	*(to come)*	**geliyor**	*(He / she is coming)*
gitmek	*(to go)*	**gidiyor**	*(He / she is going)*
yemek	*(to eat)*	**yiyor**	*(He / she is eating)*
uyumak	*(to sleep)*	**uyuyor**	*(He / she is sleeping)*
yürümek	*(to walk)*	**yürüyor**	*(He / she is walking)*
kalmak	*(to stay)*	**kalıyor**	*(He / she is staying)*
bakmak	*(to look (at))*	**bakıyor**	*(He / she is looking (at))*
atlamak	*(to jump))*	**atlıyor**	*(He / she is jumping)*

STEP 2

Then, the question endings are added to the end separately. The question endings for each person are given below: (The ending–**iyor** or **–yor** for the 3rd singular person (**o**, *he / she / it*) added in **STEP 1** is underlined.)

(Ben)	-(i)yor muyum?	*Am I ...-ing?*
(Sen)	-(i)yor musun?	*Are you ...-ing?*
(O)	-(i)yor mu?	*Is he / she / it ...-ing?*
(Biz)	-(i)yor muyuz?	*Are we ...-ing?*
(Siz)	-(i)yor musunuz?	*Are you (pl) ...-ing?*
Onlar	-(i)yor mu?	*Are they ...-ing?*

Example:

Ben geliyor muyum?   *Am I coming?*
(Step 1) (Step 2)

More examples:

Sen geliyor musun?	*Are you coming?*
O geliyor mu?	*Is he / she / it coming?*
Biz geliyor muyuz?	*Are we coming?*
Siz geliyor musunuz?	*Are you (pl) coming?*
Çocuklar geliyor mu?	*Are the children coming?*
Arabalar geliyor mu?	*Are the cars coming?*

More examples with other verbs:

Ben içiyor muyum?	*Am I drinking?*
Ben bakıyor muyum?	*Am I looking (at)?*
Ben uyuyor muyum?	*Am I sleeping?*
Ben görüyor muyum?	*Am I seeing?*

Note that there are two ending options for **onlar**, *they:* **-(i)yor** or **-(i)yorlar**. In case the plural ending is preferred, then it should be **-(i)yorlar mı?** Remember the vowel change in the personal endings, too. (Both ending possibilities are given in the examples.)

Examples:

Çocuklar geliyor mu? / geliyorlar mı?	*Are the children coming?*
Çocuklar içiyor mu? / içiyorlar mı?	*Are the children drinking?*
Çocuklar bakıyor mu? / bakıyorlar mı?	*Are the children looking?*
Çocuklar uyuyor mu? / uyuyorlar mı?	*Are the children sleeping?*
Çocuklar görüyor mu? / görüyorlar mı?	*Are the children seeing?*

exercise 4

Form questions in the present progressive tense with the given clues. Pay attention to the vowel change before adding the ending. Also note that numbers 4 and 5 have two conjugations since there are two ending options for **onlar**, *they*.

Example:

Ben / çay / içmek   **Ben çay içiyor muyum?**
I / tea / to drink   *Am I drinking tea?*

1. sen/beni/bilmek   ....

2. biz/dinlenmek   ....

3. o/otele/gitmek   ....

4. onlar/sahanda yumurta/yemek   ....

5. insanlar/menüye/bakmak   ....

6. siz/kafede menüden yemek/seçmek ....

7. ben/seni/görmek   ....

8. sen/ gezmek / istemek   ....

9. biz/ uyumak   ....

Bölüm 3
Part 3

Dialogue 3

Anıtkabir'de at Anıtkabir

İbrahim and Michelle arrive at Anıtkabir after a short walk.

İbrahim:	Michelle, işte! Anıtkabir'e geldik bile! *Michelle, look! We (surprisingly early) reached to Anıtkabir!*
Michelle:	Evet! Çok görkemli! Ayrıca, burası çok kalabalık. Burada çok insan var. *Yes! Very majestic! In addition, it's very crowded here. There're a lot of people here.*
İbrahim:	Evet, epey insan var. Anıtkabir'i ziyaret etmek için geliyorlar. Gençler, yaşlılar, çocuklar. *Yes, there are quite many people. They're coming here to visit Anıtkabir. Youngsters, old people, children.*
Michelle:	Anıtkabir biraz yüksekte değil mi? Buradan bütün Ankara'yı görüyorum. Hem açık alan hem yeşillik. *Anıtkabir's a little high, right? I see Ankara as a whole from here. The field is both open and green.*
İbrahim:	Aynen, bir tepe üzerinde ve yemyeşil. Ankara'nın ortasında bir vaha gibi. Bak, şurada Aslanlı Yol var. Önce oradan geçeriz, sonra tören alanını görürüz ve en son kabri ziyaret ederiz. *Exactly, it's on a hill and it's lush green. Like an oasis in the middle of Ankara. Look, there's Aslanlı Yol here. We'll pass through it first then see the parade ground and finally visit the tomb.*
Michelle:	En son, buradaki müzeyi de görmek isterim. Ve buradaki kafede bir şeyler atıştırırız. *At the end, I also want to see the museum here and let's have a snack at the cafe here.*
İbrahim:	Tabii. *Of course.*

1. What do the people come to Anıtkabir for?
2. Did Michelle like the location of Anıtkabir?

Vocabulary

Aslanlı Yol	*a wailking road in Anıtkabir*	kabir	*tomb*
açık	*open*	kalabalık	*crowded*
alan	*field*	müze	*museum*
atıştırmak	*to eat sneaks*	ortasında	*in the middle*
ayrıca	*in addition*	tepe	*hill*
bütün	*whole*	tören alanı	*parade ground*
en son	*finally*	üzerinde	*on top of*
epey	*rather*	vaha	*oasis*
geçmek	*to pass*	yaşlı	*old people*
genç	*youngster*	yemyeşil	*lush green*
gibi	*like*	yeşillik	*green*
görkemli	*majestic*	yüksek	*high*
için	*for*	ziyaret etmek	*to visit*

In the dialogue above, İbrahim points out Anıtkabir and says, **İşte!**, *Look!* It can also be used like *over here* or *over there* in English, e.g. **İşte Anıtkabir!**, *Look, Anıtkabir is over there!*

Again in İbrahim's part, he says **bile**. This can be translated in English as *already*, but it has a meaning of surprise, too. So, **Anıtkabir'e geldik bile** should be translated as *We surprisingly early reached to Anıtkabir!* rather than *We already reached to Anıtkabir.*

Also note that some nouns have spelling exceptions when in the accusative form (in the object position in a sentence). **Kabir** is one of them and is written as **kabri** in the accusative form. Even though grammatically incorrect, it is also acceptable to say **kabiri**, anyway.

exercise 5

Which is the odd one out in each row?

ortasında	içeride	üzerinde	tepe
geçmek	görkemli	boş	kalabalık
şekerli	sade	şekersiz	alan
zeytin	peynir	vaha	tereyağı

sayılar numbers

Find the Turkish cardinal (counting) numbers from 0 to 20 below.

Sayılar / Numbers

sıfır	zero	on bir	eleven
bir	one	on iki	twelve
iki	two	on üç	thirteen
üç	three	on dört	fourteen
dört	four	on beş	fifteen
beş	five	on altı	sixteen
altı	six	on yedi	seventeen
yedi	seven	on sekiz	eighteen
sekiz	eight	on dokuz	nineteen
dokuz	nine	yirmi	twenty
on	ten		

Using cardinal numbers with the nouns is the opposite of that in English. The nouns remain singular even after modified with numbers.

Examples:

beş arabalar	beş araba	*five cars*
iki kardeşler	iki kardeş	*two brothers/sisters*
üç yollar	üç yol	*three ways*
dört öğrenciler	dört öğrenci	*four students*
altı uçaklar	altı uçak	*six planes*

The uncountable nouns can be modified with cardinal numbers, too.

Examples:

iki çaylar	iki çay	*two (cups of) tea*
üç sular	üç su	*three (glasses of) water*
dört reçeller	dört reçel	*four (plates of) jam*
altı kahveler	altı kahve	*six (cups of) coffee*

Bölüm 4
Part 4

dilbilgisi grammar

geniş zaman the present tense

The present tense is usually used to express an action is done repeatedly or regularly. It's also possible to express plans by using the present tense. For the conjugation of the verbs, special personal endings are added to the bare form of the verbs.

However, the endings depend on the final letter of the verbs. The endings following a consonant or a vowel differ. These differences will be studied step by step in the following pages.

•   In case the verb ends with a consonant, the following endings are added:

(Ben)	-irim	I V*
(Sen)	-irsin	You V
(O)	-ir	He / She / It Vs
(Biz)	-iriz	We V
(Siz)	-irsiniz	You (pl) V
Onlar	-ir / -irler	They V

(*) "V" represents any verb in the present tense.

Examples: **gel mek** *(to come)*

Ben gelirim.	*I come.*
Sen gelirsin.	*You come.*
O gelir.	*He/She comes.*
Biz geliriz.	*We come.*
Siz gelirsiniz.	*You (pl) come.*
Çocuklar gelir / gelirler.	*The children come.*
Arabalar gelir.	*The cars come.*

NB Since the endings added to the verbs bear the personal information, the subjects can be omitted. That's why the subjects are written in brackets. One exception to this is **onlar**, *they*. **Onlar** cannot be omitted.
In addition, note that there are two ending options for the 3rd plural person, **onlar**, *they*, singular (**-ir**) and plural (**-irler**). However, for the nonhumans in the subject position, plural ending cannot be preferred.

Examples:

Çocuklar *(human)* **gelir/gelirler**   *The children come.*
Arabalar *(nonhuman)* **gelir/~~gelirler~~.**   *The cars come.*

the vowel harmony

The letter "**i**" in the present tense endings may change to "**ı**", "**u**", or "**ü**" depending on the last vowel of the verb.

Last vowel of the preceding verb	a,ı	e,i	o,u	ö,ü
The vowel in the ending	a, ı	e, i	a, u	e, ü

Examples:

iç mek	Ben içerim.	*I drink.*
bak mak	Sen bakarsın.	*You look (at).*
gör mek	Biz görürüz.	*We see.*
uç mak	Onlar uçarlar.	*They fly.*

NB Remember that there are two ending options for the 3rd plural person, **onlar**, *they*, singular (**-ir**) and plural (**-irler**). In case the plural ending (**-irler**) is used, the vowel "**e**" must also change depending on the preceding vowel.

The endings **-ler** or **-lar** depend on the preceding vowel.

Last vowel of the preceding verb	a,ı, o, u	e,i, ö, ü
the endings –ler / -lar	**-lar**	**-ler**

Examples:

iç mek	Çocuklar içerler.	*The children drink.*
bak mak	Çocuklar bakarlar.	*The children look (at).*
gör mek	Çocuklar görürler.	*The children see.*
uç mak	Çocuklar uçarlar.	*The children fly.*

- In case the verb ends with a vowel, he following personal endings are added to the verbs.

(Ben)	-rim	*I V**
(Sen)	-rsin	*You V*
(O)	-r	*He / She / It Vs*
(Biz)	-riz	*We V*
(Siz)	-rsiniz	*You (pl) V*
Onlar	-r / -rler	*They V*

(*) "V" represents any verb in the present tense.

Examples: **iste mek** *(to want)*

Ben isterim.	*I want.*
Sen istersin.	*You want.*
O ister.	*He / She / It wants.*
Biz isteriz.	*We want.*
Siz istersiniz.	*You (pl) want.*
Çocuklar ister / isterler.	*The children want.*
Atlar ister.	*The horses want.*

NB Note that there are two ending options for the 3rd plural person, **onlar**, *they*, singular (**-r**) and plural (**-rler**). However, for the nonhumans in the subject position, plural ending cannot be preferred.

Examples:

Çocuklar *(human)* **ister/isterler**   *The children want.*
Atlar *(nonhuman)* **ister/~~isterler~~**.   *The horses want.*

the vowel harmony

The letter "i" in the present tense endings may change to "ı", "u", or "ü" depending on the last vowel of the verb.

Last vowel of the preceding verb	a,ı	e,i	o,u	ö,ü
The vowel in the ending	ı	i	u	ü

(Only the ending for **ben**, *I* is given in the examples to show the vowel change better. Additionally, the words given here were selected only to show the vowel changes. So, please pay attention to the vowel changes rather than the meaning.)

Examples:

söyle mek	**Ben söylerim.**	*I tell.*
atla mak	**Ben atlarım.**	*I jump.*
uyu mak	**Ben uyurum.**	*I sleep.*
yürü mek	**Ben yürürüm.**	*I walk.*

NB Remember that there are two ending options for the 3rd plural person, **onlar**, *they*, singular (**-r**) and plural (**-rler**). In case the plural ending (**-rler**) is used, the vowel "**e**" must also change depending on the preceding vowel. The previous **-ler** / **-lar** table is applicable here, too.

Examples:

söyle mek	**Çocuklar söylerler.**	*The children tell.*	**x**
atla mak	**Çocuklar atlarlar.**	*The children jump.*	
uyu mak	**Çocuklar uyurlar.**	*The children sleep.*	
yürü mek	**Çocuklar yürürler.**	*The children walk.*	

NB The verb **gitmek** and **etmek** has a special spelling in the present tense.

Examples:

git mek	*(to go)*

Giderim.	*I go.*
Gidersin.	*You go.*
Gider.	*He / She / It goes.*
Gideriz.	*We go.*
Gidersiniz.	*You (pl) go.*
Onlar giderler.	*They go.*

etmek	*(to do or to perform)*

Ederim.	*I do.*
Edersin.	*You do.*
Eder.	*He / She / It does.*
Ederiz.	*We do.*
Edersiniz.	*You (pl) do.*
Onlar ederler.	*They do.*

exercise 6

Form positive sentences in the present tense with the given clues. Pay attention to the vowel change before adding the ending. Also note that numbers 4 and 5 have two conjugations since there are two ending options for **onlar**, *they*.

Example:

Ben / çay / içmek   **Ben çay içerim.**
I / tea / to drink   *I drink tea.*

1. **sen/beni/bilmek**   ....

2. **biz/dinlenmek**   ....

3. **o/otele/gitmek**   ....

4. **onlar/sahanda yumurta/yemek** ....

5. **insanlar/menüye/bakmak**   ....

6. **siz/kafede menüden yemek/seçmek** ....

7. **ben/seni/görmek**   ....

8. **sen/ gezmek / istemek**   ....

9. **biz/ uyumak**   ....

the negative form

To form negative sentences in the present tense, the negative ending **–me / -ma** is added <u>right before</u> the personal ending.
The negative ending **–me / -ma** and the personal ending following is a 2 way vowel harmony meaning it changes depending on the preceding vowel.

Last vowel of the preceding verb	a,ı, o, u	e,i, ö, ü
the endings –me / -ma	-ma	-me

Examples:

gel mek *(to come)*   **ge<u>lme</u>**   *don't / doesn't come*
bak mak *(to look (at))*   **b<u>akma</u>**   *don't / doesn't look (at)*

Both possibilities of the negative ending with the personal ending are studied in the following pages:

• The negative ending **–ma** with the personal ending is as given below:

(Ben)	-mam	*I don't ...*
(Sen)	-mazsın	*You don't ...*
(O)	-maz	*He / She It doesn't ...*
(Biz)	-mayız	*We don't ...*
(Siz)	-mazsınız	*You (pl) don't ..*
Onlar	-maz / -mazlar	*They don't ...*

Examples: **bak mak** *(to look (at))*

Ben bakmam.	*I don't look (at).*
Sen bakmazsın.	*You don't look (at).*
O bakmaz.	*He/She / It doesn't look (at).*
Biz bakmayız.	*We don't look (at).*
Siz bakmazsınız.	*You (pl) don't look (at).*
Çocuklar bakmaz / bakmazlar.	*The children don't look (at).*
Atlar bakmaz.	*The horses don't look (at).*

• And, the negative ending **–me** with the personal ending is as given below:

(Ben)	-mem	*I don't ...*
(Sen)	-mezsin	*You don't ...*
(O)	-mez	*He / She It doesn't ...*
(Biz)	-meyiz	*We don't ...*
(Siz)	-mezsiniz	*You (pl) don't ..*
Onlar	-mez / -mezler	*They don't ...*

Examples: **gel mek** *(to come)*

Ben gelmem.	*I don't come.*
Sen gelmezsin.	*You don't come.*
O gelmez.	*He/She / It doesn't come.*
Biz gelmeyiz.	*We don't come.*
Siz gelmezsiniz.	*You (pl) don't come.*
Çocuklar gelmez / gelmezler.	*The children don't come.*
Arabalar gelmez.	*The cars don't come.*

NB Remember that there are two ending options for the 3rd plural person, **onlar**, *they*, singular (**-mez / -maz**) and plural (**-mezler / -mazlar**). However, for the nonhumans in the subject position, plural ending cannot be preferred.

Examples:

Çocuklar bakmaz / bakmazlar.	*The children don't look (at).*
Atlar ~~bakmaz~~.	*The horses don't look (at).*
Çocuklar gelmez / gelmezler.	*The children don't come.*
Arabalar ~~gelmez~~.	*The cars don't come.*

exercise 7

Form negative sentences in the present tense with the given clues. Pay attention to the vowel change before adding the ending. Also note that numbers 4 and 5 have two conjugations since there are two ending options for **onlar**, *they*.

Example:

Ben / çay / içmek   **Ben çay içmem.**
I / tea / to drink   *I don't drink tea.*

1. sen/beni/bilmek   ....
2. biz/dinlenmek   ....
3. o/otele/gitmek   ....
4. onlar/sahanda yumurta/yemek   ....
5. insanlar/menüye/bakmak   ....
6. siz/kafede menüden yemek/seçmek   ....
7. ben/seni/görmek   ....
8. sen/ gezmek / istemek   ....
9. biz/ uyumak   ....

the question form

To form a question in the present tense, two steps are needed.

STEP 1

First, the verb is conjugated for the 3rd singular person (**o**, *he / she / it*). Remember that for the 3rd singular person (**o**, *he / she / it*) the ending is either **–ir** or **–r**. See the present tense verb conjugations above. Also remember the vowel change.

Examples:

The verb is conjugated for the 3rd <u>singular person</u> (**o**, *he / she / it*).

söylemek	*(to say)*	**söyler**	*(He / she says)*
gelmek	*(to come)*	**gelir**	*(He / she comes)*
gitmek	*(to go)*	**gider**	*(He / she goes)*
yemek	*(to eat)*	**yer**	*(He / she eats)*
uyumak	*(to sleep)*	**uyur**	*(He / she sleeps)*
yürümek	*(to walk)*	**yürür**	*(He / she walks)*
kalmak	*(to stay)*	**kalır**	*(He / she stays)*
bakmak	*(to look (at))*	**bakar**	*(He / she looks (at))*
atlamak	*(to jump))*	**atlar**	*(He / she jumps)*

STEP 2

Then, the question endings are added to the end separately. The question endings for each person are given below: (The ending **–ir** or **–r** for the 3rd singular person (**o**, *he / she / it*) added in **STEP 1** is underlined.)

(Ben)	**-(i)r miyim?**	*Do I ...?*
(Sen)	**-(i)r misin?**	*Do you ..?*
(O)	**-(i)r mi?**	*Does he / she / it ..?*
(Biz)	**-(i)r miyiz?**	*Do we ...?*
(Siz)	**-(i)r misiniz?**	*Do you (pl) ...?*
Onlar	**-(i)r mi?**	*Do they ...?*

Example:

Ben <u>gelir</u> <u>miyim</u>?   *Do I come?*
　　(Step 1) (Step 2)

More examples:

Sen gelir misin?	*Do you come?*
O gelir mi?	*Does he / she/ it come?*
Biz gelir miyiz?	*Do we come?*
Siz gelir misiniz?	*Do you (pl) come?*
Çocuklar gelir mi?	*Do the children come?*
Arabalar gelir mi?	*Do the cars come?*

More examples with other verbs. Remember the vowel change in the personal endings:

Ben içer miyim?	*Do I drink?*
Ben bakar mıyım?	*Do I look?*
Ben uyur muyum?	*Do I sleep?*
Ben görür müyüm?	*Do I see?*

Note that there are two ending options for **onlar**, *they*: **-(i)r** or **-(i)rler**. In case the plural ending is preferred, then it should be **-(i)rler mi?** Remember the vowel change in the personal endings, too. (Both ending possibilities are given in the examples.)

Examples:

Çocuklar gelir mi? / gelirler mi?	*Do the children come?*
Çocuklar içer mi? / içerler mi?	*Do the children drink?*
Çocuklar bakar mı? / bakarlar mı?	*Do the children look?*
Çocuklar uyur mu? / uyurlar mı?	*Do the children sleep?*
Çocuklar görür mü? / görürler mi?	*Do the children see?*

exercise 8

Form questions in the present tense with the given clues. Pay attention to the vowel change before adding the ending. Also note that numbers 4 and 5 have two conjugations since there are two ending options for **onlar**, *they*.

Example:

Ben / çay / içmek	**Ben çay içer miyim?**
I / tea / to drink	*Do I drink tea?*

1. **sen/beni/bilmek** ....
2. **biz/dinlenmek** ....
3. **o/otele/gitmek** ....
4. **onlar/sahanda yumurta/yemek** ....
5. **insanlar/menüye/bakmak** ....
6. **siz/kafede menüden yemek/seçmek** ....
7. **ben/seni/görmek** ....
8. **sen/ gezmek / istemek** ....
9. **biz/ uyumak** ....

mastar: belirtili nesne infinitive as the direct object

In Turkish, the infinitive form of verbs can be used as the direct object.

Examples: (The infinitive forms are underlined below.)

Çay içmek istiyorum.	*I want to drink tea.*
Biraz su almak istiyorum.	*I want to take some water.*
Biraz gezmek isterim.	*I want to take a little walk.*
Kahve almak ister misin?	*Do you want to take coffee?*

It is also possible to make an infinitive negative by adding the negative suffix **me** before **–mek** or **ma** before **–mak.**

Examples: (The negative suffixes are underlined below.)

gelmek	*to come*	gelmemek	*not to come*
gitmek	*to go*	gitmemek	*not to go*
içmek	*to drink*	içmemek	*not to drink*
yemek	*to eat*	yememek	*not to eat*
atlamak	*to jump*	atlamamak	*not to jump*
uyumak	*to sleep*	uyumamak	*not to sleep*
bakmak	*to look (at)*	bakmamak	*not to look (at)*

Examples with the sentences:

Çay içmemek istiyorum.	*I want not to drink tea.*
Su almamak istiyorum.	*I want not to take water.*
Gezmemek isterim.	*I want not to take a walk.*

expressing wishes

In Turkish, it is possible to express wishes by using several ways. One is by using the verb of **istemek**. As mentioned before, there are two tenses that can be translated in English as present tenses. The verb **istemek** can be conjugated in these tenses to express wishes, and inquire about others's wishes.

Examples:

Ben biraz zeytin istiyorum.	*I want some olives.*
Ben biraz zeytin isterim.	*I want some olives.*

The negative form of "expressing wishes" is formed by using the negative sentences. Examples:

Zeytin istemiyorum.	*I don't want olives.*
Zeytin istemem.	*I don't want olives.*

Note that **biraz**, *some* can be used both in positive sentences and questions. However, **hiç**, *any* can only be used in negative sentences.

Examples:

Biraz zeytin ister misin?	*Do you want some olives?*
Biraz zeytin istiyor musun?	*Do you want some olives?*
Hiç zeytin istemiyorum.	*I don't want any olives.*
Hiç zeytin istemem.	*I don't want any olives.*

It's also possible to use the short forms. Examples:

Hiç istemem.	*I don't want any.*
Hiç istemiyorum.	*I don't want any.*
Biraz isterim.	*I want some.*
Biraz istiyorum.	*I want some.*

expressing plans

In Turkish, it is possible to express plans by using several ways. One is by using the present tense. As mentioned before, it is also suitable for making plans. Then it's possible to translate is as "Let's".

Examples:

Önce biraz dinleniriz, sonra yemek yeriz.
First, let's rest a little and then eat.
First, we can/should/shall rest a little and then eat.

Kahvaltımızı burada yaparız.
Let's have breakfast here.
We can/should/shall have breakfast here.

Kahvaltıda çay alır mıyız?
Shall we take tea at the breakfast?

Kahvaltıda çay alır mısın?
Will you take tea at the breakfast?

İstanbul'a benimle gelir misin?
Will you come to İstanbul with me?

Unit Four: Eski bir arkadaşla buluşma

Meeting an old friend

With this unit, you will be able to:
• Talk about regular actions, hobbies, habits, places, and people • Give advice and options • Make comparisons • Use the adverbs of manner

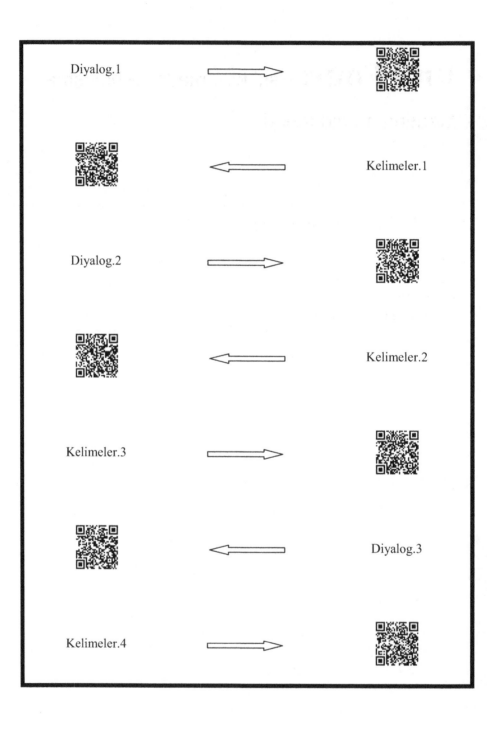

Diyalog.1

Kelimeler.1

Diyalog.2

Kelimeler.2

Kelimeler.3

Diyalog.3

Kelimeler.4

Bölüm 1
Part 1

Dialogue 1

İbrahim, sen misin? İbrahim, is it you?

İbrahim calls a friend of his old friends, Ali on the phone. Ali lives in Ankara.

İbrahim:	Alo! Merhaba! Ben İbrahim Korkmaz. Ali ile mi görüşüyorum? *Hello! I'm İbrahim Korkmaz. Am I speaking to Ali?*
Ali:	İbrahim, sen misin? *İbrahim, is it you?*
İbrahim:	Evet, Ali. Benim. Biz Ankara'dayız. *Yes, Ali. It's me. We're in Ankara.*
Ali:	Hoş geldiniz! Nasılsın? Michelle yenge nasıl? *Welcome! How are you? How is Michelle?*
İbrahim:	Çok şükür, ikimiz de iyiyiz. Sen nasılsın? Kızın, yeğenim Yağmur nasıl? *Thanks God, both of us are fine. How are you? How is your daughter, Yağmur, my niece?*
Ali:	Biz de iyiyiz, teşekkürler. Bu akşam yemekte birlikteyiz. Uygunsunuz, değil mi? *We're fine, too, thanks. We're together for dinner. You're available, aren't you?*
İbrahim:	Uygunuz, uygunuz! Görüşürüz! *We're available! See you!*
Ali:	Tamam ben seni ararım. Görüşmek üzere! *Okay, I'll call you. See you!*

1. Did Ali recognize İbrahim at once?
2. Will they meet tonight for dinner?

Vocabulary

akraba	*relative*	**kuzen**	*cousin*
abi	*elder brother*	**oğul**	*son*
abla	*elder sister*	**uygun**	*available*
enişte	*brother-in-law*	**yeğen**	*nephew, niece*

kız	daughter	yenge	sister-in-law
Çok şükür!	*Thanks God!*		

In the dialogue above, İbrahim wants to talk to his friend, Ali. He wants to verify the one he's talking to is his friend. He asks, **Ali ile mi görüşüyorum?**, *Is it Ali speaking?* This kind of verification is quite common while speaking on the phone. The phrase literally means *Am I speaking to Ali?* In his respond, Ali asks a similar question, again for verification, **İbrahim, sen misin?**, *İbrahim, is it you?* Here, he expresses his surprise. The verb **görüşmek** actually means *to talk to or see each other*. It's also possible to use it in the following patterns: **Görüşmek üzere!**, and **Görüşürüz!** They both mean *See you!*

İbrahim replies, **benim**. Here, this **benim** is not the same as **benim**, *my* used in possessives. Here it means, *it's me*. There is an intonation difference between them. Note the marked syllables for stress in the following phrases: **be<u>nim</u> arabam**, *my car* and **<u>be</u>nim**, *it's me*.

Note that in Türkiye it's very common to address and behave friends as if they're relatives. Therefore men can address their friends wifes as **yenge**, *sister-in-law* or **abla**, *elder sister* and women can address their friends husbands as **enişte**, *brother-in-law* or **abi**, *elder brother*. And, it's common to address the friends son and daughter as **yeğen**, *nephew* or *niece*. Apart from that, it's possible to hear the words **abi** and **abla** right after introduction.

Dialogue 2

sohbet, muhabbet a warm conversation

After meal, they have a warm conversation.

Ali:

Eee, İbrahim, daha daha nasılsın, bakalım?
Tell me, İbrahim, how are you?

İbrahim:

İyi be Ali. Bildiğin, gibi. Senden n'aber?
Fine Ali. As you know. What about you?

Ali:

Ne olsun be İbrahim? Çok şükür, her şey yolunda. Yağmur okulunda, ben işteyim.
Fine İbrahim. Thanks God, everything is fine. Yağmur is at school, I'm at work.

İbrahim:

Çok şükür.
Thanks God.

Ali:

Tatiliniz ne kadar? Ankara'da mı kalırsınız?
How long is your vacation? Will you stay in Ankara?

İbrahim:

İki hafta civarı. Buradan İstanbul'a geçmek istiyoruz.
Around two weeks. We want to go to İstanbul from here.

Ali:	Arabayla mı gidersiniz yoksa uçakla mı?
	Will you go by car or by plane?
İbrahim:	Araba kiralamak istiyorum. Onu tercih ederim. Hem daha fazla yer görürürüz. Hem araba sürmek isterim.
	I want to rent a car. I prefer it. In addition, we can see more places. And, I want to drive.
Ali:	Bence de arabayla gitmelisiniz.
	I also think that you should go by car.

1. How long is their vacation?
2. Will they stay in Ankara for the rest of their vacation?

Vocabulary

bence	*in my opinion*	**muhabbet etmek**	*to have a warm conversation*
bilmek	*to know*	**ne kadar?**	*how long?, how many/much?*
civarı	*around*	**sence**	*in your opinion*
daha	*more than*	**sohbet**	*a warm conversation*
geçmek	*to pass, to go*	**sohbet etmek**	*to have a warm conversation*
hafta	*week*	**sürmek**	*to drive*
hem	*by this way, and*	**tercih etmek**	*to prefer*
kiralamak	*to rent*	**yer**	*place*
muhabbet	*a warm conversation*		
Herşey yolunda.	*Everything is fine.*		
Ne olsun be?	*Everything is fine.*		

In the second dialogue, Ali starts his sentence with **Eee**. This is not a word. But, it can be translated in English as *say*, or *tell me*. It is very common in conversations between sincere friends. Again, **daha daha nasılsın?**, *how are you?* and **bakalım**, *let's see* are common phrases used among sincere friends. **Be** is another exclamation word without a translation. It is more common to use before the names when addressing directly. It can be used to make the conversation warmer, more intimate.

Additionally, **Çok şükür**, *Thanks God* is another way of saying that everything is fine, like **Ne olsun be?**. In fact, **Ne olsun be?** literally *means What (else) should be?* Even if it's appropriate for every conversation, it's used in sincere occassions more often.

Bölüm 2
Part 2

dilbilgisi grammar

tavsiye advice

In Turkish, to form sentences expressing advice, the advice ending **–meli / -malı**, *should* is added <u>right before</u> the personal ending.

the vowel harmony

The ending **–meli / -malı**, *should* depend on the last vowel of the verb.

Last vowel of the verb	a,ı,o,u	e,i,ö,ü
The ending –meli / -malı	-malı	-meli

Examples:

gel mek *(to come)*	**gelmeli**	*should come*
bak mak *(to look (at))*	**bakmalı**	*should look (at)*

Both possibilities of the ending and the personal ending following are studied in the following pages:

• The ending **–meli** and the personal ending following is as given below:

(Ben)	-meliyim	*I should*
(Sen)	-melisin	*You should*
(O)	-meli	*He / She / It should*
(Biz)	-meliyiz	*We should*
(Siz)	-melisiniz	*You (pl) should*
Onlar	-meli/meliler	*They should*

Examples:

Ben gelmeliyim.	*I should come.*
Sen gelmelisin.	*You should come.*
O gelmeli.	*He / She It should come.*
Biz gelmeliyiz.	*We should come.*
Siz gelmelisiniz.	*You should come.*

Çocuklar gelmeli/gelmeliler.		*The children should come.*
Arabalar gelmeli.		*The cars should come.*

- The ending **–malı** and the personal ending following is as given below:

(Ben)	-malıyım	*I should*
(Sen)	-malısın	*You should*
(O)	-malı	*He / She / It should*
(Biz)	-malıyız	*We should*
(Siz)	-malısınız	*You (pl) should*
Onlar	-malı/malılar	*They should*

Examples:

Ben bakmalıyım.	*I should look (at)*
Sen bakmalısın.	*You should look (at).*
O bakmalı.	*He / She / It should look (at)*
Biz bakmalıyız.	*We should look (at)*
Siz bakmalısınız.	*You should look (at)*
Çocuklar bakmalı/ bakmalılar.	*The children should look (at)*
Atlar bakmalı.	*The horses should look (at)*

NB Since the endings added to the verbs bear the personal information, the subjects can be omitted. That's why the subjects are written in brackets in the tables. One exception to this is **onlar**, *they*. **Onlar** cannot be omitted.
In addition, note that there are two ending options for the 3rd plural person, **onlar**, *they*, singular (**-meli / -malı**) and plural (**-meliler / -malılar**). However, for the nonhumans in the subject position, plural ending cannot be preferred.

Examples:

Çocuklar *(human)* **gelmeli/gelmeliler.**	*The children should come.*
Arabalar *(nonhuman)* **gelmeli/~~gelmeliler~~.**	*The cars should come.*
Çocuklar bakmalı/bakmalılar.	*The children should look.*
Atlar bakmalı bakmalı/~~bakmalılar~~.	*The horses should look.*

exercise 1

Form sentences that express advices with the given clues. Pay attention to the vowel change before adding the ending. Also note that numbers 4 and 5 have two conjugations since there are two ending options for **onlar**, *they*.

Example:

Ben / çay / içmek
I / tea / to drink

Ben çay içmeliyim.
I should drink tea.

1. sen/beni/bilmek ....
2. biz/dinlenmek ....
3. o/otele/gitmek ....
4. onlar/sahanda yumurta/yemek ....
5. insanlar/menüye/bakmak ....
6. siz/kafede menüden yemek/seçmek ....
7. ben/seni/görmek ....
8. sen/ araba kiralamak ....
9. biz/ uyumak ....

the negative form

To form negative advices, the negative ending **–memeli / -mamalı**, *shouldn't* is added <u>right before</u> the personal ending.
The negative ending **–memeli / -mamalı**, *shouldn't* and the personal ending following is a 2 way vowel harmony meaning it changes depending on the preceding vowel.

the vowel harmony

The ending **–memeli / -mamalı**, *shouldn't* depend on the last vowel of the verb.

Last vowel of the verb	a,ı,o,u	e,i,ö,ü
The ending –memeli / -mamalı	-mamalı	-memeli

Examples:

gel mek *(to come)*   **gelmemeli**   *shouldn't come*

bak mak *(to look (at))*   **bakmamalı**   *shouldn't look (at)*

For the vowel change tables of the ending and the personal ending, see positive formation above.

Examples:

Ben gelmemeliyim.	*I should not come.*
Sen gelmemelisin.	*You should not come.*
O gelmemeli.	*He / She It should not come.*
Biz gelmemeliyiz.	*We should not come.*
Siz gelmemelisiniz.	*You should not come.*
Çocuklar gelmemeli/gelmemeliler.	*The children should not come.*
Arabalar gelmemeli.	*The cars should not come.*
Ben bakmamalıyım.	*I should not look (at)*
Sen bakmamalısın.	*You should not look (at).*
O bakmamalı.	*He/She/It should not look (at)*
Biz bakmamalıyız.	*We should not look (at)*
Siz bakmamalısınız.	*You should not look (at)*
Çocuklar bakmamalı/ bakmamalılar.	*The children should not look (at)*
Atlar bakmamalı.	*The horses should not look (at)*

exercise 2

Form sentences that express negative advices with the given clues. Pay attention to the vowel change before adding the ending. Also note that numbers 4 and 5 have two conjugations since there are two ending options for **onlar**, *they*.

Example:

Ben / çay / içmek   **Ben çay içmemeliyim.**
I / tea / to drink   *I should not drink tea.*

1.   sen/beni/bilmek
2.   biz/dinlenmek
3.   o/otele/gitmek
4.   onlar/sahanda yumurta/yemek
5.   insanlar/menüye/bakmak
6.   siz/kafede menüden yemek/seçmek
7.   ben/seni/görmek
8.   sen/ araba kiralamak
9.   biz/ uyumak

the question form

To form a question with the advices, two steps are needed.

STEP 1

First, the verb is conjugated for the 3rd singular person (**o**, *he / she / it*). Remember that for the 3rd singular person (**o**, *he / she / it*) the ending is either **–meli** or **–malı**. See the verb conjugations above. Also remember the vowel change.

Examples:

The verb is conjugated for the 3rd <u>singular person (**o**, *he / she / it*)</u>.

söyle mek	*(to say)*	**söylemeli**	*(He / she should say)*
gel mek	*(to come)*	**gelmeli**	*(He / she should come)*
git mek	*(to go)*	**gitmeli**	*(He / she should go)*
ye mek	*(to eat)*	**yemeli**	*(He / she should eat)*
uyu mak	*(to sleep)*	**uyumalı**	*(He / she should sleep)*
yürü mek	*(to walk)*	**yürümeli**	*(He / she should walk)*
kal mak	*(to stay)*	**kalmalı**	*(He / she should stay)*
bak mak	*(to look (at))*	**bakmalı**	*(He / she should look (at))*
atla mak	*(to jump))*	**atlamalı**	*(He / she should jump)*

STEP 2

Then, the question endings are added to the end separately. The question endings for each person are given below.

Only the ending with **–meli** is given in the table. The previous vowel change table is also applicable here.

(The ending **–meli** or **–malı** for the 3rd singular person (**o**, *he / she / it*) added in **STEP 1** is underlined.)

(Ben)	<u>-meli</u> miyim?	*Should I ...?*
(Sen)	<u>-meli</u> misin?	*Should you ..?*
(O)	<u>-meli</u> mi?	*Should he / she / it ..?*
(Biz)	<u>-meli</u> miyiz?	*Should we ...?*
(Siz)	<u>-meli</u> misiniz?	*Should you (pl) ...?*
Onlar	<u>-meli</u> mi?	*Should they ...?*

Example:

Ben gelmeli miyim?   *Should I come?*
(Step 1) (Step 2)

More examples:

Sen gelmeli misin?	*Should you come?*
O gelmeli mi?	*Should he / she/ it come?*
Biz gelmeli miyiz?	*Should we come?*
Siz gelmeli misiniz?	*Should you (pl) come?*
Çocuklar gelmeli mi?	*Should the children come?*
Arabalar gelmeli mi?	*Should the cars come?*

More examples with other verbs. Remember the vowel change in the personal endings:

Ben içmeli miyim?	*Should I drink?*
Sen bakmalı mısın?	*Should you look (at)?*
O uyumalı mı?	*Should he / she / it sleep?*
Biz görmeli miyiz?	*Should we see?*

Also note that there are two ending options for **onlar**, *they*: **-meli** or **meliler**. In case the plural ending is preferred, then it should be **-meliler mi?** Remember the vowel change in the personal endings, too.

Examples:

Çocuklar gelmeli mi? / gelmeliler mi?	*Should the children come?*
Çocuklar içmeli mi? / içmeliler mi?	*Should the children drink?*
Çocuklar bakmalı mı? / bakmalılar mı?	*Should the children look?*
Çocuklar uyumalı mı? / uyumalılar mı?	*Should the children sleep?*
Çocuklar görmeli mi? / görmeliler mi?	*Should the children see?*

exercise 3

Form questions with advices with the given clues. Pay attention to the vowel change before adding the ending. Also note that numbers 4 and 5 have two conjugations since there are two ending options for **onlar**, *they*.

Example:

Ben / çay / içmek   **Ben çay içmeli miyim?**
I / tea / to drink   *Should I drink tea?*

1. **sen/beni/bilmek**   ....
2. **biz/dinlenmek**   ....
3. **o/otele/gitmek**   ....
4. **onlar/sahanda yumurta/yemek** ....
5. **insanlar/menüye/bakmak**   ....
6. **siz/kafede menüden yemek/seçmek** ....
7. **ben/seni/görmek**   ....
8. **sen/ araba kiralamak**   ....
9. **biz/ uyumak**   ....

Ülke, Millet, Lisan / Country, Nation, Language

Alman	German person	**İspanya**	Spain
Almanca	German language	**İspanyol**	Spanish person
Almanya	Germany	**İspanyolca**	Spanish language
Arap	Arab	**İtalya**	Italy
Arapça	Arabic	**İtalyan**	Italian person
Çin	China	**İtalyanca**	Italian language
Çince	Chinese	**Japon**	Japanese person
Çinli	Chinese person	**Japonca**	Japanese language
Fransa	France	**Japonya**	Japan
Fransız	French person	**Rus**	Russian person
Fransızca	French language	**Rusça**	Russian language
Hindistan	India	**Rusya**	Russia
Hintçe	Indian language	**Suudi Arabistan**	Saudi Arabia
Hintli	Indian person	**Türk**	Turk
İngiliz	English person	**Türkçe**	Turkish language
İngilizce	English language	**Türkiye**	Türkiye
İngiltere	England		

giving options

It is possible to give options by using "-mi (yoksa) –mi?". The present and progressive tenses are applicable to this usage. Examples:

Arabayla mı gidersiniz yoksa uçakla mı?
Will you go by car or by plane?

Şarkı söylemek mi, dinlemek mi?
(Which do you like) to sing a song or listen to it?

İngilizceyi mi daha çok seversin yoksa İspanyolcayı mı?
Which do you like more, English or Spanish?

Kahvaltıda kahve mi içersin yoksa çay mı tercih edersin?
Will you drink tea at the breakfast or do you prefer tea?

Dinlenmek mi istiyorsun gezmek mi?
Do you want to rest or take a trip?

the adverbs, the adverbs of manner

In general, adverbs give the answer of the "how?", "when", "how many/much?", "where?" and "when?" questions asked to the verb of the sentence. They are derived from adjectives or verbs.

The adverbs of manner, are the adverbs that give the answer to the "how?" questions. There are **several** ways to derive adverbs.

1.   The suffix **–ce / ca**, *-ly* is added to adjectives. Note the vowel and consonant harmony.

Last vowel of the verb	a,ı,o,u	e,i,ö,ü
The ending –ce / -ca	-ca	-ce

Examples:

zeki ce   **Yağmur zekice konuşuyor.**
clever ly   *Yağmur speaks cleverly.*

akıllı ca   **Yağmur akıllıca konuşuyor.**
clever ly   *Yağmur speaks cleverly.*

hızlı ca   **Talha arabayı hızlıca sürer.**
                           Talha drives the car fast.

Note that **zeki** and **akıllı** mean the same.

The letter "c" in the ending may change to "ç" depending on the last letter of the preceding word:

the consonant harmony

In case the word ends with one the consonants **'f'**, **'s'**, **'t'**, **'k'**, **'ç'**, **'ş'**, **'h'**, or **'p'**, the letter "c" in the ending changes to "ç":

Last letter of the preceding word	f	s	t	k	ç	ş	h	p
The ending –ce / -ca change to	-çe / -ça							

Example:

yavaş ça   **İbrahim çayını yavaşça içiyor.**
(slow ly)   *İbrahim drinks his tea slowly.*

2.   Adjectives are used twice.

yavaş yavaş   **İbrahim çayını yavaş yavaş içiyor.**
                                      İbrahim drinks his tea slowly.

hızlı hızlı   **Talha arabayı hızlı hızlı sürer.**
                                      Talha drives the car fast.

3.   Adjectives are used without changing.

yavaş   **İbrahim çayını yavaş içiyor.**
                                      İbrahim drinks his tea slowly.

hızlı   **Talha arabayı hızlı sürer.**
                                      Talha drives the car fast.

4.   The suffix "-erek/-arak" is added to bare form of the verbs. Note the vowel harmony.

Examples:

çalış mak   **çalışarak**
(to work/study)   *(by working/studying)*

İbrahim <u>çalışarak</u> dinlenir.   *İbrahim rests <u>by working/studying</u>.*

uçmak   **uçarak**
(to fly)   *(by flying)*

İbrahim ve Michelle Ankara'ya   *İbrahim and Michelle are coming to*
<u>uçarak</u> geliyor.   *Ankara <u>(by) flying</u>.*

koşmak	koşarak
(to run)	*(by running)*

Talha otele <u>koşarak</u> gider.   *Talha goes to the hotel (by) running.*

NB The derivation is not suitable to all the verbs and all the adjectives. In addition, not all the adjectives are suitable for each method.

the comparisons

It's possible make comparison of adjectives and adverbs by using the ending **-den daha**, *more than*. Note that –den daha is a 2 way harmony meaning it changes depending on the preceding vowel.

Last vowel of the word	a,ı,o,u	e,i,ö,ü
The ending –den / -dan	-dan	-den

Examples:

İngilizce İspanyolcadan daha yaygındır.   *English is more common than Spanish*

Ama İspanyolca İngilizceden daha şiirseldir.   *But Spanish sounds more poetic than English.*

The letter "d" in the ending may change to "t" depending on the last letter of the preceding word:

the consonant harmony

In case the word ends with one the consonants '**f**', '**s**', '**t**', '**k**', '**ç**', '**ş**', '**h**', or '**p**', the letter "d" in the ending changes to "**t**":

Last letter of the preceding word	f	s	t	k	ç	ş	h	p
The ending –den / -dan change to	-ten / -tan							

Examples:

Araba uçaktan daha yavaştır.
The car is slower than the plane.

Şarkı söylemek dinlemekten daha zordur.
To sing a song is harder than to listen.

More examples:

Uçak arabadan daha hızlıdır.
The plane is faster than the car.

Kahvaltıda kahveyi çaydan daha çok severim.
I like coffee more than tea at breakfast.

Dinlenmek gezmekten daha kolay. Ancak gezmek daha eğlenceli.
To rest is easier than to take a trip. But, to take a trip is more entertaining.

Kahvaltıda akşam yemeğinden daha fazla yiyecek var.
There's more food at breakfast than at dinner.

expressing the equal degree

Expression of the equal degree is formed by using **kadar**, *as as.*

Examples:

Araba uçak <u>kadar</u> hızlı değildir.
The car isn't <u>as</u> fast <u>as</u> the plane.

Şarkı söylemek dinlemek <u>kadar</u> kolay.
To sing a song is <u>as</u> easy <u>as</u> to listen.

İngilizce İspanyolca <u>kadar</u> şiirseldir. Ve İspanyolca İngilizce kadar yaygındır.
English sounds <u>as</u> poetic <u>as</u> Spanish. And Spanish is as common as English.

Kahvaltıda kahveyi çay <u>kadar</u> (çok)* sevmem.
I don't like coffee <u>as</u> much <u>as</u> tea at breakfast.

Dinlenmek gezmek <u>kadar</u> eğlenceli değildir.
To rest isn't <u>as</u> entertaining <u>as</u> to take a trip.

Kahvaltıda akşam yemeğindeki <u>kadar</u> (çok)* yiyecek var.
There's <u>as</u> much food at breakfast <u>as</u> at dinner.

(*) Note that it is optional to add **çok**, *much* in these sentences since the meaning already provides the meaning.

Bölüm 3
Part 3

Dialogue 3

zekice! clever!

While İbrahim and Ali having a conversation, Michelle and Yağmur start talking at the other end of the table.

Michelle:	Ders dışında neler yaparsın, Yağmur? Hobin falan var mı?
	What do you do in your time out of lessons, Yağmur? Do you have any hobbies?
Yağmur:	Fazla zamanım kalmıyor aslında, ama müzikle ilgilenmek güzel.
	I don't have much time left in fact, but it's nice to be interested in music.
Michelle:	Nasıl yani? Şarkı söylemek mi, yoksa dinlemek mi?
	How? To sing a song or listen to it?
Yağmur:	Her ikisi de. Boş zamanımda bir de ud çalıyorum.
	Both of them. I also play the ud in my free time.
Michelle:	Harika!
	Wonderful!
Yağmur:	Ayrıca, ileride mesleğimde fayda sağlamak istiyorum ve yabancı dil öğreniyorum.
	Apart from that, I like to gain advantage for my profession in the future and learn foreing languages.
Michelle:	Çok zekice! Ne öğreniyorsun?
	Very clever! What do you learn?
Yağmur:	İngilizce ve İspanyolca birlikte.
	English and Spanish, together.
Michelle:	Hangisini daha çok seviyorsun? İngilizceyi mi, İspanyolcayı mı?
	Which one do you like more? English or Spanish?
Yağmur:	İngilizce İspanyolcadan daha kolay. İspanyolca İngilizce kadar yaygın değil, ama daha şiirsel.
	English is easier than Spanish. Spanish isn't as common as English, but it's more poetic.
Michelle:	Kesinlikle seninle aynı fikirdeyim!
	Certainly, I agree with you!

---

1. Does Yağmur have hobbies? What are they?

2. How many foreign languages does Yağmur study?

Vocabulary

aslında	in fact	ileride	in the future
aynı	the same	ilgilenmek	to be interested in
ayrıca	in addition	İspanyolca	Spanish
boş zaman	free time	keman	violin
çalmak	to play	kolay	easy
ders	lesson	meslek	profession
dışında	outside, out of, apart from	müzik	music
dinlemek	to listen to	nasıl?	how?
düşünce	thought	piyano	piano
falan	or else	şarkı	song
fayda	advantage	şarkı söylemek	to sing
fayda sağlamak	to gain advantage	şiirsel	poetic
fikir	opinion	ud	ud
gitar	guitar	yabancı dil	foreign language
hangisi?	which?	yapmak	to do
her ikisi de	both	yaygın	common, widespread
herkes	everyone	zamanı kalmak	to have time left
herşey	everything	zor	difficult
hobi	hobby		
Seninle aynı fikirdeyim.	I agree with you.		

In the dialogue above, they talk about hobbies or activities. In Michelle's question **Hobin falan var mı?**, **falan** can be translated as *something like*. **Falan** is more appropriate to use in sincere conversations, not with the people just introduced to.

exercise 4

Which is the odd one out in each row?

yabancı dil	söylemek	sağlamak	kalmak
gitar	fikir	piyano	ud
müzik	keman	çalmak	ayrıca
dinlemek	şiirsel	aynı	zor

Bölüm 4
Part 4

herkes, her şey everyone, everything

Herkes and **her şey** are considered singular even though they mean plural. In addition, they can only be used in affirmative sentences.

Examples:

Burada herkes var.	*There's eveyone here.*
Burada her şey var.	*There's eveything here.*

hiç, hiçbir şey, hiç kimse any, anything, anyone

Hiç can be translated into English as *any*, but in the context it is actually used to intensify the negative meaning. It can be used in the questions, too. It is also used with **bir şey**, *something* and **(bir) kimse**, *someone* to make those negative. Examples:

hiç, *any*

Paran var mı?	*Do you have money?*
Hiç paran var mı?	*Do you have any money?*
Evet, (biraz) param var.	*Yes, I have (some) money.*
Paran yok mu?	*Don't you have money?*
Hiç paran yok mu?	*Don't you have any money?*
Hayır, (hiç) param yok.	*No, I don't have (any) money.*
Hiç mi yok? / Hiç yok mu?	*Don't you have any?*
Hayır, hiç yok.	*No, I don't have any.*

bir şey, *something*

Burada bir şey var mı?	*Is there something here?*
Evet, burada bir şey var.	*Yes, there's something here.*
Burada (hiç)bir şey yok mu?	*Isn't there anything here?*
Hayır, burada (hiç)bir şey yok.	*No, there isn't anything here.*

(bir) kimse, *someone*

Burada (bir) kimse var mı?	*Is there someone here?*
Evet, burada biri/birisi* var.	*Yes, there's someone here.*
Burada (hiç) kimse yok mu?	*Isn't there anyone here?*
Hayır, burada (hiç) kimse yok.	*No, there isn't anyone here.*

(*) **Kimse**, *one* or **bir kimse**, *someone* usually isn't used in positive sentences. Instead, **biri** or **birisi** is preferred with the same meaning.

Burada kimse* yok mu?	*Isn't there anyone here?*
Burada biri/birisi* yok mu?	*Isn't there anyone here?*

Hayır, burada kimse* yok.	*No, there's no one here.*
Hayır, burada biri/birisi* yok.	*No, there's no one here.*

(*) **Kimse** can be also be used in negative sentences or questions alone. As said above, **hiçbir** is added to intensify the meaning.

hiçbir şey, *nothing*

Burada hiçbir şey yok mu?	*Isn't there anything here?*
Hayır, burada hiçbir şey yok.	*No, there's nothing here.*

hiçbir kimse, *no one*

Burada hiçbir kimse yok mu?	*Isn't there anyone here?*
Hayır, burada hiçbir kimse yok.	*No, there's no one here.*

more on there is / there are

In Turkish, it is also possible to use **var**, *there is / there* are with the persons, (I, You, He / She / It, We, You, and They).

To form to be sentences with persons, the special endings are added to **var**, *there is / there are*.

Var and the personal endings are given in the table:

(Ben)	varım	*I'm (there)**
(Sen)	varsın	*You are (there)**
(O)	var	*He / She / It is (there)**
(Biz)	varız	*We are (there)**
(Siz)	varsınız	*You (pl) are (there)**
Onlar	var / varlar	*They are (there)**

(*) There represents any place information. See the examples.

Examples:

Ben bu işte varım.	*I'm <u>in</u> this business.*
Biz sizinle her şeye varız.	*We're <u>in</u> everything with you.*

NB Since the endings added to the verbs bear the personal information, the subjects can be omitted. That's why the subjects are written in brackets in the table. One exception to this is **onlar**, *they*. **Onlar** cannot be omitted.

In addition, note that there are two ending options for the 3rd plural person, **onlar**, *they*, singular (**var**) and plural (**varlar**). However, for the nonhumans in the subject position, plural ending cannot be preferred.

Example:

Onlar bu işte kesin var / varlar.   *They're certainly in this business.*

NB This structure, in fact, a "to be" sentence is with place information. Note that both sentences below mean the same.

Example:

Odada ben varım.   *I'm in the room.*
Ben odadayım.   *I'm in the room.*

more on there isn't / there aren't

In Turkish, it is also possible to use **yok**, *there isn't / there* aren't with the persons, (I, You, He / She / It, We, You, and They).

To form to be sentences with persons, the special endings are added to **yok**, *there isn't / there aren't*.

Yok and the personal endings are given in the table:

(Ben)	yokum	*I'm not (there)**
(Sen)	yoksun	*You aren't (there)**
(O)	yok	*He / She / It isn't (there)**
(Biz)	yokuz	*We aren't (there)**
(Siz)	yoksunuz	*You (pl) aren't (there)**
Onlar	yok / yoklar	*They aren't (there)**

(*) There represents any place information. See the examples.

Examples:

Ben bu işte yokum.   *I'm not <u>in</u> this business.*

Biz sizinle hiçbir işte yokuz.   *We aren't <u>in</u> any business with you.*

NB Since the endings added to the verbs bear the personal information, the subjects can be omitted. That's why the subjects are written in brackets in the table. One exception to this is **onlar**, *they*. **Onlar** cannot be omitted.
In addition, note that there are two ending options for the 3rd plural person, **onlar**, *they*, singular (**yok**) and plural (**yoklar**). However, for the nonhumans in the subject position, plural ending cannot be preferred.

Example:

Onlar bu işte kesin yok / yoklar.   *They're certainly not in this business.*

NB This structure, in fact, is a "to be" sentence with place information. Note that both sentences below mean the same.

Example:

| **Odada ben yokum.** | *I'm not in the room.* |
| **Ben odada değilim.** | *I'm not in the room.* |

more on is there? / are there?

The question is formed by placing the question word **mı?** at the end separately right before the personal ending.

Var mı?, *is there? / are there?* and the personal endings are given in the table:

(Ben)	var mıyım?	*Am I there?**
(Sen)	var mısın?	*Are you there?**
(O)	var mı?	*Is he / she / it there?**
(Biz)	var mıyız?	*Are we there?**
(Siz)	var mısınız?	*Are you (pl) there?**
Onlar	var mı?/ varlar mı?	*Are they there?**

(*) There represents any place information.

Examples:

| **Sen bu işte var mısın?** | *Are you in this business?* |
| **Siz bizimle her şeye var mısınız?** | *Are you in everything with us?* |

Note that there are two ending options for the 3rd plural person, **onlar**, *they*, singular (**var mı?**) and plural (**varlar mı?**).

Example:

| **Onlar bu işte kesin var mı?** | *Are they certainly in this business?* |
| **Onlar bu işte kesin varlar mı?** | *Are they certainly in this business?* |

NB This structure, in fact, is a "to be" sentence with place information. Note that both sentences below mean the same.

Example:

| **Ben odada var mıyım?** | *Am I in the room?* |
| **Ben odada mıyım?** | *Am I in the room?* |

more on isn't there? / aren't there?

The question is formed by placing the question word **mu?** at the end separately <u>right before</u> the personal ending.

Yok mu?, *isn't there? / aren't there?* and the personal endings are given in the table:

(Ben)	yok muyum?	*Aren't I there?* *
(Sen)	yok musun?	*Aren't you there?* *
(O)	yok mu?	*Isn't he / she / it there?* *
(Biz)	yok muyuz?	*Aren't we there?* *
(Siz)	yok musunuz?	*Aren't you (pl) there?* *
Onlar	yok mu?/ yoklar mı?	*Aren't they there?* *

(*) There represents any place information. See the examples.

Examples:

Sen bu işte yok musun?   *Aren't you <u>in</u> this business?*

Siz bizimle her şeye yok musunuz?   *Aren't you <u>in</u> everything with us?*

Note that there are two ending options for the 3rd plural person, **onlar**, *they*, singular (**yok mu?**) and plural (**yoklar mı?**).

· Example:

Onlar bu işte yok mu?   *Aren't they in this business?*

Onlar bu işte yoklar mı?   *Aren't they in this business?*

NB This structure, in fact, is a "to be" sentence with place information. Note that both sentences below mean the same.

Example:

Ben odada yok muyum?   *Aren't I in the room?*

Ben odada değil miyim?   *Aren't I in the room?*

exercise 5

Answer the question with the subject given. Make positive or negative sentences.

Example: **Odada kimse var mı?**   **Evet/ben**
                (Is there anyone in the room?)   *(Yes / I)*

                                              Evet, odada ben varım.
                                              (Yes, I'm in the room.)

1. **Evet/sen**   ....
2. **Evet/çocuklar**   ....
3. **Evet/biz**   ....
4. **Evet/siz**   ....
5. **Evet/Michelle**   ....
6. **Evet/herkes**   ....
7. **Evet/bir şey**   ....
8. **Evet/birisi**   ....
9. **Hayır/hiç kimse** ....
10. **Hayır/hiç bir şey** ....

düzenli uğraşı & hobiler regular activity & hobbies

Read the examples about asking and answering about the regular activities and hobbies.

Genellikle ne(ler) yaparsın?	*What do you do regularly?*
Düzenli olarak müzik dinlerim.	*I listen to music regularly.*
Başka neler yaparsın?	*What else do you do?*
Sabahları kitap okurum.	*I read books in the mornings.*
Hobin var mı?	*Do you have a hobby?*
Düzenli bir uğraşın var mı?	*Do you have a regular activity?*
Düzenli olarak ders çalışırım.	*I study my lessons regularly.*
Ders dışında ne yaparsın?	*What do you do in your free time?*
Ders dışında ud çalarım.	*I play the ud in my free time.*
Bir de akşamları şarkı söylerim.	*And, I sing songs in the evenings.*

Unit Five: İstanbul'a gidiyoruz.

We're going to İstanbul.

With this unit, you will be able to:

- Book a room and register at a hotel
- Rent a car
- Inquire about needs, ideas, and plans
- Express ability/possibility
- Use the gerund
- Learn the numbers, 21-1,000,000

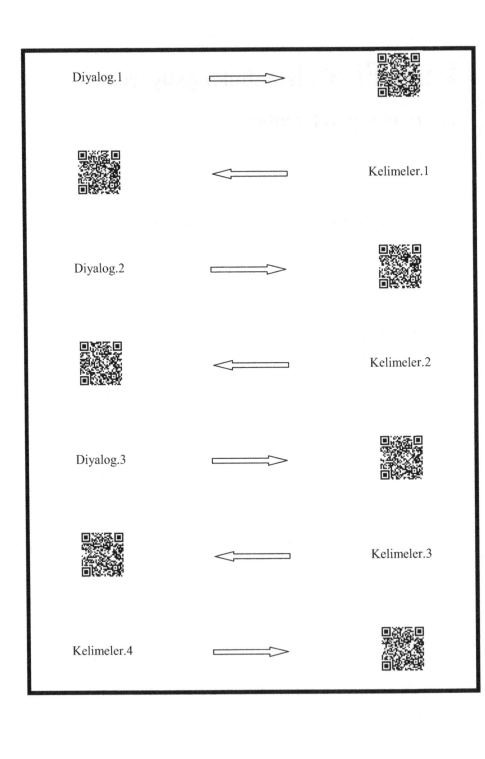

Bölüm 1
Part 1

Dialogue 1

araç kiralama car renting

Michelle and İbrahim decided to rent a car. İbrahim calls a car renting agency on the phone.

Zeynep:	Merhaba, Yıldırım Araç Kiralama. Ben, Zeynep. Size nasıl yardımcı olabilirim?
	Hello, Yıldırım Car Renting. I'm Zeynep. How can I help you?
İbrahim:	Merhaba, ismim İbrahim Korkmaz. Küçük bir araç kiralamak istiyorum.
	Hello, my name's İbrahim Korkmaz. I want to rent a small car.
Zeynep:	Tabii İbrahim Bey. Nasıl bir araba istersiniz?
	Alright, Mr. İbrahim. What kind of car do you want?
İbrahim:	Küçük olsun yeterli.
	A small car is enough.
Zeynep:	Vites nasıl olsun? Düz – otomatik? Ya yakıt? Dizel – benzinli?
	What about the transmission? Standard – automatic? What about the fuel? Diesel – gasoline?
İbrahim:	Otomatik daha iyi. Yakıt farketmez. İkisi de olur.
	Automatic is better. The fuel doesn't matter. Both would be okay.
Zeynep:	Kaç günlüğüne istiyorsunuz?
	For how many days do you want the car?
İbrahim:	Bir haftalık istiyorum. Ücreti ne kadar?
	I want it for a week. What's the price?
Zeynep:	Günlük beş yüz tl. Yedi çarpı beş yüz, yani toplam üç bin beş yüz tl. artı günlük sigorta masrafı, İbrahim Bey.
	It's 500 TL for a day. 7 times 500, so it's total 3,500 TL plus daily insurance cost, Mr. İbrahim.

1. Does İbrahim want to buy a car?
2. How many days does he want it for?

Vocabulary

araç	vehicle	kiralama	renting
artı	added to	masraf	cost
aylık	for a month, monthly	olmak	to be
benzin	gasoline	otomatik	automatic
bölü	divided by	saatlik	for an hour, hourly
çarpı	multiplied by	sigorta	insurance
dizel	diesel	toplam	total
düz	standart	ücret	price
eksi	subtracted from	vites	transmission
fark etmek	to make a difference	yakıt	fuel
günlük	for a day, daily	yardımcı	helper
haftalık	for a week, weekly	yıllık	for a year, yearly
Size nasıl yardımcı olabilirim?		How can I help you?	

In the dialogue above, we see **olsun** both in question and in answer. It can be translated as *can/shall it be?* and *let it be* respectively. We also see the same verb, **olmak** in **olur**. Here it's translated as *it is possible or acceptable*.

Note that the currency in Turkish can be said in two ways. One is by saying **lira** and the other is by saying the letters in the abreviation, i.e. **te**, **le**.

exercise 1

Which is the odd one out in each row?

artı	eksi	ücret	çarpı
saatlik	otomatik	aylık	günlük
araç	uçak	araba	masraf
vites	sigorta	yakıt	olmak

Dialogue 2

otelde yer ayırtma booking room at a hotel

Before starting their trip to İstanbul, İbrahim wants to book their room at a hotel. He searched for hotels in İstanbul and found one.

İbrahim:	Merhabalar, Satürn Otel mi?
	Hello, is it the Saturn Hotel?
Nâlân:	Evet, beyefendi. Buyurun, Satürn Otel. Ben Nâlân. Nasıl yardımcı olabilirim?
	Yes, sir. Welcome, this is the Saturn Hotel. I'm Nâlân. How can I help?
İbrahim:	Bir oda için yer ayırtmak istiyorum.
	I want to make a reservation for a room.
Nâlân:	Tabii, kaç günlük tutmak istiyorsunuz? Kaç kişilik olsun?
	Sure, how many days do you want the reservation for? For how many people?
İbrahim:	Yedi günlük. Eşim ve benim için.
	For 7 days. For myself and my wife.
Nâlân:	Tabii efendim. Sizin için yerimiz var. Yerinizi ayırıyorum.
	Sure, sir. We have room for you. I'm makink your reservation.
İbrahim:	Ücret internet sayfasındaki gibi değil mi? Ayrıca, oda boğaz manzaralı olsun.
	Is the price as said on the internet page, right? In addition, the room should be with the Bosphorus scenery.
Nâlân:	Evet efendim. Tüm odalarımız boğaz manzaralı. Fiyatta da ayrıca bir kolaylık yaparız.
	Yes, sir. All our rooms are with the Bosphorus scenery. We'll make an additional discount as well.

1. Does İbrahim know about the price?
2. Can they see the Bosphorus from their room?

Vocabulary

Boğaz	*the Bosphorus*	**oda**	*room*
fiyat	*price*	**oda tutmak**	*to stay in a hotel*
internet sayfası	*internet page*	**yer ayırmak**	*to approve the reservation*
kişilik	*for a person*	**yer ayırtmak**	*to apply for a hotel reservation*

manzara	view
Fiyatta da ayrıca bir kolaylık yaparız.	*We'll make an extra discount on the price.*

In the dialogue above, Nâlân says, **Fiyatta da ayrıca bir kolaylık yaparız.** This means that the price may be lower, discounted. These types of phrases are widely heard when buying and selling something and even in booking a hotel room.

Bölüm 2
Part 2

dilbilgisi grammar

the gerund

In Turkish, the gerund is derived from the infinitive by separating the last letter "k". The gerund form of a verb is considered as a noun and it can be used with modifiers and suffixes. Examples:

içmek	*to drink*	içme	*drinking*
bakmak	*to look*	bakma	*looking*
uyumak	*to sleep*	uyuma	*sleeping*
görmek	*to see*	görme	*seeing*
söylemek	*to say*	söyleme	*saying*

The verbs with more pieces are also included. The final letter "k" is omitted to turn it into the gerund form. Examples:

tercih etmek	*to prefer*	tercih etme	*preferring*
yardım etmek	*to help*	yardım etme	*helping*
banyo yapmak	*to take a bath*	banyo yapma	*taking a bath*
seçim yapmak	*to choose*	seçim yapma	*choosing*
indirim yapmak	*to discount*	indirim yapma	*discounting*

Derival of the negative gerund is also possible in Turkish. The negative ending -me/-ma is added to the gerund to make it negative. **–me** or **–ma** depends on the last vowel of the verb.

Last vowel of the verb	a,ı,o,u	e,i,ö,ü
The ending –me / -ma	-ma	-me

Examples:

içme	*drinking*	içmeme	*not drinking*
bakma	*looking*	bakmama	*not looking*
uyuma	*sleeping*	uyumama	*not sleeping*
görme	*seeing*	görmeme	*not seeing*
söyleme	*saying*	söylememe	*not saying*
tercih etme	*preferring*	tercih etmeme	*not preferring*
yardım etme	*helping*	yardım etmeme	*not helping*
banyo yapma	*taking a bath*	banyo yapmama	*not taking a bath*

| **seçim yapma** | *choosing* | **seçim yapmama** | *not choosing* |
| **indirim yapma** | *discounting* | **indirim yapmama** | *not discounting* |

It is also possible to use the possessives with the gerunds. See Unit 2 for the formation of the possessives if necessary.

Examples:

(benim) içmem	**(senin) içmen**	**(onun) içmesi, vb.**
my drinking	*your drinking*	*his/her drinking, etc.*
(that I drink)	*(that you drink)*	*(that he/she drinks), etc.*

(benim) uyumam	**(senin) uyuman**	**(onun) uyuması, vb.**
my sleeping	*your sleeping*	*his/her sleeping, etc.*
(that I sleep)	*(that you sleep)*	*(that he/she sleeps), etc.*

(benim) görmem	**(senin) görmen**	**(onun) görmesi, vb.**
my seeing	*your seeing*	*his/her seeing, etc.*
(that I see)	*(that you see)*	*(that he/she sees), etc.*

ability/possibility-I

In Turkish, the ability and possibility is expressed in several ways. One is to use **mümkün** or **mümkündür**, *it's possible* with an infinitive or a gerund. Examples:

İstanbul'a araba ile gitmek mümkün. (infinitive **gitmek**, *to go*)
It's possible to go to İstanbul by car.
(One can go to İstanbul by car.)

Talha'nın hızlı araba sürmesi mümkündür. (gerund **sürme**, *driving*)
It's possible that Talha drives fast.
(Talha can drive fast.)

Otelden Anıtkabir'e yürümek mümkündür. (infinitive **yürümek**, *to walk*)
It's possible to walk to Anıtkabir from the hotel.
(One can walk to Anıtkabir from the hotel.)

Otelden Kızılay Meydanı'na yürümeniz de mümkün. (gerund **yürüme**, *walking*)
It's possible for you to walk to Kızılay Square from the hotel, too.
(You can walk to the Kızılay Square from the hotel, too.)
(Lit. Your walking to the Kızılay Square from the hotel is possible.)

Michelle için İngilizce konuşmak mümkündür. (infinitive **konuşmak**, *to speak*)
It's possible for Michelle to speak English.
(Michelle can speak English.)

Michelle'in Türkçe konuşması da mümkündür. (Here the gerund **konuşma**, *speaking* is used.)
It's also possible for Michelle to speak Turkish.
(Michelle can also speak Turkish.)
(Lit. Michelle's speaking Turkish is also possible.)

exercise 2

Make sentences expressing ability/possibility with the given clues and **mümkün** or **mümkündür**. Use the gerund form in your answers.

Example:

Ben / çay / içmek   **Benim çay içmem mümkündür.**
I / tea / to drink   *It's possible that I can drink tea.*
                    (Lit. My drinking tea is possible.)

1. sen/beni/bilmek   ....

2. biz/dinlenmek   ....

3. o/otele/gitmek   ....

4. onlar/sahanda yumurta/yemek   ....

5. insanlar/menüye/bakmak   ....

6. siz/kafede menüden yemek/seçmek   ....

7. ben/seni/görmek   ....

8. sen/ araba kiralamak   ....

9. biz/ uyumak   ....

the negative form

To form a negative sentence, **değil**, *not* is added after **mümkün**, *possible*. **Değil**, *not* can be used both with infinitives and gerund. Examples:

İstanbul'a araba ile gitmek mümkün değil.
It's not possible to go to İstanbul by car.
(You (One) cannot go to İstanbul by car.)

Talha'nın hızlı araba sürmesi mümkün değildir.
It's not possible that Talha drives fast.
(Talha cannot drive fast.)
(Lit. Talha's driving a fast car isn't possible.)

Otelden Anıtkabir'e yürümek mümkün değildir.
It's not possible to walk to Anıtkabir from the hotel.
(You cannot walk to Anıtkabir from the hotel.)

Otelden Kızılay Meydanı'na yürümeniz de mümkün değildir.
It's not possible for you to walk to Kızılay Square from the hotel, either.
(You cannot walk to the Kızılay Square from the hotel, either.)
(Lit. Your walking to the Kızılay Square from the hotel also isn't possible.)

Michelle için İngilizce konuşmak mümkün değildir.
It's not possible for Michelle to speak English.
(Michelle isn't able to speak English.)

Michelle'in Türkçe konuşması da mümkün değildir.
It's also not possible for Michelle to speak Turkish.
Michelle cannot to speak Turkish, either.
(Lit. Michelle's speaking Turkish also isn't possible.)

the question form

To form a question, the question suffix **mü?** or **müdür?** is added after **mümkün** separately.Examples:

İstanbul'a araba ile gitmek mümkün mü?
Is it possible to go to İstanbul by car?
Can you (one) go to İstanbul by car?

Talha'nın hızlı araba sürmesi mümkün müdür?
It's possible that Talha drives fast?
Can Talha drive fast?

Otelden Anıtkabir'e yürümek mümkün müdür?
Is it possible to walk to Anıtkabir from the hotel?
Can you walk to Anıtkabir from the hotel?

Otelden Kızılay Meydanı'na yürümeniz de mümkün mü?
Is it possible also for you to walk to Kızılay Square from the hotel?
Can you also walk to the Kızılay Square from the hotel?

Michelle için İngilizce konuşmak mümkün müdür?
Is it possible for Michelle to speak English?
Can Michelle speak English?

Michelle'in Türkçe konuşması da mümkün müdür?
Is it also possible for Michelle to speak Turkish?
Can Michelle also speak Turkish?

exercise 3

Make questions about ability/possibility with the given clues and **mümkün mü?** or **mümkün müdür?** Then give both positive and negative short answers to the questions.

Example:

Ben / çay / içmek   **Benim çay içmem mümkün müdür?**
I / tea / to drink   *Is it possible that I drink tea?*
                        Evet, mümkündür.
                        Yes, it's possible.
                        Hayır, mümkün değildir.
                        No, It's not possible.

1. sen/beni/bilmek ....

2. biz/dinlenmek ....

3. o/otele/gitmek ....

4. onlar/sahanda yumurta/yemek ....

5. insanlar/menüye/bakmak ....

6. siz/kafede menüden yemek/seçmek ....

7. ben/seni/görmek ....

8. sen/ araba kiralamak ....

9. biz/ uyumak ....

ability/possibility-II

In Turkish, the ability and possibility is also expressed by adding the ending **–ebilmek / -abilmek**, *to be able to*, to the verb before the personal ending. In other words, the verbs are conjugated for each person by using the ending **–ebilmek / -abilmek**. See Unit 1 for the personal endings if necessary.

However, the endings depend on the final letter of the verb. The endings following a consonant or a vowel differ. These differences will be studied step by step in the following pages.

• In case the verb ends with a consonant, the following endings are added:

(Ben)	**-ebilirim**	*I can*
(Sen)	**-ebilirsin**	*You can*
(O)	**-ebilir**	*He / She can*
(Biz)	**-ebiliriz**	*We can*
(Siz)	**-ebilirsiniz**	*You (pl) can*
Onlar	**-ebilir / -ebilirler**	*They can*

Examples: **gel mek** *(to come)*

Ben gelebilirim.	*I can come.*
Sen gelebilirsin.	*You can come.*
O gelebilir.	*He/She can come.*
Biz gelebiliriz.	*We can come.*
Siz gelebilirsiniz.	*You (pl) can come.*
Çocuklar gelebilir / gelebilirler.	*The children can come.*
Arabalar gelebilir.	*The cars can come.*

NB Since the endings added to the verbs bear the personal information, the subjects can be omitted. That's why the subjects are written in brackets. One exception to this is **onlar**, *they*. **Onlar** cannot be omitted.
In addition, note that there are two ending options for the 3rd plural person, **onlar**, *they*, singular (**-ebilir**) and plural (**-ebilirler**). However, for the nonhumans in the subject position, plural ending cannot be preferred.

Examples:

Çocuklar *(human)* **gelebilir/gelebilirler**	*The children can come.*
Arabalar *(nonhuman)* **gelebilir/~~gelebilirler~~.**	*The cars can come.*

the vowel harmony

The endings **-ebilmek** or **-abilmek** and the personal endings depend on the last vowel of the verb.

Last vowel of the verb	a, ı, o, u	e, i, ö, ü
the endings −ebilmek / -abilmek	**-abilmek**	**-ebilmek**

Examples:

iç mek	**Ben <u>içebilirim</u>.**	*I can drink.*
bak mak	**Sen b<u>akabilirsin</u>.**	*You can look (at).*
gör mek	**Biz g<u>örebiliriz</u>.**	*We can see.*
uç mak	**Siz <u>uçabilirsiniz</u>.**	*You can fly.*
iç mek	**Çocuklar <u>içebilir</u> / <u>içebilirler</u>.**	*The children can drink.*

NB The verb **gitmek** and **etmek** have a special spelling:

gi̱t mek	*(to go)*
Gidebilirim.	*I can go.*
Gidebilirsin.	*You can go.*
Gidebilir.	*He / She / It can go.*
Gidebiliriz.	*We can go.*
Gidebilirsiniz.	*You (pl) can go.*
Onlar gidebilirler.	*They can go.*
etmek	*(to do or to perform)*
Edebilirim.	*I can do.*
Edebilirsin.	*You can do.*
Edebilir.	*He / She / It can do.*
Edebiliriz.	*We can do.*
Edebilirsiniz.	*You (pl) can do.*
Onlar edebilirler.	*They can do.*

- In case the verb ends with a vowel, the "**y**" is added right after the bare form of the verb.

Examples: **iste mek** *(to want)*

Ben iste̱yebilirim.	*I can want.*
Sen iste̱yebilirsin.	*You can want.*
O iste̱yebilir.	*He / She / It can want.*
Biz iste̱yebiliriz.	*We can want.*
Siz iste̱yebilirsiniz.	*You (pl) can want.*
Çocuklar iste̱yebilir / iste̱yebilirler.	*The children can want.*
Atlar iste̱yebilir.	*The horses can want.*

More examples: (Only the person **ben**, *I* is used to show the formation better.)

söyle mek	**Ben söyle̱yebilirim.**	*I can tell.*
atla mak	**Ben atla̱yabilirim.**	*I can jump.*
uyu mak	**Ben uyu̱yabilirim.**	*I can sleep.*
yürü mek	**Ben yürü̱yebilirim.**	*I can walk.*

NB The verbs **demek** and **yemek** have a special spelling.

y**e** mek	*(to eat)*
Yiyebilirim.	*I can eat.*
Yiyebilirsin.	*You can eat.*
Yiyebilir.	*He / She / It can eat.*
Yiyebiliriz.	*We can eat.*
Yiyebilirsiniz.	*You (pl) can eat.*
Onlar yiyebilirler.	*They can eat.*
d**e** mek	*(to say)*
Diyebilirim.	*I can say.*
Diyebilirsin.	*You can say.*
Diyebilir.	*He / She / It can say.*
Diyebiliriz.	*We can say.*
Diyebilirsiniz.	*You (pl) can say.*
Onlar yiyebilirler.	*They can say.*

exercise 4

Form positive sentences expressing ability / possiblity with the given clues. Pay attention to the vowel change before adding the ending. Also note that numbers 4 and 5 have two conjugations since there are two ending options for **onlar**, *they*.

Example:

Ben / çay / içmek	**Ben çay <u>içebilirim</u>.**
I / tea / to drink	*I can drink tea.*

1. sen/beni/bilmek ....

2. biz/dinlenmek ....

3. o/otele/gitmek ....

4. onlar/sahanda yumurta/yemek ....

5. insanlar/menüye/bakmak ....

6. siz/kafede menüden yemek/seçmek ....

7. ben/seni/görmek ....

8. sen/ araba kiralamak ....

9. biz/ uyumak ....

the negative form

To form negative sentences about ability and possibility is possible by adding the ending **–ememek / -amamak**, *not to be able to*, to the verb before the personal ending. In other words, the verbs are conjugated for each person by using the ending **–ememek / -amamak**. See Unit 1 for the personal endings if necessary.

However, the endings depend on the final letter of the verb. The endings following a consonant or a vowel differ. These differences will be studied step by step in the following pages.

•   In case the verb ends with a consonant, the following endings are added:

(Ben)	-emem	*I cannot*
(Sen)	-emezsin	*You cannot*
(O)	-emez	*He / She cannot*
(Biz)	-emeyiz	*We cannot*
(Siz)	-emezsiniz	*You (pl) cannot*
Onlar	-emez / -emezler	*They cannot*

(*) "V" represents any verb in the present tense.

Examples: **gel mek** *(to come)*

Ben gelemem.	*I cannot come.*
Sen gelemezsin.	*You cannot come.*
O gelemez.	*He / She / It cannot come.*
Biz gelemeyiz.	*We cannot come.*
Siz gelemezsiniz.	*You (pl) cannot come.*
Çocuklar gelemez / gelemezler.	*The children cannot come.*
Arabalar gelemez.	*The cars cannot come.*

NB Since the endings added to the verbs bear the personal information, the subjects can be omitted. That's why the subjects are written in brackets. One exception to this is **onlar**, *they*. **Onlar** cannot be omitted.
In addition, note that there are two ending options for the 3rd plural person, **onlar**, *they*, singular (**-emez**) and plural (**-emezler**). However, for the nonhumans in the subject position, plural ending cannot be preferred.

Examples:

Çocuklar *(human)* **gelemez/gelemezler**   *The children cannot come.*

Arabalar *(nonhuman)* **gelemez/~~gelemezler~~.**   *The cars cannot come.*

the vowel harmony

The endings **-ememek** or **-amamak** and the personal endings depend on the last vowel of the verb.

Last vowel of the verb	a, ı, o, u	e, i, ö, ü
the endings –ememek / -amamak	-amamak	-ememek

Examples:

iç mek	Ben i̱çemem.	*I cannot drink.*
bak mak	Sen ba̱ka̱mazsın.	*You cannot look (at).*
gör mek	Biz gö̱reme̱yiz.	*We cannot see.*
uç mak	Siz u̱çama̱zsınız.	*You cannot fly.*
iç mek	Çocuklar i̱çeme̱z / i̱çeme̱zler.	*The children can't drink.*

NB The verbs **gitmek** and **etmek** has a special spelling:

gi̱t mek   *(to go)*

Gidemem.	*I cannot go.*
Gidemezsin.	*You cannot go.*
Gidemez.	*He / She / It cannot go.*
Gidemeyiz.	*We cannot go.*
Gidemezsiniz.	*You (pl) cannot go.*
Onlar gidemezler.	*They cannot go.*

etmek   *(to do or to perform)*

Edemem.	*I cannot do.*
Edemezsin.	*You cannot do.*
Edemez.	*He / She / It cannot do.*
Edemeyiz.	*We cannot do.*
Edemezsiniz.	*You (pl) cannot do.*
Onlar edemezler.	*They cannot do.*

• In case the verb ends with a vowel, the "**y**" is added right after the bare form of the verb.

Examples: **iste mek** *(to want)*

Ben isteyemem.	*I cannot want.*
Sen isteyemezsin.	*You cannot want.*
O isteyemez.	*He / She / It cannot want.*
Biz isteyemeyiz.	*We cannot want.*
Siz isteyemezsiniz.	*You (pl) cannot want.*
Çocuklar isteyemez / isteyemezler.	*The children cannot want.*
Atlar isteyemez.	*The horses cannot want.*

More examples: (Only the person **ben**, *I* is used to show the formation better.)

söyle mek	**Ben söyleyemem.**	*I cannot tell.*
atla mak	**Ben atlayamam.**	*I cannot jump.*
uyu mak	**Ben uyuyamam.**	*I cannot sleep.*
yürü mek	**Ben yürüyemem.**	*I cannot walk.*

NB The verbs **demek** and **yemek** have a special spelling.

ye mek	*(to eat)*
Yiyemem.	*I cannot eat.*
Yiyemezsin.	*You cannot eat.*
Yiyemez.	*He / She / It cannot eat.*
Yiyemeyiz.	*We cannot eat.*
Yiyemezsiniz.	*You (pl) cannot eat.*
Onlar yiyemezler.	*They cannot eat.*
de mek	*(to say)*
Diyemem.	*I cannot say.*
Diyemezsin.	*You cannot say.*
Diyemez.	*He / She / It cannot say.*
Diyemeyiz.	*We cannot say.*
Diyemezsiniz.	*You (pl) cannot say.*
Onlar diyemezler.	*They cannot say.*

exercise 5

Form negative sentences expressing ability / possiblity with the given clues. Pay attention to the vowel change before adding the ending. Also note that numbers 4 and 5 have two conjugations since there are two ending options for **onlar**, *they*.

Example:

Ben / çay / içmek   **Ben çay içemem.**
I / tea / to drink   *I cannot drink tea.*

1. **sen/beni/bilmek**   ....

2. **biz/dinlenmek**   ....

3. **o/otele/gitmek**   ....

4. **onlar/sahanda yumurta/yemek** ....

5. **insanlar/menüye/bakmak**   ....

6. **siz/kafede menüden yemek/seçmek** ....

7. **ben/seni/görmek**   ....

8. **sen/ araba kiralamak**   ....

9. **biz/ uyumak**   ....

the question form

To form a question, two steps are needed.

STEP 1

First, the verb is conjugated for the 3rd singular person (**o**, *he / she / it*). Remember that for the 3rd singular person (**o**, *he / she / it*) the ending is either **–(y)ebilir** or **–(y)abilir**. Also remember the vowel change.

Examples:
The verb is conjugated for the 3rd singular person (**o**, *he / she / it*).

söylemek	*(to say)*	**söyleyebilir**	*(He / she can say)*
gelmek	*(to come)*	**gelebilir**	*(He / she can come)*
gitmek	*(to go)*	**gidebilir**	*(He / she can go)*
yemek	*(to eat)*	**yiyebilir**	*(He / she can eat)*
uyumak	*(to sleep)*	**uyuyabilir**	*(He / she can sleep)*
yürümek	*(to walk)*	**yürüyebilir**	*(He / she can walk)*
kalmak	*(to stay)*	**kalabilir**	*(He / she can stay)*
bakmak	*(to look (at))*	**bakabilir**	*(He / she can look (at))*
atlamak	*(to jump))*	**atlayabilir**	*(He / she can jump)*

STEP 2

Then, the question endings are added to the end separately. The question endings for each person are given below: (Only the ending –(y)ebilir is given in the table. See the positive formation for the vowel change.

(Ben)	–(y)ebilir miyim?	*Can I?*
(Sen)	–(y)ebilir misin?	*Can you?*
(O)	–(y)ebilir mi?	*Can he / she / it?*
(Biz)	–(y)ebilir miyiz?	*Can we?*
(Siz)	–(y)ebilir misiniz?	*Can you (pl)?*
Onlar	–(y)ebilir/ler mi?	*Can they?*

Example:
Ben <u>gelebilir</u> <u>miyim</u>?   *Can I come?*
     (Step 1) (Step 2)

More examples:

Sen gelebilir misin?   *Can you come?*

O gelebilir mi?   *Can he / she / it come?*

Biz gelebilir miyiz?   *Can we come?*

Siz gelebilir misiniz?   *Can you (pl) come?*

Çocuklar gelebilir mi? / gelebilirler mi?   *Can the children come?*

Arabalar gelebilir mi?   *Can the cars come?*

More examples with other verbs:

Ben içebilir miyim?   *Can I drink?*

Sen bakabilir misin?   *Can you look (at)?*

O uyuyabilir mi?   *Can he / she / it sleep?*

Biz görebilir miyiz?   *Can we see?*

Note that there are two ending options for **onlar**, *they*: **-(y)ebilir** or **-(y)ebilirler** In case the plural ending is preferred, then it should be **-(y)ebilirler mi?** Remember the vowel change in the personal endings, too. (Both ending possibilities are given in the examples.)

Examples:

Çocuklar gel<u>ebilir</u> mi? / gel<u>ebilirler</u> mi?   *Can the children come?*

Çocuklar iç<u>ebilir</u> mi? / iç<u>ebilirler</u> mi?   *Can the children drink?*

Çocuklar bak<u>abilir</u> mi? / bak<u>abilirler</u> mi?   *Can the children look?*

Çocuklar uyu<u>yabilir</u> mi?/ uyu<u>yabilirler</u> mi?   *Can the children sleep?*

Çocuklar gör<u>ebilir</u> mi? / gör<u>ebilirler</u> mi?   *Can the children see?*

Bölüm 3
Part 3

Dialogue 3

otele giriş registering in the hotel

İbrahim and Michelle arrive at the hotel. They talk to the person at the desk.

İbrahim:	Merhaba! Ben İbrahim Korkmaz. Burada yerimiz var.
	Hello! I'm İbrahim Korkmaz. We have room here.
Bülent:	Evet İbrahim Bey, Michelle Hanım. Hoş geldiniz! Odanız hazır. Hemen çıkmak ister misiniz?
	Yes, Mr. İbrahim, Mrs. Michelle. Welcome! Your room is ready. Would you like to go up immediately?
İbrahim:	Evet, eşyalarımızı bırakır biraz dinleniriz.
	Yes, we'll leave our luggage and rest for a while.
Michelle:	Haklısın, çok iyi olur.
	You're right, it would be good.
Bülent:	Size eşyalarınızla Kerim yardımcı olsun.
	Kerim will help you with your belongings.
Michelle:	Bir şey sormak istiyorum. Yemek saatlerini öğrenebilir miyim?
	I'd like to ask something. Can I learn about the meal hours?
Bülent:	Tabii efendim. Yemek saatleri ve diğer tüm bilgiler odadaki tanıtım kitapçığınızda mevcut. İlâve sorunuz olursa, biz buradan cevaplarız.
	Sure ma'am. The meal hours and all the other information is included in the booklet in your room. In case of additional inqueries, we'll help you from here.

1. Did İbrahim and Michelle need to wait before their room was ready?
2. Do they have to take their luggage themselves?

Vocabulary

bırakmak	*to leave*	**hazır**	*ready*
bilgi	*information*	**ilâve**	*additional*

cevaplamak	*to answer*	**mevcut**	*there is*
çanta	*bag*	**saat**	*hour*
çıkmak	*to go up to the room*	**sormak**	*to ask*
diğer	*other*	**soru**	*question*
eşya	*belonging*	**tanıtım kartı**	*the introductory booklet*
haklı	*right*	**yer**	*room, place*
Haklısın.		*You're right./ It's a good idea.*	

In the dialogue above, İbrahim says, **eşyalarımızı bırakır biraz dinleniriz**. Here the verbs both **bırakmak** and **dinlenmek** should be conjugated for the same subject, **biz**, *we*. But the first verb, **bırakmak** looks like it is conjugated for the subject of **o**, *he/she*. In Turkish, it is grammatically correct to leave the first verbs conjugated for the 3rd person if more than one verb is used. However, it is not necessary. See both types of usage in the examples:

Eşyalarımızı <u>bırakır</u>, biraz <u>dinlenir</u>, biraz su <u>içer</u>, biraz da yemek <u>yeriz</u>.

Eşyalarımızı <u>bırakırız</u>, biraz <u>dinleniriz</u>, biraz su <u>içeriz</u>, biraz da yemek <u>yeriz</u>.

sayılar numbers

Find the Turkish numbers from 21 to 1,000,000 below.

sayılar / numbers

yirmi bir	*twenty one*	**yüz on bir**	*a hundred and eleven*
yirmi iki	*twenty two*	**iki yüz**	*two hundred*
yirmi üç	*twenty three*	**üç yüz**	*three hundred*
otuz	*thirty*	**bin**	*a thousand*
kırk	*forty*	**iki bin**	*two thousand*
elli	*fifty*	**on bin**	*ten thousand*
altmış	*sixty*	**yirmi bin**	*twenty thousand*
yetmiş	*seventy*	**yüz bin**	*a hundred thousand*
seksen	*eighty*	**dokuz yüz bin**	*nine hundred thousand*
doksan	*ninety*	**bir milyon**	*one million*
yüz	*a hundred*		

Unit Six: Alışveriş yapıyoruz.

We're shopping.

With this unit, you will be able to:

- Talk about shopping, money, colours, clothes, and grocery items
- Talk about time
- Use prepositions of place
- Use the declension of "with"
- Use the object in a sentence

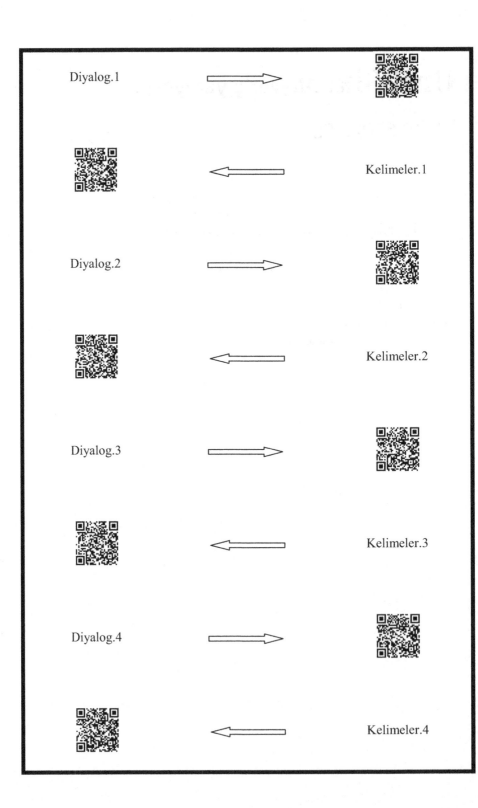

Bölüm 1
Part 1

Dialogue 1

önce alışveriş shopping first

Michelle and İbrahim are talking in their hotel room.

Michelle:	İbrahim, ben tatil için İstanbul'dan bazı kıyafetler almak istiyorum.
İbrahim:	Tabii ki, tatlım. Çok iyi fikir. Ne düşünüyorsun?
Michelle:	Aklımda bir kaç şey var. Ama dükkâna gidince de karar veririm.
İbrahim:	Tamamdır. Alışverişe ne zaman çıkmak istersin?
Michelle:	Bugün öğleden sonra olabilir. Saat ikiden sonra. Ne dersin?
İbrahim:	İyi iyi. Akşam saat altıda yemek başlıyor. Alışveriş için dört saatimiz var.
Michelle:	Alışverişe birlikte gidelim. Dükkândan otele dönerken bana yardım edersin.
İbrahim:	Tabii ki. Çok güzel alışveriş çantası taşırım, bilirsin.

1. Is Michelle sure about what to buy?
2. Will they go shopping together?

Vocabulary

akıl	*mind*	**gece**	*night*
aklımda	*in my mind*	**karar vermek**	*to decide*
akşam	*evening*	**karar**	*decision*
alışveriş	*shopping*	**kıyafet**	*cloth, clothing*
alışverişe çıkmak	*to go shopping*	**öğleden önce**	*before noon*
başlamak	*to start*	**öğleden sonra**	*afternoon*
bazı	*some*	**öğlen**	*at noon*

dönmek	*to return*	sabah	*morning*
dükkân	*store, shop*	taşımak	*to take, to move, to transport*
düşünmek	*to think*	tatil	*vacation*
gece yarısı	*midnight*		
Ne dersin?		*What do you think?*	

In the dialogue above, we see **Ama dükkâna gidince de karar veririm**. Here, **de** should be translated as *again* or *one more time* instead of *also*. The meaning is *I made up my mind, but I may decide in the store one more time*.

Also note that some nouns have spelling exceptions when in the accusative form (in the object position in a sentence). **Akıl** is one of them and is written as **aklı** in the accusative form. Normally, it should be **akılı** in the accusative form, but the first "ı" drops as a rule. There are other examples, such as **şehir**, *city* for example. In the accusative form, it's spelled as **şehri** not **şehiri**. Here, the first "i" drops. Such exceptions will be mentioned whenever necessary in the following units of the book.

exercise 1

Which is the odd one out in each row?

öğlen	akşam	gece	tatil
başlamak	taşımak	dükkân	dönmek
bazı	hepsi	hiç	karar
birlikte	akıl	fikir	karar

Dialogue 2

Kapalıçarşı'ya doğru towards Kapalıçarşı

On the way to Kapalıçarşı.

Michelle:	İbrahim, Kapalıçarşı'ya mı gidiyoruz? Neden orası?
İbrahim:	Evet. Çünkü Kapalıçarşı'da çok fazla seçenek ve ilginç şeyler bulabiliriz. Farklı alanlarda ve çok sayıda dükkân var.
Michelle:	Ne gibi farklı alanlar?
İbrahim:	Kuyumcular, hediyelik eşya dükkânları, lokantalar, kafeler, kıyafet dükkânları ve daha birçok şey.
Michelle:	Evet. Çok kalabalık aynı zamanda.
İbrahim:	İnsanlar buradan pek çok ihtiyacını karşılar. O yüzden kalabalık olur. Kapalıçarşı aynı zamanda merkezî bir yerde ve diğer turistik mekânlara da yürüme mesafesinde.
Michelle:	Çok eski bir yere benziyor. Öyle değil mi?
İbrahim:	Evet, tarihî bir çarşı. Osmanlı döneminden. Ve günümüzde oldukça turistik ve meşhurdur.

1. Was the Grand Bazaar crowded that day?
2. Was the Grand Bazaar built lately?

Vocabulary

alan	*area, field*	**neden?**	*why?*
bulmak	*to find*	**o nedenle**	*because of that*
çünkü	*because*	**o sebeple**	*because of that*
farklı	*different, various*	**o yüzden**	*since*
günümüzde	*in these days, today*	**ondan dolayı**	*because of that*
hediyelik eşya	*souvenir shop*	**pek**	*much, many, a lot*
ihtiyacını karşılamak	*to satisfy, to meet one's need*	**sayı**	*number, quantity*
ihtiyaç	*need*	**seçenek**	*choice*
ilginç	*interesting*	**tarihî**	*historic*

kıyafet dükkânı	clothing store	tuhaf	strange
kuyumcu	jewelery store	turistik	touristic
mesafe	distance	yürüme mesafesi	walking distance
meşhur	famous		

Kapalıçarşı	the Grand Bazaar
Osmanlı dönemi	the Ottoman period

In the dialogue above, **o yüzden** and **çünkü** mean similar. They both show the reason. In addition, **ondan dolayı**, **o nedenle**, **onun için**, or **o sebeple**, *because of the fact that*, can be used in the similar way.

talking about time

In Turkish, talking about the time is similar to that in English. It's both possible to use **buçuk**, *half* and **çeyrek**, *quarter* and use the minutes to tell the time.

Examples:

Saat kaç?   *What is the time? / What time is it?*

Saat on.   10:00   *It's ten o'clock.*
Saat iki.   02:00   *It's two o'clock.*

Saat on buçuk.   10:30   *It's half past ten.*
Saat on otuz.   10:30   *It's ten thirty.*

Saat iki buçuk.   02:30   *It's half past two.*
Saat iki otuz.   02:30   *It's two thirty.*

Saat onu çeyrek geçiyor.   10:15   *It's a quarter past ten.*
Saat on çeyrek.   10:15   *It's a quarter past ten.*
Saat on on beş.   10:15   *It's ten fifteen.*

Saat ikiyi çeyrek geçiyor.   02:15   *It's a quarter past two.*
Saat iki çeyrek.   02:15   *It's a quarter past two.*
Saat iki on beş.   02:15   *It's two fifteen.*

Saat ona çeyrek var.   09:45   *It's a quarter to ten.*
Saat dokuz kırk beş.   09:45   *It's nine forty five.*

Saat ikiye çeyrek var.   01:45   *It's a quarter to two.*
Saat bir kırk beş.   01:45   *It's one forty five.*

Saat ikiye on (dakika) var.   01:50   *It's ten (minutes) to two.*
Saat biri beş (dakika) geçiyor.   01:05   *It's five (minutes) past one.*

NB In Turkish, use sabah, öğlen, or gündüz for am and akşam or gece for pm. Examples:

Saat <u>sabah</u> on.	10:00	It's ten <u>am.</u>
Saat <u>gündüz</u> sekiz.	08:00	It's eight <u>am.</u>
Saat <u>akşam</u> sekiz.	20:00	It's eight <u>pm.</u>
Saat <u>gece</u> iki.	02:00	It's two <u>am.</u>

Bölüm 2
Part 2

dilbilgisi grammar

to, towards

The direction ending "**-e/-a**" is used in place of the preposition of place "to or towards" in English. The direction ending "**-e/-a**" depends on the preceding vowel.

the vowel harmony

Last vowel of the preceding word	a, ı, o, u	e, i, ö, ü
the endings –e / -a	-a	-e

Examples:

ot**ele**	*to the hotel*
dükk**âna**	*to the store*

In case of a preceding letter is a vowel, the letter "**y**" is added before the direction ending "**-e/-a**".

Examples:

lokanta**ya**	*to the restaurant*
oda**ya**	*to the room*

In case of the word is a proper name, the direction ending "**-e/-a**" is separated by an apostrophe.

Examples:

Michelle'e	*to Michelle*
Talha'ya	*to Talha*
İrem'e	*to İrem*
ABD'ye	*to the USA.*
İstanbul'a	*to İstanbul*

In case the word ends with one the consonants "**ç**", "**k**", "**p**", or "**t**", this letter changes accordingly as given in the table below before the direction ending "**-e/-a**" is added.

the consonant harmony

Last consonant of the first word	ç	k	p	t
It changes to	c	g / ğ	b	d

Examples:

ağaç	*tree*	**ağaca**	*to the tree*
renk	*colour*	**renge**	*to the colour*
çocuk	*child*	**çocuğa**	*to the child*
çorap	*sock*	**çoraba**	*to the socks*
cilt	*skin*	**cilde**	*to the skin*

Note that there are some exceptions with the consonants "**p**" and "**t**".

Examples:

ip	*rope*	**ipe**	*to the rope*
at	*horse*	**ata**	*to the horse*

NB The consonant harmony is not applied when the word is a proper name.

Examples:

Tunç	**Tunç'a**	*to Tunç*
Irak	**Irak'a**	*to Iraq*
Mehtap	**Mehtap'a**	*to Mehtap*
Murat	**Murat'a**	*to Murat*

It's also possible to use the direction ending "**-e/-a**" with the persons. Below are given the direction ending "-e/-a" for each person:

bana	*to me*
sana	*to you*
ona	*to him / her / it*
bize	*to us*
size	*to you (pl)*
onlara	*to them*

Examples:

Bana bir çay getirir misin?	*Can you bring a cup of tea to me?*
Sana gelmek istiyorum.	*I want to come to you (your place).*
Bunu ona verebilir miyim?	*Can I give this to her / him?*
Bize bir şarkı söyler misin?	*Will you sing a song to us?*
Size geliyoruz.	*We're going to you (your place).*
Onlara gidiyoruz.	*We're going to them (their place).*

exercise 2

Add the direction ending "**-e/-a**" to the each word. Note the vowel and the consonant change.

Example:	**otel**	**otele**
	(hotel)	*(to the hotel)*
İbrahim	Eymen	Jack
Ankara	Londra	Kahvaltı
Birleşik Krallık	Çocuklar	Ağaç
Direk	Kulüp	Çorap

at, in, on

The direction ending "**-de/-da**" is used in place of the preposition of place "at, in, or on" in English. The direction ending "**-de/-da**" depends on the preceding vowel. The previous vowel harmony table is also applicable here.

Examples:

otelde	*at / in the hotel*
dükkânda	*at / in the store*
lokantada	*at / in the restaurant*
odada	*at / in the room*

In case of the word is a proper name, direction ending "**-de/-da**" is separated by an apostrophe.

Examples:

Michelle'de	*at Michelle (at Michelle's place)*
Talha'da	*at Talha (at Talha's place)*
İrem'de	*at İrem (at İrem's place)*
ABD'de	*in the USA.*
İstanbul'da	*in İstanbul*

In case the word ends with one the consonants 'f', 's', 't', 'k', 'ç', 'ş', 'h', or 'p', this letter changes accordingly as given in the table below before the direction ending "**-de/-da**" is added.

the consonant harmony

Last letter of the preceding word	f	s	t	k	ç	ş	h	p
the direction ending –de / -da **change to:**	-te / -ta							

Examples:

şef	*chef*	**şefte**	*at the chef*
sos	*sauce*	**sosta**	*on the sauce*
çift	*couple*	**çiftte**	*at the couple*
renk	*colour*	**renkte**	*at the colour*
ağaç	*tree*	**ağaçta**	*on the tree*
kuş	*bird*	**kuşta**	*on the bird*
çorap	*sock*	**çorapta**	*on the socks*

It's also possible to use the direction ending "**-de/-da**" with the persons. Below are given the direction ending "-de/-da" for each person:

bende	*at me*	*(at my place)*
sende	*at you*	*(at your place)*
onda	*at him / her / it*	*(at his / her place)*
bizde	*at us*	*(at our place)*
sizde	*at you (pl)*	*(at your place)*
onlarda	*at them*	*(at their place)*

Examples:

Bende yeni bir haber yok.	*There's nothing new with me*.*
Sende ne var?	*What's with you?*
Onda tuhaf bir şey var.	*There's something weird with him/her.*
Bu akşam bizdeyiz.	*We're at us (our place) tonight.*

(*) In these examples, the direction ending "**-de/-da**" can also be translated as "with".

exercise 3

Add the direction ending "**-de/-da**" to the each word. Note the vowel and the consonant change.

| Example: | **otel** | **oteld<u>e</u>** |
| | *(hotel)* | *(at / in the hotel)* |

İbrahim	Eymen	Jack
Ankara	Londra	Kahvaltı
Birleşik Krallık	Çocuklar	Ağaç
Direk	Kulüp	Çorap

from

The direction ending "**-den/-dan**" is used in place of the preposition of place "from" in English. The direction ending "**-den/-dan**" depends on the preceding vowel. The previous vowel harmony table is also applicable here.

Examples:

otel<u>den</u>	*from the hotel*
dükk<u>ân</u>d<u>an</u>	*from the store*
lokant<u>ad</u>a<u>n</u>	*from the restaurant*
od<u>ad</u>a<u>n</u>	*from the room*

In case of the word is a proper name, the direction ending "**-den/-dan**" is separated by an apostrophe.

Examples:

Michelle'den	*from Michelle (from Michelle's place)*
Talha'dan	*from Talha (from Talha's place)*
İrem'den	*from İrem (from İrem's place)*
ABD'den	*from the USA.*
İstanbul'dan	*from İstanbul*

In case the word ends with one the consonants 'f', 's', 't', 'k', 'ç', 'ş', 'h', or 'p', this letter changes accordingly as given in the table below before the direction ending "**-den/-dan**" is added.

the consonant harmony

Last letter of the preceding word	f	s	t	k	ç	ş	h	p
the direction ending –den / -dan **change to:**	-ten / -tan							

Examples:

şef	*chef*	**şeften**	*from the chef*
sos	*sauce*	**sostan**	*from the sauce*
çift	*couple*	**çiftten**	*from the couple*
renk	*colour*	**renkten**	*from the colour*
ağaç	*tree*	**ağaçtan**	*from the tree*
kuş	*bird*	**kuştan**	*from the bird*
sabah	*morning*	**sabahtan**	*from the morning*
çorap	*sock*	**çoraptan**	*from the socks*

It's also possible to use the direction ending "**-den/-dan**" with the persons. Below are given the direction ending "**-den/-dan**" for each person:

benden	*from me*	*(from my place)*
senden	*from you*	*(from your place)*
ondan	*from him / her / it*	*(from his / her place)*
bizden	*from us*	*(from our place)*
sizden	*from you (pl)*	*(from your place)*
onlardan	*from them*	*(from their place)*

Examples:

Benden bir şey ister misin?   *Do you want anything from me?*

Senden n'aber?   *What's the news from you?*

Onlardan geliyoruz.   *We're coming from them (their place).*

Bu hediye bizden size! Buyurun!   *This gift is from us to you! Please take it!*

exercise 4

Add the direction ending "**-den / -dan**" to the each word. Note the vowel and the consonant change.

Example: **otel**   **otelden**
              (hotel)   *(from the hotel)*

İbrahim	Eymen	Jack
Ankara	Londra	Kahvaltı
Birleşik Krallık	Çocuklar	Ağaç
Direk	Kulüp	Çorap

the declension of "with"

In Turkish, it is also possible to use **ile**, *with* as an ending attached. In this case, the ending is **–le / -la**, *with*.
The ending is **–le / -la** depends on the preceding vowel. The previous vowel harmony table is also applicable here.

Examples:

uçak ile	**uçak<u>la</u>**	*with the airplane*
ablam ile	**abl<u>am</u><u>la</u>**	*with my sister*
abim ile	**ab<u>im</u><u>le</u>**	*with my brother*
öğretmen ile	**öğretm<u>en</u><u>le</u>**	*with the teacher*

In case of a preceding letter is a vowel, the letter "**y**" is added before the adding the ending "**-le / -la**".

Examples:

araba ile	**araba<u>y</u>la**	*with the car*
yumurta ile	**yumurta<u>y</u>la**	*with the egg*
su ile	**su<u>y</u>la**	*with the water*
hava ile	**hava<u>y</u>la**	*with the air*

In case of the word is a proper name, the ending "**-le / -la**" is separated by an apostrophe.

Examples:

İbrahim ile	**İbrahim'le**	*with İbrahim*
Michelle ile	**Michelle'le**	*with Michelle*
Talha ile	**Talha'yla**	*with Talha*
İstanbul ile	**İstanbul'la**	*with İstanbul*

It's also possible to use the ending "**-le / -la**" with the persons. Below are given the direction ending "**-le/-la**" for each person:

benim ile	**benimle**	*with me*
senin ile	**seninle**	*with you*
onun ile	**onunla**	*with him / her / it*
bizim ile	**bizimle**	*with us*
sizin ile	**sizinle**	*with you (pl)*
onlar ile	**onlarla**	*with them*

Examples:

Benimle gelir misin?	*Will you come <u>with me</u>?*
Seninle kalabilir miyim?	*Can I stay <u>with you</u>?*
Şimdi **onunla** konuşuyorum.	*I'm talking with him / her now.*
Bizimle misiniz?	*Are you (pl) <u>with us</u>?*

the accusative form (the object of a sentence)

In Turkish, accusative form ending "**-i**" is added to the words when they are used in the object position.

Example:

                                         (the accusative form)

otel (*the hotel*)   **otel<u>i</u>** (*the hotel*)

Oteli görüyorum.   *I see <u>the hotel</u>.*

The ending -i is a 4 way vowel harmony, meaning **-i** can change to **-i / -ı / -u / -ü**, depending on the preceding vowel.

the vowel harmony

Last vowel of the preceding word	a,ı	e,i	o,u	ö,ü
the ending -i (x4)	-ı	-i	-u	-ü

Examples:

                                     (the accusative form)

çay (*the tea*)   **çay<u>ı</u>** (*the tea*)
pantolon (*the pants*)   **pantolon<u>u</u>** (*the pants*)
otel (*the hotel*)   **otel<u>i</u>** (*the hotel*)
süt (*the milk*)   **süt<u>ü</u>** (*the milk*)

Çayı severim.	*I like <u>the tea</u>.*
Oteli görüyorum.	*I see <u>the hotel</u>.*
Pantolonu alıyorum.	*I buy <u>the pants</u>.*
Sütü içiyorum.	*I drink <u>the milk</u>.*

In case of a preceding letter is a vowel, the letter "**y**" is added before the accusative form ending "**-i**" (x4).

Examples:

	(the accusative form)
lokanta (*the restaurant*)	**lokantayı** (*the restaurant*)
oda (*the room*)	**odayı** (*the room*)
kuyumcu (*the jewelry store*)	**kuyumcuyu** (*the jewelry store*)
kahve (*the coffee*)	**kahveyi** (*the coffee*)

<u>**Lokantayı**</u> **görüyorum.**	*I see <u>the restaurant</u>.*
<u>**Odayı**</u> **görüyorum.**	*I see <u>the room</u>.*
<u>**Kuyumcuyu**</u> **biliyorum.**	*I know <u>the jewelry store</u>.*
<u>**Kahveyi**</u> **içiyorum.**	*I drink <u>the coffee</u>.*

In case of the word is a proper name, the accusative form ending "**-i**" (x4) is separated by an apostrophe.

Examples:

Michelle'i	**Michelle'i görüyorum.**	*I see <u>Michelle</u>.*
Talha'yı	**Talha'yı görüyorum.**	*I see <u>Talha</u>.*
İrem'i	**İrem'i görüyorum.**	*I see <u>İrem</u>.*
ABD'yi	**ABD'yi biliyorum.**	*I know the USA.*
İstanbul'u	**İstanbul'u dinliyorum.**	*I listen to İstanbul.*

In case the word ends with one the consonants "**ç**", "**k**", "**p**", or "**t**", this letter changes accordingly as given in the table below before the accusative ending "**-i**" (x4) is added.

the consonant harmony

Last consonant of the first word	ç	k	p	t
It changes to	c	g / ğ	b	d

Examples:

ağaç	*tree*	**ağacı**	*the tree*
renk	*colour*	**rengi**	*the colour*
çocuk	*child*	**çocuğu**	*the child*
çorap	*sock*	**çorabı**	*the socks*
cilt	*skin*	**cildi**	*the skin*

Note that there are some exceptions with the consonants "**p**" and "**t**".

Examples:

| **ip** | *rope* | **ipi** | *the rope* |
| **at̲** | *horse* | **at̲ı** | *the horse* |

NB The consonant harmony is not applied when the word is a proper name.

Examples:

Tunç	**Tunç'u**	*Tunç*
Irak	**Irak'ı**	*Irak*
Mehtap	**Mehtap'ı**	*Mehtap*
Murat	**Murat'ı**	*Murat*

It's also possible to use the accusative form ending "**-i**" with the persons.

Below are given the accusative form ending "**-i**" for each person:

beni	*me*
seni	*you*
onu	*him / her / it*
bizi	*us*
sizi	*you (pl)*
onları	*them*

Examples:

Beni tanıyor musun?	*Do you know me?*
Seni görüyorum.	*I see you.*
Onu sevmiyorum.	*I don't like her / him.*
Bizi hatırlıyor musunuz?	*Do you remember us?*
Sizi ziyaret edebilir miyiz?	*Can we visit you?*
Onları tanımıyorum.	*I don't know them.*

More examples with the accusative form:

Çayı şekerli istiyorum.	*I want the tea with sugar.*
Kahveyi sade severim.	*I like the coffee black.*
Bunu alabilir miyim?	*Can I take it?*
Sütü sıcak tercih ederim.	*I prefer the milk hot.*

Michelle'i hemen aramalısın.	*You should call Michelle right away.*
Talha'yı tanıyor musun?	*Do you know Talha?*
İrem'i işten alırız.	*We'll take İrem from work.*
ABD'yi görmem mümkün mü?	*Can I see the USA?*
İstanbul'u ziyaret edebilir miyim?	*Can I visit İstanbul?*
Seni hemen görmek istiyorum.	*I want to see you immediately.*

ağaç	**Bu ağacı tanıyorum.**	*I know this tree.*
renk	**Bu rengi severim.**	*I like this colour.*
çocuk	**Çocuğu görmeliyim.**	*I should see the child.*
dolap	**Bu dolabı satın alamam.**	*I can't buy the cabinet.*

It's also possible to use gerunds in the accusative case.

Examples:

infinitive	*gerund*
yemek *(to eat)*	**yeme** *(eating)*
çalışmak *(to work / study)*	**çalışma** *(working / studying)*
şarkı söylemek *(to sing a song)*	**şarkı söyleme** *(singing a song)*
Türkçe konuşmak *(to speak Turkish)*	**Türkçe konuşma** *(speaking Turkish)*

Yemeyi severim.	*I like eating.*
Çalışmayı pek sevmem.	*I don't like working much.*
Şarkı söylemeyi severim.	*I like singing a song.*
Türkçe konuşmayı seviyoruz.	*We like speaking Turkish.*

It's also possible to use possessives with gerunds in the accusative case.

Examples:

infinitive	*gerund*	*gerund with possessives*
bakmak *(to look)*	**bakma** *(looking)*	**(senin) bakman** *(your looking) or (you to look)*
içmek *(to drink)*	**içme** *(drinking)*	**(onun) içmesi** *(his/her drinking) or (him/her to drink)*
almak *(to take)*	**alma** *(taking)*	**(benim) almam** *(my taking) or (me to take)*
yemek *(to eat)*	**yeme** *(eating)*	**(sizin) yemeniz** *(your eating) or (you to eat)*

Bana bakmanı istemiyorum.	*I don't want you to look at me.*

(Lit. I don't want your looking at me.)

Bunu içmesini istiyorum. I want him/her to drink this.
(Lit. I want his/her drinking this.)

Bir bardak çay almamı ister Do you want me to take a cup of tea?
misin?
(Lit. Do you want my taking a cup of tea?)

Bunu yemenizi isterim. I want you to eat this.
(Lit. I want your eating this.)

exercise 5

Add the accusative ending "-i" (x4) to the each word. Note the vowel and the consonant change.

Example:	**otel**	**oteli**
	(hotel)	*(the hotel)*

İbrahim	Eymen	Jack
Ankara	Londra	Kahvaltı
Birleşik Krallık	Çocuklar	Ağaç
Direk	Kulüp	Çorap

Bölüm 3
Part 3

Dialogue 3

alışveriş zamanı time for shopping

İbrahim and Michelle arrive in Kapalıçarşı. Fascinated by the historical atmosphere of Kapalıçarşı, Michelle entered a clothing store that they saw.

Satıcı:	Efendim, hoş geldiniz. Size nasıl yardımcı olabilirim? Ne bakıyorsunuz?
Michelle:	Teşekkür ederim. Açık renk bluz ve pantolon alacağım. Eşim için de yine yazlık bir gömlek istiyorum.
Satıcı:	Tabii efendim, bedeniniz nedir ve ne renk bakıyorsunuz?
Michelle:	İkimiz de orta beden giyiyoruz. Bluz ve gömlek beyaz olsun.
Satıcı:	Efendim, bluz ve gömlekler şu tarafta. Şurada, karşıdaki rafta. Pantolonlar ise bu tarafta. Sağda. Gömleklerin tam karşısında.
Michelle:	Peki bunların fiyatını öğrenebilir miyim? Meselâ bluzler kaça? Pantolon ne kadar olur? Ayrıca, bunları sonra değiştirebilir miyim?
Satıcı:	Bluzlerin tanesi 20, gömleklerin ise 30 lira. Ama size bir indirim yaparız. Eşyaları iade almıyoruz ama değişim yaparız. Akşam saat altıya kadar değişim yaparız. Ama fişini de getirmelisiniz.

1. Was it easy to find clothes in the store? Or, were they able to see the clothes from where they stand?
2. Can they change the clothes later?

Vocabulary

açık	*light*	**kalın kıyafet**	*warm clothes*
ak	*white*	**kara**	*black*

beden numarası	*size number*	**karşı**	*opposite*
beden	*size*	**kırmızı**	*red*
beyaz	*white*	**kışlık**	*for winter*
bluz	*blouse*	**koyu**	*dark*
büyük beden	*large size*	**küçük beden**	*small size*
çorap	*socks*	**mavi**	*blue*
değişim yapmak	*to exchange*	**meselâ**	*for instance*
değişim	*exchange*	**mor**	*purple*
değiştirmek	*to exchange, to change*	**orta beden**	*medium size*
elbise	*dress*	**pantolon**	*pants*
etek	*skirt*	**pembe**	*pink*
fiş	*receipt*	**raf**	*shelf*
getirmek	*to bring*	**renk**	*colour*
gömlek	*shirt*	**sarı**	*yellow*
gri	*grey*	**satmak**	*to sell*
iade almak	*to (accept) refund*	**siyah**	*black*
iade etmek	*to (apply for the) refund*	**şapka**	*hat*
iç çamaşırı	*underwear*	**tane**	*each*
ince kıyafet	*light clothes*	**taraf**	*side*
indirim	*discount*	**turuncu**	*orange*
indirmek	*to discount*	**yazlık**	*for summer*
kadar	*until*	**yeşil**	*green*
kahverengi	*brown*		

Ne bakıyorsunuz?	*What do you want to take?*
kaça?	*how much?*
ne kadar olur?	*how much?*

In the dialogue above, **satıcı,** *the seller* asks his question **Ne renk bakıyorsunuz?**, *What colour do you want?* Here, **bakmak** is used in place of *to want, to buy* or *to look for*. It's commonly used in the colloquial Turkish.

Also note the suffix **–ki** in **karşıdaki** and **sağdaki**. It adds the meaning of *the one*. Examples: **sağdaki**, *the one on the right*, **karşıdaki**, *the one on the other side*, **bu taraftaki**, *the one one this side*, etc. It can also be in the plural form. Examples: sağdakiler, karşıdakiler, **bu taraftakiler**, etc..

In addition, **indirim yapmak**, *to make a discount* and **indirmek**, *to discount* are synonyms; likewise, **değişim yapmak**, *to make an exhange* and **değiştirmek**, *to exchange* can be used in the same meaning.

Finally, **iade etmek**, *to refund* is performed by the customer and **iade almak** *to accept the refund* is performed by the seller. To put it differently, while **müşteri iade eder,** *the customer refunds*, **satıcı iade alır** *the seller accepts the refund*.

exercise 6

List the names of the clothes, colors, and verbs related to buying and selling you have learned in this lesson into three groups below. Then check your work with the vocabulary section of this lesson.

Example: <u>clothes</u>   <u>colors</u>   <u>verbs</u>
                       elbise   ak   satmak

Dialogue 4

markette in the market

İbrahim and Michelle enter a market, grocery store while they're on their way to the hotel. They need a few things to buy.

Michelle:	İbrahim, şu tarafa gidelim. Bak, orada meyve-sebze reyonu var.
İbrahim:	İyi fikir. Ne almak istersin?
Michelle:	Bir kilo yeşil elma ve yarım kilo şeftali.
İbrahim:	Ben de yeni bir diş fırçası alabilirim.
Michelle:	Tamam. Sonra da bir litre soğuk meyve suyu ve beş yüz gram çerez alırız.
İbrahim:	Senin alışveriş yapmanı çok beğeniyorum. Tamamdır. Alışveriş arabaları şu tarafta.
Michelle:	Ben de seninle alışveriş yapmayı seviyorum.

Vocabulary

alışveriş arabası	*shopping cart*	**portakal**	*orange*
armut	*pear*	**poşet**	*bag*
ayna	*mirror*	**reçel**	*jam*
baharat	*spice*	**sabun**	*soap*
biber	*pepper*	**salam**	*salami*
çay	*tea*	**salatalık**	*cucumber*
çerez	*nuts*	**sarımsak**	*garlic*
çilek	*strawberry*	**sebze**	*vegetable*
dilim	*slice*	**sıcak içecek**	*hot drink*
diş fırçası	*tooth brush*	**siyah zeytin**	*black olive*
diş macunu	*tooth paste*	**soğan**	*onion*
domates	*tomatoes*	**soğuk içecek**	*cold drink*
dondurma	*ice cream*	**su**	*water*
ekmek	*bread*	**sucuk**	*sausage*
elma	*apple*	**süt**	*milk*
erik	*plum*	**şampuan**	*shampoo*
et	*meat*	**şeftali**	*peach*
fasulye	*bean*	**şeker**	*sugar*
gram	*gram*	**şişe**	*bottle*
havuç	*carrot*	**tane**	*piece*
içecek	*drinks*	**tarak**	*comb*
kahvaltılık	*food for breakfast*	**tavuk**	*chicken*
kahve	*coffee*	**temizlik malzemeleri**	*cleaning materials*
karpuz	*watermelon*	**tereyağı**	*butter*
kavun	*melon*	**tırnak makası**	*nail scissors*
kayısı	*apricot*	**traş malzemeleri**	*shaving materials*
kutu	*box*	**turşu**	*pickle*
litre	*liter*	**tuvalet kâğıdı**	*toilet paper*
marul	*lettuce*	**tuz**	*salt*
meyve	*fruit*	**üzüm**	*grape*

muz	*banana*	**vişne**	*sour cherry*
parça	*piece*	**yeşil zeytin**	*green olive*
patates	*patatoes*	**yiyecek**	*food*
patlıcan	*eggplant*	**yoğurt**	*yogurt*
peçete	*paper towel*	**yumurta**	*eggs*
peynir	*cheese*		

Unit Seven: Tatil güzel geçiyor.

The vacation is going well.

With this unit, you will be able to:

- Talk about past actions
- Use the past tense
- Express possession in the past tense
- Use 'there was/were'
- Use the ordinal numbers
- Talk about the days of the week

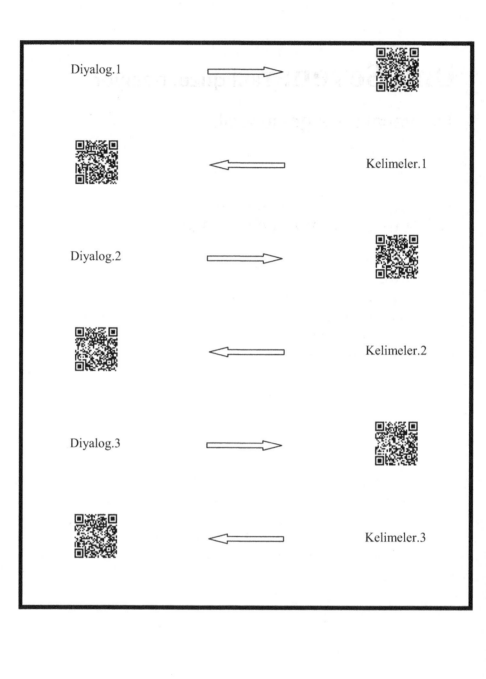

Bölüm 1
Part 1

Dialogue 1

Haber var. There's news.

When they returned to their room in the evening, Michelle noticed that her mom sent her an email.

Michelle:	Annemden haber var.
İbrahim:	İyiler değil mi? Annem ve babam nasıl?
Michelle:	Çok şükür iyiler. Sağlıkları iyi. Köpekleri de iyi.
İbrahim:	Onu nasıl öğrendin?
Michelle:	Mesajda bir de fotoğraf vardı. Resimde köpek Çanko da vardı.
İbrahim:	Çok iyi. Sevindim.
Michelle:	Bizi ve tatilimizi merak ediyorlar. Biliyorsun onlar da bizimle birlikte gelmek istedi.
İbrahim:	Evet biliyorum, malesef zamanları yoktu. Ve çok üzüldüler.
Michelle:	Onlar da önceden Türkiye'ye geldiler. Hâttâ Türkiye'de arkadaşları vardı. Kâmuran amca ile Fahriye teyze. Ayrıca onların Londra'da kızları vardı, Sema. Onlar şimdi emekli oldular ve Türkiye'ye yerleştiler.

1. What do Michelle's parents want to learn?
2. Did Michelle's parents have friends in Türkiye, too? If any, who are they?

Vocabulary

amca	*uncle*	**meraklı**	*curious*
emekli	*retired*	**mesaj**	*message*
fotoğraf	*photograph*	**öğrenmek**	*to figure out, to learn*
haber	*news*	**resim**	*picture*

hâttâ	even	sağlık	health
kedi	cat	sevinmek	to be happy
köpek	dog	teyze	aunt
merak etmek	to wonder	üzülmek	to be sad
merak	curiosity	yerleşmek	to settle

In the dialogue above, we see **Zamanları yoktu,** *They didn't have time.* Notice that **zaman**, *time* can be made plural in Turkish.

Dialogue 2

tatil nasıl geçiyor? how is the vacation going?

Michelle wanted to read the email aloud.

Michelle:	Mesajı sesli okuyorum: Sevgili kızım Michelle. Nasılsın? Sevgili damadım İbrahim nasıl? Tatiliniz nasıl geçiyor? Önce Ankara'ya indiniz. Ankara nasıldı? Ankara'yı beğendin mi? İstanbul'a geçtiniz mi? Ne zaman geçtiniz? İstanbul'a uçakla mı gittiniz yoksa arabayla mı? Oteli kolayca buldunuz mu? Biliyorsun biz de sizinle gelmek istedik. Arkadaşlarımız Kâmuran bey ve Fahriye hanımı çok özledik. Bu arada, Londra'da herşey çok iyi. Baban ve ben iyiyiz. Köpeğimiz Çanko da şimdi daha iyi oldu. Senin için onun bir fotoğrafını çektim. Resmi sana gönderiyorum. Sana ve İbrahim'e iyi bir tatil diliyoruz. Hoşçakalın. Annen ve Baban.
İbrahim:	Biz de onları özledik.

1. How was Çanko before?
2. Why did Michelle's parents also want to come with them?

Vocabulary

bu arada	in the meantime	kolayca	easily
bulmak	to find	okumak	to read
damat	son-in-law	özlemek	to miss
dilemek	to wish	randevu	appointment

fotoğraf çekmek	to take photographs	resim çizmek	to draw pictures
geçirmek	to spend time	sesli	loud
geçmek	to pass, to go	sessiz	silent
gelin	daughter-in-law	sevgili	dear
göndermek	to send	yazmak	to write
Hoşçakalın!		Goodbye!	
Malesef!		Unfortunately!	

In the dialogue above, Michelle's mom says, **sevgili kızım and sevgili damadım.** Note that **sevgili** can be translated as *dear*, and *beloved* and it's common to use it in letters, messages, and in face to face conversations.

Also note that **geçmek**, *to pass* can be used in place of *to spend time, to move* or *to go*.

exercise 1

List the names of the family members and relatives you have learned into two groups below. Then check your work with the vocabulary section of this lesson.

Example: <u>family members</u>   <u>relatives</u>

                  anne   amca

_____

_____

_____

_____

_____

Bölüm 2
Part 2

dilbilgisi grammar

vardı there was / there were

In Turkish, "there was / there were" is expressed by using **vardı**. Note that a place information is also given in the sentences. (See Unit 2 for "there is / there are".)

Examples:

Otelde (bir) taksi vardı.	*There was a taxi at the hotel.*
Okulda öğrenciler var.	*There were students in the school.*

NB It's also possible to use **vardı**, *there was / were*, without the place information. But in this case, <u>possessives are used</u>. **Pay attention to the change in the meaning.**

Examples.

Michelle'in (bir) piyanosu vardı.	*Michelle had a piano.*
Çocukların (bir) odası vardı.	*The children had a room.*
Ali'nin (bir) oteli vardı.	*Ali had a hotel.*
Ali'nin otelleri vardı.	*Ali had hotels.*
Benim (bir) kız kardeşim vardı.	*I had a sister.*

yoktu there wasn't / there weren't

In Turkish, "there wasn't / there weren't" is expressed by using **yoktu**. Note that a place information is also given in the sentences. (See Unit 2 for "there isn't / there aren't".)

Otelde (hiç) taksi yoktu.	*There weren't any taxis at the hotel.*
Okulda (hiç) öğrenci yoktu.	*There weren't any students in the school.*
Burada (hiç) çocuk yoktu.	*There weren't any children here.*
Orada (hiç) çocuk yoktu.	*There weren't any children over there.*

NB It's also possible to use **yoktu**, *there wasn't / weren't*, without the place information. But in this case, <u>possessives are used</u>. **Pay attention to the change in the meaning.**

Examples.

Michelle'in (hiç) piyanosu yoktu.	*Michelle didn't have any pianos.*
Çocukların (hiç) odası yoktu.	*The children didn't have any rooms.*
Ali'nin (hiç) oteli yoktu.	*Ali didn't have any hotels.*
Benim (hiç) kız kardeşim yoktu.	*I didn't have any sisters.*

the question form of "vardı / yoktu"

The question is formed by placing the question word at the end separately. (See Unit 2 for "the question form of there is / there are".)

- For **vardı**, the question ending is **var mıydı?**, *was there? / were there?*

Examples:

Otelde taksi var mıydı?	*Were there taxis at the hotel?*
Okulda öğrenci var mıydı?	*Were there students in the school?*
Orada çocuk var mıydı?	*Were there children over there?*

More examples with the possessives:

Michelle'in piyanosu var mıydı?	*Did Michelle have a piano?*
Çocukların odası var mıydı?	*Did the children have a room?*
Ali'nin oteli var mıydı?	*Did Ali have a hotel?*
Senin kız kardeşin var mıydı?	*Did you have a sister?*

- For **yok**, the question ending is **yok muydu?**, *wasn't there? / weren't there?*

Examples:

Otelde (hiç) taksi yok muydu?	*Weren't there (any) taxis at the hotel?*
Okulda (hiç) öğrenci yok muydu?	*Weren't there (any) students in the school?*
Orada (hiç) çocuk yok muydu?	*Weren't there (any) children over there?*

More examples with the possessives:

Michelle'in (hiç) piyanosu yok muydu?	*Didn't Michelle have (any) pianos?*
Çocukların (hiç) odası yok muydu?	*Didn't the children have (any) rooms?*
Ali'nin (hiç) oteli yok muydu?	*Didn't Ali have (any) hotels?*
Senin (hiç) kız kardeşin yok muydu?	*Didn't you have (any) sisters?*

"vardı / yoktu" with the persons

In Turkish, it is also possible to use **vardı**, *there was / there were* with the persons, (I, You, He / She / It, We, You, and They).

To form to be sentences with persons, the special endings are added to **vardı**, *there was / there were*.

Vardı and the personal endings are given in the table:

(Ben)	vardım	*I was (there)**
(Sen)	vardın	*You were (there)**
(O)	vardı	*He / She / It was (there)**
(Biz)	vardık	*We were (there)**
(Siz)	vardınız	*You (pl) were (there)**
Onlar	vardı / varlardı	*They were (there)**

(*) There represents any place information. See the examples.

Examples:

Ben bu işte vardım.	*I was <u>in</u> this business.*
Biz sizinle her şeye vardık.	*We were <u>in</u> everything with you.*

Similarly, it is also possible to use **yoktu**, *there wasn't / there weren't* with the persons, (I, You, He / She / It, We, You, and They).

To form to be sentences with persons, the special endings are added to **yoktu**, *there wasn't / there weren't*.

Yoktu and the personal endings are given in the table:

(Ben)	yoktum	*I wasn't (there)**
(Sen)	yoktun	*You weren't (there)**
(O)	yoktu	*He / She / It wasn't (there)**
(Biz)	yoktuk	*We weren't (there)**
(Siz)	yoktunuz	*You (pl) weren't (there)**
Onlar	yoktu / yoklardı	*They weren't (there)**

(*) There represents any place information. See the examples.

Examples:

Ben bu işte yoktum. *I wasn't in this business.*

Biz sizinle hiçbir işte yoktuk. *We weren't in any business with you.*

exercise 2

Answer the question with the given words. Make positive or negative sentences according to the words given.

Example: **Odada kimse var mıydı?** **Evet/ben**
(Was there anyone in the room?) *(Yes / I)*

Evet, odada ben vardım.
(Yes, I was in the room.)

1. **Evet/sen** ....

2. **Evet/çocuklar** ....

3. **Evet/biz** ....

4. **Evet/siz** ....

5. **Evet/Michelle** ....

6. **Evet/herkes** ....

7. **Evet/bir şey** ....

8. **Evet/birisi** ....

9. **Hayır/hiç kimse** ....

10. **Hayır/hiç bir şey** ....

exercise 3

Make a question with possessives by using the given words. Then give a positive and a negative answer to the question you just formed. Use the word pairs in your questions and answers.

Example: **otel / şoför / ?** **Otelin şoförü var mıydı?**
(hotel / driver) *(Did the hotel have a driver?)*

Evet, otelin şoförü vardı.
(Yes, the hotel had a driver.)

Hayır, otelin şoförü yoktu.
(No, the hotel didn't have a driver.)

1. **sen / eş**   ....

2. **otel / lokanta**   ....

3. **okul / öğrenci**   ....

4. **Michelle / kardeş** ....

5. **biz / iş**   ....

6. **otel / yönetici**   ....

geçmiş zaman the past tense

The past tense is unique in Turkish and corresponds to the Simple Past Tense in English. Turkish does not have Simple Past Tense, Present Perfect Tense and Past Perfect Tense distinctions as in English.

In Turkish, these distinctions are expressed through the use of various conjunctions, prepositions, clauses, etc. and are interpreted in this way.

Therefore, Simple Past Tense, Present Perfect Tense and Past Perfect Tense structures, which can be expressed separately in translations from Turkish to English, are expressed only in Simple Past Tense in translations from English to Turkish.

The past tense is used to express an action is done in the past. For the conjugation of the verbs, special personal endings are added to the bare form of the verbs.

(Ben)	**-dim**	*I V$_{ed}$**
(Sen)	**-din**	*You V$_{ed}$**
(O)	**-di**	*He / She V$_{ed}$**
(Biz)	**-dik**	*We V$_{ed}$**
(Siz)	**-diniz**	*You (pl) V$_{ed}$**
Onlar	**-di / -diler**	*They V$_{ed}$**

(*) "*V$_{ed}$**" represents any verb in the past tense.

Examples: **gel mek** *(to come)*

Ben geldim.	*I came.*
Sen geldin.	*You came.*
O geldi.	*He / She / It came.*
Biz geldik.	*We came.*
Siz geldiniz.	*You (pl) came.*
Çocuklar geldi / geldiler.	*The children came.*
Arabalar geldi.	*The cars came.*

NB Since the endings added to the verbs bear the personal information, the subjects can be omitted. That's why the subjects are written in brackets. One exception to this is **onlar**, *they*. **Onlar** cannot be omitted.

In addition, note that there are two ending options for the 3rd plural person, **onlar**, *they*, singular (**-di**) and plural (**-diler**). However, for the nonhumans in the subject position, plural ending cannot be preferred. Examples:

Çocuklar *(human)* **geldi/geldiler**   *The children came.*

Arabalar *(nonhuman)* **geldi/~~geldiler~~.**   *The cars came.*

the vowel harmony

The letter "i" in the past tense endings may change to "ı", "u", or "ü" depending on the last vowel of the verb.

Last vowel of the preceding verb	a,ı	e,i	o,u	ö,ü
The vowel in the ending	ı	i	u	ü

(Only the ending for **ben**, *I* is given in the examples to show the vowel change better.)

Examples:

söyle mek	**Ben söyledim.**	*I told.*
atla mak	**Ben atladım.**	*I jumped.*
uyu mak	**Ben uyudum.**	*I slept.*
yürü mek	**Ben yürüdüm.**	*I walked.*

NB Remember that there are two ending options for the 3rd plural person, **onlar**, *they*, singular (**-di**) and plural (**-diler**). In case the plural ending (**-diler**) is used, the vowel "**e**" must also change depending on the preceding vowel.

The endings **-ler** or **-lar** depend on the preceding vowel.

Last vowel of the preceding verb	a,ı, o, u	e,i, ö, ü
the endings –ler / -lar	**-lar**	**-ler**

Examples:

söyle mek	**Çocuklar söylediler.**	*The children told.*
atla mak	**Çocuklar atladılar.**	*The children jumped.*
uyu mak	**Çocuklar uyudular.**	*The children slept.*
yürü mek	**Çocuklar yürüdüler.**	*The children walked.*

the consonant harmony

The first letter of the ending "d" changes into 't' when the preceding consonant, which is the last letter of the preceding verb ends with one of the letters of 'f', 's', 't', 'k', 'ç', 'ş', 'h', and 'p'.

To put it differently;

Last letter of the verb	f	s	t	k	ç	ş	h	p
the first letter of the ending –d changes to:	-t						

(Only the ending for **ben**, *I* is given in the examples to show the consonant change better.)

Examples:

iç mek	Ben içtim.	*I drank.*
bak mak	Ben baktım.	*I looked (at).*
git mek	Ben gittim.	*I went.*
uç mak	Ben uçtum.	*I flew.*

exercise 4

Make positive sentences in the past tense. Note the vowel and consonant change.

Example:

Ben / çay / içmek   **Ben çay içtim.**
I / tea / to drink   *I drank tea.*

1. sen/beni/bilmek   ....

2. biz/dinlenmek   ....

3. o/otele/gitmek   ....

4. onlar/sahanda yumurta/yemek   ....

5. insanlar/menüye/bakmak   ....

6. siz/kafede menüden yemek/seçmek   ....

7. ben/seni/görmek   ....

8. sen/ araba kiralamak   ....

9. biz/ uyumak   ....

the negative form

To form negative sentences in the past tense, the negative ending **–me** is added right before the personal ending.

The negative ending **–me** added right before the personal endings are given in the table below:

(Ben)	-medim	*I didn't V**
(Sen)	-medin	*You didn't V**
(O)	-medi	*He / She didn't V**
(Biz)	-medik	*We didn't V**
(Siz)	-mediniz	*You (pl) didn't V**
Onlar	-medi / -mediler	*They didn't V**

(*) "*V**" represents any verb in the present tense.

Examples: **gel mek** *(to come)*

Ben gelmedim.	*I didn't come.*
Sen gelmedin.	*You didn't come.*
O gelmedi.	*He / She / It didn't come.*
Biz gelmedik.	*We didn't come.*
Siz gelmediniz.	*You (pl) didn't come.*
Çocuklar gelmedi / gelmediler.	*The children didn't come.*
Arabalar gelmedi.	*The cars didn't come.*

Note that the negative ending **–me** is a 2 way vowel harmony meaning it changes to "**-ma**" depending on the preceding vowel.

Last vowel of the preceding verb	a,ı,o,u	e,i,ö,ü
The negative ending –me / -ma	-ma	-me

(Only the ending for **ben**, *I* is given in the examples to show the vowel change better.)

Examples:

söyle mek	**Ben söylemedim.**	*I didn't tell.*
atla mak	**Ben atlamadım.**	*I didn't jump.*
uyu mak	**Ben uyumadım.**	*I didn't sleep.*
yürü mek	**Ben yürümedim.**	*I didn't walk.*

exercise 5

Make negative sentences in the past tense. Note the vowel change.

Example:

Ben / çay / içmek   **Ben çay içmedim.**
I / tea / to drink   *I didn't drink tea.*

1. **sen/beni/bilmek**   ....

2. **biz/dinlenmek**   ....

3. **o/otele/gitmek**   ....

4. **onlar/sahanda yumurta/yemek**   ....

5. **insanlar/menüye/bakmak**   ....

6. **siz/kafede menüden yemek/seçmek** ....

7. **ben/seni/görmek**   ....

8. **sen/ araba kiralamak**   ....

9. **biz/ uyumak**   ....

the question form

To form questions in the past tense, the question ending **mi?** is added separately to the end of the positive endings.

The question ending **mi?** with the positive personal endings are given in the table below:

(Ben)	-dim mi?	*Did I V*?*
(Sen)	-din mi?	*Did you V*?*
(O)	-di mi?	*Did he / she / it V*?*
(Biz)	-dik mi?	*Did we V*?*
(Siz)	-diniz mi?	*Did you (pl) V*?*
Onlar	-di mi?/ -diler mi?	*Did they V*?*

(*) "*V**" represents any verb in the present tense.

Examples: **gel mek** *(to come)*

Ben geldim mi?	*Did I come?*
Sen geldin mi?	*Did you come?*
O geldi mi?	*Did he / she / it come?*
Biz geldik mi?	*Did we come?*
Siz geldiniz mi?	*Did you (pl) come?*
Çocuklar geldi / geldiler mi?	*Did the children come?*
Arabalar geldi mi?	*Did the cars come?*

the vowel harmony

The question ending **mi?** is a 4 way vowel harmony meaning it changes to **mı?**, **mu?**, or **mü?** depending on the preceding vowel.

The preceding vowel	a,ı	e,i	o,u	ö,ü
The question ending mi? (x4)	mı?	mi?	mu?	mü?

(Only the ending for **ben**, *I* is given in the examples to show the vowel change better.)

Examples:

söyle mek	**Ben söyledim mi?**	*Did I tell?*
atla mak	**Ben atladım mı?**	*Did I jump?*
uyu mak	**Ben uyudum mu?**	*Did I sleep?*
yürü mek	**Ben yürüdüm mü?**	*Did I walk?*

More examples:

Ben istedim mi?	*Did I want?*
Sen gittin mi?	*Did you go?*
Sen baktın mı?	*Did you look?*
O uyudu mu?	*Did he / she / it sleep?*
Biz gördük mü?	*Did we see?*
Siz söylediniz mi?	*Did you tell?*
Onlar atladılar mı?	*Did they jump?*
Onlar uçtular mı?	*Did they fly?*

exercise 6

Make questions in the past tense. Note the vowel and consonant change.

Example:

Ben / çay / içmek   **Ben çay içtim mi?.**
I / tea / to drink   *Did I drink tea?*

1. **sen/beni/bilmek**   ....

2. **biz/dinlenmek**   ....

3. **o/otele/gitmek** ....

4. **onlar/sahanda yumurta/yemek** ....

5. **insanlar/menüye/bakmak** ....

6. **siz/kafede menüden yemek/seçmek** ....

7. **ben/seni/görmek** ....

8. **sen/ araba kiralamak** ....

9. **biz/ uyumak** ....

"to be" sentences in the past tense

In Turkish, "to be" isn't used in the past tense either. Remember, it's not used in the present tense. Instead, there are personal endings. However, the endings depend on the final letter of the word. The endings following a consonant or a vowel differ.

- In case the word ends with a consonant, the following endings are added:

(Ben)	-dim	*I was*
(Sen)	-din	*You were*
(O)	-di	*He / She / It was*
(Biz)	-dik	*We were*
(Siz)	-diniz	*You (pl) were*
Onlar	-di / -diler	*They were*

Examples:

Ben öğretmendim.	*I was a teacher.*
Sen öğretmendin.	*You were a teacher.*
O öğretmendi.	*He / She / It was a teacher.*
Biz öğretmendik.	*We were teachers.*
Siz öğretmendiniz.	*You (pl) were teachers.*
Onlar öğretmendi / öğretmendiler.	*They were teachers.*

NB Since the endings added to the verbs bear the personal information, the subjects can be omitted. That's why the subjects are written in brackets. One exception to this is **onlar**, *they*. **Onlar** cannot be omitted.
In addition, note that there are two ending options for the 3rd plural person, **onlar**, *they*, singular (**-di**) and plural (**-diler**). However, for the nonhumans in the subject position, plural ending cannot be preferred.

the vowel harmony

The letter "**i**" in the past tense "to be" endings may change to "**ı**", "**u**", or "**ü**" depending on the last vowel of the verb.

Last vowel of the preceding word	a,ı	e,i	o,u	ö,ü
The vowel in the ending	ı	i	u	ü

(Only the ending for **ben**, *I* is given in the examples to show the vowel change better.)

Examples:

öğretmen	**Ben öğretmendim.**	*I was a teacher.*
yorgun	**Ben yorgundum.**	*I was tired.*
üzgün	**Ben üzgündüm.**	*I was sad.*
manav	**Ben manavdım.**	*I was a greengrocer.*

NB In case the plural ending (**-diler**) is used, the vowel "**e**" must change depending on the preceding vowel. The previous "**-ler / -lar** table" is also applicable here.

Examples:

Çocuklar yorgundular (yorgunlardı)*.	*The children were tired.*
Çocuklar üzgündüler (üzgünlerdi)*.	*The children were sad.*
Çocuklar çalışkandılar (çalışkanlardı)*.	*The children were hardworking.*
Çocuklar tembeldiler (tembellerdi)*.	*The children were lazy.*

* also possible.

the consonant harmony

The first letter of the ending "d" changes into 't' when the preceding consonant, which is the last letter of the preceding verb ends with one of the letters of 'f', 's', 't', 'k', 'ç', 'ş', 'h', and 'p'.

To put it differently;

Last letter of the verb	f	s	t	k	ç	ş	h	p
the first letter of the ending –d changes to:	-t							

(Only the ending for **ben**, *I* is given in the examples to show the consonant change better.)

Examples:

Ben kasaptım (kasapdım).   *I was a butcher.*

Ben şeftim (şefdim).   *I was a chef.*

Ben mühendistim (mühendisdim).   *I was an engineer.*

• In case the word ends with a vowel, the ending connector "**y**" is added right before the personal endings. In other words, the following endings are added:

(Ben)	-ydim	*I was*
(Sen)	-ydin	*You were*
(O)	-ydi	*He / She / It was*
(Biz)	-ydik	*We were*
(Siz)	-ydiniz	*You (pl) were*
Onlar	-ydi / -ydiler	*They were*

Examples:

Ben öğrenciydim.   *I was a student.*

Sen öğrenciydin.   *You were a student.*

O öğrenciydi.   *He / She / It was a student.*

Biz öğrenciydik.   *We were students.*

Siz öğrenciydiniz.   *You (pl) were students.*

Onlar öğrenciydi / öğrenciydiler.   *They were students.*

NB The vowel harmony is also necessary here. See the previous vowel harmony tables.

Examples:

öğrenci	Ben öğrenciydim.	*I was a student.*
hızlı	Garson hızlıydı.	*The waiter was fast.*
uslu	Çocuk usluydu.	*The child was docile.*
türkücü	Sen türkücüydün.	*You were a singer.*

the negative form

To form negative "to be" sentences, **değil**, *not* is used as studied in Unit 1. Then the personal endings are added to **değil**.

Below are given the special personal endings:

(Ben)	değildim	*I wasn't*
(Sen)	değildin	*You weren't*
(O)	değildi	*He / She / It wasn't*
(Biz)	değildik	*We weren't*
(Siz)	değildiniz	*You (pl) weren't*
Onlar	değildi / değillerdi	*They weren't*

Examples:

Bu yemek çok lezzetli değildi.	*This meal wasn't very delicious.*
Otelimiz pahalı değildi.	*Our hotel wasn't expensive.*
Dün çok yorgun değildim.	*I wasn't tired yesterday.*
Arkadaşlarımız üzgün değillerdi.	*Our friends weren't sad.*
Siz çok hızlı değildiniz.	*You weren't very fast.*
Senin çayın da sıcak değildi.	*Your tea wasn't hot, either.*

the question form

To form a question with the "to be" sentences in the past tense, the question word **mi?** is added right before the personal endings. Then the question word **mi? and** the personal endings are written separately.

The question ending **mi?** added separately to the end of the positive endings is given in the table below:

(Ben)	miydim?	*Was I?*
(Sen)	miydin?	*Were you?*
(O)	miydi?	*Was he / she / it?*
(Biz)	miydik?	*Were we?*
(Siz)	miydiniz?	*Were you (pl)?*
Onlar	miydi?	*Were they?*

Examples:

Ben öğretmen miydim?   *Was I a teacher?*

Sen öğretmen miydin?   *Were you a teacher?*

O öğretmen miydi?   *Was he / she / it a teacher?*

Biz öğretmen miydik?   *Were we teachers?*

Siz öğretmen miydiniz?   *Were you (pl) teachers?*

Onlar öğretmen miydi?   *Were they teachers?*
Onlar öğretmenler miydi?   *Were they teachers?*

the vowel harmony

The question word **mi?** is a 4 way vowel harmony meaning it changes to "**mı?, mu?,** or **mü?** depending on the preceding vowel. Remember, the personal endings are also change according to the question word.

The preceding vowel	a,ı	e,i	o,u	ö,ü
The question word mi? (x4)	mı?	mi?	mu?	mü?

Examples:

öğrenci	**Ben öğrenci miydim?**	*Was I a student?*
hızlı	**Garson hızlı mıydı?**	*Was the waiter fast?*
uslu	**Çocuk uslu muydu?**	*Was the child docile?*
türkücü	**Sen türkücü müydün?**	*Were you a singer?*

More examples:

Bu yemek lezzetli miydi?	*Was this meal delicious?*
Otelimiz pahalı mıydı?	*Was our hotel expensive?*
Dün çok yorgun muyduk?	*Were we tired yesterday?*
Arkadaşlarımız üzgünler miydi?	*Were our friends sad?*
Siz çok hızlı mıydınız?	*Were you very fast?*
Senin çayın da sıcak mıydı?	*Was your tea hot, too?*
Jack eskiden bir mühendis miydi?	*Was Jack an engineer in the past?*
Memnunlar mıydı?	*Were they pleased?*

exercise 7

Change the "to be" sentences into the past tense. Note the vowel and consonant changes.

Example:

Ben yorgunum.   **Ben yorgundum.**
I'm tired.   *I was tired.*

1. **Sen evlisin.**   ....

2. **Michelle çok aç.**   ....

3. **Yemek hiç lezzetli değil.**   ....

4. **Manzara harika.**   ....

5. **Biz garsonuz.**   ....

6. **Serra bir öğrenci.**   ....

7. **Köpek Çanko hasta değil.**   ....

8. **Michelle'in babası bir mühendistir.** ....

9. **Biz Türkiye'deyiz.**   ....

Bölüm 3
Part 3

talking about the days of the week

In Turkish, talking about the days of the week is done in a special way.

Examples:

Bugün günlerden ne?	*What's the day today? / What day is it?*
Bugün (günlerden) Salı.	*Today is Tuesday. / It's Tuesday today.*
Dün günlerden neydi?	*What day was yesterday?*
Dün (günlerden) Pazardı.	*Yesterday was Sunday.*
Yarın günlerden ne?	*What day is tomorrow?*
Yarın (günlerden) Cuma.	*Tomorrow is Friday.*

ordinal numbers

In Turkish, ordinal numbers are formed by adding the ordinal endings at the end of the numbers.

In case the number ends with a vowel, the ending –**nci** is used. When the number ends with a consonant, then the ending is **–inci**. The vowel/vowels change adpending on the preceding vowel in the number.

The vowel harmony table for the ordinal endings is given below:

The preceding vowel	a,ı	e,i	o,u	ö,ü
The ordinal endings –nci / -inci	–ncı / -ıncı	–nci / -inci	–ncu / -uncu	–ncü / -üncü

Some examples with the ordinal numbers:

ilk	*first*		**ikinci**	*second*
birinci	*first*		**dördüncü**	*fourth*
üçüncü	*third*		**altıncı**	*sixth*
beşinci	*fifth*		**sekizinci**	*eighth*
yedinci	*seventh*		**onuncu**	*tenth*
dokuzuncu	*ninth*		**sonuncu**	*last*

Examples:

Bugün haftanın kaçıncı günü?	*What day of the week is today?*
Bugün haftanın ilk günü.	*Today is the first day of the week.*
Bugün haftanın birinci günü.	*Today is the first day of the week.*
Bugün haftanın beşinci günü.	*Today is the fifth day of the week.*
Bugün yedinci gün.	*Today is the seventh day.*
Bugün haftanın sonuncu günü.	*Today is the last day of the week.*

talking about the past actions

Read the examples about asking and answering about the past actions.

Bugün ne(ler)* yaptın?	*What did you today?*
Bugün güzel bir kahvaltı yaptım.	*I had a nice breakfast today.*
Dün neler yaptın?	*What did you yesterday?*
Dün hiç yemek yemedim.	*I didn't eat food yesterday.*
Evvelsi gün kahvaltı yaptın mı?	*Did you eat breakfast the day before yesterday?*
Hayır, malesef. Yine bir şey yemedim.	*No, unfortunately. I didn't eat anything, either.*

(*) Note that in Turkish, it's also possible to make the question word **ne?**, *what?* plural. However the translation remains the same.

Dialogue 3

otele giriş registering in the hotel

Michelle wrote an email back to her mom. She wants to read this email aloud, too.

Michelle:	Anneme şöyle yazdım: Sevgili anneciğim ve babacığım. Nasılsınız? Çanko nasıl? Tamamen iyileşti mi? Bu arada, ben de İbrahim de gayet iyiyiz. Tatilimiz güzel geçiyor. Önce Ankara'ya indik. Ankara'daki otelimiz çok güzeldi. Orada Talha ve kardeşi Serra ile tanıştık. Ayrıca, evvelsi gün İbrahim'in arkadaşı Ali ile de buluştuk. Ali'nin kızını çok sevdim. Ankara'da üç gün kaldık sonra Ankara'dan ayrıldık. Araba ile İstanbul'a geldik. Bugün Kapalıçarşı'ya alışveriş için gittik. Çok tarihî ve çok görkemliydi. Sonra otele döndük. Biraz yorulduk ve şimdi dinlenmek istiyoruz. Biz de size selâm söylüyoruz. Hoşçakalın. Kızınız ve damadınız.
İbrahim:	Eline sağlık!

1. Did Michelle meet with new people in Ankara?
2. How was the shopping day?

In the dialogue above, Michelle says, **anneciğim** and **babacığım**. In Turkish, it's very common to add these suffixes while addressing directly to the people beloved. It's also possible to add the suffix to proper names, then an apostrophe is needed, e.g. **İbrahim'ciğim**, **Michelle'ciğim**, etc.

Also note that **geçmek**, *to pass* is used in this dialogue, too. Here **geçmek** is used for the time. **Tatil geçiyor**, *The vacation is passing.* **Geçmek** can be used in the following structures, too: **Ben akşam size geçiyorum.**, *I'll drop in on you in the evening.* or **Ben senin arabanı yolda geçiyorum.**, *I'm passing your car on the road.*

Vocabulary

ayrılmak	*to leave*	**yarın**	*tomorrow*
böyle	*like this*	**evvelsi gün**	*the day before yesterday*
buluşmak	*to meet*	**dün**	*yesterday*
hoşlanmak	*to like*	**sevmek**	*to love*
inmek	*to land, get off*	**şöyle**	*like this*
iyileşmek	*to get well*	**tamamen**	*completely*
kalmak	*to stay*	**tanışmak**	*to meet, to introduce*
selâm söylemek	*to send best regards*	**yorulmak**	*to get tired*
Eline sağlık!		*Good job!, Bless your hands!*	

exercise 8

Which is the odd one out in each row?

dün	akşam	evvelsi gün	bugün
çizmek	yazmak	okumak	iyileşmek
sevmek	hoşlanmak	beğenmek	yorulmak
tamamen	sevinmek	üzülmek	merak etmek

Unit Eight: İstanbul'da bir gezi

A trip in İstanbul

With this unit, you will be able to:

- Buy tickets for public transportation vehicles
- Talk about weather and directions
- Use the parallel conjunctions such as 'and', 'also, etc.'
- Use the 'how often' questions
- Use the 'how long' questions
- Use the adverbs of frequency

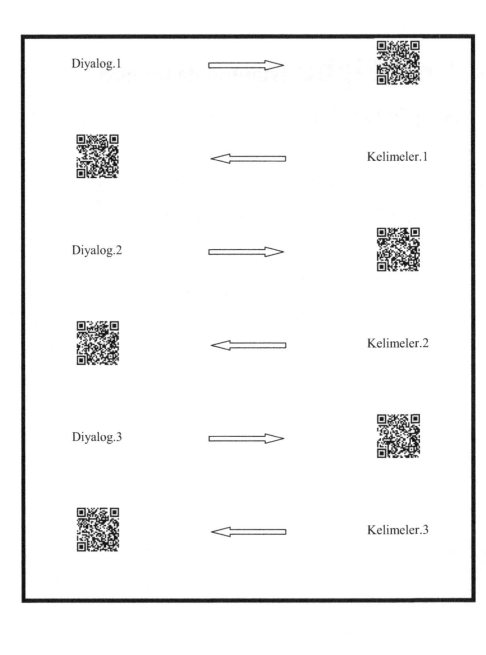

Bölüm 1
Part 1

Dialogue 1

gezi hazırlığı preparation for the trip

Michelle and İbrahim want to travel in İstanbul via public transportation vehicles.

Michelle:	Bence şehir içinde araba yerine toplu taşıma araçlarını tercih edebiliriz.
Michelle:	
İbrahim:	Ben de aynı fikirdeyim. Toplu taşıma vasıtasıyla İstanbul'un her yerine gidebiliriz.
Michelle:	Nasıl yani?
İbrahim:	Örneğin otelin hemen yanındaki metro durağından metroya binebiliriz. Sonra da tramvaya aktarma yaparız.
Michelle:	Peki ya vapur seyahati? Bir boğaz turuna hayır demem!
İbrahim:	Aynı biletle vapura da bineriz.
Michelle:	Yani bilet sadece metro için değil aynı zamanda vapur için de geçerli, değil mi?
İbrahim:	Aynen öyle. Ve başka bilet almayız, aynı biletle geri döneriz.

1. Where can they get on metro?
2. Can they get on every transportation vehicles with one ticket?

Vocabulary

aktarma yapmak	*to transfer*	**geri dönmek**	*to return*
aynı	*the same*	**örneğin**	*for instance*
bilet	*ticket*	**seyahat**	*trip*
binmek	*to get on/in a vehicle*	**tercih etmek**	*to prefer*
farklı	*different*	**toplu taşıma**	*public transportation*
geçerli	*valid*	**vapur**	*ferry*

| Aynen öyle! | *Just like that!* |
| Nasıl yani? | *How come?* |

In the dialogue above, we see **bence** used with a suggestion. It's common to add **bence** to suggestions, in Turkish. It's also common to add **sence** to the questions about suggestions. Examples: **Bence şimdi çay içebiliriz.**, *In my opinion, we can drink tea now.* and **Sence şimdi çay içebilir miyiz?**, *In your opinion, can we drink tea now?*

In spoken Turkish, it's common to give short answers when in the same opinion with the others. Note that **aynen öyle**, **ben de aynı fikirdeyim**, and **bence de** are used for these situations. They substitute long sentences, just like the similar phrases used in English, e.g. *I thinks so, too.*, *Me, too*, or *That's right.*

Dialogue 2

İstanbulkart İstanbulkart: an electronic ticket

Michelle and İbrahim decided to go directly to Sirkeci Port from their hotel to take a ferry for Bosphorus Tour. But, they know that they need tickets first. They came to a kiosk at the metro station.

İbrahim:	Merhabalar, İki tane İstanbulkart istiyorum.
Satıcı:	Tabii, beyefendi. Öğrenci mi yoksa tam mı?
İbrahim:	İki tam bilet.
Satıcı:	Tabii, tek seferlik mi yoksa iki seferlik mi? Kaç seferliğine istiyorsunuz?
İbrahim:	Ne tek seferlik ne de iki. Sürekli olarak kullanmak istiyorum.
Satıcı:	O zaman, geçici değil devamlı bilet almalısınız. Buyurun. İki kişilik 20 lira. Ücretini şuradaki makinelerden yükleyebilirsiniz.
İbrahim:	Hangi makineden ödeme yapabilirim? Sağdaki mi soldaki mi?
Satıcı:	Aslında hem sağdaki hem de soldaki olur. Fakat sağdaki makine bazen çalışmaz, soldaki her zaman çalışır.

1. Will they buy a temporary or a permanent ticket?
2. How can they load money into their İstanbulkart tickets?

Vocabulary

arka	*back*	**ödeme yapmak**	*to make a payment*
baş	*the beginning of*	**ödemek**	*to pay*
bazen	*sometimes*	**ön**	*ahead*
devamlı	*permanent*	**sağ**	*right*
geçici	*temporary*	**sol**	*left*
geri	*reverse*	**sürekli**	*permanent*
gidiş geliş	*round trip*	**tek sefer**	*one way*
ileri	*forward*	**tek yön**	*one way*
İstanbulkart	*an electronic ticket for public transportation in İstanbul*	**yüklemek**	*to load*
makine	*machine*		

Note that the seller says, "**o zaman ....**". It can be translated as *then ...* In addition to that, **öyleyse**, *if so*, can also be used in the similar meaning.

Also note that **tam** means *regular* in this concept. For example, tam bilet is a ticket for regular passengers, but there are other versions, too, such as **öğrenci bileti**, a ticket for students or **yaşlılar için bilet**, a ticket for the old people, etc.

exercise 1

Which is the odd one out in each row?

sağ	sol	makine	arka
geri	toplu taşıma	bilet	seyahat
ödemek	sürekli	gidiş geliş	tek yön
binmek	inmek	aktarma yapmak	geçerli

Bölüm 2
Part 2

dilbilgisi grammar

çeşitli bağlaçlar various conjunctions

In Turkish, parallel meaning is expressed by using several conjunctions or connectors. These conjunctions can be used to connect nouns, adjectives, adverbs, and verbs.

"de" bağlacı the conjunction "also, too, both"

Talha bir öğrencidir.	*Talha is a student.*
Serra da bir öğrencidir.	*Serra is a student, too.*
Talha da Serra da birer öğrencidir.	*Both Talha and Serra are students.*
Her ikisi de birer öğrencidir.	*Both of them are students (each).*

NB In Turkish, pluralization of **bir**, *a* is also possible, i.e. **birer**. In fact, it means *each*.

İbrahim çok çalışır.	*İbrahim works a lot.*
İbrahim çok okur da.	*İbrahim reads a lot, too.*
İbrahim çok da okur.	*İbrahim reads a lot, too.*
İbrahim çok çalışır, çok da okur.	İbrahim works alot, and reads a lot, too.
Eymen çok akıllıdır.	*Eymen is very smart.*
Eymen çok yaramazdır da.	*Eymen is very naughty, too.*
Eymen çok da yaramazdır.	*Eymen is very naughty, too.*

NB In Turkish, the conjunction "**de**" can be placed at the end, too.
Also note that, **aynı zamanda**, *at the same time* is generally used with the conjunction "**de**". Examples:

Talha bir öğrencidir. Aynı zamanda Serra da bir öğrencidir.
Talha is a student. At the same time, Serra is a student, too.

İbrahim çok çalışır. Aynı zamanda çok da okur.
İbrahim works a lot. At the same time, he reads a lot, too.

Eymen çok akıllıdır. Aynı zamanda çok da yaramazdır.
Eymen is very clever. At the same time, he's very naughty, too.

"hem - hem" bağlacı the conjunction "also, too, both"

Hem Talha hem de Serra birer öğrencidir.
Both Talha and Serra are students.

İbrahim hem çok çalıştı hem de çok okudu.
İbrahim both worked and read a lot.

Eymen hem çok akıllı hem de çok yaramazdır.
Eymen is both very smart and very naughty.

"ve" bağlacı the conjunction "and"

Talha ve Serra birer öğrencidir.
Talha and Serra are students.

İbrahim çok çalıştı ve çok okudu.
İbrahim worked a lot and read a lot.

Eymen çok akıllı ve çok yaramazdır.
Eymen is very smart and very naughty.

"sadece –değil, aynı zamanda -da" bağlacı
the conjunction "not only, but also"

Sadece Talha değil, aynı zamanda Serra da bir öğrencidir.
Not only Talha but also Serra is a student.

İbrahim sadece çok çalışmadı, aynı zamanda çok da okudu.
İbrahim not only worked a lot but also read a lot.

Eymen sadece çok akıllı değil aynı zamanda çok da yaramazdır.
Eymen is not only very smart but also very naughty.

"ne, ne de" bağlacı the conjunction "neither, nor"

Ne Talha ne de Serra muhasebeci değil. İkisi de öğrenci.
Neither Talha nor Serra is an accountant. Both are students.

İbrahim ne uyur ne de dinlenir. O sadece çok çalışır ve çok okur.
İbrahim neither sleeps nor rests. He just works a lot and read a lot.

Eymen ne çalışkan ne de usludur. O sadece çok akıllı ve yaramazdır.
Eymen is neither studious nor docile. He's just very smart and naughty.

exercise 2

Fill in the blanks with the correct conjunction according to the given clues.

Example: **Senin araban kırmızı. Benim arabam da kırmızı.**

<u>Hem</u> senin araban <u>hem de</u> benim arabam kırmızı.

1.   **Senin araban kırmızı. Benim arabam yeşil.**

            _____ senin araban _____ benim arabam sarı.

2.   **Senin araban yeni. Benim arabam da yeni.**

            _____ senin araban _____ benim arabam da yeni.

3.   **Anıtkabir Ankara'da. İlkbahar Otel Ankara'da.**

            Anıtkabir _____ İlkbahar Otel Ankara'da.

4.   **Çay sıcak. Kahve sıcak.**

            Çay _____ kahve _____ sıcak.

5.   **Ud çalmayı severim. Şarkı söylemeyi severim.**

            _____ ud çalmayı _____ şarkı söylemeyi severim.

sıklık soruları how often questions

In Turkish, the how often questions can be used in every tense as they can be in English. The important point is to point the frequence in the question and in the answer. Expression of the frequency can be done in several ways. Below are the examples of expression of the frequency:

questions

Ne sıklıkta Türkiye'ye gidersiniz?
How often do you go to Türkiye?

Ne sıklıkta yemek pişirirsin?
How often do you cook meal?

Size ne sıklıkta ödeme yapmam gerekiyor?
How often do I have to pay you?

Burada ne sıklıkta yağmur yağar?
How often does it rain here?

sıklık bildiren zarflar the adverbs of frequency

The formation of the sentences with the adverbs of frequency is given below.

hep, her zaman always

Hep/her zaman kitap okur musun?	*Do you always read books?*
Evet, hep/zaman okurum.	*Yes, I always read.*
Kahvaltıyı hep/her zaman burada mı yaparsın?	*Do you always have breakfast here?*
Evet, kahvaltımı hep/her zaman burada yaparım.	*Yes, I always have my breakfast here.*
Hep/her zaman böyle misindir?	*Are you always like this?*
Evet, hep/her zaman.	*Yes, always.*

hiç, asla ever, never

Hiç kitap okur musun?	*Do you ever read books?*
Hayır, hiç/asla okumam.	*No, I never read books.*
Burada hiç kahvaltı yaptın mı?	*Have you ever had breakfast here?*
Hayır, hiç/asla yapmadım.	*No, I haven't ever.*
Hiç Türkiye'ye gittiniz mi?	*Have you ever gone to Türkiye?*
Hayır, hiç/asla gitmedik.	*No, we have never gone.*

NB Even though **hiç** and **asla** have a similar meaning, **asla** can only be used in negative sentences.

sık sık, bazen, ara sıra often, sometimes, occasionally

Bazen deniz kıyısında koşarım.	*I sometimes run on the sea side.*
Sık sık şehir içinde koşarım.	*I often run in the city center.*
Ara sıra yürüyüş de yaparım.	*I occasionally take a walk, too.*
Bazen evde pişiririm.	*I sometimes cook at home.*
Sık sık alışverişe giderim.	*I often go shopping.*
Ara sıra da kafeye giderim.	*I occasionally go to the cafe, too.*

nadiren, pek (-) seldom

Nadiren çay içerim.	*I seldom drink tea.*
Pek çay içmem.	*I seldom drink tea.*
Nadiren kitap okurum.	*I seldom read books.*
Pek kitap okumam.	*I seldom read books.*
Nadiren hasta olurum.	*I seldom get sick.*
Pek hasta olmam.	*I seldom get sick.*

NB Even though **nadiren** and **pek** have a similar meaning, **pek** can only be used in negative sentences.

diğerleri others

Üç günde bir deniz kıyısında koşarım.	*I run on the sea side every three days.*
Haftada bir şehir içinde koşarım.	*I run in the city center once in a week.*
Her gün yürüyüş yaparım.	*I take a walk everyday.*
İki günde bir evde pişiririm.	*I cook at home every other day.*

exercise 3

Write the frequency adverbs on the rows according to their frequency. More than one answer is possible for each row.

hiç, sabahları, haftasonları, sık sık, her zaman, bazen, ara sıra, nadiren

most frequent ↑ _____

_____

_____

_____

least frequent ↓ _____

süre soruları how long questions

In Turkish, the how long questions can be used in every tense as they can be in English. The important point is to point the duration in the question and in the answer. Expression of the duration can be done in several ways. Below are the examples of expression of the duration:

questions

Kaç gündür Türkiye'desiniz?
How many days have you been in Türkiye?

Ne zamandır Türkiye'desiniz?
How long have you been in Türkiye?

Ne zamandan beri Türkiye'desiniz?
Since when have you been in Türkiye?

Ne zamandan bu yana Türkiye'desiniz?
Since when have you been in Türkiye?

Kaç günlüğüne Türkiye'ye geldiniz?
For how many days did you come to Türkiye?

Türkiye'ye kaç gün için geldiniz?
For how many days did you come to Türkiye?

Ne kadar zaman için Türkiye'ye geldiniz?
For how long did you come to Türkiye?

Kaç günlüğüne Türkiye'de kalmak istiyorsunuz?
For how many days do you want to stay in Türkiye?

Ne kadarlığına Türkiye'de kalmak istiyorsunuz?
For how long do you want to stay in Türkiye?

Türkiye'de kaç gün kaldınız?
How many days did you stay in Türkiye?

Türkiye'de ne kadar kaldınız?
How long did you stay in Türkiye?

answers

Beş gündür Türkiye'deyiz.
We have been in Türkiye for five days.

Bir haftadır Türkiye'deyiz.
We have been in Türkiye for a week.

Salı gününden beri Türkiye'deyiz.
We have been in Türkiye since Tuesday.

Salıdan bu yana Türkiye'deyiz.
We have been in Türkiye since Tuesday.

Türkiye'ye beş günlüğüne geldik.
We came to Türkiye for five days.

Türkiye'ye beş gün için geldik.
We came to Türkiye for five days.

Türkiye'ye bir haftalığına geldik.
We came to Türkiye for a week.

Türkiye'de beş günlüğüne kalmak istiyoruz.
We want to stay in Türkiye for five days.

Türkiye'de bir haftalığına kalmak istiyoruz.
We want to stay in Türkiye for a week.

Türkiye'de beş gün kaldık.
We stayed in Türkiye for five days.

Türkiye'de beş günlüğüne kaldık.
We stayed in Türkiye for five days.

Bölüm 3
Part 3

Dialogue 3

Asya ile Avrupa'nın arasında between Asia and Europe

Michelle and İbrahim took metro to Beşiktaş Port first. Then they got on a ferry. When the ferry was in the middle of Bosphorus, İbrahim started talking excitedly.

İbrahim:	Michelle, bak! Şu anda tam Boğaz'ın ortasındayız. Yani Asya ile Avrupa'nın arasındayız.
Michelle:	Ya!? Ne heyecanlı!
İbrahim:	Bak sağımız Asya, solumuz Avrupa kıtası. İstanbul Boğazı iki kıtayı ayırıyor.
Michelle:	Evet, kesinlikle öyle!
İbrahim:	Boğaz hem iki kıtayı ayırıyor hem de iki denizi birleştiriyor.
Michelle:	Ya!? Hangi denizler?
İbrahim:	Şu anda Marmara Denizi'ndeyiz. Kuzeyde Karadeniz ve güneyde Ege Denizi Marmara Denizi'nde birleşiyor. Tabii, aynı şekilde doğu ile batı yani Asya ile Avrupa da köprülerde birleşiyor.
Michelle:	Fevkalâde! Kuzeyden ve güneyden gelen rüzgârlar da tam burada birleşiyor. Hava hem güneşli hem de serin. Biraz üşüdüm. Ya sen?

1. What continents does the Bosphorus connect?
2. What seas does the Marmara Sea connect?

Vocabulary

arasında	*between*	karlı	*snowy*
Asya	*Asia*	kesilmek	*to (wind, snow, or rain) stop*
Avrupa	*Europe*	kıta	*continent*
ayırmak	*to split*	köprü	*bridge*
batı	*west*	kuzey	*north*
birleşmek	*to merge*	rüzgâr esmek	*to (wind) blow*
birleştirmek	*to join*	rüzgâr	*wind*
bulut	*cloud*	rüzgârlı	*windy*
bulutlu	*cloudy*	serin	*cool*
deniz	*sea*	sıcak	*hot*
dinmek	*to (wind, snow, or rain) stop*	sıcaklamak	*to get hot*
doğu	*east*	soğuk	*cold*
güneş açmak	*to (sun) shine*	şu anda	*for the moment*
güneşli	*sunny*	üşümek	*to get cold*
güney	*south*	yağmur yağmak	*to rain*
hava	*weather*	yağmur	*rain*
ılık	*warm*	yağmurlu	*rainy*
kar yağmak	*to snow*	yani	*in other words*
kar	*snow*		
Ne heyecanlı!	*How exciting!*		
Ya!?	*How exciting!*		

In the dialogue above, Michelle says, **ya!?**. This is an exclamation word used upon shocking, or surprise. **Ya** has another usage as in **ya sen?** In this situation, it means *what about you?* or *how is it from you side?* And the concept should be taken into consideration.

Also note that **tam** means *exactly* here, i. e. **tam ortası**, *exactly in the middle.*

exercise 4

List the names of the directions, nouns and adjectives related to the weather
you have learned in this lesson into three groups below. Then check your
work with the vocabulary section of this lesson.

Example:	directions	nouns	adjectives
	kuzey	bulut	bulutlu

_____

_____

_____

_____

_____

hava hakkında konuşmak talking about the weather

In Turkish, the following phrases are widely used when talking about weather
conditions.

Hava nasıl?	*How is the weather?*
Bugün yağmur yağacak mı?	*Will it rain today?*
Hava bugün biraz serin.	*It's a little cool today.*
Bugün hava çok sıcak.	*It's very hot today.*
Hava rüzgârlı.	*It's windy.*
Dışarıda rüzgâr var.	*It's windy outside.*
Yağmur yağıyor.	*It's raining.*
Kar yağıyor.	*It's snowing.*
Rüzgâr esiyor.	*The wind is blowing.*
Rüzgâr/yağmur/kar durdu.	*The wind/rain/snow stopped.*
Rüzgâr/yağmur/kar kesildi.	*The wind/rain/snow stopped.*
Rüzgâr/yağmur/kar dindi.	*The wind/rain/snow stopped.*
Güneş açtı.	*The sun is shining.*
Üşüdüm.	*I got cold.*
Sıcakladım.	*I got hot.*

yönler hakkında konuşmak talking about the directions

In Turkish, the following phrases are widely used when talking about directions.

İstanbul nerede?	*Where is İstanbul?*
Kuzeyde.	*In the north.*
Türkiye'nin kuzeyinde.	*In the north of Türkiye.*
Ankara'nın kuzeyinde.	*North of Ankara.*
Senin evin nerede?	*Where is your house?*
Ankara'nın kuzeyinde.	*In the north of Ankara.*
Eczanenin karşısında.	*Opposite of the pharmacy.*
Otobüs durağının yanında.	*Next to the bus stop.*
Okulun arkasında.	*In back of the school.*
Otelin önünde.	*In front of the hotel.*
Sokağın sonunda.	*At the end of the street.*
Sokağın başında.	*At the beginning of the street.*
Sokağın tam ortasında.	*In the very middle of the street.*
Sokağın sağında.	*On the right of the street.*
Sağda.	*On the right.*
Sağdaki ev.	*The house on the right.*

Unit Nine: Bir arkadaş daveti

An invitation of a friend

With this unit, you will be able to:

- Talk about directions and addresses
- Make an invitation
- Make suggestions with 'let's'
- Reject and accept invitations
- Use the Future Tense
- Use conjunctions 'or' and 'else'

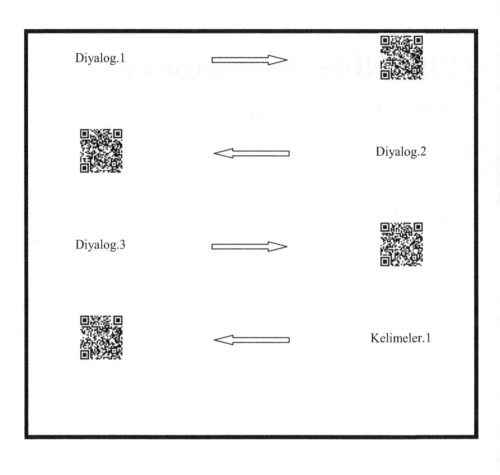

Bölüm 1
Part 1

Dialogue 1

arkadaşlara bir telefon a call to the friends

Michelle calls Kâmuran and Fahriye. They want to extend the regards that Michelle's mom and dad sent them.

Michelle:	Merhaba, Kâmuran amca ile görüşebilir miyim, acaba?
Fahriye:	Merhabalar. Kim, arıyor?
Michelle:	Fahriye teyze, sizsiniz değil mi? Ben Michelle.
Fahriye:	Michelle, kızım. Sen misin? Neredesin sen?
Michelle:	Evet, Fahriye teyze benim. İbrahim'le birlikte İstanbul'dayız.
Fahriye:	Aaa! Hiç haberim yoktu. Hoş geldiniz. Mutlaka bize de bekliyorum. Bak, Kâmuran amcanın da selâmı var. O da çağırıyor. Çok sevindik. Annen babanlar nasıl, iyiler mi?
Michelle:	İyiler iyiler, çok şükür. Onların da selâmı var size. Ayrıca siz de Kâmuran amcaya selâm söyleyin.
Fahriye:	Geliyorsunuz, değil mi? Bugün gelin. Bekliyoruz.
Michelle:	Fahriye teyze, davetiniz için teşekkür ederim. Tabii ki, geliriz. Çok memnun oluruz. İbrahim'le konuşmalıyım, ama bugün olmayabilir. Biz sizi ararız.

1. Did Fahriye know Michelle and İbrahim were in İstanbul?
2. Did Michelle accept the invitation right away?

In the dialogue above, Michelle says, **acaba.** Even though it means *I wonder*, it's common to add **acaba** in questions to intensify the meaning.

Also note that **Aaa!** is used to show surprise.

NB In Turkish, it is very common to send regards to others by saying for example; **İbrahim'e selâm söyle**, or **Michelle'e selâm söyle**. And when someone sends **selâm** to someone, it is *almost* necessary to the one receiving it to send it back, by saying **sen de ona selâm söyle**.

Dialogue 2

ziyaret zamanını belirleme planning the visit time

Michelle and İbrahim talks about the visit to Uncle Kâmuran and Aunt Fahriye.

Michelle:	Sağolsunlar, bizi hemen çağırıyorlar.
İbrahim:	Evet, ben de onları özledim. Aslında hemen gitmek isterim.
Michelle:	Ben de. Ne zaman gidelim, sence?
İbrahim:	Yarın ya da yarından sonraki gün olabilir. Ama bugün biraz zor. Çünkü seninle bugün yemeğe gideceğiz.
Michelle:	Yarın da sahilde yürüyüşe çıkacağız, unutma!
İbrahim:	Tamam, o zaman. Ziyarete yarından sonra gidebiliriz. Hemen arayacak mısın?
Michelle:	Evet, hemen arayacağım. Fahriye teyze bir an önce öğrenmek ister.

1. Do they have plans for today and tomorrow? What are the plans?
2. When will they call Fahriye that they'll be able to visit the day after tomorrow?

Note that **hemen** has many usages, e.g. *immediately, now, soon*, and *as soon as possible*.

Bölüm 2
Part 2

dilbilgisi grammar

gelecek zaman the future tense

For the conjugation of the verbs for the future tense, special personal endings are added to the bare form of the verbs.

However, the endings depend on the final letter of the verbs. The endings following a consonant or a vowel differ. These differences will be studied step by step in the following pages.

- In case the verb ends with a consonant, the following endings are added. However, the vowels in the future tense endings may change depending on the last vowel of the verb. Actually, there are two ending possibilities depending on the preceding vowels.

the vowel harmony

Both ending possibilities are given in the table below:

Last vowel of the preceding verb	a,ı, o, u		e,i, ö, ü	
the future tense endings	(Ben) -acağım	*I will*	(Ben) –eceğim	*I will*
	(Sen) -acaksın	*You will*	(Sen) –eceksin	*You will*
	(O) –acak	*He / She / It will*	(O) –ecek	*He / She / It will*
	(Biz) -acağız	*We will*	(Biz) –eceğiz	*We will*
	(Siz) -acaksınız	*You (pl) will*	(Siz) –eceksiniz	*You (pl) will*
	Onlar -acak / -acaklar	*They will*	Onlar -ecek / -ecekler	*They will*

Examples: **gel mek** *(to come)*

Ben geleceğim.	*I will come.*
Sen geleceksin.	*You will come.*
O gelecek.	*He / She / It will come.*
Biz geleceğiz.	*We will come.*
Siz geleceksiniz.	*You (pl) will come.*
Çocuklar gelecek / gelecekler.	*The children will come.*
Arabalar gelecek.	*The cars will come.*

kal mak *(to stay)*

Ben kalacağım.	*I will stay.*
Sen kalacaksın.	*You will stay.*
O kalacak.	*He / She / It will stay.*
Biz kalacağız.	*We will stay.*
Siz kalacaksınız.	*You (pl) will stay.*
Çocuklar kalacak / kalacaklar.	*The children will stay.*
Arabalar kalacak.	*The cars will stay.*

NB Since the endings added to the verbs bear the personal information, the subjects can be omitted. That's why the subjects are written in brackets. One exception to this is **onlar**, *they*. **Onlar** cannot be omitted.

In addition, note that there are two ending options for the 3rd plural person, **onlar**, *they*, singular (**-ecek / -acak**) and plural (**-ecekler / -acaklar**). However, for the nonhumans in the subject position, plural ending cannot be preferred.

Examples:

Çocuklar *(human)* **gelecek/gelecekler**	*The children will come.*
Arabalar *(nonhuman)* **gelecek/~~gelecekler~~.**	*The cars will come.*

Çocuklar *(human)* **kalacak/kalacaklar**	*The children will stay.*
Arabalar *(nonhuman)* **kalacak/~~kalacaklar~~.**	*The cars will stay.*

• In case the verb ends with a vowel, the suffix connector letter "**y**" is added right before the future tense endings:

Examples: (Only the ending for **ben**, *I* is given in the examples to show the consonant change better.)

söyle mek	**Ben söyleyeceğim.**	*I will tell.*
atla mak	**Ben atlayacağım.**	*I will jump.*
uyu mak	**Ben uyuyacağım.**	*I will sleep.*
yürü mek	**Ben yürüyeceğim.**	*I will walk.*

NB The verbs **gitmek, etmek,** and **yemek** have a special spelling in the future tense.

Examples:

| git mek | *(to go)* |

Gideceğim.	*I will go.*
Gideceksin.	*You will go.*
Gidecek.	*He / She / It will go.*
Gideceğiz.	*We will go.*
Gideceksiniz.	*You (pl) will go.*
Onlar gidecekler.	*They will go.*

etmek	*(to do or to perform)*
Edeceğim.	*I will do.*
Edeceksin.	*You will do.*
Edecek.	*He / She / It will do.*
Edeceğiz.	*We will do.*
Edeceksiniz.	*You (pl) will do.*
Onlar edecekler.	*They will do.*

| ye mek | *(to eat)* |

Yiyeceğim.	*I will eat.*
Yiyeceksin.	*You will eat.*
Yiyecek.	*He / She / It will eat.*
Yiyeceğiz.	*We will eat.*
Yiyeceksiniz.	*You (pl) will eat.*
Onlar yiyecekler.	*They will eat.*

More examples with the future tense:

iç mek	**Ben içeceğim.**	*I will drink.*
bak mak	**Sen bakacaksın.**	*You will look.*
uyu mak	**O uyuyacak.**	*He / She / It will sleep.*
gör mek	**Biz göreceğiz.**	*We will see.*
iste mek	**Ben isteyeceğim.**	*I will want.*
söyle mek	**Biz söyleyeceğiz.**	*We will tell.*
atla mak	**Sen atlayacaksın.**	*You will jump.*
uç mak	**Onlar uçacak / uçacaklar.**	*They will fly.*
yürü mek	**Sız yürüyeceksiniz.**	*You will walk.*

exercise 1

Form positive sentences in the future tense with the given clues. Pay attention to the vowel change before adding the ending. Also note that numbers 4 and 5 have two conjugations since there are two ending options for **onlar**, *they*.

Example:

Ben / çay / içmek
I / tea / to drink

Ben çay içeceğim.
I will drink tea.

1. **sen/beni/bilmek** ....
2. **biz/dinlenmek** ....
3. **o/otele/gitmek** ....
4. **onlar/sahanda yumurta/yemek** ....
5. **insanlar/menüye/bakmak** ....
6. **siz/kafede menüden yemek/seçmek** ....
7. **ben/seni/görmek** ....
8. **sen/ araba kiralamak** ....
9. **biz/ uyumak** ....

the negative form

To form negative sentences in the future tense, the negative ending **–me / -ma** is added right before the personal ending.

The negative ending **–me / -ma** with the personal ending changes depending on the preceding vowel which is the last vowel of the verb. However, there are two ending possibilities depending on the preceding vowels.

the vowel harmony

Both ending possibilities are given in the table below:

Last vowel of the preceding verb	a, ı, o, u		e, i, ö, ü	
the future tense endings	(Ben) –mayacağım	*I won't*	(Ben) –meyeceğim	*I won't*
	(Sen) –mayacaksın	*You won't*	(Sen) –meyeceksin	*You won't*
	(O) –mayacak	*He / She / It won't*	(O) –meyecek	*He / She / It won't*
	(Biz) –mayacağız	*We won't*	(Biz) –meyeceğiz	*We won't*
	(Siz) –mayacaksınız	*You (pl) won't*	(Siz) –meyeceksiniz	*You (pl) won't*
	Onlar -mayacak / -mayacaklar	*They won't*	Onlar -meyecek / -meyecekler	*They won't*

Examples:

gel mek *(to come)*

Ben gelmeyeceğim.	*I won't come.*
Sen gelmeyeceksin.	*You won't come.*
O gelmeyecek.	*He / She / It won't come.*
Biz gelmeyeceğiz.	*We won't come.*
Siz gelmeyeceksiniz.	*You (pl) won't come.*
Çocuklar gelmeyecek / gelmeyecekler.	*The children won't come.*
Arabalar gelmeyecek.	*The cars won't come.*

kal mak *(to stay)*

Ben kalmayacağım.	*I won't stay.*
Sen kalmayacaksın.	*You won't stay.*
O kalmayacak.	*He / She / It won't stay.*
Biz kalmayacağız.	*We won't stay.*
Siz kalmayacaksınız.	*You (pl) won't stay.*
Çocuklar kalmayacak / kalmayacaklar.	*The children won't stay.*
Arabalar kalmayacak.	*The cars won't stay.*

More examples with the future tense:

iç mek	**Ben içmeyeceğim.**	*I won't drink.*
bak mak	**Sen bakmayacaksın.**	*You won't look.*
uyu mak	**O uyumayacak.**	*He / She / It won't sleep.*
gör mek	**Biz görmeyeceğiz.**	*We won't see.*
iste mek	**Ben istemeyeceğim.**	*I won't want.*
söyle mek	**Biz söylemeyeceğiz.**	*We won't tell.*
atla mak	**Sen atlamayacaksın.**	*You won't jump.*
uç mak	**Onlar uçmayacak/ uçmayacaklar.**	*They won't fly.*
yürü mek	**Siz yürümeyeceksiniz.**	*You won't walk.*

exercise 2

Form positive sentences in the future tense with the given clues. Pay attention to the vowel change before adding the ending. Also note that numbers 4 and 5 have two conjugations since there are two ending options for **onlar**, *they*.

Example:

Ben / çay / içmek   **Ben çay içmeyeceğim.**
I / tea / to drink   *I won't drink tea.*

1. **sen/beni/bilmek**   ....

2. **biz/dinlenmek**   ....

3. **o/otele/gitmek**   ....

4. **onlar/sahanda yumurta/yemek**   ....

5. **insanlar/menüye/bakmak** ....

6. **siz/kafede menüden yemek/seçmek**   ....

7. **ben/seni/görmek**   ....

8. **sen/ araba kiralamak**   ....

9. **biz/ uyumak**   ....

the question form

To form a question in the future tense, two steps are needed.

STEP 1

First, the verb is conjugated for the 3rd singular person (**o**, *he / she / it*). Remember that for the 3rd singular person (**o**, *he / she / it*) the ending is either **–ecek** or **–acak**. See the future tense verb conjugations above. Also remember the vowel change.

Examples:
The verb is conjugated for the 3rd <u>singular person (**o**, *he / she / it*).</u>

söylemek	*(to say)*	**söyleyecek**	*(He / she will say)*
gelmek	*(to come)*	**gelecek**	*(He / she will come)*
gitmek	*(to go)*	**gidecek**	*(He / she will go)*
yemek	*(to eat)*	**yiyecek**	*(He / she will eat)*
uyumak	*(to sleep)*	**uyuyacak**	*(He / she will sleep)*
yürümek	*(to walk)*	**yürüyecek**	*(He / she will walk)*
kalmak	*(to stay)*	**kalacak**	*(He / she will stay)*
bakmak	*(to look (at))*	**bakacak**	*(He / she will look (at))*
atlamak	*(to jump))*	**atlayacak**	*(He / she will jump)*

STEP 2

Then, the question endings are added to the end separately. The question endings for each person are given below: (The ending–**ecek** or –**acak** for the 3rd singular person (**o**, *he / she / it*) added in **STEP 1** is underlined.)

Last vowel of the preceding verb	a,ı, o, u		e,i, ö, ü	
the future tense endings	(Ben) –acak mıyım?	*Will I?*	(Ben) –ecek miyim?	*Will I?*
	(Sen) –acak mısın?	*Will you?*	(Sen) –ecek misin?	*Will you?*
	(O) –acak mı?	*Will he / she / it?*	(O) –ecek mi?	*Will he / she / it?*
	(Biz) –acak mıyız?	*Will we?*	(Biz) –ecek miyiz?	*Will we?*
	(Siz) -acak mısınız?	*Will you (pl)?*	(Siz) -ecek misiniz?	*Will you (pl)?*
	Onlar -acak mı? / - acaklar mı?	*Will they?*	Onlar -ecek mi?/ - ecekler mi?	*Will they?*

Example:
Ben <u>gelecek</u> <u>miyim</u>?   *Will I come?*
(Step 1) (Step 2)

More examples:

Sen gelecek misin?   *Will you come?*

O gelecek mi?   *Will he / she/ it come?*

Biz gelecek miyiz?   *Will we come?*

Siz gelecek misiniz?   *Will you (pl) come?*

Çocuklar gelecek mi?   *Will the children come?*

Arabalar gelecek mi?   *Will the cars come?*

More examples with other verbs. Remember the vowel change in the personal endings:

Ben içecek miyim?   *Will I drink?*

Ben bakacak mıyım?   *Will I look?*

Ben uyuyacak mıyım?   *Will I sleep?*

Ben görecek miyim?   *Will I see?*

More examples with the future tense:

iç mek	**Ben içecek miyim?**	*Will I drink?*
bak mak	**Sen bakacak mısın?**	*Will you look?*
uyu mak	**O uyuyacak mı?**	*Will he / she / it sleep?*

gör mek	Biz görecek miyiz?	*Will we see?*
iste mek	Ben isteyecek miyim?	*Will I want?*
söyle mek	Biz söyleyecek miyiz?	*Will we tell?*
atla mak	Sen atlayacak mısın?	*Will you jump?*
uç mak	Onlar uçacak mı? / uçacaklar mı?	*Will they fly?*
yürü mek	Siz yürüyecek misiniz?	*Will you walk?*

exercise 3

Form questions in the future tense with the given clues. Pay attention to the vowel change before adding the ending. Also note that numbers 4 and 5 have two conjugations since there are two ending options for **onlar**, *they*.

Example:

Ben / çay / içmek
I / tea / to drink

Ben çay içecek miyim?
Will I drink tea?

1. sen/beni/bilmek ....

2. biz/dinlenmek ....

3. o/otele/gitmek ....

4. onlar/sahanda yumurta/yemek ....

5. insanlar/menüye/bakmak ....

6. siz/kafede menüden yemek/seçmek ....

7. ben/seni/görmek ....

8. sen/ araba kiralamak ....

9. biz/ uyumak ....

Bölüm 3
Part 3

çeşitli bağlaçlar various conjunctions

In Turkish, the existance of two equal possibilities is expressed in several ways. These conjunctions can be used to connect nouns, adjectives, adverbs, and verbs.

"veya, ya da, ya ya" bağlacı the conjunction "or"

Note that by using **ama ... kesinlikle**, *but ... certainly*, it is possible to reach to a certainty. Also note that the conjuction **ya ya** can only be used in positive sentences.

Serra gelebilir veya gelmeyebilir.	*Serra may come or not.*
Serra gelebilir ya da gelmeyebilir.	*Serra may come or not.*
Serra ya gelir ya gelmez.	*Serra may come or not.*
Ama bize kesinlikle haber verir.	*But she certainly informs us.*
Talha çalışır veya dinlenir.	*Talha either works or rests.*
Talha çalışır ya da dinlenir.	*Talha either works or rests.*
Talha ya çalışır ya dinlenir.	*Talha either works or rests.*
Ama kesinlikle boş durmaz.	*But he certainly does something.*
Eymen evdedir veya dışarıdadır.	*Eymen is either at home or outside.*
Eymen evdedir ya da dışarıdadır.	*Eymen is either at home or outside.*
Eymen evdedir ya da dışarıdadır.	*Eymen is either at home or outside.*
Ama kesinlikle oyun oynar.	*But he certainly plays a game.*

"başka" bağlacı the conjunction "else"

Note that the conjunction **başka**, *else*, can only be used in negative sentences and questions.

Otelde Talha ve Serra var. Otelde (Talha ve Serra'dan) başka kim var?
Talha and Serra are at the hotel. Who else is at the hotel?

Otelde Talha ve Serra'dan başka kimse yok.
There's no one else apart from Talha and Serra.

İbrahim çalışır ve okur. Başka ne yapar?
İbrahim works and reads. What else does he do?

İbrahim başka bir şey yapmaz.
İbrahim doesn't do anything else.

Eymen akıllı ve yaramazdır. Başka nedir?
Eymen is clever and naughty. What else is he?

tavsiye verme giving advice with let's

It's possible to give advice by using the ending **–alım / -elim**, *let's*. In this formation, only the 1st plural person, **biz**, *we* is used.
The ending depends on the final letter of the verbs. The ending following a consonant or a vowel differs.

•   In case the verb ends with a consonant, the following endings are added. However, the vowels in the endings may change depending on the last vowel of the verb. Actually, there are two ending possibilities depending on the preceding vowels.

the vowel harmony

Both ending possibilities are given in the table below:

Last vowel of the preceding verb	a, ı, o, u	e, i, ö, ü
the ending –alım / -elim	**(Biz) –alım** *Let's*	**(Biz) –elim** *Let's*

Examples:

iç mek	**(Biz) içelim.**	*Let's drink.*
gel mek	**(Biz) gelelim.**	*Let's come.*
bak mak	**(Biz) bakalım.**	*Let's look.*
gör mek	**(Biz) görelim.**	*Let's see.*
uç mak	**(Biz) uçalım.**	*Let's fly.*

•   In case the verb ends with a vowel, the suffix connector letter "**y**" is added right before the ending.

Examples:

söyle mek	**(Biz) söyleyelim.**	*Let's tell.*
atla mak	**(Biz) atlayalım.**	*Let's jump.*
uyu mak	**(Biz) uyuyalım.**	*Let's sleep.*
yürü mek	**(Biz) yürüyelim.**	*Let's walk.*

NB The verbs **gitmek**, *to go*, **etmek**, *to do* or *to perform*, **yemek**, *to eat*, and **demek**, *to say* have a special spelling.

Examples:

Diyelim.	*Let's say.*
Gidelim.	*Let's go.*
Edelim.	*Let's do.*
Yiyelim.	*Let's eat.*

NB Some additions such as **haydi**, *come on*, **bence**, *for me*, or **bana sorarsan**, *if you ask me*, are used very commonly with the advice sentences in the daily Turkish.

Examples:

Haydi sinemaya gidelim.	*Come on let's go to the movies.*
Bence bugün evde yiyelim.	*If you ask me, let's eat at home today.*
Birazdan dışarı çıkalım.	*Let's get out soon.*
İbrahim'i aralayım.	*Let's call İbrahim.*
Haydi biraz çay içelim.	*Come on let's drink some tea.*
Haydi kahvaltı edelim.	*Come on let's have breakfast*

the negative form

To form negative advices, the negative ending **–me / -ma** is added right before the personal ending.

The negative ending **–me / -ma** with the personal ending changes depending on the preceding vowel which is the last vowel of the verb. However, there are two ending possibilities depending on the preceding vowels.

the vowel harmony

Both ending possibilities are given in the table below:

Last vowel of the preceding verb	a, ı, o, u	e, i, ö, ü
the ending –mayalım / -meyelim	**(Biz) –mayalım** *Let's not*	**(Biz) – meyelim** *Let's not*

Examples:

iç mek	(Biz) içmeyelim.	*Let's not drink.*
gel mek	(Biz) gelmeyelim.	*Let's not come.*
bak mak	(Biz) bakmayalım.	*Let's not look.*
gör mek	(Biz) görmeyelim.	*Let's not see.*
uç mak	(Biz) uçmayalım.	*Let's not fly.*
söyle mek	(Biz) söylemeyelim.	*Let's not tell.*
atla mak	(Biz) atlamayalım.	*Let's not jump.*
uyu mak	(Biz) uyumayalım.	*Let's not sleep.*
yürü mek	(Biz) yürümeyelim.	*Let's not walk.*

NB Şimdi, *now*, **şimdilik**, *for now*, or similar additions are used very commonly with the negative advice sentences in the daily Turkish.

Examples:

Bugün evde kalmayalım.	*Let's not stay at home today.*
Şimdi dışarı çıkmayalım.	*Let's not get out now.*
Şimdilik oraya gitmeyelim.	*Let's not go there for now.*
Bence artık yemeyelim.	*Let's not go there for now.*

the question form

To ask for advice, the question ending **–mi? / -mı?** is added right before the personal ending.

The question ending **–mi / -mı** with the personal ending changes depending on the preceding vowel which is the last vowel of the verb. However, there are two ending possibilities depending on the preceding vowels.

the vowel harmony

Both ending possibilities are given in the table below:

Last vowel of the preceding verb	a,ı, o, u	e,i, ö, ü
the ending -(y)alım/-(y)elim	(Biz) –(y)alım mı? *Shall we?*	(Biz) –(y)elim mi? *Shall we?*

Examples:

iç mek	(Biz) içelim mi?	*Shall we drink?*
gel mek	(Biz) gelelim mi?	*Shall we come?*
bak mak	(Biz) bakalım mı?	*Shall we look?*
gör mek	(Biz) görelim mi?	*Shall we see?*
uç mak	(Biz) uçalım mı?	*Shall we fly?*

Remember to add the suffix connector letter "**y**" right before the ending in case the verb ends with a vowel,:

Examples:

söyle mek	**(Biz) söyleyelim mi?**	*Shall we tell?*
atla mak	**(Biz) atlayalım mı?**	*Shall we jump?*
uyu mak	**(Biz) uyuyalım mı?**	*Shall we sleep?*
yürü mek	**(Biz) yürüyelim mı?**	*Shall we walk?*

NB The verbs **gitmek**, **etmek**, **yemek**, **demek** have a special spelling.

Examples:

Diyelim mi?	*Shall we say?*
Gidelim mi?	*Shall we go?*
Yiyelim mi?	*Shall we eat?*
Edelim mi?	*Shall we do?*

It's also possible to ask for advice by using question words.

Examples:

Ne yapalım?	*What shall we do?*
Nereye gidelim?	*Where shall we go?*
Ne yiyelim?	*What shall we eat?*
Nerede kahvaltı edelim?	*Where shall we have breakfast?*

NB Using **sence**, *for you*, when asking for advice is common in the daily Turkish.

Examples:

Sence şimdi ne yapalım?	*For you, what shall we do now?*
Sence Michelle'i görelim mi?	*For you, shall we see Michelle?*
Sence kimi arayalım?	*For you, who shall we call?*

Bölüm 4
Part 4

Dialogue 3

arkadaşlara bir telefon daha one more call to the friends

Michelle calls Kâmuran and Fahriye. They want to fix a date for the visit.

Michelle:	Merhaba, Fahriye teyze. Ben Michelle.
Fahriye:	Merhaba, Michelle. Söyle bakayım. Bugün geleceksiniz, değil mi?
Michelle:	Fahriye teyzeciğim, Biz ancak Perşembe günü gelebiliriz.
Fahriye:	Öyle mi? Tamam o zaman.
Michelle:	Evet, Fahriye teyzeciğim. Fahriye teyze sizin eve nasıl gelebiliriz? Adresi verebilir misin?
Fahriye:	Tabii. Nerede oteliniz?
Michelle:	Sarayburnu'ndayız. Arabamız da var.
Fahriye:	Tamam. Önce kuzeye doğru 5 km. gidin. Bahçelievler kavşağından doğuya dönün. Viraja dikkat edin. 5 blok düz ilerleyin. Caddenin sonunda, köşede eczaneyi göreceksiniz. Oradan sağa kıvrılın. Okulun tam karşısına arabayı park edeceksiniz. Evimiz o sokakta, sondaki ev.
Michelle:	Anladım Fahriye teyzeciğim. Ancak biz yine de adresinizi alalım. Navigasyon cihazına kaydedelim. N'olur n'olmaz!

1. Did Michelle know where Fahriye lives?
2. Is Michelle sure about finding their address only by using Fahriye's directions?

Vocabulary

adres	*address*	**kavşak**	*intersection*
aramak	*to try to find*	**kıvrılmak**	*to turn*
bir an önce	*as soon as possible*	**köşe**	*corner*

birazdan	soon	mutlaka	for sure
blok	bloc	navigasyon cihazı	navigation device
cadde	avenue	okul	school
çağırmak	to call	park etmek	to park
dikkat	attention	sokak	street
dikkat etmek	to pay attention	son	end
düz	straight	telefonla aramak	to call on the phone
eczane	pharmacy	viraj	curve
N'olur n'olmaz!		Just in case!	
Kim arıyor?		Who's calling?	
Aaa!		What!	
acaba		I wonder	

In the dialogue above, Fahriye teyze says, **bakayım**. Literally, it means *let me look*. However, it's used as *tell me*. It's also possible to use it in plural form i.e. **bakalım**. These pharases are widely used in spoken Turkish. However, it's not suitable to say **bakalım** or **bakayım** to older or to people with higher status, or to people just introduced to.

exercise 4

Which is the odd one out in each row?

kavşak	yol	viraj	eczane
cadde	aramak	blok	sokak
otel	dikkat	okul	ev
doğu	köşe	batı	kuzey

Unit Ten: Bir arkadaşa ziyaret

A visit to a friend

With this unit, you will be able to:

- Talk about houses, furniture and neighborhood
- Give and accept presents
- Express purpose
- Express possession in the future tense
- Use 'there will be and there won't be'
- Form sentences in the future tense
- Use the prepositions for –ful and -less

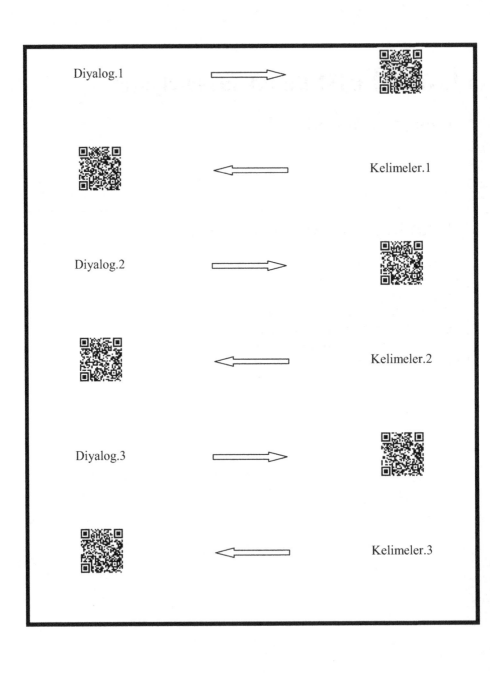

Bölüm 1
Part 1

Dialogue 1

Fahriye Teyze'lerde at Aunt Fahriye's home

Michelle and İbrahim followed the directions the navigation device through the route. They found the address easily and quickly. They didn't stick in trafic, either.

Kâmuran:	Hoş geldiniz, çocuklar. Adresi kolay buldunuz mu?
İbrahim:	Evet, Kâmuran amca. Kolayca geldik.
Fahriye:	Hoş geldiniz, İbrahim oğlum. Hoş geldiniz, Michelle kızım. Şükür Kavuşturana.
Michelle:	Biz de sizi çok özledik Fahriye teyze, Kâmuran amca. Bu arada, eviniz çok güzel. Bahçesi de çok hoş. Kaç yıldır burada oturuyorsunuz?
Kâmuran:	Sağolun kızım. Buraya yeni taşındık. Ev de mahalle de çok güzel. Memnunuz. Komşular da iyi.
İbrahim:	Sakin bir mahalle. Aynı zamanda merkezî de.
Fahriye:	Ana caddenin hemen arkası. Çarşıya ve Sema'nın işyerine yürüme mesafesinde. Buraya Sema işe yürüyerek gitsin diye taşındık.
Michelle:	Çok şanslı. Şu anda çalışıyor, değil mi?
Kâmuran:	O da birazdan gelir. İşi saat altıda bitecek.

1. Did Michelle and İbrahim had difficulty finding the address?
2. Have Fahriye and Kâmuran been living in the same house long?

Vocabulary

bahçe	*garden*	**mahalle**	*neighborhood*
civar	*vicinity*	**mesâi**	*working shift*
gürültülü	*noisy*	**oturmak**	*to live in a place*

hareketli	with lots of activity	sakin	calm
hareketsiz	still	sessiz	quiet
hoş	cute	sokak	street
komşu	neighbor	son	end
köşe	corner		
Şükür Kavuşturana.		Thanks God.	

In the dialogue above, we see **Şükür Kavuşturana.** It's used widely in spoken Turkish with the meaning of thanks God. Again, this is common in every situation, not only in religious ones.

In Turkish, it's common that old people usually address the youngesters as **kızım**, *my daughter* and **oğlum**, *my son*. In return, the young people can call them as **amca**, *uncle* or **teyze**, *aunt.*

Dialogue 2

bahçede in the garden

Right after entering the garden, Kâmuran invites them to sit in the garden.

Kâmuran:	Tekrar hoş geldiniz, bakalım. Buyurun şöyle oturun. Daha daha nasılsınız? İyi misiniz? Bizim arkadaşlarımız nasıllar?
Michelle:	Çok şükür iyiyiz, Kâmuran amca. Bizimkilerin de çok selâmı var.
Fahriye:	Siz de onlara söyleyin. Onları da çok özledik. İyi ki geldiniz.
Michelle:	Fahriye teyze, size küçük bir hediye aldık. Umarız beğenirsiniz.
Kâmuran:	Neden zahmet ettiniz kızım.
Fahriye:	Biz yabancı mıyız, Michelle? Ne gerek vardı?
İbrahim:	Ne zahmeti Fahriye teyze? Küçük bir şey zaten. Size lâyık değil ama ...
Michelle:	Güle güle kullanın. Kullandıkça bizi hatırlayın.

1. What did Michelle's parents want to do?
2. Did Michelle and İbrahim bring a present?

Vocabulary

bizimkiler	*our parents, kids, friends, etc.*	**oturmak**	*to sit*
hediye	*present*	**yabancı**	*foreign*
ummak	*to hope*		

Biz yabancı mıyız?	*We're close to each other, not strangers.*
Kullandıkça bizi hatırlayın.	*Remember us when using it.*
Ne gerek vardı?	*You shouldn't have done it.*
Ne zahmeti?	*It's not a big thing.*
Neden zahmet ettiniz?	*Why did you do that?*
Size lâyık değil ama ...	*It's too little for you but ...*

In the dialogue above, Kâmuran says, **daha daha nasılsınız?**, *how are you again and again?* This phrase is very widely used especially by the older people.

Neden zahmet ettiniz? and **Ne gerek vardı?**, *You shouldn't have bought this!* are the common phrases used after receiving a present. Then, the other person replies by **Ne zahmeti? Güle güle kullanın. Kullandıkça bizi hatırlayın.** These phrases can be used with different verbs, too, e.g. **Güle güle giyin. Giydikçe bizi hatırlayın.** Literally it means, *Use it in good mood and remember us while using.*

Also note that **bizimkiler** in Michelle's part means *her parents*. **Bizimkiler** can mean *the parents, the kids* or *some close people* and the listener knows who they are.

Bölüm 2
Part 2

dilbilgisi grammar

complements in the future tense

In Turkish, the verb **olmak**, *to be*, is used in the future tense. Remember, in the present and the past tense, only personal suffixes are used instead of the verb. Even though the future tense is studied, here the conjugation of the verb **olmak** is given one more time in positive, negative, and question forms.

Positive:

(Ben)	olacağım	*I'll be*
(Sen)	olacaksın	*You'll be*
(O)	olacak	*He / She / It will be*
(Biz)	olacağız	*We will be*
(Siz)	olacaksınız	*You (pl) will be*
Onlar	olacak / olacaklar	*They will be*

Examples:

Bugün Ankara'da olacağım. — *I'll be in Ankara today.*

O yakında evli olacak. — *He / she will be married soon.*

Akşama evde olacaklar. — *They'll be home in the evening.*

Negative:

(Ben)	olmayacağım	*I won't be*
(Sen)	olmayacaksın	*You won't be*
(O)	olmayacak	*He / She / It won't be*
(Biz)	olmayacağız	*We won't be*
(Siz)	olmayacaksınız	*You (pl) won't be*
Onlar	olmayacak / olmayacaklar	*They won't be*

Examples:

Artık üzgün olmayacağız. — *We'll not be sad any longer.*

Siz bugün bizimle olmayacaksınız. — *You won't be with us, today.*

Akşama evde olmayacaklar. — *They won't be home in the evening.*

Question:

(Ben)	olacak mıyım?	*Will I be?*
(Sen)	olacak mısın?	*Will you be?*
(O)	olacak mı?	*Will he / she / it be?*
(Biz)	olacak mıyız?	*Will we be?*
(Siz)	olacak mısınız?	*Will you (pl) be?*
Onlar	olacaklar mı? / olacaklar mı?	*Will they be?*

Examples:

Bugün Ankara'da olacak mısın?   *Will you be in Ankara today?*

Sen ne zaman burada olacaksın?   *When will you be here?*

Akşama evde olacaklar mı?   *Will they be home in the evening?*

NB In Turkish, it is common to use the adverbs of time such as **sabah**, *morning*, **öğle(n)**, *noon*, **akşam**, *evening*, **gece**, *night*, **hafta**, *week*, or **ay**, *month*, etc. as **sabaha**, **öğlene**, **akşama**, **geceye**, **haftaya**, or **aya**, etc. with the sentences in the future tense. Note that there's no change in the meaning between these words.

However, in this way it's also possible to use the present tense in place of for the future sense, since the suffixes of –e or –a have the meaning of –e **kadar**, *until*.

Examples: (Note that the meaning remains the same even different tenses are used.)

Sabah(a) burada olacağım. / Sabaha buradayım.
I'll be here in the (until) morning.

Kızımız gelecek ay(a) doğacak. / Kızımız gelecek aya doğuyor.
Our daughter will be born (until) next month.

Yemek öğlen(e) hazır olacak. / Yemek öğlene hazır.
The food will be ready at (until) noon.

Kardeşim sabah(a) gelecek. / Kardeşim sabaha burada.
My brother will be here in the (until) morning.

Akşam(a) yanınızda olacağız. / Akşama yanınızdayız.
We will be with you at (until) evening.

olacak, olmayacak, olacak mı?   there will be, there won't be, will there be?

In Turkish, "there will be", "there won't be" or "will there be?" is expressed by using the verb **olmak**, *to be*. Note that a place information is also given in the sentences. (See Unit 2 for "there is / there are".)

Examples:

Otelde (bir) taksi olacak.	*There will be a taxi <u>at the hotel.</u>*
Okulda öğrenciler olacak.	*There will be students <u>in the school.</u>*
Otelde (hiç) taksi olmayacak.	*There won't be (any) taxis <u>at the hotel.</u>*
Okulda (hiç) öğrenci olmayacak.	*There won't be (any) students <u>in the school.</u>*
Otelde taksi olacak mı?	*Will there be a taxi <u>at the hotel?</u>*
Okulda öğrenciler olacak mı?	*Will there be students <u>in the school?</u>*
Otelde taksi olmayacak mı?	*Won't there be a taxi <u>at the hotel?</u>*
Okulda öğrenciler olmayacak mı?	*Won't there be students <u>in the school?</u>*

NB It's also possible to use the verb **olmak**, *to be*, without the place information. But in this case, <u>possessives are used</u>. **Pay attention to the change in the meaning.**

Examples.

Michelle'in (bir) piyanosu olacak.	*Michelle will have a piano.*
Çocukların (bir) odası olacak.	*The children will have a room.*
Ali'nin (bir) oteli olacak.	*Ali will have a hotel.*
Ali'nin otelleri olacak.	*Ali will have hotels.*
Benim (bir) kız kardeşim olacak.	*I will have a sister.*
Michelle'in (hiç) piyanosu olmayacak.	*Michelle won't have (any) pianos.*
Çocukların (hiç) odası olmayacak.	*The children won't have (any) rooms.*
Ali'nin (hiç) oteli olmayacak.	*Ali won't have (any) hotels.*
Benim (hiç) kız kardeşim olmayacak.	*I won't have (any) sisters.*
Michelle'in piyanosu olacak mı?	*Will Michelle have a piano?*
Çocukların odası olacak mı?	*Will the children have a room?*
Ali'nin oteli olacak mı?	*Will Ali have a hotel?*
Benim kız kardeşim olacak mı?	*Will I have a sister?*

Michelle'in piyanosu olmayacak mı?	*Won't Michelle have a piano?*
Çocukların odası olmayacak mı?	*Won't the children have a room?*
Ali'nin oteli olmayacak mı?	*Won't Ali have a hotel?*
Benim kız kardeşim olmayacak mı?	*Won't I have a sister?*

exercise 1

Answer the question with the given words. Make positive or negative sentences according to the words given.

Example: **Odada kimse olacak mı?**   **Evet/ben**
           (Will there anyone in the room?)   *(Yes / I)*

           Evet, odada ben olacağım.
           (Yes, I will be in the room.)

1.   **Evet/sen**   ....
2.   **Evet/çocuklar**   ....
3.   **Evet/biz**   ....
4.   **Evet/siz**   ....
5.   **Evet/Michelle**   ....
6.   **Evet/herkes**   ....
7.   **Evet/bir şey**   ....
8.   **Evet/birisi**   ....
9.   **Hayır/hiç kimse**   ....
10. **Hayır/hiç bir şey** ....

exercise 2

Make <u>a question</u> with possessives by using the given words. Then give <u>a positive</u> and <u>a negative</u> answer to the question you just formed. Use the word pairs in your questions and answers.

Example: **otel / şoför / ?**   **Otelin şoförü olacak mı?**
           (hotel / driver)   *(Will the hotel have a driver?)*

                                     Evet, otelin şoförü olacak.
                                     (Yes, the hotel will have a driver.)

                                     Hayır, otelin şoförü olmayacak.
                                     (No, the hotel won't have a driver.)

1. **sen / eş**   ....

2. **otel / lokanta**   ....

3. **okul / öğrenci**   ....

4. **Michelle / kardeş** ....

5. **biz / iş**   ....

6. **otel / yönetici**   ....

amaç ifadeleri expressing purpose

In Turkish, expression of purpose is possible in several ways.

-sin diye for, in order that

It's possible to express purpose by using the ending **-sin diye**, *in order that*. (Note that, this formation is the same formation you learned about advice. But remember with the advice, only the 1st plural person, **biz**, *we* is used.)
The ending depends on the final letter of the verbs. The ending following a consonant or a vowel differs.

In addition to that, in this formation, the endings of the 3rd singular person, **o**, *he / she / it*, and the 3rd plural person, **onlar**, *they* are different from the endings of the other persons. So, they will be studied in different charts.

the vowel harmony (for O and Onlar)

The endings of the 3rd singular person, **o**, *he / she / it*, and the 3rd plural person, **onlar**, *they* are given in the table below:

Last vowel of the preceding verb	(O) (In order that he / she / it)	Onlar (In order that they)
a,ı	-sın diye	-sın / -sınlar diye
o,u	-sun diye	-sun / -sunlar diye
e,i	-sin diye	-sin / -sinler diye
ö,ü	-sün diye	-sün / -sünler diye

Examples:

(O) söylesin diye	*In order that he / she says*
Onlar söylesin / söylesinler diye	*In order that they say*
(O) atlasın diye	*In order that he / she/ it jumps*
Onlar atlasın / atlasınlar diye	*In order that they jump*
(O) uyusun diye	*In order that he / she/ it sleeps*
Onlar uyusun / uyusunlar diye	*In order that they sleep*
(O) yürüsün diye	*In order that he / she/ it walks*
Onlar yürüsün / yürüsünler diye	*In order that they walk*

the negative form (for O and Onlar)

The negative endings of the 3rd singular person, **o**, *he / she / it*, and the 3rd plural person, **onlar**, *they* are given in the table below:

Last vowel of the preceding verb	(O) (In order that he/she /it doesn't)	Onlar (In order that they don't)
a,ı,o,u	-masın diye	-masın / -masınlar diye
e,i,ö,ü	-mesin diye	-mesin / -mesinler diye

Examples:

(O) söylemesin diye	*In order that he / she doesn't say*
Onlar söylemesin / söylemesinler diye	*In order that they don't say*
(O) atlamasın diye	*In order that he/she/it doesn't jump*
Onlar atlamasın / atlamasınlar diye	*In order that they don't jump*
(O) uyusun diye	*In order that he/she/it doesn't sleep*
Onlar uyumasın / uyumasınlar diye	*In order that they don't sleep*
(O) yürümesin diye	*In order that he/she/it doesn't walk*

Onlar yür<u>ümesi</u>n / yür<u>ümesi</u>nler diye   *In order that they don't walk*

the vowel harmony (for other persons)

• In case the verb ends with a consonant, the following endings are added. However, the vowels in the endings may change depending on the last vowel of the verb. Actually, there are two ending possibilities depending on the preceding vowels.

the vowel harmony

Both ending possibilities are given in the table below:

Last vowel of the preceding verb	a, ı, o, u		e, i, ö, ü	
the ending *diye*	(Ben) –ayım	*In order that I*	(Ben) –eyim	*In order that I*
	(Sen) –asın	*In order that you*	(Sen) –esin	*In order that you*
	(Biz) –alım	*In order that we*	(Biz) –elim	*In order that we*
	(Siz) –asınız	*In order that you (pl)*	(Siz) –esiniz	*In order that you (pl)*

Examples:

iç mek	(Ben) içeyim diye	*In order that I drink*
gel mek	(Sen) gelesin diye	*In order that you come*
bak mak	(Biz) bakalım diye	*In order that we look*
gör mek	(Siz) göresiniz diye	*In order that you (pl) see*
uç mak	(Ben) uçayım diye	*In order that I fly*

• In case the verb ends with a vowel, the suffix connector letter "**y**" is added right before the ending:

Examples:

söyle mek	(Ben) söyleyeyim diye	*In order that I tell*
atla mak	(Ben) atlayayım diye	*In order that I jump*
uyu mak	(Ben) uyuyayım diye	*In order that I sleep*
yürü mek	(Ben) yürüyeyim diye	*In order that I walk*

NB The verbs **gitmek**, **etmek**, **demek**, and **yemek**, have a special spelling.
Examples:

gi̲t mek   *(to go)*

Gideyim diye   *In order that I go*
Gidesin diye   *In order that you go*
Gitsin diye   *In order that he / she / it goes*
Gidelim diye   *In order that we go*
Gidesiniz diye   *In order that you (pl) go*
Onlar gitsinler diye   *In order that they go*

e̲t mek   *(to do)*

Edeyim diye   *In order that I do*
Edesin diye   *In order that you do*
Etsin diye   *In order that he / she / it does*
Edelim diye   *In order that we do*
Edesiniz diye   *In order that you (pl) do*
Onlar etsinler diye   *In order that they do*

ye̲ mek   *(to eat)*

Yiyeyim diye   *In order that I eat*
Yiyesin diye   *In order that you eat*
Yesin diye   *In order that he / she / it eats*
Yiyelim diye   *In order that we eat*
Yiyesiniz diye   *In order that you (pl) eat*
Onlar yesinler diye   *In order that they eat*

de̲ mek   *(to say)*

Diyeyim diye   *In order that I say*
Diyesin diye   *In order that you say*
Desin diye   *In order that he / she / it say*
Diyelim diye   *In order that we say*
Diyesiniz diye   *In order that you (pl) say*
Onlar desinler diye   *In order that they say*

the negative form (for other persons)

To form negative sentences, the negative ending **–me / -ma** is added right before the personal ending.

The negative ending **–me / -ma** with the personal ending changes depending on the preceding vowel which is the last vowel of the verb. However, there are two ending possibilities depending on the preceding vowels.

the vowel harmony

Both ending possibilities are given in the table below:

Last vowel of the preceding verb	a, ı, o, u		e, i, ö, ü	
the ending diye	(Ben) – mayayım	*In order that I don't*	(Ben) – meyeyim	*In order that I don't*
	(Sen) – mayasın	*In order that you don't*	(Sen) –meyesin	*In order that you don't*
	(Biz) –mayalım	*In order that we don't*	(Biz) –meyelim	*In order that we don't*
	(Siz) – mayasınız	*In order that you (pl) don't*	(Siz) – meyesiniz	*In order that you (pl) don't*

Examples:

iç mek	(Ben) içmeyeyim diye	*In order that I don't drink*
gel mek	(Sen) gelmeyesin diye	*In order that you don't come*
bak mak	(Biz) bakmayalım diye	*In order that we don't look*
gör mek	(Siz) görmeyesiniz diye	*In order that you (pl) don't see*
uç mak	(Ben) uçmayayım diye	*In order that I don't fly*
söyle mek	(Sen) söylemeyesin diye	*In order that you don't tell*
atla mak	(Siz) atlamayasınız diye	*In order that you don't jump*
uyu mak	(Biz) uyumayalım diye	*In order that we don't sleep*
yürü mek	(Ben) yürümeyeyim diye	*In order that I don't walk*

More examples:

Çay içeyim diye kafeye gittim.*
I went to the cafe in order that I drink tea.

Sen bakasın diye resmimi göndereceğim.*
I'll send my picture in order that you look (at it).

O rahatça uyusun diye sessiz olalım.**
Let's be quiet in order that he / she / it sleeps well.

Biz görelim diye cama çıktılar.*
They came to the window in order that we see (them).

Uçsunlar diye uçağa bindiler.*
They got on the plane in order that they fly.

(*) In the spoken Turkish, it is also possible to use the same structure in a different way.

Examples:

Kafeye <u>çay içeyim diye</u> gittim.
I went to the cafe in order that I drink tea.

Resmimi <u>sen bakasın diye</u> göndereceğim.
I'll send my picture in order that you look (at it).

Cama <u>biz görelim diye</u> çıktılar.
They came to the window in order that we see (them).

Uçağa <u>uçsunlar diye</u> bindiler.
They got on the plane in order that they fly.

(**) The variation is not applicable to all.

Examples:

~~**Sessiz o rahatça uyusun diye olalım.**~~*

Examples with the negatives:

Çay <u>içmeyeyim</u> diye kafeye gitmedim.
I didn't go to the cafe in order that I wouldn't drink tea.

Sen <u>bakmayasın</u> diye resmimi göndermeyeceğim.
I won't send my picture in order that you won't look (at it).

O rahatça <u>uyumasın</u> diye gürültü yapalım.
Let's make noice in order that he/she won't sleep well.

Biz <u>görmeyelim</u> diye cama çıkmıyorlar.
They don't come to the window in order that we won't see (them).

<u>Uçmasınlar</u> diye onlara uçak bileti almadım.
I didn't buy them a flight ticket in order that they won't fly.

exercise 3

Form an adverb clause of purpose with the given clues. Then complete the sentence with a standart main clause of **buraya gelmek** in the past tense. Pay attention to the vowel change before adding the ending. Also note that numbers 4 and 5 have two conjugations since there are two ending options for **onlar**, *they*.

Example:

Ben / çay / içmek   **Ben çay içeyim diye buraya geldim.**
I / tea / to drink   *In order that I drink tea, I came here.*

Sen / çay / içmek   **Sen çay içesin diye buraya geldin.**
You / tea / to drink   *In order that you drink tea, you came here.*

1. sen/beni/bilmek   ....

2. biz/dinlenmek   ....

3. o/otele/gitmek ....

4. onlar/menemen/yemek ....

5. insanlar/menüye/bakmak ....

6. siz/kafede menüden yemek/seçmek ....

7. ben/seni/görmek ....

8. sen/ araba kiralamak ....

9. biz/ uyumak ....

için, amacıyla, niyetiyle in order to

It's also possible to express purpose by using **için** or **amacıyla** with an infinitive. Examples:

<u>Çay içmek için/amacıyla/niyetiyle</u> **kafeye gittim.**
I went to the cafe in order to drink tea.

<u>Bakmak için/amacıyla/niyetiyle</u> **bir ayna aldım.**
I bought a mirror to look (at).

<u>Rahatça uyumak için/amacıyla/niyetiyle sessiz bir yere gidelim.</u>
Let's go to a quiet place in order to sleep well.

<u>Bizi görmek için/amacıyla/niyetiyle</u> **cama çıktınız.**
You came to the window in order to see us.

<u>Uçmak için/amacıyla/niyetiyle</u> **uçağa bindiler.**
They got on the plane in order to fly.

Bölüm 3
Part 3

Dialogue 3

üst kat, alt kat upstairs, downstairs

While Kâmuran and İbrahim are having a conversation in the garden, Fahriye wants to show their new house to Michelle.

Fahriye:	Üst katta iki odamız var. Bak, burası misafir odası, şurası da Sema'nın yatak odası. Bu katta iki de banyo-tuvalet var.
Michelle:	Gayet geniş duruyor.
Fahriye:	Evet, genişler. Çok güzel ama kışın ısıtmak zor olacak. Isıtmak kolay olsun diye kışın Sema alt kata inecek ve üst katla alt katın arasındaki kapıyı kapatacağız.
Michelle:	Akıllıca!
Fahriye:	Daha fazla ısınmak için Kâmuran amcan çatıyı ve bacayı da tamir edecek. Haydi alt kata inelim. Orada da yemek odası, oturma odası ve mutfak var.
Michelle:	Mobilyalarınız da çok güzel. Güle güle oturun.
Fahriye:	Koltukları, masayı, sehpa ve sandalyeleri yeniledik. Ancak halıları değiştirmedik. Ha, bir de, perdeleri de yeni aldık. Sizin hediye saatinizi de oturma odasına baş köşeye asacağım.
Michelle:	Güle güle kullanın, Fahriye teyzeciğim.

1. How many floors does the house have?
2. In which room will Michelle's and İbrahim's present stay?

Vocabulary

ayna	mirror	masa	table
baca	chimney	misafir odası	guest room
balkon	balcony	mobilya	furniture
banyo	bathroom	mutfak	kitchen
cam	glass, window	oturma odası	living room

çatı	roof	orta sehpa	coffee table
çıkmak	to go up	pencere	window
dar	narrow	perde	curtains
geniş	wide	saat	clock
halı	carpet	sandalye	chair
ısıtmak	to heat	soğutmak	to cool
inmek	to go down	tamir etmek	to repair
kenar sehpası	end table	tuvalet	restroom
koltuk	sofa	yatak odası	sleeping room
kat	story, floor	yemek odası	dining room
baş köşe		the best place in the room	
Güle güle oturun.		Stay in good health.	

In the dialogue above, Fahriye says, **Sizin hediye saatinizi de baş köşeye asacağım**. Here **baş köşe** implies *the best place* and it's used to show respect to the person.

dilbilgisi grammar

-li / -siz –ful / -less

In Turkish, the endings **-li / -siz**, are added to some nouns to make adjectives with the meaning of *with / without* the same as the endings *–ful / -less* in English.

the vowel harmony

The endings **–li / -siz** , *with / without* are 4 way vowel harmony meaning they change depending on the preceding vowel.

Last vowel of the preceding word	a,ı	e,i	o,u	ö,ü
The endings -li / -siz	-lı / -sız	-li / -siz	-lu / -suz	-lü / -süz

Examples:

Noun	**Adjective**	**Adjective**
şeker *sugar*	**şekerli** *with sugar*	**şekersiz** *without sugar*
cam *glass*	**camlı** *with glass*	**camsız** *without glass*
tuz *salt*	**tuzlu** *salty*	**tuzsuz** *without salt*
süt *milk*	**sütlü** *with milk*	**sütsüz** *without milk*

Note the spelling exception of **dikkât**.

dikkât *attention*	**dikkâtli** *with attention*	**dikkâtsiz** *without attention*

NB These endings are not applicable to all nouns. In addition, some nouns accept only one of the endings:

us *mind*	**uslu** *mindful (docile)*	~~ussuz~~ -
hız *speed*	**hızlı** *speedy*	~~hızsız~~ -
yaş *age*	**yaşlı** *old*	~~yaşsız~~ -

exercise 4

List the names of the rooms, furniture, and other nouns related to a house you have learned in this lesson into three groups below. Then check your work with the vocabulary section of this lesson.

Example:	<u>rooms</u> yemek odası	<u>furniture</u> koltuk	<u>other nouns</u> pencere

Unit Eleven: Bahçede mangal

Barbeque in the yard

With this unit, you will be able to:

- Express reason 'because'
- Use the adverb clauses of time (when, before, after)
- Talk about kitchen utensils
- Talk about nature
- Talk about renting a flat

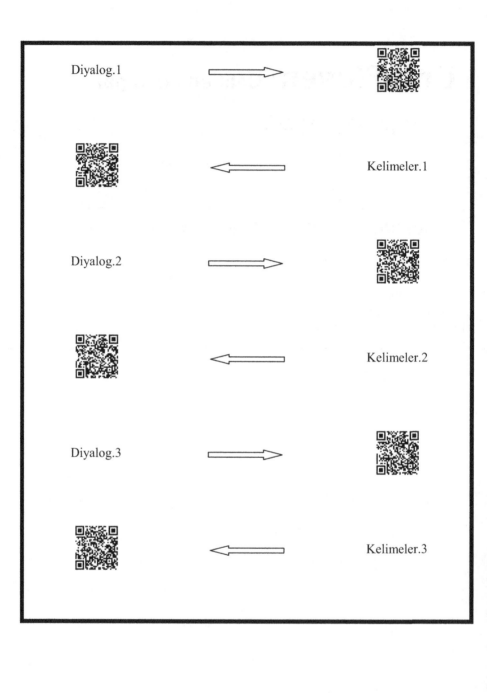

Bölüm 1
Part 1

Dialogue 1

mangal zamanı time for barbeque

Fahriye and Kâmuran planned a meal in the garden. Fahriye prepared many things in the kitchen while Kâmuran arranged the barbeque and the table in the garden.

Kâmuran:	Michelle, Fahriye teyzen sizin için çok hazırlık yaptı.
Michelle:	Eline sağlık Fahriye teyze. Neler yaptın yine? Ben senin yemeklerini çok severim, bilirsin.
Fahriye:	Sağol kızım. Pek bir şey yok, aslında. Sen çok sevdiğin için dürüm sardım. Sonra patates salatası yapmak için biraz patates haşladım, ayrıca biraz da kızarttım. Sen öyle sevdiğin için patatesleri ince ince dilimledim. Domatesleri de büyük büyük doğradım.
Michelle:	Çok sağol Fahriye teyze. Çok zahmet ettin yine.
Fahriye:	Kâmuran amcan da bahçede mangal yaktı. Ayrıca, masaya örtü serdi ve tabak, kaşık, bardak ve çatalı koydu. En son peçeteleri yerleştirdi. Yemekten sonra da semaverden çay içeceğiz. Kâmuran amcan çayı semaverde demleyecek. Semaveri yeni yaktı. Biz yemek yerken çay demlenecek. Sonra sohbet edeceğiz.
Kâmuran:	Çay çoktan demlendi Fahriye hanım! Artık içebiliriz!

1. Where did Kâmuran make preparations for the meal?
2. Will they brew tea before or after the meal?

Vocabulary

bardak	*glass, cup*	**kaşık**	*spoon*
çatal	*fork*	**kızartmak**	*to fry*
demlemek	*to brew*	**koymak**	*to put*
demlenmek	*to be brewed*	**mangal**	*barbecue*

dilimlemek	*to slice*	**örtü**	*cover, cloth*
doğramak	*to chop*	**patates**	*patatoes*
domates	*tomatoes*	**peçete**	*tissue*
dürüm	*roll*	**salata**	*salad*
düzenleme yapmak	*to make arrangements*	**sarmak**	*to wrap*
düzenlemek	*to arrange*	**semaver**	*samovar*
en son	*finally*	**sohbet etmek**	*to have a conversation*
haşlamak	*to boil*	**tabak**	*plate*
hazırlamak	*to prepare*	**yakmak**	*to light*
hazırlık	*preparation*	**yerleştirmek**	*to put*
hazırlık yapmak	*to make preparations*		

In the dialogue above, we see **neler yaptın yine?** literally it means *what did you do again?* But the meaning is *Thank you for what you did.* The answer is usually, **pek bir şey yok, aslında,** *in fact, it's nothing much.*

exercise 1

List the names of the kitchen utensils needed for a dinner table and verbs about food preparation and cooking methods you have learned in this lesson into two groups below. Then check your work with the vocabulary section of this lesson.

Example: <u>dinner table</u> <u>verbs for food preparation & cooking</u>
peçete doğramak

_____

_____

_____

_____

_____

Dialogue 2

bahçede sebze yetiştirmek growing vegetables in the garden

Michelle notices vegetables in the garden.

Michelle:	Fahriye teyze, sebzelerinizi gördüm. Çok güzeller. Neler yetiştiriyorsunuz.
Fahriye:	Domates, biber, patlıcan, nane, soğan, sarımsak, salatalık, havuç ve maydanoz var. Ama meyve de yetiştirmek istiyoruz. Çilek, kavun, karpuz falan. Henüz ürün alamadık çünkü buraya daha yeni taşındık.
Michelle:	Çok sağlıklı ve eğlenceli bir uğraşı.
Fahriye:	Haklısın. Hem bahçeden sebzeleri taze taze toplamak mümkün hem de tabîat ile iç içe olmak çok dinlendirici.
Kâmuran:	Sabahları bahçede hem kahvaltımızı ediyoruz hem de sofradan kalkmadan sebze, ağaç, çiçek ve çimenleri suluyoruz. Kahvaltı süresinde onlar sulanıyor.

1. Are they growing fruit in the garden?
2. Have they collected any products from the garden yet?

Vocabulary

bayat	*stale*	**sağlıklı**	*healthy*
biber	*pepper*	**salatalık**	*cucumber*
boyunca	*during, long*	**sarımsak**	*garlic*
çilek	*strawberry*	**sebze**	*vegetable*
çimen	*grass*	**sofra**	*dining table*
dinlendirici	*relaxing*	**soğan**	*onion*
eğlenceli	*entertaining*	**sulamak**	*to water*
falan	*etc.*	**sulanmak**	*to be watered*
havuç	*carrot*	**süresinde**	*during*
iç içe olmak	*to be intertwined*	**tabîat**	*nature*
kalkmak	*to stand up*	**taşınmak**	*to move*
karpuz	*watermelon*	**taze**	*fresh*
kavun	*melon*	**toplamak**	*to collect*

maydanoz	*parsley*	tüm gün boyunca	*all daylong*
meyve	*fruit*	uğraşı	*activity*
mümkün	*possible*	ürün	*product*
nane	*mint*	yetiştirmek	*to grow*
patlıcan	*eggplant*		

Fahriye'nin menüsü / Fahriye's menu

iskender	*meat served on top of bread topped with tomato sauce and melted butter*	karnıyarık	*minced meat in an eggplant boat*
ayran	*yogurt drink*	lahmacun	*minced meat on thin dough*
baklava	*piscatios/walnuts in between many layers of thin phyllo*	mevsim salata	*salad made with the vegetables of the season*
cacık	*chopped cucumber in diluted yogurt*	pilav üstü döner	*rice covered with grilled beef*
çoban salatası	*salad made with tomatoes, cucumbers, peppers, onions, and parsley*	porsiyon	*portion*
dondurma	*ice cream*	sütlaç	*rice pudding*
kadayıf	*shredded pastry with piscaito/walnut filling*	tatlı	*dessert*

Note that it's common to grow own vegetable in the garden if any and even in balconies.

exercise 2

List the names of the vegetables and fruit you have learned in this lesson into two groups below. Then check your work with the vocabulary section of this lesson.

Example: <u>vegetable</u>   <u>fruit</u>
                        nane   kavun

_____

_____

_____

_____

_____

Bölüm 2
Part 2

dilbilgisi grammar

sebep bildiren zarflar the adverbs of reason

In Turkish, there are several ways to express reason.

çünkü because, since

It's possible to express reason by using **çünkü**, *because* or *since* in the adverb clauses. Examples:

Çok yoruldum çünkü çok çalıştım.
I got very tired because I worked hard.

Çok acıktım çünkü bütün gün boyunca bir şey yemedim.
I got hungry a lot since I didn't eat anything all day long.

Çocuk hastanede yatıyor çünkü hasta oldu.
The child is at the hospital because he got sick.

Sınavda başarılı olamadım çünkü hiç çalışmadım.
I couldn't succeed in the exams since I didn't study at all.

Şimdi para harcayabilirsin çünkü artık zengin oldun.
You can spend money (now that) because you got rich.

-diği için because, since, for

It's also possible to express reason by using **–diği için**, *because, since, for*. To form the structure, special endings are used for each person. Note that it is usually more suitable for <u>the past tense</u>.

The ending **–diği için**, *because, since, for* and the personal endings are given in the table below:

(Ben)	**-diğim için**	*Since I*
(Sen)	**-diğin için**	*Since you*
(O)	**-diği için**	*Since he / she / it*
(Biz)	**-diğimiz için**	*Since we*
(Siz)	**-diğiniz için**	*Since you (pl)*
Onlar	**-diği için/-dikleri için**	*Since they*

Examples:

Ben geldiğim için	*Since I came*
Sen geldiğin için	*Since you came*
O geldiği için	*Since he/she came*
Biz geldiğimiz için	*Since we came*
Siz geldiğiniz için	*Since you came*
Çocuklar geldiği / geldikleri için	*Since the children came*
Arabalar geldiği için	*Since the cars came*

the vowel harmony

The letter "**i**" in the endings may change to "**ı**", "**u**", or "**ü**" depending on the last vowel of the verb.

Last vowel of the preceding verb	a,ı	e,i	o,u	ö,ü
The vowel in the ending	ı	i	u	ü

Examples:

söyle mek	**Ben söyle<u>diğim</u> için**	*Since I told*
atla mak	**Ben atla<u>dığım</u> için**	*Since I jumped*
uyu mak	**Ben uyu<u>duğum</u> için**	*Since I slept*
yürü mek	**Ben yürü<u>düğüm</u> için**	*Since I walked*

The letter "d" in the ending may change to "t" depending on the last letter of the preceding word:

the consonant harmony

In case the word ends with one the consonants 'f', 's', 't', 'k', 'ç', 'ş', 'h', or 'p', the letter "d" in the ending changes to "t":

Last letter of the preceding word	f	s	t	k	ç	ş	h	p
The ending –diği için change to	-tiği için							

Examples:

Ben içtiğim için   *Since I drank*

Sen baktığın için   *Since you looked*

Onlar uçtukları için   *Since they flew*

More examples:

Çok çalıştığım için çok yoruldum.
I got very tired because I worked hard.

Bütün gün boyunca bir şey yemediğim için çok acıktım.
I got hungry a lot since I didn't eat anything all day long.

Çocuk hasta olduğu için hastanede yatıyor.
The child is at the hospital because he got sick.

Hiç çalışmadığım için sınavda başarılı olamadım.
I couldn't succeed in the exams since I didn't study at all.

Artık zengin olduğun için şimdi para harcayabilirsin.
You can spend money (now that) because you got rich.

the negative form

It's also possible to form negative sentences by adding the negative ending **–me / -ma** right before the ending.

The negative ending **–me / -ma** is a 2 way vowel harmony meaning it changes depending on the preceding vowel.

Last vowel of the preceding verb	a, ı, o, u	e, i, ö, ü
the endings –me / -ma	**-ma**	**-me**

Examples:

Ben söylemediğim için	*Since I didn't tell*
Ben atlamadığım için	*Since I didn't jump*
Ben uyumadığım için	*Since I didn't sleep*
Ben yürümediğim için	*Since I didn't walk*
Ben içmediğim için	*Since I didn't drink*
Ben bakmadığım için	*Since I didn't look*
Ben uçmadığım için	*Since I didn't fly*

exercise 3

Answer the questions. Express the reason by using **-diği için**. Note the vowel and the consonant change.

Examples:

Neden başarılı oldun? / çok çalışmak
Why did you succeed? / to study hard

Çok çalıştığım için başarılı oldum.
I succeeded because I studied hard.

zaman zarfları the adverbs of time

In Turkish, there are several ways to express time in the adverb clauses. One is expressing two actions occurring at the same time, and the other is expressing two actions before and after one another. They will be studied in two groups below:

aynı anın ifadesi two actions occurring at the same time

iken when, while

In Turkish, the adverb of time **iken**, *when* or *while* is used as adverb phrases to express two actions occurring at the same time. In this structure, the verb is conjugated for the 3rd singular person, **o**, *he / she / it* in the present progress tense or in the present tense. See Unit 3 for the present progressive and present tenses.

Examples:

Çalışır iken	*While working*
Çalışıyor iken	*While working*

Note that the person (subject) isn't given here. The person or the subject is figured out by looking at the main sentence that follow this adverbial phrase:

Examples:

Çalışır iken müzik dinlerim.   *While working, I listen to music.*

Çalışır iken müzik dinlersin.   *While working, you listen to music.*

Çalışıyor iken müzik dinlerim.   *While working, I listen to music.*

Çalışıyor iken müzik dinlersin. *While working, you listen to music.*

However, it's also possible to add a subject in the front in case the person in the adverb and the main clauses are different.

Examples:

(The person who works and the person who listens to music are the same.)

Çalışır iken müzik dinlerim.   *While working, I listen to music.*

Çalışır iken müzik dinlersin. *While working, you listen to music.*

Çalışır iken müzik dinler.   *While working, he / she listens to music.*

(The person who works and the person who listens to music are different.)

Ben çalışır iken *(sen)* **müzik dinlersin.**   *While I work, you listen to music.*

Sen çalışır iken (ben) müzik dinlerim.   *While you work, I listen to music.*

O çalışır iken (biz) müzik dinleriz.   *While he / she works, I listen to music.*

Biz çalışır iken (o) müzik dinler.   *While we work, he / she listens to music.*

Also note that it's possible to use this structure with all tenses. Therefore, the time of the sentence can only be figured out by looking at the main sentence that follow this adverbial phrase:

Examples:

Çalışır / Çalışıyor iken müzik dinliyorum.   *While working, I'm listening to music.*

Çalışır / Çalışıyor iken müzik dinlerim.   *While working, I listen to music.*

Çalışır / Çalışıyor iken müzik dinledim.   *While working, I listened to music.*

Çalışır / Çalışıyor iken müzik dinleyeceğim.   *While working, I will listen to music.*

It's also possible to use the adverb **iken**, *when* or *while* as an ending. In this case, the ending "-ken" is added to the verb.

Examples:

Çalışır iken / Çalışırken   *While working*

Çalışıyor iken / Çalışıyorken   *While working*

Examples with the sentences:

Çalışır iken / çalışırken müzik dinlerim.
While working, I listen to music.

Çalışır iken / çalışırken müzik dinlersin.
While working, you listen to music.

Çalışıyor iken / Çalışıyorken müzik dinlerim.
While working, I listen to music.

Çalışıyor iken / Çalışıyorken müzik dinlersin.
While working, you listen to music.

More examples:

Kahvaltı ediyorken / ederken Ali'yi gördüm.
While I was having breakfast, I saw Ali.

Ali kahvaltı ediyorken / ederken onu gördüm.
While Ali was having breakfast, I saw him.

Giderken beni de götür.
While you leave, take me, too.

Giderken seni de alırım.
While I leave, I'll take you, too.

It's also possible to use the adverb **iken**, *when* or *while* or the ending **–ken** with the adjectives and nouns.

Examples:

Açken / aç iken üzgün hissederim.   *While hungry, I feel sad.*

Tokken / tok iken neşeli olurum.   *While full, I become joyful.*

In case the word ends with a vowel, the connector letter "**y**" is added right before the ending **-ken**.

Mutluyken / mutlu iken çok yerim.   *While happy, I eat much.*

Öğrenciyken / öğrenci iken çok   *While I was a student, I studied a lot.*
çalıştım.

Evdeyken / evde iken hep uyurum.   *While at home, I sleep all the time.*

aynı zamanda at the same time

In Turkish, it is also possible to express that two actions occur at the same time by using the conjunction **aynı zamanda**, *at the same time*.

Examples:

Çalıştım. Aynı zamanda, müzik dinledim.
I worked. I listened to music, at the same time.

Çalışırım. Aynı zamanda, müzik dinlerim.
I work. I listen to music, at the same time.

Çalışacağım ve aynı zamanda müzik dinleyeceğim.
I'll work and listen to music, at the same time.

Kahvaltımı ediyorum, aynı zamanda Ali ile sohbet ediyorum.
I'm having my breakfast and at the same time, I'm having a conversation with Ali.

Ali çayını içiyor aynı zamanda telefonda konuşuyor.
Ali's drinking his tea and at the same time, he's talking on the phone.

Sen git, aynı zamanda beni de götür.
You leave and take me at the same time, too.

Giderim, aynı zamanda seni de alırım.
I'll leave and take you at the same time, too.

-diğinde when

In Turkish, another way is to express that two actions occur at the same time is by using the ending **-diğinde**, when. The ending **-diğinde** and the personal endings are added to the bare form of the verb.

The ending **–diğinde**, *when* and the personal endings are given in the table below:

(Ben)	**-diğimde**	*When I*
(Sen)	**-diğinde**	*When you*
(O)	**-diğinde**	*When he / she / it*
(Biz)	**-diğimizde**	*When we*
(Siz)	**-diğinizde**	*When you (pl)*
Onlar	**-diğinde /-diklerinde**	*When they*

Examples:

Ben geldiğimde	*When I come*
Sen geldiğinde	*When you come*
O geldiğinde	*When he / she comes*
Biz geldiğimizde	*When we come*
Siz geldiğinizde	*When you come*
Çocuklar geldiğinde/geldiklerinde	*When the children come*
Arabalar geldiğinde	*When the cars come*

the vowel harmony

The ending **–diğinde**, *when* and the personal endings are 4 way vowel harmony meaning they change depending on the preceding vowel.

All 4 possibilities of the ending **–diğinde** with the personal ending are given in the table below:

Last vowel of the preceding verb	Persons	a,ı	e,i	o,u	ö,ü
The ending	(Ben) (Sen) (O) (Biz) (Siz) Onlar	-dığımda -dığında -dığında -dığımızda -dığınızda -dığında /- dıklarında	-diğimde -diğinde -diğinde -diğimizde -diğinizde -diğinde /- diklerinde	-duğumda -duğunda -duğunda -duğumuzda -duğunuzda -duğunda /- duklarında	-düğümde -düğünde -düğünde -düğümüzde -düğünüzde -düğünde /- düklerinde

Examples:

söyle mek	**Ben söyle<u>diğimde</u>**	*When I tell*
atla mak	**Ben atla<u>dığımda</u>**	*When I jump*
uyu mak	**Ben uyu<u>duğumda</u>**	*When I sleep*
yürü mek	**Ben yürü<u>düğümde</u>**	*When I walk*

The letter "d" in the ending may change to "t" depending on the last letter of the preceding word:

the consonant harmony

In case the word ends with one the consonants '**f**', '**s**', '**t**', '**k**', '**ç**', '**ş**', '**h**', or '**p**', the letter "**d**" in the ending changes to "**t**":

Last letter of the preceding word	f	s	t	k	ç	ş	h	p
The ending –diğinde **change to**				-tiğinde				

Examples:

Ben iç<u>t</u>iğimde	*When I drink*
Sen bak<u>t</u>ığında	*When you look*

Onlar uçtuğunda	*When they fly*

More examples:

O uyuduğunda	*When he / she sleeps*
Biz gördüğümüzde	*When we see*
Ben istediğimde	*When I want*
Ben söylediğimde	*When I tell*
Siz atladığınızda	*When you (pl) jump*
Onlar uçtuklarında	*When they fly*

Note that this structure can be used with all the tenses like the previous adverbs. Therefore, the time of the sentence can only be figured out by looking at the main sentence that follow this adverbial phrase:

Examples:

Çalıştığımda çok yoruldum.
I got very tired when I worked.

Çalıştığımda çok yorulurum.
I get very tired when I work.

Seni son gördüğümde daha küçük bir çocuktun.
When I saw you the last time, you were a little child.

Kitap okuduğumda müzik de dinledim.
When I read a book, I listened to music, too.

Sen müzik dinlediğinde ben rahatsız oluyorum.
When you listen to music, I get disturbed.

Ali kahvaltı ettiğinde mutlaka çay içer.
When Ali eats breakfast, He drinks tea, for sure.

Gittiğinde beni de götür.
When you leave, take me, too.

Gittiğimde seni de alırım.
When I leave, I'll take you, too.

exercise 3

Combine the two clauses in a complete sentence. Express that the two actions occur at the same time. Make three sentences in the present tense by using **–iken**, **-diğinde**, and **aynı zamanda**.

Examples:

ben / uyumak/dinlenmek
I / to sleep / to rest

> **Uyurken dinlenirim.**
> *While sleeping, I rest.*
>
> **Uyuduğumda dinlenirim.**
> *When sleeping, I rest.*
>
> **Uyurum, aynı zamanda dinlenirim.**
> *I sleep, at the same time I rest.*

1. o / kitap okumak / müzik dinlemek   ....
2. biz / evi taşımak / yorulmak   ....
3. siz / gezmek / yeni yerler görmek   ....
4. Michelle / yemek pişirmek / yemek   ....
5. İbrahim / araba sürmek / konuşmak   ....

iki farklı anın ifadesi two actions occurring at different times

-dikten sonra after

In order to express that one action occurs after another, the ending **-dikten sonra**, *after* is added to form an adverb clause of time.

The ending **–dikten sonra**, *after* is used for all the persons:

Examples:

Ben geldikten sonra	*After I come*
Sen geldikten sonra	*After you come*
O geldikten sonra	*After he / she comes*
Biz geldikten sonra	*After we come*
Siz geldikten sonra	*After you come*
Çocuklar geldikten sonra	*After the children come*
Arabalar geldikten sonra	*After the cars come*

the vowel harmony

The ending **–dikten sonra**, *after* is 4 way vowel harmony meaning it changes depending on the preceding vowel.

All 4 possibilities of the ending **–dikten sonra** are given in the table below:

Last vowel of the preceding verb	a,ı	e,i	o,u	ö,ü
The ending	-dıktan sonra	-dikten sonra	-duktan sonra	-dükten sonra

Examples:

söyle mek	**Ben söyledikten sonra**	*After I tell*
atla mak	**Ben atladıktan sonra**	*After I jump*
uyu mak	**Ben uyuduktan sonra**	*After I sleep*
yürü mek	**Ben yürüdükten sonra**	*After I walk*

The letter "d" in the ending may change to "t" depending on the last letter of the preceding word:

the consonant harmony

In case the word ends with one the consonants 'f', 's', 't', 'k', 'ç', 'ş', 'h', or 'p', the letter "d" in the ending changes to "t":

Last letter of the preceding word	f	s	t	k	ç	ş	h	p
The ending –dikten sonra change to	-tikten sonra							

Examples:

Ben içtikten sonra	*After I drink*
Sen baktıktan sonra	*After you look*
Onlar uçtuktan sonra	*After they fly*

More examples:

O uyuduktan sonra	*After he / she sleeps*
Biz gördükten sonra	*After we see*
Ben istedikten sonra	*After I want*
Ben söyledikten sonra	*After I tell*
Siz atladıktan sonra	*After you (pl) jump*
Onlar uçtuktan sonra	*After they fly*

Note that this structure can be used with all the tenses like the previous adverbs. Therefore, the time of the sentence can only be figured out by looking at the main sentence that follow this adverbial phrase:

Examples:

Çay içtikten sonra kalkacağım.	*I'll get up (leave) after I drink tea.*
Sen çay içtikten sonra kalkacağım.	*I'll leave after you drink tea.*
O uyuduktan sonra biz geldik.	*We arrived after he/she slept.*
Biz onları gördükten sonra çıktık.	*We left after we saw them.*
Ben istedikten sonra sen de istedin.	*After I wanted, you wanted, too.*
Söyledikten sonra vaz geçtim.	*I changed my mind after I said.*
Çalıştıktan sonra dinleneceğim.	*I'll rest after I work.*

-meden önce before

In order to express that one action occurs before another, the ending **–meden önce**, *before* is added to form an adverb clause of time.

The ending **–meden önce**, *before* is used for all the persons:

Examples:

Ben gelmeden önce	*Before I come*
Sen gelmeden önce	*Before you come*
O gelmeden önce	*Before he / she comes*
Biz gelmeden önce	*Before we come*
Siz gelmeden önce	*Before you come*
Çocuklar gelmeden önce	*Before the children come*
Arabalar gelmeden önce	*Before the cars come*

the vowel harmony

The ending **–meden önce**, *before* is 2 way vowel harmony meaning it changes depending on the preceding vowel.

Both possibilities of the ending **–meden önce** are given in the table below:

Last vowel of the preceding verb	a,ı,o,u	e,i,ö,ü
The ending	-madan önce	-meden önce

Examples:

söyle mek	Ben söylemeden önce	*Before I tell*
atla mak	Ben atlamadan önce	*Before I jump*
uyu mak	Ben uyumadan önce	*Before I sleep*
yürü mek	Ben yürümeden önce	*Before I walk*

Note that this structure can be used with all the tenses like the previous adverbs. Therefore, the time of the sentence can only be figured out by looking at the main sentence that follow this adverbial phrase:

Examples:

Kalkmadan önce çay içeceğim.	*I'll drink tea before I leave.*
Sen kalkmadan önce çay içeceğim.	*I'll drink tea before you leave.*
O uyumadan önce geldik.	*We arrived before he/she slept.*
Biz onları görmeden önce çıktık.	*We left before we saw them.*
Ben istemeden önce sen istedin.	You wanted before I wanted.
Söylemeden önce vaz geçtim.	*I changed my mind before I said.*
Çalışmadan önce dinleneceğim.	*I'll rest before I work.*

exercise 4

Combine the two clauses in a complete sentence. Express that the two actions occur at different times. Make two sentences in the present tense by using **–dikten sonra** and **–meden önce**.

Examples:

ben / önce çalışmak / sonra dinlenmek
I / first to sleep / then to rest

> **Çalıştıktan sonra dinlenirim.**
> *I rest after I work.*

> **Dinlenmeden önce çalışırım.**
> *I work before I rest.*

1. o/ önce kitap okumak/ sonra müzik dinlemek   ....

2. biz/ önce evi satın almak/sonra taşınmak   ....

3. siz/ önce gezmek/sonra yeni yerler görmek   ....

4. Michelle/ önce yemek pişirmek/ sonra yemek   ....

5. İbrahim/ önce araba sürmek/sonra konuşmak   ....

Bölüm 3
Part 3

Dialogue 3

ev kiralama konusu the house renting issue

Sema, the daughter of Fahriye and Kâmuran, came home from work. After she graduated from the university in London, she returned to Türkiye and started working here. She engaged with Lütfi, a collauge from work last month. She's still living with her parents and there's three months ahead of their wedding. However, she's has already started looking for a house for rent in the vicinity.

İbrahim:	Bahçeli bir ev mi tutmak istiyorsunuz?
Sema:	Aslında çok isterim. Çünkü Lütfi de bahçeyi ve doğayı çok seviyor. Aynı zamanda, kendisi evde kedi besliyor. Onun için ev mutlaka bahçeli ve balkonlu olmalı. Kedi evde yaşarsa rahatsız oluyorum.
Michelle:	Eşya alacak mısınız yoksa ev mobilyalı mı olacak?
Sema:	Önce mobilyalı istedik ama sonradan vazgeçtik. Hem benim hem de Lütfi'nin eşyası var. Onun için ev mobilyasız olmalı. Ama bize 3 oda bir salon ev yeterli olur çünkü fazla eşyamız yok. Ayrıca bir ocak ve buzdolabımız eksik. Diğer eşyalarımız tamam.
Michelle:	Evde ısıtma ve soğutma nasıl olmalı?
Sema:	Evde ısıtma için doğalgaz yakıtlı bir kombi olmalı ve yaz için bir kaç klima olmalı.

1. Why do they need a house with a garden?
2. Will they need the house with furniture?

Vocabulary

beslemek	*to feed*	**mobilyalı**	*furnished*
buzdolabı	*refrigerator*	**mobilyasız**	*unfurnished*
doğa	*nature*	**ocak**	*oven*

doğal gazlı kombi	natural gas boiler	rahatsız olmak	to get irritated
eksik	missing, lacking	salon	living room
eşya (mobilya)	things, furniture	soğutma	cooling
fırın	stove	tam	full
ısıtma	heating	tutmak	to rent
klima	airconditioner	vaz geçmek	to change mind

Note that **tutmak** is used instead of **kiralamak**, *to rent* in the dialogue above. Both can be used.

Also note that **bahçeli**, means *with garden* and **mobilyalı** means *with furniture*. It's also possible to say **bahçesiz**, *without garden* or **mobilyasız**, *without furniture*. The suffixes of **–li** and **–siz**, *with* and *without* can be used with other nouns, too when necessary.

Unit Twelve: Konserde

At the concert

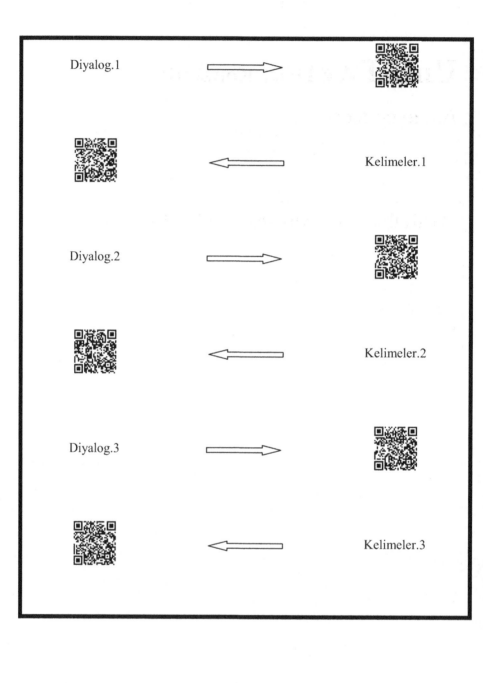

Bölüm 1
Part 1

Dialogue 1

konser salonunda at the concert hall

While Michelle and İbrahim visited Kâmuran and Fahriye, they started a conversation with Sema about likes, dislikes and about music. Sema wanted to go to a concert with them. She also wanted to bring her fiance Lütfi to the concert and introduce him to her friends.

Sema:	İyi ki geldik. Ve eminim ki siz de çok beğeneceksiniz.
Michelle:	Ben pop müzikten çok hoşlanırım. Ama İbrahim folklorik müziği daha çok sever.
Lütfi:	Ben de. Beni pop müzikle Sema tanıştırdı.
İbrahim:	Beni de Michelle. Ama şimdi o kadar çok seviyorum ki başka bir şey dinlemiyorum.
Sema:	Sevgi böyle bir şey!
Michelle:	Aynen. Örneğin ben korku filmlerinden hiç hoşlanmam. Bundan dolayı, İbrahim de benim için artık korku filmi seyretmiyor.
Sema:	Hangi tür filmlerden hoşlanırsınız?
Michelle:	Komedi ve macera filmlerinden. Ayrıca spor müsabakalarını seyrederim. Ha bir de, belgeseller ve yemek tarifleri.
İbrahim:	Michelle yemek tarifi programlarını izlemeyi o kadar çok seviyor ki, ben de alıştım.

1. What kind of music do both İbrahim and Lütfi like?
2. What kind of movies does Michelle not like?

Vocabulary

alışmak	*to get used to*	**macera filmi**	*adventure movie*
belgesel	*documentary*	**müsabaka**	*competition*
çeşit	*kind*	**müzik**	*music*

dolu	*full of*	pop müzik	*pop music*
folklorik	*folkloric*	program	*program*
hafif müzik	*soft music*	seyretmek	*to watch*
hoşlanmak	*to like*	şarkı	*song*
izlemek	*to watch*	tür	*kind*
komedi filmi	*comedy movie*	türkü	*folkloric song*
korku filmi	*scary movie*	yemek tarifi	*recipe*
Eminim ki,		*I'm sure that*	
İyi ki,		*Fortunately,*	
Ne yazık ki,		*Unfortunately,*	

In the dialogue above, we see the exclamation phrase **ha bir de.** It's common to use it when you realize you forgot to say something.

Dialogue 2

konser salonunda (devam) at the concert hall (cont.)

The conversation, of course, came to the football and teams.

Lütfi:	Ben Başakşehir Sporu tutuyorum. Çok başarılı değiller ama ben onları yine de destekliyorum.
İbrahim:	Ben artık futbol izlemiyorum. Michelle maçtan hoşlanmaz. Sonuç olarak, ben de artık hoşlanmıyorum.
Sema:	Ne harika! Ne sevgi dolu bir çift!
Michelle:	Evet, kendisi çok kibardır.
İbrahim:	Teşekkür ederim hayatım, beni utandırıyorsun.
Michelle:	Neden? Eşini seviyorsun, sonuç olarak ona kibar davranıyorsun.
Sema:	Tabii ki. Keşke Lütfi de artık takım tutmasa ve benimle birlikte dizi seyretse.
Lütfi:	Ben mi? Ben takım tutmayı çoktan bıraktım. Ve artık sadece dizi izlemek istiyorum.
İbrahim:	Aferin Lütfi, hızlı öğreniyorsun. Mutluluğun anahtarı eşine "sen haklısın" demektir.

1. Does İbrahim watch sports?
2. Will Lütfi continue watching sports?

Vocabulary

anahtar	*key*	**dizi**	*tv series*
Başakşehir Spor	*a famous soccer team in Türkiye*	**futbol**	*soccer*
bırakmak	*to stop*	**kibar**	*kind*
çift	*a couple*	**maç**	*match*
davranmak	*to behave*	**mutluluk**	*happiness*
demek	*to mean*	**tutmak**	*to support*
demek, anlatmak	*to say, to tell*	**utandırmak**	*to make someone feel ashamed*
desteklemek	*to support*	**utanmak**	*to feel ashamed*
Aferin!	*Good job!*		
Keşke	*I wish*		
Sonuç olarak,	*As a result,*		

Note that **tutmak** is used instead of **desteklemek**, *to support* in the dialogue above. Both can be used.

exercise 1

Which is the odd one out in each row?

demek	söylemek	anlatmak	tutmak
müzik	türkü	şarkı	mutluluk
korku	çift	macera	komedi
müsabaka	hafif	pop	folklorik

Bölüm 2
Part 2

dilbilgisi grammar

dilek ifadeleri the wish clauses

In Turkish, expressing wishes is possible in two ways (see Unit 3). The wish clauses are formed by adding **–se / -sa** with the personal ending to the bare form of the verb.

The "wish" ending **–se / -sa**, and the personal ending following is a 2 way vowel harmony meaning it changes depending on the preceding vowel.

Both possibilities of the "wish" ending **–se / -sa** with the personal ending are given in the table below:

Last vowel of the preceding verb	a,ı, o, u		e,i, ö, ü	
the endings – se / -sa	(Ben) -sam	*I wish I would*	(Ben) -sem	*I wish I would*
	(Sen) -san	*I wish you would*	(Sen) -sen	*I wish you would*
	(O) -sa	*I wish he/she/it would*	(O) -se	*I wish he/she/it would*
	(Biz) -sak	*I wish we would*	(Biz) -sek	*I wish we would*
	(Siz) -sanız	*I wish you (pl) would*	(Siz) -seniz	*I wish you (pl) would*
	Onlar -sa/-salar	*I wish they would*	Onlar -se/-seler	*I wish they would*

Examples:

gel mek	*to come*
Ben gel+sem	*I wish I would come*
Sen gelsen	*I wish you would come*
O gelse	*I wish he / she would come*
Biz gelsek	*I wish we would come*
Siz gelseniz	*I wish you (pl) would come*
Çocuklar gelse / gelseler	*I wish the children would come*
Arabalar gelse	*I wish the cars would come*

More examples:

bak mak	*to look (at)*
Ben bak+sam	*I wish I would look (at)*
Sen baksan	*I wish you would look (at)*
O baksa	*I wish he / she would look (at)*
Biz baksak	*I wish we would look (at)*
Siz baksanız	*I wish you (pl) would look (at)*
Çocuklar baksa / baksalar	*I wish the children would look (at)*

Here, it is important to remind that is is also possible to form the negative wish clauses. To form negative wish clauses, the negative ending **–me** or **–ma** is added right before the wish ending. Note the vowel change. The negative ending **–me** or **–ma** should be in accordance with the ending **–se / -sa**. See the previous table for the vowel harmony.

Examples:

gel mek	*to come*
Ben gel+mesem	*I wish I wouldn't come*
Sen gelmesen	*I wish you wouldn't come*
O gelmese	*I wish he / she wouldn't come*
Biz gelmesek	*I wish we wouldn't come*
Siz gelmeseniz	*I wish you (pl) wouldn't come*
Çocuklar gelmese / gelmeseler	*I wish the children wouldn't come*
Arabalar gelmese	*I wish the cars wouldn't come*

bak mak	*to look (at)*
Ben bak+masam	*I wish I wouldn't look (at)*
Sen bakmasan	*I wish you wouldn't look (at)*
O bakmasa	*I wish he / she wouldn't look (at)*
Biz bakmasak	*I wish we wouldn't look (at)*
Siz bakmasanız	*I wish you (pl) wouldn't look (at)*
Çocuklar bakmasa / bakmasalar	*I wish the children wouldn't look (at)*

NB It's very common to use **keşke**, *if only* with the wish clauses.

Examples:

Keşke zengin olsan.	*If only/I wish you became rich.*
Keşke sizi görsek.	*If only/I wish (We wish) we could/would see you. (We wish to see you.)*
Keşke rahatça uyusa.	*If only/I wish he/she could/would sleep well.*
Keşke gelseler.	*If only/I wish they could/would come.*
Keşke tekrar çocuk olsam.	*If only/I wish I could/would become a child once again.*
Keşke siz de isteseniz.	*If only/I wish you could/would also want.*
Keşke bugün aramasa.	*If only/I wish he/she wouldn't call today.*
Keşke uyanmasam.	*If only/I wish not to wake up.*
Keşke hiç yağmur durmasa.	*If only/I wish the rain wouldn't stop.*

sonuç bildirme zarfları the adverb clauses of result

In Turkish, expressing result is possible in several ways.

o kadar ... ki, so ... that

One is using **o kadar ... ki**, *so ... that* in adverb clauses. Examples:

O kadar çalıştım ki, çok yoruldum.
I worked so hard that I got very tired.

O kadar acıktım ki, herşeyi yiyebilirim.
I got so hungry that I can eat everything.

Çocuk o kadar hasta oldu ki, hastanede yatıyor.
The child got so sick that he/she is at the hospital.

O kadar akıllı ki, hiç çalışmadan başarılı oluyor.
He/She's so clever that he/she succeeds without studying.

O kadar zengin oldun ki, artık para harcayabilirsin.
You got so rich that you can spend money now.

o kadar (bir) ... ki, such that

Another is using **o kadar (bir) ... ki,** *such (a / the) ... that* in adverb clauses.
Examples:

O kadar çalışkan bir insanım ki, hiç durmam.
I'm such a hardworking person that I never stop.

O kadar aç bir çocuk ki, herşeyi yiyebilir.
He/She's such a hungry child that he/she can eat everything.

Çocuk o kadar ciddî bir tedavi gördü ki, hemen iyileşti.
The child received such an intense treatment that he/she got well instantly.

O kadar akıllı birisi ki, hiç çalışmadan başarılı oluyor.
He/She's such a clever person that he/she succeeds without studying.

exercise 2

Make a sentence in the past tense with the clues given. Express result in your sentences by using **o kadar ki**, *so that / such that.*
Examples:

ben/ çok çalışmak / başarılı olmak
I / study a lot / to succeed

O kadar çok çalıştım ki, başarılı oldum.
I studied so much that I succeeded.

1.   ben/çok yemek / doymak   ....
2.   o/fazla para harcamak / parası kalmamak   ....
3.   siz/çok sevmek / bizi ziyarete gelmek   ....
4.   biz/alışverişe ihtiyacı olmak / dükkâna gitmek ....
5.   onlar/mutlu insan / sokakta şarkı söylemek ....

böylece, sonuç olarak as a result, so that

Result is also expressed by using **böylece,** *so that* or **sonuç olarak,** *as a result.*
Examples:

Çok çalıştım, böylece çok yoruldum.
I worked hard, so that I got very tired.

Çok acıktım, sonuç olarak herşeyi yiyebilirim.
I got so hungry, as a result, I can eat everything.

Çocuk hasta oldu, sonuç olarak hastanede yatıyor.
The child got sick as a result, he/she is at the hospital.

O akıllı biri. Böylece, hiç çalışmadan başarılı oluyor.
He/She's a clever person. As a result, he/she succeeds without studying.

Artık zengin oldun. Sonuç olarak şimdi para harcayabilirsin.

You finally got rich. As a result, you can spend money now.

exercise 3

Make a sentence in the past tense with the clues given. Express result in your sentences by using **böylece**, *so that* or **sonuç olarak**, *as a result*.

Examples:

ben/ çok çalışmak / başarılı olmak
I / study a lot / to succeed

> **Çok çalıştım. Böylece / Sonuç olarak başarılı oldum.**
> *I studied a lot. So that / As a result, I succeeded.*

1. **ben/çok yemek / doymak** ....

2. **o/fazla para harcamak / parası kalmamak** ....

3. **siz/çok sevmek / bizi ziyarete gelmek** ....

4. **biz/alışverişe ihtiyacı olmak / dükkâna gitmek** ....

5. **onlar/mutlu insan / sokakta şarkı söylemek** ....

soru kelimeleri the question words

You're already familiar most of the question words used in Turkish so far. Anyway, all the question words are listed in the table below for your ease.

hangi?	*which?*	**kaç yaşında?**	*how old?*
kaç?	*how many/much?*	**kim?**	*who?*
nasıl?	*how?*	**ne sıklıkta?**	*how often?*
ne kadar?	*how many/much?*	**ne zaman?**	*when?*
ne?	*what?*	**neden?**	*why?*
nerede?	*where?*	**niçin?**	*what for?*
niye?	*why?*	**nereye?**	*to where?*
nereden?	*from where?*	**kaçıncı?**	*which?*

Examples:

Hangi dili konuşuyorsun?	*What language do you speak?*
Hangisi senin araban?	*Which is your car?*
En çok hangi rengi seversin?	*Which color do you like most?*

Yemeklerden hangisini sen pişirdin?	*Which one of the dishes did you cook?*
Bugün hangi gün?	*What day is it today?*
Bugün günlerden hangisi?	*Which day is today?*
Bu elbise kaç para?	*How much money is this dress?*
Otel odası günlük ne kadar?	*How much is the hotel room for a day?*
Arabayı kaç günlük istiyorsunuz?	*How many days do you want the car for?*
Türkiye'ye kaç günlüğüne gideceksiniz?	*How many days will you go to Türkiye for?*
Odanın günlüğü kaç lira?	*How much is the room for a day?*
Kaç yaşındasın?	*How old are you?*
Kaç kilosun?	*How much do you weigh?*
Saat kaç?	*What time is it?*
Bu ne?	*What's this?*
Bu ne kadar?	*How much is it?*
Ne yaptın?	*What did you do?*
Ne zaman gelirsin?	*When will you arrive?*
Ne sıklıkta müzik dinlersin?	*How often do you listen to music?*
Nekadar kalacaksın?	*How long will you stay?*
Bu kim?	*Who's this?*
Nasılsınız?	*How are you?*
Şarkıyı nasıl buldun?	*How did you like this song?*
Neden Türkçe konuşmak istiyorsun?	*Why do you want to speak Turkish?*
Türkiye'ye niçin geldin?	*What did you come to Türkiye for?*
Niye böyle dedin şimdi?	*Why did you say so now?*
Nereden geliyorsun?	*Where are you coming from?*
Nerede kalacaksın?	*Where will you stay?*
Nereye gideceksin?	*Where will you go to?*
Kaçıncı ayda geleceksin?	*Which month will you come?*

Evet/hayır sorusu yes/no question

As you've already learned, yes/no questions are formed by adding the question suffix "**mi**?" at the end of the sentence. However, it is also possible to place it right after the desired word to get the answer to the point. Then, as a result, the meaning changes dramatically.

NB It's also important to put stress on the part of the question you ask while speaking. You'll notice that stress is widely used in questions and answers in Turkish.

Study the questions and the answers below.

Examples:

Michelle eşi İbrahim ile Türkiye'ye tatil için geldi.

Michelle mi eşi İbrahim ile Türkiye'ye tatil için geldi?	*Who came?*
Michelle eşi İbrahim ile mi Türkiye'ye tatil için geldi?	*With whom?*
Michelle eşi İbrahim ile Türkiye'ye mi tatil için geldi?	*Where to?*
Michelle eşi İbrahim ile Türkiye'ye tatil için mi geldi?	*What for?*
Michelle eşi İbrahim ile Türkiye'ye tatil için geldi mi?	*Did she?*

Michelle çarşıya eşine bir elbise almak için gidecek.

Michelle mi çarşıya eşine bir elbise almak için gidecek?	*Who?*
Michelle çarşıya mı eşine bir elbise almak için gidecek?	*Where?*
Michelle çarşıya eşine mi bir elbise almak için gidecek?	*For whom?*
Michelle çarşıya eşine bir elbise mi almak için gidecek?	*What?*
Michelle çarşıya eşine bir elbise almak için mi gidecek?	*Why?*
Michelle çarşıya eşine bir elbise almak için gidecek mi?	*Will she?*

Talha Serra'yı Pazar günü okula arabayla götürdü.

Talha mı Serra'yı Pazar günü okula arabayla götürdü?	*Who?*
Talha Serra'yı mı Pazar günü okula arabayla götürdü?	*Whom?*
Talha Serra'yı Pazar günü mü okula arabayla götürdü?	*When?*
Talha Serra'yı Pazar günü okula mı arabayla götürdü?	*Where?*
Talha Serra'yı Pazar günü okula arabayla mı götürdü?	*How?*
Talha Serra'yı Pazar günü okula arabayla götürdü mü?	*Did he?*

Bölüm 3
Part 3

diğer zaman zarfları the other adverbs of time

The formation of the sentences with the other adverbs of time is given below.

hâlâ, daha, henüz still, yet

Note that **henüz** and **daha** , *still / yet* cannot be used in the positive questions. Additionally, **henüz** cannot be used in positive sentences.

Hâlâ/henüz/daha kalkmadın mı?	*Didn't you get up yet?*
Evet/hayır, hâlâ/henüz/daha kalkmadım.	*No, I didn't get up yet.*
Hâlâ/daha uyuyorum.	*I'm still sleeping.*
Hâlâ/henüz/daha çayını bitirmedin mi?	*Didn't you finish your tea yet?*
Evet/hayır, hâlâ/henüz/daha bitirmedim.	*No, I didn't finish (it) yet.*
Hâlâ/daha içiyorum.	*I'm still drinking (it).*

NB Both **evet** and **hayır** can be used in the answer to a negative question.

Hâlâ uyuyor musun?	*Are you still sleeping?*
Evet, hâlâ/daha uyuyorum.	*Yes, I'm still sleeping.*

çoktan already

Hâlâ/henüz/daha kalkmadın mı?	*Didn't you get up yet?*
Evet/hayır, çoktan kalktım.	*No, I already got up.*
Hâlâ/henüz/daha çayını bitirmedin mi?	*Didn't you finish your tea yet?*
Evet/hayır, çoktan bitirdim.	*No, I already finished (it).*

yeni, şimdi, artık just, now, finally

Hâlâ/henüz/daha kalkmadın mı?	*Didn't you get up yet?*
Evet/hayır, yeni/şimdi/artık kalktım.	*No, I just got up.*
Hâlâ/henüz/daha çayını bitirmedin mi?	*Didn't you finish your tea yet?*
Evet/hayır, yeni/şimdi/artık bitirdim.	*No, I just finished (it).*

artık now that

Artık zenginim, para harcayabilirim.		*Now that I'm rich, I can spend money.*
Artık doydum, artık yemeyeceğim.		*Now that I got full, I won't eat any longer.*
Artık uyandım, gidebiliriz.		*Now that I woke up, we can go.*

artık any longer

Note that **artık** with the meaning of *any longer* can only be used in negative questions and negative sentences.

Hâlâ uyuyor musun?	*Are you still sleeping?*
Hayır, artık uyumuyorum.	*No, I'm not sleeping any longer.*
Hâlâ yemeğini yiyor musun?	*Are you still eating your meal?*
Hayır, artık yemiyorum.	*No, I'm not eating any longer.*
Hâlâ üzgün müsün?	*Are you still sad?*
Hayır, artık değilim.	*No, I'm not any longer.*
Artık orada çalışmıyor musun?	*Are you not working there any longer?*
Evet/hayır, artık çalışmıyorum.	*No, I'm not any longer.*
Artık yemiyor musun?	*Are you not eating any longer?*
Evet/hayır, artık yemiyorum.	*No, I'm not any longer.*

exercise 4

Complete the sentences by using the proper adverbs of frequency.

Example:

Michelle <u>artık</u> hiç bir şey yiyemez. Çünkü o <u>çoktan</u> yedi. Ancak İbrahim <u>henüz/daha/hâlâ</u> yemedi.

1. Yağmur dersini ___ bitirdi. Ancak ___ müzik dinlemeye başlamadı.

2. Biz sizi __ davet ettik. Ancak siz bizi ___ görmeye gelmediniz.

3. Hasta çocuk ___ bir çok ilaç içti. Ancak ___ iyileşmedi.

4. Michelle sabahları koşar. Ama ___ kilo alıyor.

5. Siz ___ çok gezmediniz. Ama ____ güzel yerler gördünüz.

6. Siz ____ İstanbul'da daha güzel bir ev satın aldınız. _____ hemen taşınabilirsiniz. ____ bu evde kalmazsınız.

Dialogue 3

konser salonunun çıkışında at the concert hall exit

After the concert, they decided to go to a cafe to drink Turkish coffee.

Sema:	İyi ki geldiniz. Ama keşke daha çok kalsanız. Birlikte gezsek.
Michelle:	Ne yazık ki tatilimiz çok kısa.
İbrahim:	Evet, aslında biz de çok isteriz.
Lütfi:	Bu arada, kahvelerinizi nasıl istersiniz?
İbrahim:	Michelle sade içer. Ben de artık sade içiyorum.
Sema:	Ben ...
Lütfi:	Biliyorum, tatlım. Sen orta şekerli içersin. Tabii ben de orta içeceğim. Yanında lokum da alacağım.
Michelle:	Bak, Lütfi de çok kibar.
İbrahim:	Evet, Lütfi de bizden.
Michelle:	Kahveyle birlikte lokum da mı alacaksın? Ah keşke, her şeyden yesem ve hiç kilo almasam.
İbrahim:	Almasak!

1. Does Sema drink the coffee with sugar?
2. Will Michelle and İbrahim take lokum with coffee?

Vocabulary

bizden (biri)	*(one) of us*	**orta**	*with a little sugar*
kilo almak	*to gain weight*	**sade**	*without sugar*
lokum	*delight*	**şekerli**	*with sugar*

In the dialogue above, we see the phrases of **iyi ki**, *fortunately* and **ne yazık ki**, *unfortunately*. Note that it's common to use **iyi ki** usually with the past tense while using **ne yazık ki** with the present tense.

Unit Thirteen: İyi hissetmiyorum.

I'm not feeling well.

With this unit, you will be able to:

- Talk about health and body parts
- Describe pain and health problems
- Use conjunction 'otherwise'
- Use conditionals
- Express regulations
- Use imperatives

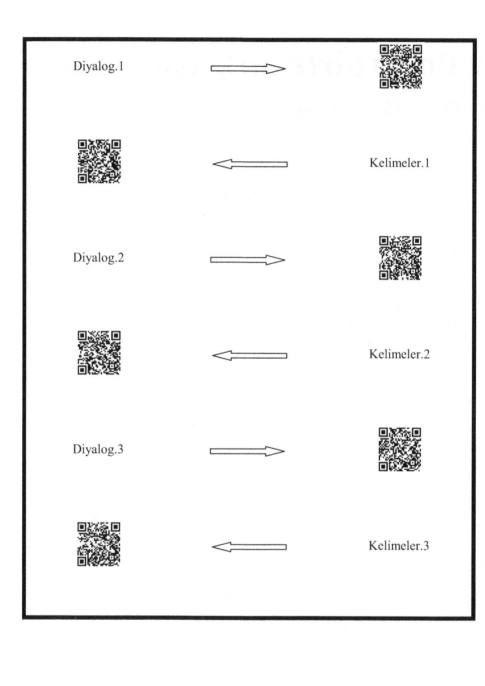

Bölüm 1
Part 1

Dialogue 1

otel odasında in the hotel room

İbrahim feels bad.

Michelle:	Şimdi nasılsın, İbrahim'ciğim?
İbrahim:	Çok şükür biraz daha iyiyim. Artık mide bulantım yok.
Michelle:	Çok sevindim. Ateşin nasıl oldu? Ya boğazın? Hâlâ öksürüyor musun?
İbrahim:	Ateşim sanki biraz düştü gibi ama çok emin değilim. Boğazım hâlâ ağrıyor. Ancak artık öksürmüyorum.
Michelle:	Sen doktora görünmek zorundasın.
İbrahim:	Biliyorum. Ama şu anda oldukça halsiz hissediyorum. Çok terledim. Bütün vücudum ve saçlarım ter içinde. Belki bir kaç saat sonra daha iyi olurum. O zaman gideriz.
Michelle:	Tamam. Sen şimdi biraz dinlen. Ateşin düşmezse, gideriz. Doktor muayene ederse, daha iyi. Hiç olmazsa, sana ilaç yazar. Ya da, en azından, uzman tavsiyesi verir.
İbrahim:	Oldu. Eğer uyuyabilirsem, kalkınca bakarız.

1. Does İbrahim still cough?
2. Can he move right now?

Vocabulary

ağrı	*pain*	**muayene etmek**	*to examine*
ağrımak	*to ache*	**saç**	*hair*
ateş	*fever*	**tavsiye**	*advice*
ateşi düşmek	*to (fever) fall*	**ter**	*sweat*
doktora görünmek	*to be seen by a doctor*	**terlemek**	*to perspire*
en azından	*at least*	**uzman**	*specialist*

| ilaç yazmak | *to write a prescription* | **vücut** | *body* |
| mide bulantısı | *nausea* | | |

In the dialogue above, we see the phrase of **hiç olmazsa**, *at least*. In addition to that, the phrase **en azından** can be used in the same manner.

Dialogue 2

doktorda at the doctor's

İbrahim didn't get well yet. But, he feels better enough to stand up and walk. Finally, they're in the hospital.

Doktor:	Şikâyetiniz nedir?
İbrahim:	Başım ağrıyor. Çok halsizim. Ayrıca boğazım ağrıyor ve yüksek ateşim var. Terden bütün gece boyunca ıslaktım.
Doktor:	Hemşire hanım şimdi ateşinizi ve nabzınızı ölçecek. Bir de kan ve idrar tahlili alalım sizden. Hastalığınız ne zaman başladı?
İbrahim:	Dün geceden beri var. Ha bir de, mide bulantım vardı, çıkardım. Ama artık bulanmıyor. Ayrıca biraz öksürdüm.
Doktor:	Kaç kez çıkardınız?
İbrahim:	İki.
Doktor:	Tamam, ben sizi bir de muayene edeyim. Şuradaki yatağa uzanın ve üzerinizi çıkarın. Gerekirse, sizden röntgen gibi başka tahliller de isterim.

1. What kind of tests will be needed for İbrahim?
2. Will the doctor also want an x-ray?

Vocabulary

acı	*pain*	**ilaç almak**	*to take medicine*
ağız	*mouth*	**ilaç yutmak**	*to take medicine*
ateşi çıkmak	*to have a high fever*	**istifra etmek**	*to throw up*
ateşi yükselmek	*to have a high fever*	**iyileşmek**	*to get well*
bacak	*leg*	**kafa**	*head*

baş	head	kan tahlili	blood test
başı dönmek	to feel dizzy	karın	abdomen
boğaz	troath	kol	arm
burun	nose	kulak	ear
çıkarmak	to throw up	kuru	dry
doktor	doctor	kusmak	to throw up
eczacı	pharmacist	mide	stomach
eczane	pharmacy	nabız	pulse
el	hand	öksürmek	to cough
geçmek	to recover from an illness	öksürük	cough
göz	eye	ölçmek	to measure
halsiz	weak	röntgen	x-ray
hap	tablet	sedye	stretcher
hasta olmak	to be sick	sırt	back
hastane	hospital	şikâyet	complaint
hemşire	nurse	uzanmak	lie down
hissetmek	to feel	üzerini çıkarmak	to uncover the upper body
ıslak	wet	yüksek ateş	high fever
idrar tahlili	urine test	yüz	face

In the dialogue above, **çıkarmak**, *to extract* is used in place of *to throw up* or *to vomit*. It's also possible to use **kusmak** or **istifra etmek** for the same meaning.

exercise 1

List the names of the parts of the body, verbs, and adjectives& nouns about sickness you have learned in this lesson into three groups below. Then check your work with the vocabulary section of this lesson.

Example: body parts   verbs   nouns & adjectives
             karın   ağrımak   ağrı

_____

_____

_____

_____

_____

Bölüm 2
Part 2

dilbilgisi grammar

"yoksa" bağlacı the conjunction "otherwise"

The conjunction **yoksa** can only be used in positive and negative sentences. It is used to talk about the other possibility.

Hemen kalkmalısın yoksa geç kalacaksın.
You have to get up now otherwise you'll be late.

Çok okumalısın yoksa başarılı olamazsın.
You have to read a lot otherwise you'll not succeed.

Soğuk su içmemelisin yoksa hasta olursun.
Don't drink cold water, otherwise you'll get sick.

Bu ilaçları almalısın yoksa iyileşemezsin.
You have to take this medicine otherwise you'll not get well.

Note that the conjuction **yoksa** can also be used in place of "or".

Talha mı yoksa Serra mı geldi? Ya da Eymen mi?
Who arrived, Talha or Serra? Or Eymen?

Kahvaltı da çay mı içersin yoksa kahve mi?
What will you drink at breakfast, tea or coffee?

şart ifadeleri the conditional clauses

The conditionals are formed in two steps. First, the verb is conjugated for the 3rd singular person in the present tense. Then the conditional ending **–se/-sa**, *if* is added with the personal endings.

STEP 1

First, the verb is conjugated for the 3rd singular person (**o**, *he / she / it*). Remember that for the 3rd singular person (**o**, *he / she / it*) the ending is either **–ir** or **–r**. See the present tense verb conjugations in Unit 3. Also remember the vowel change.

Examples:
The verb is conjugated for the 3rd <u>singular person (**o**, *he / she / it*)</u>.

söylemek	*(to say)*	**söyler**	*(He / she says)*
gelmek	*(to come)*	**gelir**	*(He / she comes)*
gitmek	*(to go)*	**gider**	*(He / she goes)*
yemek	*(to eat)*	**yer**	*(He / she eats)*
uyumak	*(to sleep)*	**uyur**	*(He / she sleeps)*
yürümek	*(to walk)*	**yürür**	*(He / she walks)*
kalmak	*(to stay)*	**kalır**	*(He / she stays)*
bakmak	*(to look (at))*	**bakar**	*(He / she looks (at))*
atlamak	*(to jump))*	**atlar**	*(He / she jumps)*

Here, it is important to remind that is is also possible to form the negative conditionals. Therefore, it is also necessary to remember the negative formation in the present tense.

Remember that for the 3rd singular person (**o**, *he / she / it*) the negative ending is either **–mez** or **–maz**. See the present tense verb conjugations in Unit 3. Also remember the vowel change.

Examples:
The verb is conjugated for the 3rd <u>singular person (**o**, *he / she / it*)</u>.

söylemek	*(to say)*	**söylemez**	*(He / she doesn't say)*
gelmek	*(to come)*	**gelmez**	*(He / she doesn't come)*
gitmek	*(to go)*	**gitmez**	*(He / she doesn't go)*
yemek	*(to eat)*	**yemez**	*(He / she doesn't eat)*
uyumak	*(to sleep)*	**uyumaz**	*(He / she doesn't sleep)*
yürümek	*(to walk)*	**yürümez**	*(He / she doesn't walk)*
kalmak	*(to stay)*	**kalmaz**	*(He / she doesn't stay)*
bakmak	*(to look (at))*	**bakmaz**	*(He / she doesn't look (at))*
atlamak	*(to jump))*	**atlamaz**	*(He / she doesn't jump)*

STEP 2

Then, the conditional ending **–se/-sa**, *if* is added with the personal endings.

the vowel harmony

The conditional ending **–se/-sa**, *if* and the personal ending following is a 2 way vowel harmony meaning it changes depending on the preceding vowel.

Both possibilities of the conditional ending with the personal ending are given in the table below:

Last vowel of the preceding verb	a,ı, o, u		e,i, ö, ü	
the endings –se / -sa	(Ben) -sam (Sen) -san (O)　-sa (Biz) -sak (Siz) -sanız Onlar -sa　/　- 　　　　larsa	*If I* *If you* *If he / she / it* *If we* *If you (pl)* *If they*	(Ben) -sem (Sen) -sen (O)　-se (Biz) -sek (Siz) -seniz Onlar -se / -lerse	*If I* *If you* *If he / she / it* *If we* *If you (pl)* *If they*

Examples:

Ben gelir+sem   *If I come*
　　(Step 1) (Step 2)

Ben bakar+sam   *If I look (at)*
　　(Step 1) (Step 2)

Ben gelmez+sem   *If I don't come*
　　(Step 1) (Step 2)

Ben bakmaz+sam   *If I don't look (at)*
　　(Step 1) (Step 2)

More examples:

Sen gelirsen   *If you come*

O gelirse   *If he / she / it comes*

Biz gelirsek   *If we come*

Siz gelirseniz   *If you (pl) come*

Çocuklar gelirse / gelirlerse   *If the children come*

Arabalar gelirse   *If the cars come*

Sen gelmezsen	*If you don't come*
O gelmezse	*If he / she / it doesn't come*
Biz gelmezsek	*If we don't come*
Siz gelmezseniz	*If you (pl) don't come*
Çocuklar gelmezse / gelmezlerse	*If the children don't come*
Arabalar gelmezse	*If the cars don't come*
Sen bakarsan	*If you look (at)*
O bakarsa	*If he / she / it looks (at)*
Biz bakarsak	*If we look (at)*
Siz bakarsanız	*If you (pl) look (at)*
Çocuklar bakarsa / bakarlarsa	*If the children look (at)*

Sen bakmazsan	*If you don't look (at)*
O bakmazsa	*If he/she/ it doesn't look (at)*
Biz bakmazsak	*If we don't look (at)*
Siz bakmazsanız	*If you (pl) don't look (at)*
Çocuklar bakmazsa / bakmazlarsa	*If the children don't look (at)*

cümle kurma forming sentences

In Turkish, it's possible to form the conditional sentences both in the present and in the future tenses. Also remember that the present tense bears the meaning of the future tense.

NB It's not necessary but very common to use **eğer** with the conditional clauses.

Examples:

(Eğer) zengin olursan, bana para verirsin.
If you become rich, you'll give me money.

(Eğer) sizi görürsek, biz de sizinle geliriz.
If we see you, we'll come with you, too.

(Eğer) rahatça uyursa, daha çabuk iyileşir.
If he/she sleeps well, he/she will get well sooner.

(Eğer) gelirlerse, ben giderim.
I'll leave if they come.

(Eğer) tekrar çocuk olursam, oyunlar oynarım.

I'll play games if I become a child once again.

(Eğer) siz de isterseniz, yapabilirsiniz.
If you also want, you can do it.

(Eğer) bugün aramazsa, üzülürüm.
I'll be sad if he/she doesn't call today

(Eğer) zamanında uyanmazsam, kesin geç kalırım.
If I don't wake up on time, I'll certainly be late.

(Eğer) hiç yağmur durmazsa, bugün evde kalırız.
If the rain doesn't stop, we'll stay at home today.

It's also possible to form the conditional clauses with the verb "to be".

Examples: (The conditional clauses with the verb "to be" are underlined.)

(Eğer) açsan, sana yemek sipariş edeyim.
I'll order food for you if you're hungry.

(Eğer) öğrenciysen, çok çalışmalısın.
You have to study a lot if you're a student.

exercise 2

Form conditional sentences with the given clues as shown in the example.

Example:
Türkiye'ye gidersin. / İstanbul'u görürsün.
You go to Türkiye. / You see İstanbul.

> **Eğer Türkiye'ye gidersen, İstanbul'u görürsün.**
> *If you go to Türkiye, you'll see İstanbul.*

1. Açsın. / Yemek sipariş edeceğim.   ....

2. Yağmur yağar. / Biz ıslanırız.   ....

3. Paraları çok olur. / Yeni bir araba alırlar.   ....

4. İstersiniz. / Başarırsınız.   ....

5. Gelirim. / Sevinir misin?   ....

emir/rica ifadeleri the imperative

The imperative is formed by using the bare form of the verb which means the verb without the endings of **–mek** or **–mak**. (See Unit 3 for the infinitive and bare forms of the verb.)

In Turkish, the imperative is formed for the second singular, **sen**, *you* and plural persons, **siz**, *you (pl)*.

Below are given the special personal endings for the 2nd persons, **sen**, *you* and **siz**, *you (pl)*:

(Sen)	**-**
(Siz)	**-in**

Note that there's no ending for the 2nd singular person, **sen**, *you*. It's the same in English. In English, bare forms of the verbs are also the imperative forms of the verbs:

Examples:

infinitive form	**bare form (the imperative form)**
içmek	**(Sen) iç!**
to drink	*(You) drink!*
gelmek	**(Sen) gel!**
to come	*(You) come!*

For the 2nd singular person, **siz**, *you (pl)*, the imperative ending is **–in**. However, it's a 4 way vowel harmony meaning it changes depending on the preceding vowel.

the vowel harmony

The imperative ending "**–in**" may change to "**-ın**", "**-un**", or "**-ün**" depending on the last vowel of the verb.

Last vowel of the verb	a,ı	e,i	o,u	ö,ü
The vowel in the ending	-ın	-in	-un	-ün

Examples:

iç mek	**(Siz) için!**	*(You (pl)) drink!*
bak mak	**(Siz) bakın!**	*(You (pl)) look!*
gör mek	**(Siz) görün!**	*(You (pl)) see!*
uç mak	**(Siz) uçun!**	*(You (pl)) fly!*

In case the verb ends with a vowel, the connector letter "y" is added right before the imperative ending.

Examples:

söyle mek	**(Siz) söyle̲yin!**	*(You (pl)) tell!*
atla mak	**(Siz) atla̲yın!**	*(You (pl)) jump!*
uyu mak	**(Siz) uyu̲yun!**	*(You (pl)) sleep!*
yürü mek	**(Siz) yürü̲yün!**	*(You (pl)) walk!*

The verbs **gitmek, etmek** and **yemek** have a special spelling.

Examples:

git mek	**(Sen) git!**	**(Siz) gidin!**
to go	*(You) go!*	*(You (pl)) go!*
et mek	**(Sen) et!**	**(Siz) edin!**
to do or *to perform*	*(You) do!*	*(You (pl)) do!*
ye mek	**(Sen) ye!**	**(Siz) yiyin!**
to eat	*(You) eat!*	*(You (pl)) eat!*

olumsuz emir/rica ifadeleri the negative imperative

The negative imperative is formed by adding the negative imperative endings of **–me** or **–ma** right after the bare form of the verb.

The negative imperative ending **–me/-ma**, and the personal ending following is a 2 way vowel harmony meaning it changes depending on the preceding vowel.

Both possibilities of the negative imperative ending with the personal ending are given in the table below:

Last vowel of the preceding verb	a,ı, o, u			e,i, ö, ü		
the endings – me / -ma	(Sen)	-ma	*Don't*	(Sen)	-me	*Don't*
	(Siz)	-mayın	*Don't*	(Siz)	-meyin	*Don't*

Examples:

git mek	**(Sen) gitme!**	**(Siz) gitmeyin!**
to go	*(You) don't go!*	*(You (pl)) don't go!*
ye mek	**(Sen) yeme!**	**(Siz) yemeyin!**
to eat	*(You) don't eat!*	*(You (pl)) don't eat!*
iç mek	**(Sen) içme!**	**(Siz) içmeyin!**
to drink	*(You) don't drink!*	*(You (pl)) don't drink!*
bak mak	**(Sen) bakma!**	**(Siz) bakmayın!**
to look	*(You) don't look!*	*(You (pl)) don't look!*
gör mek	**(Sen) görme!**	**(Siz) görmeyin!**
to see	*(You) don't see!*	*(You (pl)) don't see!*
uç mak	**(Sen) uçma!**	**(Siz) uçmayın!**
to fly	*(You) don't fly!*	*(You (pl)) don't fly!*
söyle mek	**(Sen) söyleme!**	**(Siz) söylemeyin!**
to tell	*(You) don't tell!*	*(You (pl)) don't tell!*
atla mak	**(Sen) atlama!**	**(Siz) atlamayın!**
to jump	*(You) don't jump!*	*(You (pl)) don't jump!*
uyu mak	**(Sen) uyuma!**	**(Siz) uyumayın!**
to sleep	*(You) don't sleep!*	*(You (pl)) don't sleep!*
yürü mek	**(Sen) yürüme!**	**(Siz) yürümeyin!**
to walk	*(You) don't walk!*	*(You (pl)) don't walk!*

NB It's necessary to add **asla** or **sakın**, *never* in front of a negative imperative in case it's a warning.

Examples:

Asla / sakın atlama!	*Don't jump (because it's dangerous)!*
Asla / sakın atlamayın!	*Don't jump (because it's dangerous)!*
Asla / sakın suyu içme!	*Don't drink the water (because it's dangerous)!*
Asla / sakın suyu içmeyin!	*Don't drink the water (because it's dangerous)!*

Note that **asla** and **sakın** have similar meanings. However, **sakın** is more suitable for instant warnings.

Examples:

Sakın onu yeme!	*Don't eat this (because it's dangerous)!*
Sakın onu yemeyin!	*Don't eat this (because it's dangerous)!*
Asla fazla yeme!	*Don't eat much (because it's dangerous)!*
Asla fazla yemeyin!	*Don't eat much (because it's dangerous)!*

exercise 3

Form imperatives with the given clues. Use **sakın** or **asla** with the negatives. Use them in the conditional sentences as shown in the example.

Example:

Eğer Türkiye'ye giderseniz / Siz / İstanbul'u da görmek
If you go to Türkiye / You (pl) / to see İstanbul, too

> **Eğer Türkiye'ye giderseniz, İstanbul'u da görün.**
> *If you go to Türkiye, (you (pl)) see İstanbul, too.*

1. eğer açsan / sen / yemek sipariş etmek.   ....

2. eğer yağmur yağarsa / siz / evde kalmak.   ....

3. eğer çok paranız olursa / sen / yeni bir araba almak.   ....

4. eğer başarmak istersiniz / siz / çok çalışmak.   ....

5. eğer gelirsem / sen de / gelmek   ....

6. eğer kar yağarsa / siz / dışarı çıkmamak   ....

7. eğer kilo almak istemezsen / sen / fazla yememek   ....

zorunluluk ifadeleri expression of regulation

In Turkish, it's possible to express regulation by using the imperatives and the conjunctions **yoksa** or **aksi takdirde**, *otherwise.*

Examples:

Bu ilacı iç. Yoksa iyileşemezsin.
Take this medicine. Otherwise you can't get well.

Sakın dışarı kalın kıyafetler giymeden çıkma.
Don't get out without putting on warm clothes.

Derslerine iyi çalış. Aksi takdirde başarılı olamazsın.
Study your lessons well. Otherwise you can't be successful.

Asla geç yatma. Yoksa işe geç kalırsın.
Don't stay up late. Otherwise you'll be late to work.

Lütfen fazla yeme. Aksi takdirde kilo alırsın.
Please, don't eat much, otherwise you'll gain weight.

It's also possible to express regulation by using the same structure of giving advice. See Unit 4 for the construction.

NB It's common to add **kesinlikle** or **mutlaka,** *for sure* for the possitive and **kesinlikle**, or **asla**, *never* for the negative sentences. Note that **kesinlikle** can be used with negatives and positives. It's also important to put stress on the regulation sentence in order to distinguish it from an advice.

Examples:

Bu ilacı mutlaka / kesinlikle içmelisin.
You must take this medicine.

Dışarı kalın kıyafetler giymeden kesinlikle / asla çıkmamalısın.
You must not get out without putting on warm clothes.

Derslerine mutlaka / kesinlikle iyi çalışmalısın.
You must study you lessons well.

Asla / kesinlikle geç yatmamalısın.
You must not stay up late.

Asla / kesinlikle fazla yememelisin.
You must not eat much.

It's also possible to express regulation by using the adjective **zorunda**, *must* with an infinitive. Note that **zorunda** can be used in positives and negatives.

Examples:

Bu ilacı içmek zorundasın.
You must take this medicine.

Dışarı kalın kıyafetler giyerek çıkmak zorundasın.
You must get out by putting on warm clothes.

Derslerine çalışmak zorundasın.
You must study you lessons.

Geç yatmamak zorundasın.
You must not stay up late.

Fazla yememek zorundasın.
You must not eat much.

Bölüm 3
Part 3

ağrı ve sağlık sorunları pain and health problems

In Turkish, the following phrases are commonly used when talking about pain and health problems.

Ne şikayetiniz var?	*What's your complaint?*
Neyiniz var?	*What's your problem?*
Neden şikayetçisiniz?	*What are you complaining from?*
Nereniz ağrıyor?	*Where's the pain?*
Başım ağrıyor	*I have a headache.*
Başımda bir ağrı var	*There's a pain on my head.*
Başım dönüyor.	*I feel dizzy.*
Midem bulanıyor.	*I feel nausea.*
İstifra ettim.	*I vomitted.*
Çıkardım.	*I vomitted.*
Kustum.	*I vomitted.*
Öksürüyorum.	*I'm coughing.*
Öksürüğüm var.	*I have a cough.*
Ateşim var.	*I have fever.*
Ateşim yükseldi.	*I have a high fever.*
Ateşim çıktı.	*I have a high fever.*
Ateşim düştü.	*I don't have a high fever any longer. (It fell down.)*
İyi hissetmiyorum.	*I don't feel well.*
Fazla terliyorum.	*I perspire too much.*

Dialogue 3

eczanede at the pharmacy

The doctor examined İbrahim and checked his blood and urine test results. He ended up writing a prescription. He also urged him to call him immediately in case his situation gets worse.

Fazıl:	Hoş geldiniz. Geçmiş olsun. Reçetenize bakabilir miyim?
Michelle:	Buyurun.
Fazıl:	Bakalım. Evet, bir ağrı kesici, bir de ateş düşürücü yazıyor.
İbrahim:	Hepsi o kadar mı? Başka bir şey yok mu? Ben çok fenayım.
Fazıl:	İlaçlar çok tesirli. Sorun yok, endişelenmeyin.
Michelle:	İlaçları nasıl alacak?
Fazıl:	Bakalım. Evet, ağrı kesiciyi tok karnına günde üç kere, ateş düşürücüyü ise sabah kalkınca ve akşam yatarken.
İbrahim:	Tamam, harfiyen uyarım.
Fazıl:	Evet, harfiyen uymak zorundasınız yoksa iyileşemezsiniz. İlâçları tam saatinde alın. Sakın geciktirmeyin ve erken içmeyin aksi takdirde durumunuz daha kötü olur.

1. According to the pharmacist, will the medicine be helpful?
2. What may happen in case İbrahim won't take the medicine regularly?

In the dialogue above, we see the phrase of **tok karnına**, *to a full stomach.* It's also possible to say **aç karnına**, *to an empty stomach.* Thsese are the phrases common to hear while talking about taking pills or medicine.

Vocabulary

aç karnına	*when hungry*	**harfiyen**	*exactly*
ağrı kesici	*painkiller*	**reçete**	*prescription*
aksi takdirde	*otherwise*	**tesirli**	*effective*
ateş düşürücü	*antipyretic*	**tok karnına**	*when full*
endişelenmek	*to worry*	**uymak**	*to obey*
fena	*awful*	**zorunda**	*necessary*
Hepsi o kadar mı?		*Is that all?*	
Geçmiş olsun.		*Get well soon.*	

exercise 4

Which is the odd one out in each row?

ağrı kesici	ilaç	ateş düşürücü	zorunda
reçete	ilaç	doktor	harfiyen
halsiz	sağlıklı	hasta	yorgun
kan tahlili	acı	idrar tahlili	röntgen

Unit Fourteen: Ailemi özledim.

I missed my family.

With this unit, you will be able to:

- Talk about personality traits
- Make compliments
- Make deduction
- Use superlatives
- Use reflexive pronouns
- Talk about seasons, months of the year

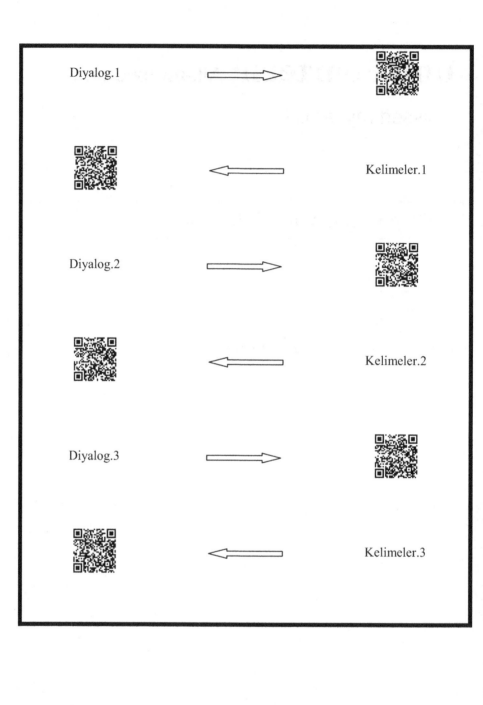

Diyalog.1 ⟹

Kelimeler.1 ⟸

Diyalog.2 ⟹

Kelimeler.2 ⟸

Diyalog.3 ⟹

Kelimeler.3 ⟸

Bölüm 1
Part 1

Dialogue 1

deniz kenarında yürüyüş a walk on the seaside

İbrahim feels better. They're taking a walk along the seaside. Michelle insisted him on getting fresh air.

Michelle:	İyi olmadı mı? Temiz hava alıyoruz. Hem biraz da hareket ediyorsun.
İbrahim:	Haklısın, çok iyi. Temiz hava bana iyi geldi. Daha iyiyim. Neredeyse tamamen iyileştim.
Michelle:	Çok iyi.
İbrahim:	Ayrıca ben senden özür dilemek istiyorum.
Michelle:	Neden? Ne oldu ki?
İbrahim:	Benim yüzümden otelde kaldık ve fazla gezemedik. Belki de biraz üşümüşümdür. Ama yine de hata bcnim. Bundan dolayı çok üzgünüm. Kusura bakma.
Michelle:	Hayatım, özür dileme lütfen. Olsun, ne güzel otelde dinlendik. Dinlenmek de tatilimizin bir parçası. Sen iyi ol. Önemli olan bu.
İbrahim:	Teşekkür ederim, Michelle. Çok anlayışlısın gerçekten.

1. What does İbrahim want to apologize for?
2. What's Michelle's response?

Vocabulary

bütün	*whole*	**neredeyse**	*almost*
gerçekten	*really*	**önemli**	*important*
hareket etmek	*to move, to be active*	**özür dilemek**	*to apologize*
hata	*fault*	**parça**	*part*
iyi gelmek	*to do good*	**temiz**	*clean*

kirli	*dirty*	yüzümden	*because of me*
Üzgünüm.	*I'm sorry.*		
Kusura bakma.	*Excuse me.*		
Ne oldu ki?	*What happened?*		

In the dialogue above, we see that **temiz,** *clean* is used for the air not **taze,** *fresh,* as in English. The opposite is **kirli** or **pis,** *polluted.*

Dialogue 2

arkadaşlar hakkında about the friends

Michelle and İbrahim liked the relationship of Sema and Lütfi.

İbrahim: Lütfi'yi çok beğendim. Çok beyefendi biri.

Michelle: Evet, Kesinlikle öyle. Sema'ya da kibar davranıyor.

İbrahim: Çok kibar birine benziyor, evet. Aynı zamanda arkadaş canlısı ve konuşkan. Üstüne, anlayışlı, düşünceli, samimi ve yakışıklı.

Michelle: Aynen. Sema da konuşkandır. Hem de çok güzel ve zarif bir kız.

İbrahim: İkisi de uyumlu. İyi anlaşıyor olmalılar.

Michelle: İkisi de uyumlu ve kibarlar. Ama senden daha uyumlu ve kibar olamazlar. Sen dünyanın en uyumlu ve en kibar insanısın.

İbrahim: Ve dünyanın en mutlu insanı benim çünkü dünyanın en güzel kadınıyla evliyim.

Michelle: İbrahim ... Beni şımartıyorsun. İltifat etme lütfen.

İbrahim: İltifat değil, canım, gerçek.

---

1. According to Michelle, who is more polite, İbrahim or Lütfi?
2. Why does İbrahim think that he's the happiest person in the world?

Vocabulary

anlaşmak	to agree	gerçek	reality
anlayışlı	considerate	iltifat etmek	to make a compliment
arkadaş canlısı	friendly	kızıl	scarlet
bekâr	single	konuşkan	talkative
beyefendi	gentleman	nişanlı	engaged
ciddî	serious	nişanlım	my fiance
dul	widow	nişanlım	my fiancee
dünya	world	samimi	sincere
düşünceli	thoughtful	sarışın	blond
esmer	brunette	şımartmak	to spoil
evli	married	yakışıklı	handsome
hanımefendi	lady	yalnız	alone
iltifat	compliment		

In the Dialogo above, İbrahim says, **...değil canım, ...** The phrase literally means *not like that darling, but like this.* However, it can be used with anyone when to attract his/her attention to the opposite direction. For example: **Otel o tarafta değil canım bu tarafta,** *The hotel is not on that direction darling, but on this direction,* **Bugün Salı değil canım Çarşamba,** *Today is not Tuesday darling, but it's Wednesday,* or **Saat beş değil canım altı,** *It's not five o'clock darling, but six o'clock,* etc.

exercise 1

Which is the odd one out in each row?

bekâr	nişanlı	evli	kızıl
dul	kızıl	sarışın	esmer
anlayışlı	hepsi	samimi	düşünceli
hayatım	tatlım	iltifat	canım

Bölüm 2
Part 2

dilbilgisi grammar

tahmin yürütme deduction, prediction

In Turkish, it is possible to express deduction or prediction by using the same structure of giving advice. See Unit 4 for the construction.

Examples:

Hava çok soğuk. Yağmur yağıyor olmalı.
It's very cold. It should / must be raining outside.

Eymen hiç çalışmadan başarılı oluyor. Çok zeki olmalı.
Eymen succeeds without studying. He should / must be very clever.

İbrahim ve Michelle odalarına şimdi girdiler. Odalarında olmalılar.
İbrahim and Michelle went in their room. They must be in their room.

Daha şimdi yemek yedin. Aç olmamalısın. Tok olmalısın.
You just ate. You shouldn't be hungry. You must be full.

Talha şimdi dinleniyor. Yorgun olmalı.
Talha is resting at the moment. He must be tired.

Çok çalıştınız. Artık Türkçe konuşuyor olmalısınız.
You studied hard. You should / must be speaking Turkish now.

exercise 2

Form a sentence expressing deduction or prediction with the given clues. Make the **–meli/-malı** type of prediction / deduction sentences.

Example: **İbrahim eşine çiçek alıyor. /kibar biri**
İbrahim is buying his wife flowers. / a kind person

> **İbrahim kibar biri olmalı.**
> *İbrahim should / must be a kind person.*

1.   **Kâmuran bahçede/sebzeleri sulamak**   ....
2.   **Fahriye mutfakta/yemek hazırlamak**   ....
3.   **Sema telefonda/nişanlısıyla konuşmak**   ....
4.   **İbrahim eczanede/hasta olmak**   ....
5.   **Michelle internette/annesine mesaj yazmak**   ....

It is possible to express deduction by using the same structure of expressing possibility. See Unit 5 for the construction.

Examples:

Hava çok soğuk. Yağmur yağabilir.
It's very cold. It could rain.

Eymen hiç çalışmadan başarılı oluyor. Çok zeki olabilir.
Eymen succeeds without studying. He could be very clever.

İbrahim ve Michelle odalarına şimdi girdiler. Odada olabilirler.
İbrahim and Michelle went in their room. They could be in the room.

Daha şimdi yemek yedin. Aç olmayabilirsin. Tok olabilirsin.
You just ate. You can't be hungry. You could be full.

Talha şimdi dinleniyor. Yorgun olabilir.
Talha is resting at the moment. He could be tired.

Çok çalıştınız. Artık Türkçe konuşuyor olabilirsiniz.
You studied hard. You could be speaking Turkish now.

exercise 3

Form sentences expressing deduction or prediction with the given clues.
Make the **–ebilmek** type of prediction / deduction sentences.

Example: **İbrahlm eşlne çiçek alıyor. /kibar biri**
İbrahim is buying his wife flowers. / a kind person

İbrahim kibar biri olabilir.
İbrahim could be a kind person.

1. **Kâmuran bahçede/sebzeleri sulamak**   ....
2. **Fahriye mutfakta/yemek hazırlamak**   ....
3. **Sema telefonda/nişanlısıyla konuşmak**   ....
4. **İbrahim eczanede/hasta olmak**   ....
5. **Michelle internette/annesine mesaj yazmak** ....

It's also possible to predict by using belki or belki de. In this form, it common to end the sentences with **–dir**. See Unit 2.

Examples:

Hava çok soğuk. Belki yağmur yağar.
It's very cold. Maybe, it will rain.
Hava çok soğuk. Belki de yağmur yağıyordur.
It's very cold. It might be raining outside.

İbrahim ve Michelle odalarına değil. Belki de dışarı çıktılar.
İbrahim and Michelle aren't in their room. Maybe they went out.

İbrahim ve Michelle odalarına değil. Belki de dışarıdalardır.
İbrahim and Michelle aren't in their room. Maybe they're outside.

Hiç yemek yemiyor. Belki de aç değildir. Belki de toktur.
He/She doesn't eat anything. Maybe he/she isn't hungry. Maybe, full.

Talha şimdi çalışmıyor. Belki de dinleniyordur.
Talha isn't studying at the moment. Maybe he's resting.

Bir arkadaş edinin. Belki de Türkçe konuşabiliyorsunuzdur.
Obtain a friend. Maybe you could speak Turkish.

exercise 4

Form three sentences expressing deduction or prediction with the given clues. Make the **-dir** type of prediction / deduction sentences.

Example:
İbrahim eşine çiçek alıyor. /kibar biri
İbrahim is buying his wife flowers. / a kind person

İbrahim belki de kibar biridir.
Maybe İbrahim is a kind person.

1. Kâmuran bahçede/sebzeleri sulamak   ....

2. Fahriye mutfakta/yemek hazırlamak   ....

3. Sema telefonda/nişanlısıyla konuşmak   ....

4. İbrahim eczanede/hasta olmak   ....

5. Michelle internette/annesine mesaj yazmak ....

kıyaslama the superlatives

In Turkish, the superlative form of the adjectives and adverbs is possible by using **"en"**, *the most / the least*. Examples:

Arkadaşlarımın içinde <u>en çok</u> İbrahim'i <u>en az</u> Kazım'ı severim.
I like İbrahim <u>the most</u> Kazım <u>the least</u> in my friends.

Talha ailedeki <u>en hızlı</u> şofördür.
Talha is <u>the fastest</u> driver in the family.

Türkçe <u>en kolay</u> dildir.
Turkish is <u>the easiest</u> language to learn.

Kahvaltı en sevdiğim öğündür.
I like breakfast the most.

Sınıfındaki kızların içinde en hızlı Serra okur.
Serra reads the fastest of the girls in class.

En çok uyumayı en az çalışmayı severim.
I like sleeping the most studying the least.

exercise 5

Form a sentence by using superlatives with the given clues.

Example:
İbrahim / bilmek / kibar
İbrahim / to know / kind

İbrahim bildiğim en kibar kişidir.
İbrahim is the kindest person I know.

1. **Kâmuran /en çok sevmek/ amca**   ....

2. **Fahriye /bilmek/ en iyi aşçı**   ....

3. **Sema telefonda/en çok/nişanlısıyla konuşmak**   ....

4. **Bugün/soğuk/gün**   ....

5. **Michelle /en çok özlemek/annesi**   ....

Bölüm 3
Part 3

dönüşlü zamirler the reflexive pronouns

The reflexive pronouns are necessary when the subject and the object are the same person.

Example:

Michelle aynada Michelle'i görüyor.
Michelle sees Michelle in the mirror.

As seen in the sentence above the subject (first Michelle) and the object (second Michelle) are the same person. Grammatically, this kind of sentences are accepted wrong. To correct, the the object (second Michelle in this example) should be changed into the reflexive pronoun. Therefore, the corrected sentence should read;

Michelle aynada <u>kendini</u> görüyor.
Michelle sees <u>herself</u> in the mirror.

Here in this example, **kendi**, *herself* is the reflexive pronoun for **o**, *she*. And, since the reflexive pronoun is in the object position in the sentence, it receives the accusative ending. See Unit 6 for the accusative form (the object of a sentence).

The full list of the reflexive pronouns are given in the table below:

(Ben)	**kendim**	*myself*
(Sen)	**kendin**	*yourself*
(O)	**kendi**	*himself / herself / itself*
(Biz)	**kendimiz**	*ourselves*
(Siz)	**kendiniz**	*yourselves*
(Onlar)	**kendileri**	*themselves*

There are several usages of the reflexive pronouns. One is using it in the accusative form.

Examples:

Aynada kendimi gördüm.   *I saw myself in the mirror.*

Kendini dinlemelisin.   *You have to listen to yourself.*

Kendine iyi bak.   *Take care of yourself.*

Gürültüden kendimizi duymuyoruz.   *We don't hear ourselves because of the noice.*

The reflexive pronouns can also be used to express that one is alone or not getting any help doing something.

Examples:

Evi kendim buldum.	*I found the house myself.*
O saçını kendi keser.	*He/She cuts his/her hair him/herself.*
Kendin öğren! Ben söylemem!	*(You) Figure (it) out yourself! I wont tell!*
Kendin pişir, kendin ye!	*Cook yourself, eat yourself!*

It's also possible to use the reflexive pronouns in this meaning by repeating them.

Examples:

Evi kendi kendime buldum.	*I found the house myself.*
Ali saçını kendi kendine keser.	*Ali cuts his hair himself.*
Kendi kendine öğren!	You figure out yourself!
Kendi kendine pişir, kendi kendine ye!	*Cook yourself, eat yourself!*

The reflexive pronouns can be used with some prepositions, too.

Examples:

Kendime elbise aldım.	*I bought myself a dress.*
Elbiseyi kendim için aldım.	*I bought the dress for myself.*
O kendinden korkar.	*He/She is afraid of him/herself.*
Benim kendimle bir sorunum yok.	*I don't have a problem with myself.*
Gerçeği önce kendine söylemelisin.	*You must tell the reality to yourself first.*

In Turkish, unlike English, it is possible to use the reflexive pronouns in the subject position.

Examples:

Talha üniversitede öğrencidir. Ayrıca kendisi çok çalışkandır.
Talha is a student in the university. And, he is very studious.

In this example, as you see, **kendisi**, *himself* is used in the subject position. However, it's not translated as *himself* but *he*. Then we can say that the sentence given below means the same:

Talha üniversitede öğrencidir. Ayrıca o çok çalışkandır.
Talha is a student in the university. And, he is very studious.

Serra lisede öğrenci. Ayrıca kendisi Arapça konuşur.
Serra is a student in the high school. And, she speaks Arabic, too.

Again in this example, **kendisi**, *herself* is used in the subject position. However, it's not translated as *herself* but s*he*. Then we can say that the sentence given below means the same:

Serra lisede öğrenci. Ayrıca o Arapça da konuşur.
Serra is a student in the high school. And, she speaks Arabic, too.

NB This usage is very common in Turkish. However, it is necessary that the listener understands who this *he* or *she* is. So, be sure to mention the person before starting a sentence with a reflexive pronoun.

Also note that using a reflexive pronoun in place of a subject pronoun is only possible for the 3rd singular person, **o**, *he, she, or it*.

exercise 6

Change the subject pronouns with reflexives. Use **aynı zamanda**, *at the same time* in your sentences.

Example:

Talha / şoför / öğrenci)
(Talha / driver / student)

> **Talha öğrenci. <u>Kendisi</u>, aynı zamanda, öğrenci.**
> *(Talha is a driver. At the same time, he's a student.)*

1.	İbrahim öğretmen. İbrahim yorgun.	4.	Eymen yaramaz. Eymen başarılı.
2.	Serra akıllı. Serra çalışkan.	5.	Annem muhasebeci Annem ev hanımı
3.	Otel büyük. Otel yeni.	6.	Anıtkabir merkezî. Anıtkabir yakın.

_____

_____

_____

_____

_____

_____

Dialogue 3

aile özlemi longing for the family

Michelle is sad that their vacation will end soon, but happy that she'll see her parents in a few days.

İbrahim:	Tatilimiz nasıldı?
Michelle:	Gayet tatil gibiydi. Gayet güzeldi. Turistik, tarihî, dinî ve kültürel bir çok mekân gördük. Aile dostlarımızla görüştük. Ama ailemi de çok özledim.
İbrahim:	Ve otelde dinlenmek zorunda kaldık ve sıkıldık. Benim hastalığımdan dolayı.
Michelle:	Hayır, İbrahim hiç sıkılmadık. Sen de bunu artık sorun etme.
İbrahim:	Aslında Türkiye'ye tatil için en güzel mevsimde, baharda geldik. Ne sıcak ne de soğuk.
Michelle:	Evet, ama Türkiye her mevsimde güzel. Kışın ayrı, yazın ayrı ve güzün ve baharda yapacak şeylerle dolu. Türkiye'de yaşasak hiç sıkılmayız.
İbrahim:	Evet, dört mevsim de çok güzeldir. Ayrıca, biliyor musun? Bazı yerlerde dört mevsimi aynı anda yaşayabilirsin.
Michelle:	İbrahim, ne dersin, yıl sonuna doğru meselâ Aralık ayında veya Ocak'ta tekrar Türkiye'ye gelelim mi? Hem o tarihte Sema'nın düğünü var.
İbrahim:	"Çok iyi bir fikir" derim.

1. Is İbrahim still sorry for causing them to stay in the hotel?
2. Do they agree to come back to Türkiye again soon?

Vocabulary

bahar	spring	kültürel	cultural
dinî	religious	mekân	site
dost	friend	mevsim	season
düğün	wedding	sıkılmak	to get bored
güz	fall	son bahar	fall
güzün	in the fall	sorun etmek	to trouble

ilk bahar	*spring*	tarihî	*historic*
kış	*winter*	yaz	*summer*
kışın	*in the winter*	yazın	*in the summer*
özlemek	*to miss, long for*	zorunda kalmak	*to have to*
Gayet tatil gibiydi.		*It was quite a vacation.*	

In the dialogue above, both **gördük**, *we saw* and **görüştük**, *we saw each other*, mean *to visit*, **ziyaret etmek**. Therefore, it's also possible to say **... bir çok mekân ziyaret ettik** and **aile dostlarımızı ziyaret ettik**. But please note that, in this case the accusative case becomes necessary, i.e. **aile dostlarımızla** görüştük and **aile dostlarımızı ziyaret ettik**.

Also note that some seasons have spelling specialties, i.e. **yaz**, *summer*, **yazın**, *in the summer*, **kış**, *winter*, **kışın**, *in the winter*, and **güz**, *fall*, **güzün**, *in the fall*, but **bahar** or **ilk bahar**, *spring*, **baharda** or **ilk baharda**, *in the spring* but not ~~baharın~~.

exercise 7

List the names of the personality traits and seasons you have learned in this lesson into two groups below. Then check your work with the vocabulary section of this lesson.

Example: personality   season
                     samimi   yaz-yazın

_____

_____

_____

_____

Unit Fifteen: İyi yolculuklar!

Have a nice trip!

With this unit, you will be able to:

- Buy airline tickets
- Ask for permission
- Give permission
- Express prohibition
- Use the passive voice
- Express general opinions
- Say goodbye

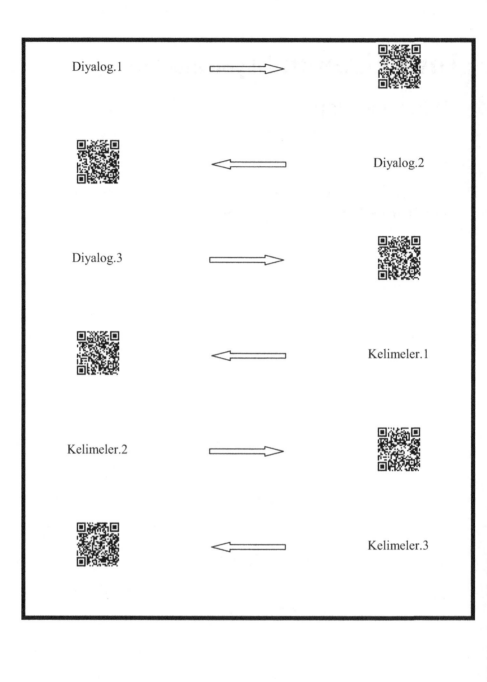

Bölüm 1
Part 1

Dialogue 1

uçak biletleri the flight tickets

İbrahim calls an agency to buy their flight tickets.

Hüsnü:	Merhaba, Son-Durak Seyâhat. Ben, Hüsnü. Size nasıl yardımcı olabilirim?
İbrahim:	Merhaba, ismim İbrahim Korkmaz. Londra'ya bilet almak istiyorum.
Hüsnü:	Tabii İbrahim Bey. Kaç kişilik olacak?
İbrahim:	İki.
Hüsnü:	Tarih? Ne zamana istiyorsunuz?
İbrahim:	Ayın dördüne.
Hüsnü:	İbrahim Bey, ayın dördünde uçakların hepsi dolu. Başka hangi güne istersiniz? Ertesi gün olur mu, meselâ?
İbrahim:	Olur olur. Biletler ne kadar ve nasıl ödeyeceğim? Ve biletleri nasıl alacağım?
Hüsnü:	İbrahim Bey, isterseniz kredi kartınızdan ödeme yapabilirsiniz ve biletinizi biz otelinize getiririz. Ya da biletinizi internet üzerinden veririz, böylece bilet almadan yani elektronik biletle uçağa binebilirsiniz.

1. Can they get on the plane that they planned?
2. How can İbrahim receive the tickets?

In the dialogue above, notice the usage of **hangi güne**. It's also possible to say **hangi gün için?**, *for which day?*

exercise 1

Write the opposite of the adjectives.

boş	_____	yavaş	_____
önce	_____	ince	_____
geç	_____	kalabalık	_____
sağlıklı	_____	ilk	_____
evli	_____	aç	_____
ıslak	_____	sıcak	_____
uzun	_____	iyi	_____
üzgün	_____	az	_____
genç	_____	dar	_____
küçük	_____	üst	_____
ağır	_____	ileri	_____
acı	_____	birlikte	_____
şekersiz	_____	sesli	_____
aynı	_____	geçici	_____

Dialogue 2

gidiş terminali departure terminal

Michelle and İbrahim stayed at Kâmuran and Fahriye's house for the extra night. They prepared the guest room for them. On the flight day, Sema and Lütfi took them to the airport. While the others are having a conversation in the departure terminal, İbrahim is at the counter fixing the check-in procedures.

İbrahim:	Merhabalar, hanımefendi. Eşim ve kendim için biletimiz var. İnternet üzerinden aldım.
Hafize:	Evet, beyefendi. Kimlikleriniz ve pasaportlarınız lütfen.
İbrahim:	Buyurun.
Hafize:	Bilet referans numaranız?
İbrahim:	858513 (seksen beş seksen beş on üç).
Hafize:	Bagajınız var mı? Yoksa eşyanızı yanınıza mı alacaksınız?
İbrahim:	Şu bavulu vermek istiyorum. Bu valizi içeri alabilir miyim?
Hafize:	Hayır efendim. Yanınıza sadece el çantalarınızı alabilirsiniz. Büyük valizleri buraya teslim etmek zorundasınız.

1. What does the teller want to see?
2. Can they take every luggage into the the plane with them?

Note that in Turkish, the numbers are usually pronounced two digits at a time.

Also note that **teslim etmek** and **vermek** mean the same.

exercise 2

Write the opposite of the verbs.

binmek	_____	hastalanmak	_____
gitmek	_____	çıkmak	_____
satmak	_____	ayrılmak	_____
uzanmak	_____	uyumak	_____
oturmak	_____	dinlemek	_____
ateşi yükselmek	_____	yatmak	_____

Bölüm 2
Part 2

dilbilgisi grammar

izin verme giving permission

In Turkish, it's possible to ask for and give permission by using the same structure as expressing ability and possibility. See Unit 5 for the construction. It's possible to add **tabii ki,** *sure* at the beginning of the positive responses.

Examples:

Bu suyu içebilir miyim?	*Can I drink the water?*
Tabii ki bu suyu içebilirsin / içebilirsiniz.	*Sure, you can drink the water.*
Dışarı çıkabilir miyim?	*Can I go out?*
Tabii ki dışarı çıkabilirsin / çıkabilirsiniz.	Sure, y*ou can go out.*
Bugün geç yatabilir miyiz?	*Can we stay up late today?*
Tabii ki bugün geç yatabilirsiniz.	*Sure, you can stay up late today.*

yasaklama expressing prohibition

In Turkish, it's possible to express prohibition by using the same structure as expressing ability and possibility in a negative way. See Unit 5 for the construction. Note that in these type of sentences, the listener is **sen**, *you* or **siz**, *you (pl)* since you talk to a person directly.

Examples:

Bu suyu içemezsin / içemezsiniz.   *You cannot drink the water.*

Bugün dışarı çıkamazsın / çıkamazsınız.   *You cannot go out.*

Asla geç yatamazsın / yatamazsınız.   *You can never stay up late.*

NB It's common to add **kesinlikle, sakın** or **asla**, *never* for the prohibition. It's also important to put stress on the regulation sentence in order to distinguish it from an advice.

exercise 3

Give a negative response to the questions below. Add **kesinlikle** at the beginning of your responses.

Example: **Bir bardak çay alabilir miyim?**
                Can I take a glass of tea?

                               Kesinlikle bir bardak çay alamazsın.
                               You can never take a glass of tea.

1.   **Bugün sizde kalabilir miyim?**   ....
2.   **Sizinle Türkçe konuşabilir miyim?**   ....
3.   **İşten bugün biraz erken çıkabilir miyim?**   ....
4.   **Sana bir şey söyleyebilir miyim?**   ....
5.   **Buraya biraz uzanabilir miyim?**   ....

It's also possible to express prohibition by using negative imperative.

Examples:

Bunu sakın yemeyin.   *Don't eat this.*

Buradan asla atlamayın.   *Don't jump from here.*

Sakın bu suyu içme.   *Don't drink the water.*

Oraya asla gitmeyin.   *Don't go there.*

exercise 4

Give a negative response to the questions by using negative imperatives.
Add **sakın** at the beginning of your responses.

Example: **Bu çayı içebilir miyim?**
                     Can I drink the tea?

                                        Hayır, sakın o çayı içme.
                                        No, don't drink the tea.

1. **Bugün size gelebilir miyim?**   ....

2. **Sizinle bir şey konuşabilir miyim?**   ....

3. **Bugün eve biraz erken gidebilir miyim?**   ....

4. **Sana bir hediye alabilir miyim?**   ....

5. **Buraya oturabilir miyim?**   ....

Bölüm 3
Part 3

Dialogue 3

İyi yolculuklar! Have a nice flight!

İbrahim came back and entered the conversation. They have only a few minutes left before the time they have to be at the departure gate.

Sema:	Geldiğiniz için çok memnun olduk. Çok sevindik.
Lütfi:	Ben de tanıştığımıza çok memnun oldum.
İbrahim:	Biz de, çok sağolun.
Michelle:	Ayrıca, nişanınızı tekrar tebrik ediyoruz. Birbirinize çok yakışıyorsunuz.
Sema:	Düğünümüze de bekliyoruz ama. Mutlaka gelin.
Michelle:	Hiç gelmez olur muyuz, canım? Siz bizim kardeşimizsiniz. Hâttâ bizimkiler de gelmek ister mutlaka.
Sema:	Onları da bekliyoruz. Çok selâm söyleyin.
Lütfi:	Hep birlikte bekliyoruz.
Michelle:	Tabii, söyleriz. Hoşçakalın.
İbrahim.:	Hoşçakalın. Görüşmek üzere.
Sema:	İyi uçuşlar. Hayırlı yolculuklar. Güle güle.
Lütfi:	İyi yolculuklar. Güle güle.

1. According to Michelle, do Sema and Lütfi match each other?
2. Will Michelle's parents also come to the wedding?

Vocabulary

bagaj	*luggage*	**Londra**	*London*
cüzdan	*wallet or purse*	**referans numarası**	*reference number*
el çantası	*hand bag*	**tarih**	*date*

kimlik	*identification*	teslim etmek	*to give*
kimlik kartı	*identification card*	vermek	*to give*
kredi kartı	*credit card*	yatmak	*to go to bed*
tebrik etmek	*to congratulate*	yatmamak	*to stay up*
pasaport	*passport*	yakışmak	*to match with*
internet üzerinden	*on the internet*		

In the dialogue above, Michelle says, **Hiç gelmez olur muyuz?** It can be translated as *Will we not come?*. But it's used to say **Of course we'll come!** Note that in Turkish, it's possible to encounter the negative questions often. And in some occasions, like the one given above, the questions are not used for getting information instead making confirmation. Just like tag questions which are also used to confirm the said information.

Note that tag questions are formed by adding **değil mi?** at the end of the posititive sentences. The tag questions can be used with any tense. In addition, the tag addition is the same for all the subject pronouns. Finally, it's necessary to place **a rising intonation** at the end of the tag questions.

Examples:

O arkadaşın, değil mi?   *He/She is your friend, isn't he/she?*

Yemek yeriz, değil mi?   *We'll eat, won't we?*

Mutlusunuz, değil mi?   *You're happy, aren't you?*

Gittiler, değil mi?   *They went, didn't they?*

Bölüm 4
Part 4

edilgen çatı the passive voice

In Turkish, there are two ways to form passive sentences.

"n" edilgen fiiller passive verbs with "n"

In Turkish, some transitive verbs (verbs which take an object in a sentence) have both active and passive versions. Even though the passive versions may be derived from the active ones, it is also possible to find these kind of passive verbs in the dictionary. You can easily spot them with the letter "**n**" right before the infinitive suffixes –**mek** or –**mak**. Some of these type passive verbs are given together with the active versions in the chart below for example:

"n" Verbs

Active Verbs		Passive Verbs	
almak	*to take*	**alınmak**	*to be taken*
başlamak	*to start*	**başlanmak**	*to be started*
beklemek	*to wait*	**beklenmek**	*to be waited*
aramak	*to call*	**aranmak**	*to be called*
bilmek	*to know*	**bilinmek**	*to be known*
bulmak	*to find*	**bulunmak**	*to be found*
hatırlamak	*to remember*	**hatırlanmak**	*to be remembered*
istemek	*to want*	**istenmek**	*to be wanted*
okumak	*to read*	**okunmak**	*to be read*
özlemek	*to miss*	**özlenmek**	*to be missed*
tanımak	*to recognize*	**tanınmak**	*to be recognized*
taşımak	*to move*	**taşınmak**	*to be moved*
ycmck	*to eat*	**yenmek**	*to be eaten*

Some examples with the active (A) and passive verbs (P):

(A) İbrahim yemeğini yedi.	*İbrahim ate his meal.*
(P) Yemek (İbrahim tarafından) yendi.	*The meal was eaten (by İbrahim).*

(A) Michelle ailesini özlüyor.	*Michelle is missing her family.*
(P) Ailesi (Michelle tarafından) özleniyor.	*Her family is being missed (by Michelle).*

(A) Ali Talha ve Serra'yı tanıyor.	*Ali recognizes Talha and Serra.*
(P) Talha ve serra (Ali tarafından) tanınıyor.	*Talha and Serra are recognized (by Ali).*

(A) Geçen yıl beş kitap okudum.	*I read five books last year.*
(P) Beş kitap geçen yıl (benim tarafımdan) okundu.	*Five books were read (by me).*

(A) Bu ay evinizi taşıyacaksınız.	*You'll move your house this month.*
(P) Eviniz bu ay (sizin tarafınızdan) taşınacak.	*Your house will be moved this month (by you).*

(A) Uçak bileti almalıyız.	*We have to buy the flight ticket.*
(P) Uçak bileti bizim tarafımızdan alınmalı.	*The flight ticket has to be bought (by us).*

Note that when the subject of the active sentence is mentioned in the passive sentence as the doer, it is necessary to turn the subject pronouns to the possessives.

Examples:

Incorrect	**Correct**
ben tarafından	benim tarafımdan
sen tarafından	senin tarafından
biz tarafından	bizim tarafımızdan

Example:

(Incorrect)   Çay ben tarafından içildi.

(Correct)   **Çay benim tarafımdan içildi.**   *The tea was drunk (by me).*

NB Not all the verbs with the letter "**n**" right before the infinitive suffix belong to this group, e.g. **dinlemek**, *to listen*, and **dinlenmek**, *to rest*. Therefore, it is important to look up in the dictionary first before using it in active or passive sentences.

"-il" edilgen fiiller passive verbs with "-il"

In Turkish, not all the transitive verbs have a passive version as mentioned previously. Then it is necessary to derive passive verbs from active ones. It is possible to turn the verbs into the passive form by adding the ending **–il / -ıl / -ul / ül** to the bare form of the verb. Note that these type of passive verbs may not be given/found in the dictionary.

The the ending **–il / -ıl / -ul / ül** changes depending on the last vowel of the verb.

Last vowel of the verb	a,ı	e,i	o,u	ö,ü
The ending –il / -ıl / -ul / ül	-ıl	-il	-ul	-ül

Examples:

"I" Verbs

Active Verbs

içmek	*to drink*
duymak	*to hear*
görmek	*to see*
satmak	*to sell*

Passive Verbs

içilmek	*to be drunk*
duyulmak	*to be heard*
görülmek	*to be seen*
satılmak	*to be sold*

Some examples with the active (A) and passive verbs (P):

(A) İbrahim çayını içti.   *İbrahim drank his tea.*
(P) Çay (İbrahim tarafından) içildi.   *The tea was drunk (by İbrahim).*

(A) Michelle Serra'yı gördü.   *Michelle saw Serra.*
(P) Serra (Michelle tarafından) görüldü.   *Serra was seen (by Michelle).*

(A) Ali Talha ve Serra'yı duydu.   *Ali heard Talha and Serra.*
(P) Talha ve Serra (Ali tarafından) duyuldu. *Talha and Serra were heard (by Ali).*

exercise 5

Change the active sentences into passive and change the passive sentences into active sentences. Use **ben** as the subject pronoun in the active sentences.

Examples:

Çay içildi.
The tea was drunk.

Ben çayı içtim.
I drank the tea.

Denizi göreceğim.
I'll see the sea.

Deniz görülecek.
The sea will be seen (by me).

1. **Anahtar bulundu.**   ....

2. **Eşyalar taşınacak.**   ....

3. **Arkadaşımı davet ettim.** ....

4. **Yemek pişirilecek.**   ....

5. **Arabamı sattım.**   ....

genel fikir belirtme expressing general opinions

In Turkish, it's possible to express general opinions by forming sentences without a definite subject. Therefore, in these type of sentences, **herkes**, *everyone* is considered the subject. Note that **–il type passive verbs** are used in these type of sentences.

Examples:

Bu suyu içilir mi?
Can everyone drink the water? / Is the water drinkable?

Tabii ki bu su içilebilir.
Sure, everyone can drink the water. / The water is drinkable.

Tatilde ne yapılır?
What everyone should / could do on vacation?

Tatilde gezilir ve yeni yerler görülür.
Everyone should / could take a trip and see new places on vacation.

Mutfakta ne yapılır?
What everyone should / could do in the kitchen?

Mutfakta yemek pişirilir.
Everyone should / could cook food in the kitchen.

Unit Sixteen: İpin Ucunu Kaçıran İnsanlar Romanından Alıntılar-1

Excerpts from the Novel **İpin Ucunu Kaçıran İnsanlar-1**

In this unit you will find:

- An authentic text from a published Turkish novel

With this unit, you will be able to:

- Capture meaning from context with / without using a dictionary
- Use the –miş past tense

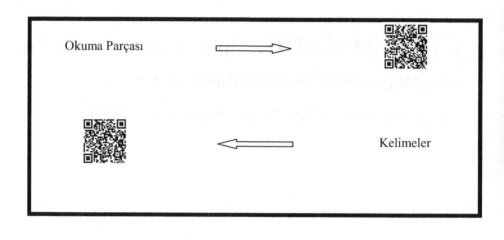

Okuma Parçası

Kelimeler

Bölüm 1
Part 1

Okuma parçası 1 / Reading Text 1

Büyük bir deponun kapısının ardında pusuya geçti, belinden tabancasını çıkardı ve etrafa bir göz attıktan sonra çok yavaş, sessiz ve dikkatli bir şekilde kapıyı araladı. Kapının ince gıcırtısı onu rahatsız etti ve yüzünü ekşiterek fevrî bir hareketle elini kulağına götürdü. Rahatsızlığı geçtikten sonra önce sağ sonra sol ayağını yavaşça içeri soktu ve tabancası elinde etrafı incelemeye girişti.

Dünya üzerinde sayılı birçok bankanın sitesini *hack*leyip müşterilerin kişisel bilgilerini ele **geçirmiş** ve bununla da kalmayıp üstüne bu bankaları **soymuş** çok uluslu bir çeteyi çökertme görevi için orada bulunuyordu. Çete üyelerini tutuklayıp adalete teslim etmesi gerekiyordu ki bunun için günlerdir doğru dürüst uyumadan **çalışmıştı**.

Tüm depoyu dolaştı ama bir tek kimseyle bile karşılaşmadı. Aldığı ihbar ve istihbarat, çetenin o depoda gizlendikleri yönündeydi. Elini kaldırdı ve parmaklarının ucuyla alnının üzerine gelmiş koyu kahverengi saçlarını kenara attı. İşaret ve orta parmağını dudağına götürerek ne olup bittiğini tekrar zihninden geçirdi. Hadi diyelim ki ihbarlar asılsızdı ama sonrasında yürütülen istihbarat çalışmasının yanlış olma ihtimali yoktu. Cebinden telefonunu çıkardı ve amirini aradı.

- Abi, burası bomboş. Kimse yok. Tuhaf bir koku alıyorum ama.

- Yok, yok. Her şey yolunda. Az önce Trinity ile konuştum. **Yoldalarmış**. Şimdi biz de gelip pusu kuracağız.

- Tamamdır abi. Bekliyorum.

Saniyeler içinde baştan aşağı siyah **giyinmiş** gözlüklü on beş kişilik bir ekip içeri girdi ve depoda bulunan eşyaların arkalarına saklandılar. Deponun içi kapkaranlıktı, âdeta göz gözü görmüyordu. Dışarıdan araba sesleri duyulunca herkes tabancasının horozunu çekti ve pür dikkat kesildi. Kapının aralandığını duyar duymaz nefeslerini tuttular. Kapı iyice açılıp da pusudan habersiz çete üyeleri içeri girince etraf birden aydınlandı ve namlular suçluların şaşkın yüzlerine doğrultuldu. Çete lideri, küfürler ederek bağırıyor ve kaçacak bir gedik arıyordu ancak bütün çabası nafileydi. Başarılı bir baskındı. Bütün çete üyeleri tutuklandı ve karakola sevk edildi.

1. Who do the police try to catch?
2. Did the police succeed in the operation?

Vocabulary

adalet	*justice*	ihbar	*notice*
âdeta	*almost*	istihbarat	*intelligence*
alın	*forehead*	işaret parmağı	*forefinger*
amir	*chief*	kapkaranlık	*full darkness*
aralamak	*to open*	karakol	*police station*
asılsız	*unfounded*	kişisel	*personal*
atmak	*to throw*	lider	*leader*
baskın	*raid*	müşteri	*customer*
bel	*waist*	nafile	*futile*
bomboş	*empty*	namlu	*barrel*
çaba	*effort*	orta parmak	*middle finger*
çete	*gang*	pusu	*ambush*
çökertmek	*to smash*	saklanmak	*to hide*
depo	*warehouse*	sevk edilmek	*to be sent*
doğrultmak	*to point at*	site	*site*
dudak	*lip*	tabanca	*pistol*
ele geçirmek	*to capture*	tabancanın horozu	*cock of a gun*
etraf	*surrounding*	teslim etmek	*to deliver*
fevrî	*impulsive*	tutuklamak	*to arrest*
gıcırtı	*creak*	tutuklanmak	*to be arrested*
girişmek	*to engage in*	ulus	*nation*
gizlenmek	*to hide*	üstüne	*over something*
görev	*task*	üye	*member*
göz atmak	*to take a glance*		

yüzünü ekşitmek	*to grimace*
bununla kalmamak	*not to stop there*
çok uluslu	*multinational*
doğru dürüst	*properly*
yönünde olmak	*to point*
ne olup bittiğini	*what's going on*
zihninden geçirmek	*to think*
yürütülen çalışmalar	*studies carried out*
pusu kurmak	*to ambush*
baştan aşağı	*all over*
göz gözü görmemek	*to be unable to see anything*
pür dikkat kesilmek	*to pay close attention*
duyar duymaz	*not later than*
nefesini tutmak	*to hold the breath*
küfür etmek	*to swear, to curse*
kaçacak bir gedik aramak	*to look for a place to hide*

Bölüm 2
Part 2

anahtar dilbilgisi ipuçları key grammar points

-mişli geçmiş zaman the -miş past tense

NB The –miş past tense is not in the scope of this book which is addressed to learners at the beginner level. However, the meaning and the construction of the –miş past tense is given here generally to give the learner an idea.

In Turkish, there are two types of past tense. The –di past tense (*See Unit 7 for the past tense construction*) and the –miş past tense. They both mean the same. However, the former has a meaning that the speaker has witnessed the action while the latter has a meaning that the speaker has not witnessed the action.

NB Since the –miş past tense has a meaning of not witnessing the mentioned action, it is more suitable for reporting. In other words, the –miş past tense is usually used for <u>only the 3rd persons</u>. (*However, it's also possible to use it with other persons.*)

For the construction of <u>the 3rd singular person</u>, the ending **-miş** is a 4 way vowel harmony, meaning **-miş** can change to **-miş / -mış / -muş / -müş**, depending on the preceding vowel.

Last vowel of the preceding word	a,ı	e,i	o,u	ö,ü
the ending -miş (x4)	-mış	-miş	-muş	-müş

Examples:

söyle mek	**Çocuk söylemiş.**	*The child told. (I didn't see.)*
atla mak	**Çocuk atlamış.**	*The child jumped. (I didn't see.)*
uyu mak	**Çocuk uyumuş.**	*The child slept. (I didn't see.)*
yürü mek	**Çocuk yürümüş.**	*The child walked. (I didn't see.)*

For the construction of <u>the 3rd plural person</u>, the ending **-mişler** is a 4 way vowel harmony, meaning **-mişler** can change to **-mişler / -mışlar / -muşlar / -müşler**, depending on the preceding vowel.

Examples:

söyle mek	**Çocuklar söylemişler.**	*The children told. (I didn't see.)*
atla mak	**Çocuklar atlamışlar.**	*The children jumped. (I didn't see.)*
uyu mak	**Çocuklar uyumuşlar.**	*The children slept. (I didn't see.)*
yürü mek	**Çocuklar yürümüşler.**	*The children walked. (I didn't see.)*

NB It is also possible to use the –miş past tense with the adjective and noun complements (the sentences without a verb). Since the –miş past tense has a meaning of not witnessing the mentioned action, it is more suitable for reporting. In other words, the –miş past tense is usually used for only the 3rd persons. (*However, it's also possible to use it with other persons.*)

For the construction, the endings are added to the adjectives and nouns. Please have the vowel change in mind. Also * note that the connector letter "y" is necessary in case the last letter is a vowel.

Examples:

Serra çalışkanmış.	*Serra was studious/hardworking.*
Talha erkenciymiş*.	*Talha was early.*
Can oyuncuymuş*.	*Can was an actor.*
Talha şoförmüş.	*Talha was a driver.*
Onlar Almanmış.	*They were German.*

Unit Seventeen: İpin Ucunu Kaçıran İnsanlar Romanından Alıntılar-2

Excerpts from the Novel **İpin Ucunu Kaçıran İnsanlar-2**

In this unit you will find:

- An authentic text from a published Turkish novel

With this unit, you will be able to:

- Capture meaning from context with / without using a dictionary
- Use the compound tenses-1

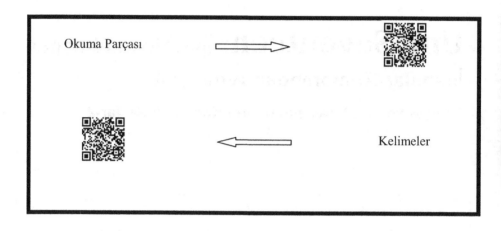

Bölüm 1
Part 1

Okuma parçası 1 / Reading Text 1

Osman resmen dükkândan kovulmuştu. Gururu incinmişti. Artık bu mahallede yaşayamazdı. Herkes onunla dalga geçecekti. Mahallenin utanç kaynağı olmuştu. Oradan ayrılmalıydı. Koşarak yurduna gitti. Herkes yemekhanede aşçı Salih'in yaptığı yemeklerden yiyordu. Odasına çıktı ve eşyalarını topladı. Gözlerinden yaşlar akıyordu. Gururu incinmişti; kaldığı yurdundan da ayrılmak zorundaydı. Çantasını aldı ve kimseye gözükmeden aşağıya indi. Kapıyı sessizce açtı ve kendini yağmurlu sokaklara attı. Sokakta koşuyordu. Nereye gideceğini bilemiyordu ama koşuyordu. Böylesi daha iyiydi. Bu mahalleden kurtulmak zorundaydı. Koştu, koştu, koştu. Dakikalarca koştu. Artık koşamıyordu. Bacağına kramp girmişti. Yere oturdu ve bacağındaki ağrının geçmesini bekledi. Oturduğu yerde düşünmeye başladı. Acaba abartmış mıydı; fazla mı tepki vermişti? Düşündükçe, düşünmeye devam ettikçe kendine sinirleniyordu. Başını sinirle kaşıdı; evet, abartmıştı. Ne olmuştu yani bir internet kafe sahibi onu kovduysa? Bir daha gitmezdi oraya, olay çözülürdü. Yaptığı yanlışı anlamıştı ancak yurda geri dönemezdi. Bir kere eşyalarını alıp orayı terk etmişti. Bir daha oraya gidemezdi.

Nasıl böyle bir şey olabilirdi? Nasıl olur da saçma sapan bir sebep yüzünden yurdundan ve mahallesinden olmuştu? Ona ne oluyordu? Kimse onu sevmiyordu. Kimse sevmemişti. Artık Orhan da yoktu. Yapayalnızdı.

---

1. Did Osman regret his decision to leave the dorm?
2. How did Osman feel at the end?

Vocabulary

abartmak	exaggerate	kurtulmak	to run away
bacak	leg	resmen	officially
böylesi	such	sinirlenmek	to get angry
dakikalarca	for minutes	yapayalnız	all alone

Turkish	English	Turkish	English
kaşımak	*to scratch*	**yemekhane**	*dining hall*
kovmak	*to fire*	**yurt**	*dorm*
kovulmak	*to get fired*		
bir sebep yüzünden	*for a reason*		
bir şeyden olmak	*to lose something*		
dalga geçmek	*to make fun of*		
fazla tepki vermek	*to overreact*		
gözlerinden yaşlar akmak	*to have tears in the eyes*		
gururu incinmek	*to feel his pride is hurt*		
kimseye gözükmeden	*without being seen by anyone*		
kramp girmek	*to have a cramp*		
Nasıl olur?	*How come?*		
Ne olmuştu yani?	*So what happened?*		
olay çözmek	*to solve a case*		
olayın çözülmesi	*solution of a case*		
saçma sapan	*nonesense*		
terk etmek	*to leave a place*		
utanç kaynağı	*embarrassment*		
yanlış anlamak	*to misunderstand*		

Bölüm 2
Part 2

anahtar dilbilgisi ipuçları key grammar points

bileşik zamanlar compound tenses

NB The compound tenses are not in the scope of this book which is addressed to learners at the beginner level. However, the meaning and the construction of the compound tenses are given here generally to give the learner an idea.

In Turkish, apart from the simple tenses, there are also compound tenses, that is, the tenses made up two simple tenses. In this structure, the first tense may be the present progressive tense, the present tense, or the future tense. And the second tense is always the past tense.

The compound tenses are used to talk about past progressive actions, past habits / intentions, and future intentions respectively.

In other words;

Comp. Tense No	First Tense	Second Tense	Meaning
1	the present progressive tense	the –di past tense	**past progressive actions**
2	the present tense	the –di past tense	**past habits / intentions**
3	the future tense	the –di past tense	**future intentions**

For the construction, the verb is conjugated for the 3rd singular person, **o**, *he / she / it* in the present progressive tense or in the present tense, or in the future tense (*See Unit 3 for the present progressive and present tense and Unit 9 for the future tense constructions*). Then the past tense personal ending is added to form a compound tense (*See Unit 7 for the past tense construction*).

To form a compound tense, two steps are needed.

STEP 1

First, the verb is conjugated for the 3rd singular person (**o**, *he / she / it*). <u>Have the vowel change in mind throughout the construction</u>.

Examples:

The verb is conjugated for the 3rd <u>singular person (**o**, *he / she / it*)</u>.

Examples: **çalışmak** & **gelmek**

Çalışıyor	*He / she is working*	**Geliyor**	*He / she is coming*
Çalışır	*He / she works*	**Gelir**	*He / she comes*
Çalışacak	*He / she will work*	**Gelecek**	*He / she will come*

STEP 2

Then, the personal endings are added to the end to form a compound tense. The personal endings of the compound tense are given for each person below:

Compound Tense. 1 (past progressive actions)

çalışmak (the present progressive tense)

(Ben)	çalışıyor	dum	*I was working*
(Sen)	çalışıyor	dun	*You were working*
(O)	çalışıyor	du	*He / She was working*
(Biz)	çalışıyor	duk	*We were working*
(Siz)	çalışıyor	dunuz	*You (pl) were working*
Onlar	çalışıyor	du / lardı	*They were working*

gelmek (the present progressive tense)

(Ben)	geliyor	dum	*I was coming*
(Sen)	geliyor	dun	*You were coming*
(O)	geliyor	du	*He / She was coming*
(Biz)	geliyor	duk	*We were coming*
(Siz)	geliyor	dunuz	*You (pl) were coming*
Onlar	geliyor	du / lardı	*They were coming*

Compound Tense. 2 (past habits / intentions)

çalışmak (the present tense)

(Ben)	çalışır	dım	*I would / used to work*
(Sen)	çalışır	dın	*You would / used to work*
(O)	çalışır	dı	*He / She would / used to work*
(Biz)	çalışır	dık	*We would / used to work*
(Siz)	çalışır	dınız	*You (pl) would / used to work*
Onlar	çalışır	dı / lardı	*They would / used to work*

gelmek (the present tense)

(Ben)	gelir	dim	*I would / used to come*
(Sen)	gelir	din	*You would / used to come*
(O)	gelir	di	*He / She would / used to come*
(Biz)	gelir	dik	*We would / used to come*
(Siz)	gelir	diniz	*You (pl) would / used to come*
Onlar	gelir	di / lerdi	*They would / used to come*

Compound Tense. 3 (future intentions)

çalışmak (the future tense)

(Ben)	çalışacak	tım	*I was (going) to work*
(Sen)	çalışacak	tın	*You were (going) to work*
(O)	çalışacak	tı	*He / She was (going) to work*
(Biz)	çalışacak	tık	*We were (going) to work*
(Siz)	çalışacak	tınız	*You (pl) were (going) to work*
Onlar	çalışacak	tı / lardı	*They were (going) to work*

gelmek (the future tense)

(Ben)	gelecek	tim	*I was (going) to come*
(Sen)	gelecek	tin	*You were (going) to come*
(O)	gelecek	ti	*He / She was (going) to come*
(Biz)	gelecek	tik	*We were (going) to come*
(Siz)	gelecek	tiniz	*You (pl) were (going) to come*
Onlar	gelecek	ti / lerdi	*They were (going) to come*

Unit Eighteen: İpin Ucunu Kaçıran İnsanlar Romanından Alıntılar-3

Excerpts from the Novel **İpin Ucunu Kaçıran İnsanlar-3**

In this unit you will find:

- An authentic text from a published Turkish novel

With this unit, you will be able to:

- Capture meaning from context with / without using a dictionary
- Use the compound tenses-2

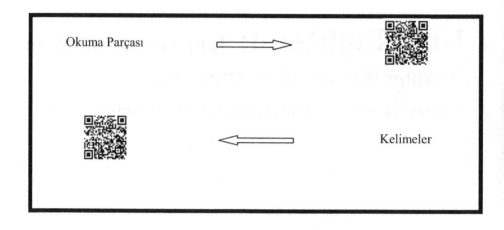

Okuma Parçası →

← Kelimeler

Bölüm 1
Part 1

Okuma parçası 1 / Reading Text 1

Osman'la Lütfi, bazı akşamlarda sıcak çikolatalarını hazırlarlar ve film izlerlerdi. Osman, melodrama ve romantik komedi filmlerinden hoşlanırken Lütfi, aksiyon ve savaş filmlerinden haz alırdı. Ne Osman Lütfi'nin ne de Lütfi Osman'ın favori filmlerini seyretmeye yanaşırdı; kısacası zevkleri bu anlamda zıttı. Çözüm olarak ikisinin de izlememekte direnmediği macera filmleri seçerlerdi. Bu sebeple bir Nicolas Cage filmi izlemeye karar verdiler. Lütfi bilgisayarı kurarken Osman sıcak çikolatayı hazırlamaya koyuldu ancak merak ettiği bir şey vardı. Lütfi Nicolas Cage'e *Nikılı Skeyc* diyordu ama neden? Lütfi önce güldü sonra açıkladı:

"Bir köyde insanlar birbirlerine hep "nikı" diye seslenirlermiş. "Günaydın, nikı. Nasılsın, nikı?" gibi. Özel bir ad değilmiş. O köyde yüzyıllarca sürmüş bu âdet. "Nikı" kelimesini o kadar çok kullanmışlar ki, orasının adı "Nikı" olarak kalmış. O köyde yaşayan Skeyc isminde bir genç varmış. Bu genç oyuncu olmak istiyormuş ve dedesinden kalma arsaları satıp Holywood'a açılmış, sonra da eksantrik karakterleri canlandırdığı filmlerle şöhret olmuş. Nikı'dan geldiği için ona *Nikı'lı Skeyc* demişler."

---

1. Did the two like the same kind of movies?
2. What kind of movies did they both like?

Vocabulary

açıklamak	*to explain*	**kurmak**	*to set up*
âdet	*tradition*	**orası**	*there, that place*
aksiyon	*action*	**savaş**	*war*
bilgisayar	*computer*	**seslenmek**	*to call*
çikolata	*chokolate*	**şöhret**	*fame*
direnmek	*to resist*	**yanaşmak**	*to approach*
haz almak	*to enjoy*	**zevk**	*pleasure*
hoşlanmak	*to like*	**zıt**	*opposite*
koyulmak	*to start doing something*		
dedesinden kalma		*inherited from his grandfather*	

Bölüm 2
Part 2

anahtar dilbilgisi ipuçları key grammar points

bileşik zamanlar compound tenses

NB The compound tenses are not in the scope of this book which is addressed to learners at the beginner level. However, the meaning and the construction of the compound tenses are given here generally to give the learner an idea.

In Turkish, apart from the simple tenses, there are also compound tenses, that is, the tenses made up two simple tenses. In this structure, the first tense may be the present progressive tense, the present tense, or the future tense. And the second tense is always the past tense.

The compound tenses are used <u>to report</u> past progressive actions, past habits / intentions, and future intentions respectively.

In other words;

Comp. Tense No	First Tense	Second Tense	Meaning
1	the present progressive tense	the –miş past tense	**reporting past progressive actions**
2	the present tense	the past –miş tense	**reporting past habits / intentions**
3	the future tense	the past –miş tense	**reporting future intentions**

For the construction, the verb is conjugated for the 3rd singular person, **o**, *he / she / it* in the present progressive tense or in the present tense, or in the future tense (*See Unit 3 for the present progressive and present tense and Unit 9 for the future tense constructions*). Then the past tense personal ending is added to form a compound tense (*See Unit 7 for the past tense construction*).

To form a compound tense, two steps are needed.

STEP 1

First, the verb is conjugated for the 3rd singular person (**o**, *he / she / it*). <u>Have the vowel change in mind throughout the construction</u>.

Examples:

The verb is conjugated for the 3rd <u>singular person (**o**, *he / she / it*)</u>.

Examples: **çalışmak & gelmek**

Çalışıyor	*He / she is working*	**Geliyor**	*He / she is coming*
Çalışır	*He / she works*	**Gelir**	*He / she comes*
Çalışacak	*He / she will work*	**Gelecek**	*He / she will come*

STEP 2

Then, the personal endings are added to the end to form a compound tense.

NB Since the –miş past tense has a meaning of not witnessing the mentioned action, it is more suitable for reporting. In other words, the –miş past tense is usually used for <u>only the 3rd persons</u>. (*However, it's also possible to use it with other persons.*)

For the construction of <u>the 3rd singular person</u>, the ending **-miş** is a 4 way vowel harmony, meaning **-miş** can change to **-miş / -mış / -muş / -müş**, depending on the preceding vowel. (*See Unit 16 for the -miş past tense construction.*)

For the construction of <u>the 3rd plural person</u>, the ending **-lermiş** is a 2 way vowel harmony, meaning **-lermiş** can change to **-lermiş / -larmış** depending on the preceding vowel. (*See Unit 7 for the vowel change of ler / lar.*)

Compound Tense. 1 (reporting past progressive actions)

çalışmak (the present progressive tense)

(O)	**çalışıyor**	**muş.**	*He / She was working. (I didn't see.)*
Onlar	**çalışıyor**	**muş / larmış.**	*They were working. (I didn't see.)*

gelmek (the present progressive tense)

(O)	**geliyor**	**muş.**	*He / She was coming. (I didn't see.)*
Onlar	**geliyor**	**muş / larmış.**	*They were coming. (I didn't see.)*

Compound Tense. 2 (reporting past habits / intentions)

çalışmak (the present tense)

(O)	çalışır	mış.		*He / She would / used to work. (I didn't see.)*
Onlar	çalışır	mış larmış.	/	*They would / used to work. (I didn't see.)*

gelmek (the present tense)

(O)	gelir	miş.	*He / She would / used to come. (I didn't see.)*
Onlar	gelir	miş / lermiş.	*They would / used to come. (I didn't see.)*

Compound Tense. 3 (reporting future intentions)

çalışmak (the future tense)

(O)	çalışacak	mış.	*He / She was (going) to work. (I didn't see.)*
Onlar	çalışacak	mış/ larmış.	*They were (going) to work. (I didn't see.)*

gelmek (the future tense)

(O)	gelecek	miş.	*He / She was (going) to come. (I didn't see.)*
Onlar	gelecek	miş / lermiş.	*They were (going) to come. (I didn't see.)*

Unit Nineteen: İpin Ucunu Kaçıran İnsanlar Romanından Alıntılar-4

Excerpts from the Novel **İpin Ucunu Kaçıran İnsanlar-4**

In this unit you will find:

- An authentic text from a published Turkish novel

With this unit, you will be able to:

- Capture meaning from context with / without using a dictionary
- Report the present actions

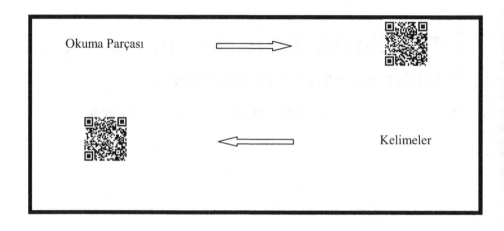

Okuma Parçası →

← Kelimeler

Bölüm 1
Part 1

Okuma parçası 1 / Reading Text 1

Aşağıya indi, o adamın yüzünü görmek istemiyordu ama başka çaresi yoktu. Tamamen aç kalmak vardı. Yemekhaneye gitti; kaşığını, çatalını ve tabağını aldı. Kafasını kaldırmadan aşçıbaşı Salih'e doğru uzattı tabağını ve masanın birine oturdu. Tabağına şöyle bir baktı; kâsede bir kepçe şehriye çorbası, üç beş domates salatalık, bir küçük kalıp peynir ve avuç içi kadar börek vardı. Nefretle yüzünü ekşitti, yine yetmeyecekti tabaktakiler. İçinden bir of çekti, ayağa kalkıp buzdolabından süt aldı ve tabağındakileri yemeye başladı. Daha çok işi vardı. Üniversite hayatına tam anlamıyla giriş yapmak için okuluna gidecekti. Ortamın kokusunu alınca havaya gireceğine inanıyordu. Kahvaltısını yaptıktan sonra yurttan ayrıldı.

Ağır adımlarla otobüs durağına doğru yürürken birden çoktan gelmiş olan otobüsün hareketlendiğini fark etti. Olabildiğince hızlı koşmaya başladı ama ne yazık ki yetişemedi. Otobüs gittikten sonra bir süre bakakaldı öylece. Yaklaşık yarım saat durakta bir sonraki otobüsün gelmesini bekledi. Ne bir yolcu geldi durağa ne de otobüs. Sonunda yoldan geçmekte olan bir amcaya sordu:

"Amca, buradan Hunat'a araba kaçta?"

---

1. Was the food enough for him?
2. Did he catch the first bus?

Vocabulary

aşçıbaşı	*chef*	**kepçe**	*ladle*
bakakalmak	*to continue looking*	**ortam**	*environment*
çare	*solution*	**şehriye çorbası**	*noodle soup*
hareketlenmek	*to start moving*	**uzatmak**	*extend*
Hunat	*A historical location in Kayseri with bus stops*	**yetmek**	*to be enough*
içinden	*from inside*	**yurt**	*dorm*
kâse	*bowl*		
avuç içi kadar		*as small as a palm (very few or little)*	
ayağa kalkmak		*to stand up*	
havaya girmek		*to get in the mood*	
nefretle yüzünü ekşitmek		*to make a wry face with hatred*	
of çekmek		*to heave a sigh*	
Şöyle bir bakmak.		*to take a glance*	
tam anlamıyla		*literally*	
Tamamen aç kalmak vardı.		*There was a possibility of starvation completely.*	

Bölüm 2
Part 2

anahtar dilbilgisi ipuçları key grammar points

şimdiki olayların aktarılması reporting the present actions

NB The reporting the present actions is not in the scope of this book which is addressed to learners at the beginner level. However, the meaning and the construction of reporting the present actions is given here generally to give the learner an idea.

In Turkish, apart from the present tense, there is another structure to report the present actions.

NB The reporting of the present actions has a meaning of witnessing the mentioned action. In other words, it is usually used for <u>only the 3rd persons</u>. (*However, it's also possible to use it with other persons.*)

For the construction, the verb is used as in the infinitive form. Then the reporting ending **–te** or **–ta** and the personal endings are added.

- For the construction of <u>the 3rd singular person</u>, the verb is used as in the infinitive form. Then the reporting ending **–te** or **–ta** is added. The ending -**te** is a 2 way vowel harmony, meaning -**te** can change to -**te** or -**ta** depending on the preceding vowel.

Last vowel of the preceding word	a, ı, o, u	e, i, ö, ü
the ending -te (x2)	-ta	-te

Examples:

söyle mek	**Çocuk söylemekte.**	*(Look,) the child is telling.*
atla mak	**Çocuk atlamakta.**	*(Look,) the child is jumping.*
uyu mak	**Çocuk uyumakta.**	*(Look,) the child is sleeping.*
yürü mek	**Çocuk yürümekte.**	*(Look,) the child is walking.*

- For the construction of <u>the 3rd plural person</u>, the verb is used as in the infinitive form, too. Then the reporting ending -**teler** or -**talar** is added. The preceding vowel table is also applicable here.

Examples:

söyle mek	**Çocuklar söylemekteler.**	*(Look,) the children are telling.*
atla mak	**Çocuklar atlamaktalar.**	*(Look,) the children are jumping.*
uyu mak	**Çocuklar uyumaktalar.**	*(Look,) the children are sleeping.*
yürü mek	**Çocuklar yürümekteler.**	*(Look,) the children are walking.*

Unit Twenty: İpin Ucunu Kaçıran İnsanlar Romanından Alıntılar-5

Excerpts from the Novel **İpin Ucunu Kaçıran İnsanlar-5**

In this unit you will find:

- An authentic text from a published Turkish novel

With this unit, you will be able to:

- Capture meaning from context with / without using a dictionary
- Use the reported speech

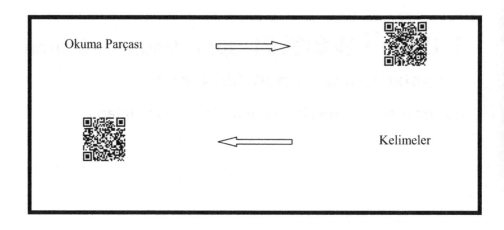

Okuma Parçası

Kelimeler

Bölüm 1
Part 1

Okuma parçası 1 / Reading Text 1

Ertesi gün derslerine devam etmek için sabah erken fakülteye gitti. Uzun bir süre ayrı kaldığı ders ortamı onu çok yormuştu. Öğle arasında aç olan karnını doyurmak için abur cubur makinesinin önüne geldi, içindekilere göz gezdirdi, hangisini alacağına karar veremiyordu. Makinenin önünde dikilmiş ciddî bir yüz ifadesiyle derin düşüncelere dalmışken aniden çok yakından duyduğu bir sesle irkildi:

"Tutku al, Tutku. Çok severim ben onu."

Orhan dehşet içerisinde etrafına bakındı, kalbi yerinden fırlayacakmış gibi atıyordu.

Yakınlarda kimse yoktu; gözlerini kocaman açmış terler içerisinde titrerken sesi bir daha işitti:

"Ne bekliyorsun hâlâ? Açım ben hadi."

"Sen de kimsin? Bu ses nereden geliyor?"

"Ben kim miyim? Ben senim. Sen de bensin. Korkacak bir şey yok."

Orhan ne olduğunu kestiremiyordu. Hayatında ilk defa duyduğu bir ses, üstelik sadece bir ses duyuluyordu, o ses de kararlı bir şekilde kendisi **olduğunu söylüyordu**. Üstelik Osman'ın favori bisküvisi Tutku alması için ısrar ediyordu. Birden aklına Osman geldi. Orhan soğuk soğuk terlemeye başlamıştı. Hızlı ve kesik nefesler alıp veriyordu.

---

1. Why did Orhan get shocked?
2. Did he see anyone around?

Vocabulary

abur cubur	*snack, junk food*	**kalp atışı**	*heart beat*
aklına gelmek	*to come to the mind*	**kalp atmak**	*(for the heart) to beat*
ayrı kalmak	*to stay apart*	**kararlı**	*determined*
dehşet içerisinde	*in horror*	**öğle arası**	*lunch break*
ders ortamı	*lesson environment*	**titremek**	*to tremble*
dikilmek	*to stand up*	**Tutku**	*a favorite chocolate brand in Türkiye*
göz gezdirmek	*to review*	**tutku**	*passion*
ısrar etmek	*to insist*	**üstelik**	*moreover*
irkilmek	*to startle*	**yormak**	*to make tired*
işitmek	*to hear*	**yüz ifadesi**	*face expression*

gözünü kocaman açmak	*to open the eyes wide (to get shocked)*
Hadi! / Haydi!	*Come on!*
hızlı ve kesik nefes alıp vermek	*to breathe fast and shallow*
kalbi yerinden fırlamak	*to get shocked*
Korkacak bir şey yok.	*There's nothing to be afraid of.*
Ne olduğunu kestirmek	*to guess what's going on*
soğuk soğuk terlemek	*to sweat cold (to be afraid of something)*

Bölüm 2
Part 2

anahtar dilbilgisi ipuçları key grammar points

ifadelerin aktarılması the reported speech

NB The reported speech is not in the scope of this book which is addressed to learners at the beginner level. However, the meaning and the construction of the reported speech is given here generally to give the learner an idea.

In Turkish, similar to English, there are four main types of reported speech. They are, reporting the positive sentences, reporting the negative sentences, reporting the Yes / No questions, and reporting the Question Word questions.

Below are given the examples fort he construction of the reported speech. Two verbs and four tenses are given here to give a general understanding of the construction. <u>Have the vowel change in mind throughout the construction</u>.

1. Reporting the positive sentences

(The present tense)

A: "Çocuk çalışır."   *A: "The child studies."*

B: A çocuğun çalıştığını söyledi.   *B: A said that the child studied.*

A: "Serra gelir."   *A: "Serra comes."*

B: A Serra'nın geldiğini söyledi.   *B: A said that Serra came.*

A: "Talha bir öğrenci."   *A: "Talha is a student."*

B: A Talha'nın bir öğrenci olduğunu söyledi. *B: A said that Talha was a student.*

(The present progressive tense)

A: "Çocuk çalışıyor."   *A: "The child is studying."*

B: A çocuğun çalıştığını söyledi.   *B: A said that the child was studying.*

B: A çocuğun çalışıyor olduğunu söyledi.   **B: A said that the child was studying.*

A: "Serra geliyor."   *A: "Serra is coming."*

B: A Serra'nın geldiğini söyledi.   *B: A said that Serra was coming.*

B: A Serra'nın geliyor olduğunu söyledi.*   *B: A said that Serra was coming.*

* Note there are two possibilities for the present progressive sentences.

(The past tense)

A: "Çocuk çalıştı."   *A: "The child studied."*

B: A çocuğun çalıştığını söyledi.   *B: A said that the child studied.*

A: "Serra geldi."   *A: "Serra came."*

B: A Serra'nın geldiğini söyledi.   *B: A said that Serra came.*

A: "Talha bir öğrenciydi."   *A: "Talha was a student."*

B: A Talha'nın bir öğrenci olduğunu söyledi.   *B: A said that Talha was a student.*

* Note the reported speech for the present and the past tense are the same.

(The future tense)

A: "Çocuk çalışacak."   *A: "The child will study."*

B: A çocuğun çalışacağını söyledi.   *B: A said that the child would study.*

A: "Serra gelecek."   *A: "Serra will come."*

B: A Serra'nın geleceğini söyledi.   *B: A said that Serra would come.*

A: "Talha bir öğrenci olacak."   *A: "Talha will be a student."*

B: A Talha'nın bir öğrenci olacağını söyledi.   *B: A said that Talha would be a student.*

2. Reporting the negative sentences

(The present tense)

A: "Çocuk çalışmaz."   *A: "The child doesn't study."*

B: A çocuğun çalışmadığını söyledi. *B: A said that the child didn't study.*

A: "Serra gelmez."   *A: "Serra doesn't come."*

B: A Serra'nın gelmediğini söyledi. *B: A said that Serra didn't come.*

A: "Talha bir öğrenci değil."   *A: "Talha isn't a student."*

B: A Talha'nın bir öğrenci olmadığını söyledi.   *B: A said that Talha wasn't a student.*

(The present progressive tense)

A: "Çocuk çalışmıyor."   *A: "The child isn't studying."*

B: A çocuğun çalışmadığını söyledi.   *B: A said that the child wasn't studying.*

B: A çocuğun çalışmıyor olduğunu   **B: A said that the child wasn't studying.*
söyledi.

A: "Serra gelmiyor."   *A: "Serra is not coming."*

B: A Serra'nın gelmediğini söyledi.   *B: A said that Serra wasn't coming.*

B: A Serra'nın gelmiyor olduğunu   *B: A said that Serra wasn't coming.*
söyledi.*

* Note there are two possibilities for the present progressive sentences.

(The past tense)

A: "Çocuk çalışmadı."   *A: "The child didn't study."*

B: A çocuğun çalışmadığını söyledi.   *B: A said that the child didn't study.*

A: "Serra gelmedi."   *A: "Serra didn't come."*

B: A Serra'nın gelmediğini söyledi.   *B: A said that Serra didn't come.*

A: "Talha bir öğrenci değildi."   *A: "Talha wasn't a student."*

B: A Talha'nın bir öğrenci olmadığını   *B: A said that Talha wasn't a student.*
söyledi.

* Note the reported speech for the present and the past tense are the same.

(The future tense)

A: "Çocuk çalışmayacak."   *A: "The child won't study."*

B: A çocuğun çalışmayacağını söyledi.   *B: A said that the child wouldn't study.*

A: "Serra gelmeyecek."   *A: "Serra won't come."*

B: A Serra'nın gelmeyeceğini söyledi.   *B: A said that Serra wouldn't come.*

A: "Talha bir öğrenci olmayacak."   *A: "Talha won't be a student."*

B: A Talha'nın bir öğrenci olmayacağını   *B: A said that Talha wouldn't be a*
söyledi.   *student.*

3.   Reporting the Yes / No questions

(The present tense)

A: "Çocuk çalışır mı?"

A: *"Does the child study?"*

B: A çocuğun çalışıp çalışmadığını sordu.

B: *A asked if the child studied.*

A: "Serra gelir mi?"

A: *"Does Serra come?"*

B: A Serra'nın gelip gelmediğini sordu.

B: *A asked if Serra came.*

A: "Talha bir öğrenci mi?"

A: *"Is Talha a student?"*

B: A Talha'nın bir öğrenci olup olmadığını sordu.

B: *A asked if Talha was a student?*

(The present progressive tense)

A: "Çocuk çalışıyor mu?"

A: *"Is the child studying?"*

B: A çocuğun çalışıp çalışmadığını sordu.

B: *A asked if the child was studying.*

A: "Serra geliyor mu?"

A: *"Is Serra coming?"*

B: A Serra'nın gelip gelmediğini sordu.

B: *A asked if Serra was coming?*

(The past tense)

A: "Çocuk çalıştı mı?"

A: *"Did the child study?"*

B: A çocuğun çalışıp çalışmadığını sordu.

B: *A asked if the child studied.*

A: "Serra geldi mi?"

A: *"Did Serra come?"*

B: A Serra'nın gelip gelmediğini sordu.

B: *A asked if Serra came.*

A: "Talha bir öğrenci miydi?"

A: *"Was Talha a student?"*

B: A Talha'nın bir öğrenci olup olmadığını sordu.

B: *A asked if Talha was a student.*

* Note the reported speech for the present and the past tense are the same.

(The future tense)

A: "Çocuk çalışacak mı?"

A: "Will the child study?"

B: A çocuğun çalışıp çalışmayacağını sordu.

B: A asked if the child would study.

A: "Serra gelecek mi?"

A: "Will Serra come?"

B: A Serra'nın gelip gelmeyeceğini sordu.

B: A asked if Serra would come.

A: "Talha bir öğrenci olacak mı?"

A: "Will Talha be a student?"

B: A Talha'nın bir öğrenci olup olmayacağını sordu.

B: A asked if Talha would be a student.

4. Reporting the Question Word questions

(The present tense)

A: "Çocuk ne çalışır?"

A: "What does the child study?"

B: A çocuğun ne çalıştığını sordu.

B: A asked what the child studied.

A: "Serra ne zaman gelir?"

A: "When does Serra come?"

B: A Serra'nın ne zaman geldiğini sordu.

B: A asked when Serra came.

A: "Talha nerede bir öğrenci?"

A: "Where is Talha a student at?"

B: A Talha'nın nerede bir öğrenci olduğunu sordu.

B: A asked where Talha was a student at.

(The present progressive tense)

A: "Çocuk ne çalışıyor?"

A: "What is the child studying?"

B: A çocuğun ne çalıştığını sordu.

B: A asked if the child was studying.

A: "Serra ne zaman geliyor?"

A: "When is Serra coming?"

B: A Serra'nın ne zaman geldiğini sordu.

B: A asked when Serra was coming.

(The past tense)

A: "Çocuk ne çalıştı?"

A: "What did the child study?"

B: A çocuğun ne çalıştığını sordu.

B: A asked what the child studied.

A: "Serra ne zaman geldi?"

A: "When did Serra come?"

B: A Serra'nın ne zaman geldiğini sordu.

B: A asked when Serra came.

A: "Talha nerede bir öğrenciydi?"

A: "Where was Talha a student at?"

B: A Talha'nın nerede bir öğrenci olduğunu sordu.
    B: A asked where Talha was a student at.

* Note the reported speech for the present, present progressive, and the past tense are the same.

(The future tense)

A: "Çocuk ne çalışacak?"   *A: "What will the child study?"*

B: A çocuğun ne çalışacağını sordu.   *B: A asked what the child would study.*

A: "Serra ne zaman gelecek?"   *A: "When will Serra come?"*

B: A Serra'nın ne zaman geleceğini sordu.   *B: A asked when Serra would come.*

A: "Talha nerede bir öğrenci olacak?"   *A: "Where will Talha be a student at?"*

B: A Talha'nın nerede bir öğrenci olacağını sordu.   *B: A asked where Talha would be a student at.*

Grammar Summary

In this unit you will find:

- Verb conjugations for the present progressive tense
- Verb conjugations for the present tense
- Verb conjugations for the past tense
- Verb conjugations for the future tense
- Preposition declensions

Verb conjugations for the present progressive tense

şimdiki zaman the present progressive tense

The present progressive is usually used to express an action on progress as the time of the conversation. It is possible to use the present progressive in place of the general present tense, too. For the conjugation of the verbs, special personal suffixes are added to the verb stems.

Below are given the special personal suffixes for personal pronouns:

(Ben)	-iyorum
(Sen)	-iyorsun
(O)	-iyor
(Biz)	-iyoruz
(Siz)	-iyorsunuz
Onlar	-iyor/iyorlar

the vowel harmony

The letter "i" in the brackets is used only when the preceding letter is a consonant. It may change depending on the preceding vowel. Find a chart below for the vowel change.

the preceding vowel	the letter in the suffix
a, ı	ı
e, i	i
o, u	u
ö, ü	ü

The vowel may change in case the verb stem ends with a vowel. Find a chart below for the vowel change.

the preceding vowel	the letter in the suffix
a, ı	-a, -ı
e, i	-e, -i
o, u	-a, -u
ö, ü	-e, -ü

the negative form

The negative suffix –me is added to the verb stem to make the present progressive tense negative.

Below are given the special negative personal suffixes for personal pronouns:

(Ben)	**-miyorum**
(Sen)	**-miyorsun**
(O)	**-miyor**
(Biz)	**-miyoruz**
(Siz)	**-miyorsunuz**
Onlar	**-miyor/miyorlar**

the question form

To form a question in the present progressive tense, first the verb is conjugated for the 3rd singular person. Then the question suffix –mu is added to the end separately.

Below are given the special personal question suffixes for personal pronouns:

(Ben)	**-iyor muyum?**
(Sen)	**-iyormusun?**
(O)	**-iyor mu?**
(Biz)	**-iyor muyuz?**
(Siz)	**-iyor musunuz?**
Onlar	**-iyor mu?/iyorlar mı?**

Verb conjugations for the present tense

geniş zaman the present tense

The present progressive is usually used to express an action is done repeatedly or regularly. For the conjugation of the verbs, special personal suffixes are added to the verb stems.

Below are given the special personal suffixes for personal pronouns:

(Ben)	**-(i)rim**
(Sen)	**-(i)rsin**
(O)	**-(i)r**
(Biz)	**-(i)riz**
(Siz)	**-(i)rsiniz**
Onlar	**-(i)r/(i)rler**

the vowel harmony

The letter "i" in the brackets is used only when the preceding letter is a consonant. And, the letter "i" may change depending on the preceding vowel. Find a chart below for the vowel change.

the preceding vowel	the letter in the suffix
a, ı	**-a, -ı**
e, i	**-e, -i**
o, u	**-a, -u**
ö, ü	**-e, -ü**

the negative form

The negative suffix –me is added to the verb stem to make the present tense negative.

Below are given the special negative personal suffixes for personal pronouns:

(Ben)	**-mem**
(Sen)	**-mezsin**
(O)	**-mez**
(Biz)	**-meyiz**
(Siz)	**-mezsiniz**
Onlar	**-mez/mezler**

the question form

To form a question in the present tense, first the verb is conjugated for the 3rd singular person. Then the question suffix –mi is added to the end separately.

Below are given the special personal question suffixes for personal pronouns:

(Ben)	**-(i)r miyim?**
(Sen)	**-(i)r misin?**
(O)	**-(i)r mi?**
(Biz)	**-(i)r miyiz?**
(Siz)	**-(i)r misiniz?**
Onlar	**-(i)r mi?/(i)rler mi?**

Verb conjugations for the past tense

geçmiş zaman the past tense

The past tense is used to express an action is done in the past. For the conjugation of the verbs, special personal suffixes are added to the verb stems.

Below are given the special personal suffixes for personal pronouns:

(Ben)	-dim
(Sen)	-din
(O)	-di
(Biz)	-dik
(Siz)	-diniz
Onlar	-di/-diler

the vowel & consonant harmony

The vowel in the suffix may change depending on the preceding vowel. Find a chart below for the vowel change.

the preceding vowel	the letter in the suffix
a, ı	ı
e, i	i
o, u	u
ö, ü	ü

The suffixes '-ler' or 'lar' in the table given above, depend on the preceding vowel.

the preceding vowel	the suffix
a, o, u, ı	-lar
e, ö, ü, i	-ler

Additionally, in case of the noun ends with one of the letters of 'f', 's', 't', 'k', 'ş', 'h', or 'p', the letter "d" changes to "t".

the negative form

The negative suffix –me is added to the verb stem to make the past tense negative. Then the personal suffixes are applied for personal pronouns. Below are given the special personal suffixes for personal pronouns:

(Ben)	**-medim**
(Sen)	**-medin**
(O)	**-medi**
(Biz)	**-medik**
(Siz)	**-mediniz**
Onlar	**-medi/-mediler**

The vowel in the suffix may change depending on the preceding vowel. Find a chart below for the vowel change.

the preceding vowel	the suffix
a, ı, o, u	**-ma**
e, i, ö, ü	**-me**

the question form

To form a question in the past tense, the question suffix –mi is added to the end of an affirmative construction separately.

Below are given the special personal suffixes for personal pronouns:

(Ben)	**-dim mi?**
(Sen)	**-din mi?**
(O)	**-di mi?**
(Biz)	**-dik mi?**
(Siz)	**-diniz mi?**
Onlar	**-di mi?/-mediler mi?**

Note that the vowel in the suffix may change. The previous vowel harmony chart is also applicable to the question suffix.

Verb conjugations for the future tense

gelecek zaman the future tense

For the conjugation of the verbs, special personal suffixes are added to the verb stems to form the future tense.

Below are given the special personal suffixes for personal pronouns:

(Ben)	-(y)eceğim
(Sen)	-(y)eceksin
(O)	-(y)ecek
(Biz)	-(y)eceğiz
(Siz)	-(y)eceksiniz
Onlar	-(y)ecek/-(y)ecekler

the vowel harmony

The letter "y" in the brackets is used only when the preceding letter is a consonant. And, the letter "e" may change to "a" depending on the preceding vowel, and the others accordingly. Find a chart below for the vowel change. Only the first personal suffix is given to point out the vowel change.

the preceding vowel	the vowels in the suffix
a, o, u, ı	-acağım
e, ö, ü, i	-eceğim

the negative form

The negative suffix –me/-ma is added to the verb stem to make the future tense negative.

Below are given the special negative personal suffixes for personal pronouns:

(Ben)	-meyeceğim
(Sen)	-meyeceksin
(O)	-meyecek
(Biz)	-meyeceğiz
(Siz)	-meyeceksiniz
Onlar	-meyecek/meyecekler

the question form

To form a question in the future tense, first the verb is conjugated for the 3rd singular person. Then the question suffix –mi is added to the end separately.

Below are given the special personal question suffixes for personal pronouns:

(Ben)	**-(y)ecek miyim?**
(Sen)	**-(y)ecek misin?**
(O)	**-(y)ecek mi?**
(Biz)	**-(y)ecek miyiz?**
(Siz)	**-(y)ecek misiniz?**
Onlar	**-(y)ecek mi?/-(y)ecekler mi?**

The letter "y" in the brackets is used only when the preceding letter is a consonant. And, the letter "e" may change to "a" depending on the preceding vowel, and the others accordingly. The previous chart is also applicable for the vowel change.

Preposition declensions

to, towards

The suffix "-e/-a" is used for the preposition of place "to or towards" in English. Below are given the declension of the preposition "-e/-a" for the personal pronouns:

(Ben)	bana
(Sen)	sana
(O)	ona
(Biz)	bize
(Siz)	size
(Onlar)	onlara

the vowel harmony

In case of a preceding letter is a vowel, the letter "y" is added before the suffix. In addition, the suffix "-e/-a" may change depending on the preceding vowel.

the preceding vowel	the vowels in the suffix
a, o, u, ı	-a
e, ö, ü, i	-e

In case of a noun is a proper name, the suffix is separated by an apostrophe.

the consonant harmony

In case of the noun ends with one of the letters of 'ç', 'k', or 'p', it changes before the suffix "-e/-a" is applied. Find a chart about the consonant change.

the preceding consonant	it changes to
ç	c
k	g, or ğ
p	b

at, in, on

The suffix "-de/-da" is used for the preposition of place "at, in, or on" in English. Below are given the declension of the preposition "-de/-da" for the personal pronouns:

(Ben)	**bende**
(Sen)	**sende**
(O)	**onda**
(Biz)	**bizde**
(Siz)	**sizde**
(Onlar)	**onlarda**

Note the previous vowel change table is also applicable to this preposition.

In case of a noun is a proper name, the suffix is separated by an apostrophe.

In case of the noun ends with one of the letters of 'f', 's', 't', 'k', 'ş', 'h', or 'p', the suffix changes to "-te/-ta".

from

The suffix "-den/-dan" is used for the preposition of place "from" in English. Below are given the declension of the preposition "-den/-dan" for the personal pronouns:

(Ben)	**benden**
(Sen)	**senden**
(O)	**ondan**
(Biz)	**bizden**
(Siz)	**sizden**
(Onlar)	**onlardan**

Note the previous vowel change table is also applicable to this preposition.

In case of a noun is a proper name, the suffix is separated by an apostrophe.

In case of the noun ends with one of the letters of 'f', 's', 't', 'k', 'ş', 'h', or 'p', the suffix changes to "-ten/-tan".

the accusative

The suffix "i" is added to the nouns for the accusative case. Below are the special personal pronouns:

(Ben)	beni
(Sen)	seni
(O)	onu
(Biz)	bizi
(Siz)	sizi
(Onlar)	onları

the vowel harmony

In case of a preceding letter is a vowel, the letter "y" is added before the suffix. In addition, the suffix may change depending on the preceding vowel.

the preceding vowel	the vowels in the suffix
a, ı	-ı
e, i	-i
o, u	-u
ö, ü	-ü

In case of a noun is a proper name, the suffix is separated by an apostrophe.

the consonant harmony

In case of the noun ends with one of the letters of 'ç', 'k', or 'p', it changes before the suffix "-e/-a" is applied. Find a chart about the consonant change.

the preceding consonant	it changes to
ç	c
k	g, or ğ
p	b

It's also possible to use gerunds with or without the possessives in the accusative case.

with

In Turkish, it is also possible to use **ile**, *with*, as the suffix, it's necessary to add "-(y)le" or "-(y)la" to the nouns.

the vowel harmony

In case of a preceding letter is a vowel, the letter "y" is added before the suffix. In addition, the suffix "-e/-a" may change depending on the preceding vowel.

the preceding vowel	the vowels in the suffix
a, o, u, ı	-a
e, ö, ü, i	-e

When used with the persons, the possessive form is used. Below are given the declension of "-le/-la" for the personal pronouns:

(Ben)	benim ile	benimle
(Sen)	senin ile	seninle
(O)	onun ile	onunla
(Biz)	bizim ile	bizimle
(Siz)	sizin ile	sizinle
(Onlar)	onlar ile	onlarla

In case of a noun is a proper name, the suffix is separated by an apostrophe.

Key to the Exercises

Unit 1

Dialogue 2
Answers: 1. No, they were late., 2. Yes, Serra is his sister.

exercise 1

Ben İbrahim Korkmaz'ım., Ben şoförüm., Ben oteldenim., Ben Türküm.
Bu Michelle., Bu şoför., Bu Serra., Bu İbrahim Korkmaz.

exercise 2

Ben şoförüm.
Sen şoförsün.
O şoför.
Biz şoförüz.
Siz şoförsünüz.
Onlar şoför/Şoförler.

Ben Türküm.
Sen Türksün.
O Türk.
Biz Türküz.
Siz Türksünüz.
Onlar Türk/Türkler.

Ben öğretmenim.
Sen öğretmensin.
O öğretmen.
Biz öğretmeniz.
Siz öğretmensiniz.
Onlar öğretmen/Öğretmenler.

Ben Almanım.
Sen Almansın.
O Alman.
Biz Almanız.
Siz Almansınız.
Onlar Alman/Almanlar.

Ben Rusum.
Sen Russun.
O Rus.
Biz Rusuz.
Siz Russunuz.
Onlar Rus/Ruslar.

exercise 3

Ben muhasebeciyim.
Biz muhasebeciyiz.

Ben öğrenciyim.
Biz öğrenciyiz.

Ben oyuncuyum.
Biz oyuncuyuz.

Ben iş insanıyım.
Biz iş insanıyız.

Ben ev hanımıyım.
Biz ev hanımıyız.

Ben Kanadalıyım.
Biz Kanadalıyız.

exercise 5

Hayır, değiliz.
Hayır, değilim.
Hayır, değilsiniz.
Hayır, değil.
Hayır, değilsin.
Hayır, değiller. / Hayır, onlar Alman değil.

exercise 6

Siz şoför değil misiniz?
Sen öğrenci değil misin?
Biz erkenci değil miyiz?
İbrahim Rus değil mi?
Ben öğretmen değil miyim?
Onlar Alman değil mi? / (Onlar) Alman değiller mi?

Unit 2

Dialogue 1

Answers: 1. No, they're only two people., 2. It's in the centre of the city.

Dialogue 2

Answers: 1. He has one brother and one sister., 2. She speaks three foreign languages. (Turkish, French, and German)

Dialogue 3

Answers: 1. They'll go the hotel room to rest., 2. They will eat something and take a short trip.

exercise 1

Hans Almandır.
Eymen akıllıdır.
Talha çalışkandır.
Otel yenidir.
İrem güzeldir.
Serra başarılıdır.
Otel merkezîdir.
Ali oyuncudur.

exercise 2

Charles Kanadalı mıdır?
Evet, Charles Kanadalıdır.
Hayır, Charles Kanadalı değildir.

İbrahim Türk müdür?
Evet, İbrahim Türktür.
Hayır, İbrahim Türk değildir.

John genç midir?
Evet, John gençtir.
Hayır, John genç değildir.

Michelle ev hanımı mıdır?
Evet, Michelle ev hanımıdır.
Hayır, Michelle ev hanımı değildir.

İrem öğrenci midir?
Evet, İrem öğrencidir.
Hayır, İrem öğrenci değildir.

Otel yeni midir?
Evet, otel yenidir.
Hayır, otel yeni değildir.

Ankara büyük müdür?
Evet, Ankara büyüktür.
Hayır, Ankara büyük değildir.

exercise 3

benim şoförüm	(my driver)
okulun şoförü	(the driver of the school / the school's driver)
öğrencinin adı	(the name of the student / the student's name)
şoförün babası	(the father of the driver / the driver's father)
İbrahim'in eşi	(the wife of İbrahim / İbrahim's wife)
Talha'nın işi	(the work of Talha / Talha's work)
Serra'nın okulu	(the school of Serra / Serra's school)
Eymen'in cevabı	(the answer of Eymen / Eymen's answer)
Kasabın çocuğu	(the child of the butcher / the butcher's child)

exercise 4

Benim şoförüm gençtir.	(My driver is young.)
Okulun şoförü yaşlıdır.	(The school's driver is old.)
Öğrencinin adı zordur.	(The student's name is difficult.)
Şoförün babası çalışkandır.	(The driver's father is hardworking.)
İbrahim'in eşi başarılıdır.	(İbrahim's wife is successful.)
Talha'nın işi kolaydır.	(Talha's work is easy.)
Serra'nın okulu büyüktür.	(Serra's school is big.)
Eymen'in cevabı doğrudur.	(Eymen's answer is correct.)
Kasabın çocuğu yaramazdır.	(The butcher's child is naughty.)

exercise 5

Senin bir eşin var mı?
Evet, benim bir eşim var.
Hayır, benim hiç eşim yok.

Otelin bir lokantası var mı?
Evet, otelin bir lokantası var.
Hayır, otelin hiç lokantası yok.

Okulun bir öğrencisi var mı?
Evet, okulun bir öğrencisi var.
Hayır, okulun hiç öğrencisi yok.

Michelle'in bir kardeşi var mı?
Evet, Michelle'in bir kardeşi var.
Hayır, Michelle'in hiç kardeşi yok.

Bizim bir işimiz var mı?
Evet, bizim bir işimiz var.
Hayır, bizim hiç işimiz yok.

Otelin bir yöneticisi var mı?
Evet, otelin bir yöneticisi var.
Hayır, otelin hiç yöneticisi yok.

Unit 3

Dialogue 1
Answers: 1. No, the cafe isn't crowded. 2. The menu is on the table.

Dialogue 2

Answers: 1. No, they ordered different things. 2. No, only Michelle will eat menemen.

Dialogue 3

Answers: 1. They come to visit. 2. Yes, she liked it a lot.

exercise 1

içeride, garson, önden, bak

exercise 2

Sen beni biliyorsun.
Biz dinleniyoruz.
O otele gidiyor.
Onlar sahanda yumurta yiyor / yiyorlar.
İnsanlar menüye bakıyor / bakıyorlar.
Siz kafede menüden yemek seçiyorsunuz.
Ben seni görüyorum.
Sen gezmek istiyorsun.
Biz uyuyoruz.

exercise 3

Sen beni bilmiyorsun.
Biz dinlenmiyoruz.
O otele gitmiyor.
Onlar sahanda yumurta yemiyor / yemiyorlar.
İnsanlar menüye bakmıyor / bakmıyorlar.
Siz kafede menüden yemek seçmiyorsunuz.
Ben seni görmüyorum.
Sen gezmek istemiyorsun.
Biz uyumuyoruz.

exercise 4

Sen beni biliyor musun?
Biz dinleniyor muyuz?
O otele gidiyor mu?
Onlar sahanda yumurta yiyor mu? / yiyorlar mı?
İnsanlar menüye bakıyor mu? / bakıyorlar mı?
Siz kafede menüden yemek seçiyor musunuz?
Ben seni görüyor muyum?
Sen gezmek istiyor musun?
Biz uyuyor muyuz?

exercise 5

tepe, geçmek, alan, vaha

exercise 6

Sen beni bilirsin.
Biz dinleniriz.
O otele gider.
Onlar sahanda yumurta yer / yerler.
İnsanlar menüye bakar / bakarlar.
Siz kafede menüden yemek seçersiniz.
Ben seni görürüm.

Sen gezmek istersin.
Biz uyuruz.

exercise 7

Sen beni bilmezsin.
Biz dinlenmeyiz.
O otele gitmez.
Onlar sahanda yumurta yemez / yemezler.
İnsanlar menüye bakmaz / bakmazlar.
Siz kafede menüden yemek seçmezsiniz.
Ben seni görmem.
Sen gezmek istemezsin.
Biz uyumayız.

exercise 8

Sen beni bilir misin?
Biz dinlenir miyiz?
O otele gider mi?
Onlar sahanda yumurta yer mi? / yerler mi?
İnsanlar menüye bakar mı? / bakarlar mı?
Siz kafede menüden yemek seçer misiniz?
Ben seni görür müyüm?
Sen gezmek ister misin?
Biz uyur muyuz?

Unit 4

Dialogue 1

Answers: 1. Yes, he did. 2. Yes, they will.

Dialogue 2

Answers: 1. Their vacation is around two weeks, 2. No, they also want to go to İstanbul.

Dialogue 3

Answers: 1. Yes, she sings songs, listens to music, and plays the ud., 2. She studies two foreign languages together, Spanish and English.

exercise 1

Sen beni bilmelisin.
Biz dinlenmeliyiz.
O otele gitmeli.
Onlar sahanda yumurta yemeli/yemeliler.
İnsanlar menüye bakmalı/bakmalılar.
Siz kafede menüden yemek seçmelisiniz.
Ben seni görmeliyim.
Sen araba kiralamalısın.
Biz uyumalıyız.

exercise 2

Sen beni bilmemelisin.
Biz dinlenmemeliyiz.
O otele gitmemeli.

Onlar sahanda yumurta yememeli/yememeliler.
İnsanlar menüye bakmamalı/bakmamalılar.
Siz kafede menüden yemek seçmemelisiniz.
Ben seni görmemeliyim.
Sen araba kiralamamalısın.
Biz uyumamalıyız.

exercise 3

Sen beni bilmeli misin?
Biz dinlenmeli miyiz?
O otele gitmeli mi?
Onlar sahanda yumurta yemeli mi? / yemeliler mi?
İnsanlar menüye bakmalı mı? / bakmalılar mı?
Siz kafede menüden yemek seçmeli misiniz?
Ben seni görmeli miyim?,
Sen araba kiralamalı mısın?
Biz uyumalı mıyız?

exercise 4

yabancı dil, fikir, ayrıca, dinlemek

exercise 5

Evet, odada sen varsın.
Evet, odada çocuklar var.
Evet, odada biz varız.
Evet, odada siz varsınız.
Evet, odada Michelle var.
Evet, odada herkes var.
Evet, odada bir şey var.
Evet, odada birisi var.
Hayır, odada hiç kimse yok.
Hayır, odada hiç bir şey yok.

Unit 5

Dialogue 1

Answers: 1. No, he just wants to rent a car., 2. He wants the car for a week.

Dialogue 2

Answers: 1. Yes, he knows about it from the internet., 2. Yes, all of their rooms are with the Bosphorus scenery.

Dialogue 3

Answers: 1. No, their room was already ready. 2. No, Kerim will help them with their belongings.

exercise 1

ücret, otomatik, masraf, olmak

exercise 2

Senin beni bilmen mümkündür.
Bizim dinlenmemiz mümkündür.
Onun otele gitmesi mümkündür.
Onların sahanda yumurta yemesi mümkündür.
İnsanların menüye bakması mümkündür.
Sizin kafede menüden yemek seçmeniz mümkündür.
Benim seni görmem mümkündür.
Senin araba kiralaman mümkündür.
Bizim uyumamız mümkündür.

exercise 3

Senin beni bilmen mümkün müdür?
Evet mümkündür. / Hayır mümkün değildir.
Bizim dinlenmemiz mümkün müdür?
Evet mümkündür. / Hayır mümkün değildir.
Onun otele gitmesi mümkün müdür?
Evet mümkündür. / Hayır mümkün değildir.
Onların sahanda yumurta yemesi mümkün müdür?
Evet mümkündür. / Hayır mümkün değildir.
İnsanların menüye bakması mümkün müdür?
Evet mümkündür. / Hayır mümkün değildir.
Sizin kafede menüden yemek seçmeniz mümkün müdür?
Evet mümkündür. / Hayır mümkün değildir.
Benim seni görmem mümkün müdür?
Evet mümkündür. / Hayır mümkün değildir.
Senin araba kiralaman mümkün müdür?
Evet mümkündür. / Hayır mümkün değildir.
Bizim uyumamız mümkün müdür?
Evet mümkündür. / Hayır mümkün değildir.

exercise 4

Sen beni bilebilirsin.
Biz dinlenebiliriz.
O otele gidebilir.
Onlar sahanda yumurta yiyebilir/yiyebilirler.
İnsanlar menüye bakabilir/bakabilirler.
Siz kafede menüden yemek seçebilirsiniz.
Ben seni görebilirim.
Sen araba kiralayabilirsin.
Biz uyuyabiliriz.

exercise 5

Sen beni bilemezsin.
Biz dinlenemeyiz.
O otele gidemez.
Onlar sahanda yumurta yiyemez/yiyemezler.

İnsanlar menüye bakamaz/bakamazlar.
Siz kafede menüden yemek seçemezsiniz.
Ben seni göremem.
Sen araba kiralayamazsın.
Biz uyuyamayız.

Unit 6

Dialogue 1
Answers: 1. No,she'll also decide later. 2. Yes.İbrahim plans to carry the bags afterwards.

Dialogue 2
Answers: 1. Yes, there are always many people shopping there. 2. No, it's from the Ottoman period.

Dialogue 3
Answers: 1. Yes, they can see the clothes over there., 2. Yes, they can change the clothes until six in the evening.

exercise 1

tatil, dükkân, karar, birlikte

exercise 2

İbrahim'e	Eymen'e	Jack'e
Ankara'ya	Londra'ya	Kahvaltıya
Birleşik Krallık'a	Çocuklara	Ağaca
Direğe	Kulübe	Çoraba

exercise 3

İbrahim'de	Eymen'de	Jack'te
Ankara'da	Londra'da	Kahvaltıda
Birleşik Krallık'ta	Çocuklarda	Ağaçta
Direkte	Kulüpte	Çorapta

exercise 4

İbrahim'den	Eymen'den	Jack'ten
Ankara'dan	Londra'dan	Kahvaltıdan
Birleşik Krallık'tan	Çocuklardan	Ağaçtan
Direkten	Kulüpten	Çoraptan

exercise 5

İbrahim'i	Eymen'i	Jack'i
Ankara'yı	Londra'yı	Kahvaltıyı
Birleşik Krallık'ı	Çocukları	Ağacı
Direği	Kulübü	Çorabı

Unit 7

Dialogue 1
Answers: 1. They wanted to learn about Michelle and İbrahim and about their vacation., 2. Yes, they have friends in Türkiye. They're Kâmuran, Fahriye, and their daughter Sema.

Dialogue 2
Answers: 1. He wasn't feeling well, but now he's better., 2. Because they missed their friends.

Dialogue 3
Answers: 1. Yes, they're Serra, Talha, and Yağmur., 2. It was tiring.

exercise 2

Evet, odada sen vardın.
Evet, odada çocuklar vardı.
Evet, odada biz vardık.
Evet, odada siz vardınız.
Evet, odada Michelle vardı.
Evet, odada herkes vardı.
Evet, odada bir şey vardı.
Evet, odada birisi vardı.
Hayır, odada hiç kimse yoktu.
Hayır, odada hiç bir şey yoktu.

exercise 3

Senin eşin var mıydı?
Evet, benim eşim vardı. / Hayır, benim eşim yoktu.

Otelin lokantası var mıydı?
Evet, otelin lokantası vardı. / Hayır, otelin lokantası yoktu.

Okulun öğrencisi var mıydı?
Evet, okulun öğrencisi vardı. / Hayır, okulun öğrencisi yoktu.

Michelle'in kardeşi var mıydı?
Evet, Michelle'in kardeşi vardı. / Hayır, Michelle'in kardeşi yoktu.

Bizim işimiz var mıydı?
Evet, bizim işimiz vardı. / Hayır, bizim işimiz yoktu.

Otelin yöneticisi var mıydı?
Evet, otelin yöneticisi vardı. / Hayır, otelin yöneticisi yoktu.

exercise 4

Sen beni bildin.
Biz dinlendik.
O otele gitti.

Onlar menemen yedi/yediler.
İnsanlar menüye baktı/baktılar.
Siz kafede menüden yemek seçtiniz.
Ben seni gördüm.
Sen araba kiraladın.
Biz uyuduk.

exercise 5

Sen beni bilmedin.
Biz dinlenmedik.
O otele gitmedi.
Onlar menemen yemedi/yemediler.
İnsanlar menüye bakmadı/bakmadılar.
Siz kafede menüden yemek seçmediniz.
Ben seni görmedim.
Sen araba kiralamadın.
Biz uyumadık.

exercise 6

Sen beni bildin mi?
Biz dinlendik mi?
O otele gitti mi?
Onlar menemen yedi mi?/yediler mi?
İnsanlar menüye baktı mı?/baktılar mı?
Siz kafede menüden yemek seçtiniz mi?
Ben seni gördüm mü?
Sen araba kiraladın mı?
Biz uyuduk mu?

exercise 7

Sen evliydin.
Michelle çok açtı.
Yemek hiç lezzetli değildi.
Manzara harikaydı.
Biz garsonduk.
Serra bir öğrenciydi.
Köpek Çanko hasta değildi.
Michelle'in babası bir mühendisti.
Biz Türkiye'deydik.

exercise 8

akşam, iyileşmek, yorulmak, tamamen

Unit 8

Dialogue 1
Answers: 1. They can get on metro at the metro station next to the hotel., 2. Yes, they can get on every transportation vehicles with one ticket. They can change vehicles when they need, too.

Dialogue 2
Answers: 1. They'll buy a permanent one., 2. They can load money into their tickets on the machines there.

Dialogue 3
Answers: 1. It connects Asia and Europe., 2. It connects the Black Sea and the Agean Sea.

exercise 1

makine, geri, ödemek, geçerli

exercise 2

Senin araban kırmızı. Benim arabam yeşil.

Ne senin araban ne de benim arabam sarı.

Senin araban yeni. Benim arabam da yeni.

senin araban da benim arabam da yeni.

Anıtkabir Ankara'da. İlkbahar Otel Ankara'da.

Anıtkabir de İlkbahar Otel Ankara'da.

Çay sıcak. Kahve sıcak.

Çay da kahve de sıcak.

Ud çalmayı severim. Şarkı söylemeyi severim.

Hem ud çalmayı hem de şarkı söylemeyi severim.

exercise 3

most frequent least frequent	her zaman
	sık sık, sabahları
	haftasonları, bazen, ara sıra
	nadiren
	hiç

Unit 9

Dialogue 1
Answers: 1. No, Fahriye didn't know that Michelle and İbrahim were in İstanbul., 2. No, she didn't accept the invitation right away, she needs to talk to İbrahim first. Then they'll call back.

Dialogue 2
Answers: 1. Yes, they have plans. They'll take a walk and go out for dinner., 2. They will call Fahriye right away because she wants to learn about the visit date immediately.

Dialogue 3
Answers: 1. No, she doesn't know the address. They need the directions., 2. No, she thinks using the navigation device might be necessary.

exercise 1

Sen beni bileceksin.
Biz dinleneceğiz.
O otele gidecek.
Onlar menemen yiyecek/yiyecekler.
İnsanlar menüye bakacak/bakacaklar.
Siz kafede menüden yemek seçeceksiniz.
Ben seni göreceğim.
Sen araba kiralayacaksın.
Biz uyuyacağız.

exercise 2

Sen beni bilmeyeceksin.
Biz dinlenmeyeceğiz.
O otele gitmeyecek.
Onlar menemen yemeyecek/yemeyecekler.
İnsanlar   menüye
bakmayacak/bakmayacaklar.
Siz kafede menüden yemek seçmeyeceksiniz.
Ben seni görmeyeceğim.
Sen araba kiralamayacaksın
Biz uyumayacağız.

exercise 3

Sen beni bilecek misin?
Biz dinlenecek miyiz?
O otele gidecek mi?
Onlar menemen yiyecek mi?/yiyecekler mi?
İnsanlar menüye bakacak mı?/bakacaklar mı?
Siz kafede menüden yemek seçecek misiniz?
Ben seni görecek miyim?
Sen araba kiralayacak mısın?
Biz uyuyacak mıyız?

exercise 4

eczane, aramak, dikkat, köşe

Unit 10

Dialogue 1
Answers: 1. No, they found it easily., 2. No, they have just moved here.

Dialogue 2
Answers: 1. They wanted to extend their best regards to Fahriye and Kâmuran., 2. Yes, they brought a present with them.

Dialogue 3
Answers: 1. It has two floors., 2. It will stay on the wall in the living room.

exercise 1

Evet, odada sen olacaksın.
Evet, odada çocuklar olacak/olacaklar.
Evet, odada biz olacağız.
Evet, odada siz olacaksınız.
Evet, odada Michelle olacak.
Evet, odada herkes olacak.
Evet, odada bir şey olacak.
Evet, odada birisi olacak.
Hayır, odada hiç kimse olmayacak.
Hayır, odada hiç bir şey olmayacak.

exercise 2

Senin eşin olacak mı?
Evet, benim eşim olacak. / Hayır, benim eşim olmayacak.

Otelin lokantası olacak mı?
Evet, otelin lokantası olacak. / Hayır, otelin lokantası olmayacak.

Okulun öğrencisi olacak mı?
Evet, okulun öğrencisi olacak. / Hayır, okulun öğrencisi olmayacak.

Michelle'in kardeşi olacak mı?
Evet, Michelle'in kardeşi olacak./ Hayır, Michelle'in kardeşi olmayacak.

Bizim işimiz olacak mı?
Evet, bizim işimiz olacak. / Hayır, bizim işimiz olmayacak.

Otelin yöneticisi olacak mı?
Evet, otelin yöneticisi olacak. / Hayır, otelin yöneticisi olmayacak.

exercise 3

Sen beni bilesin diye böyle yaptın.
Biz dinlenelim diye böyle yaptık.
O otele gitsin diye böyle yaptı.

Onlar menemen yesinler diye böyle yaptı /
yaptılar.
İnsanlar menüye baksın diye böyle yaptı /
yaptılar.
Siz kafede menüden yemek seçin diye böyle
yaptınız.
Ben seni göreyim diye böyle yaptım.
Sen araba kiralayasın diye böyle yaptın.
Biz uyuyalım diye böyle yaptı.

Biz evi taşıdıktan sonra yoruluruz.
Biz yorulmadan önce evi taşırız.

Siz gezdikten sonra yeni yerler görürsünüz.
Siz yeni yerler görmeden önce gezersiniz.

Michelle yemeği pişirdikten sonra yer.
Michelle yemeği yemeden önce pişir.

İbrahim araba sürdükten sonra konuşur.
İbrahim konuşmadan önce araba sürer.

Unit 11

Dialogue 1
Answers: 1. He made preparations in the garden.,
2. The tea will be brewed while they
eat.

Dialogue 2
Answers: 1. Not, they plan to grow fruit in the
future., 2. No, they still haven't
collected anything yet because they
just moved in this house so haven't
gotten enough time.

Dialogue 3
Answers: 1. It must have a garden because Lütfi
has a cat., 2. They already have
furniture, so they don't need a house
with furniture.

exercise 3
O kitap okurken müzik dinler.
O kitap okuduğunda müzik dinler.
O kitap okur, aynı zamanda müzik dinler.

Biz evi taşırken yoruluruz.
Biz evi taşıdığımızda yoruluruz.
Biz evi taşırız, aynı zamanda yoruluruz.

Siz gezerken yeni yerler görürsünüz.
Siz gezdiğinizde yeni yerler görürsünüz.
Siz gezersiniz, aynı zamanda yeni yerler
görürsünüz.

Michelle yemeği pişirirken yer.
Michelle yemeği pişirdiğinde yer.
Michelle yemeği pişirir, aynı zamanda yer.

İbrahim araba sürerken konuşur.
İbrahim araba sürdüğünde konuşur.
İbrahim araba sürer, aynı zamanda konuşur.

exercise 4
O kitap okuduktan sonra müzik dinler.
O müzik dinlemeden önce kitap okur.

Unit 12

Dialogue 1
Answers: 1. Both İbrahim and Lütfi like folkloric
music., 2. She doesn't like scary
movies.

Dialogue 2
Answers: 1. No, he doesn't because Michelle
doesn't like watching sports., 2. No,
he won't because Sema doesn't like
watching sports.

Dialogue 3
Answers: 1. She drinks with a little sugar., 2. They
probably won't because they
complain about gaining weight.

exercise 1
tutmak, mutluluk, çift, müsabaka

exercise 2
O kadar çok yedim ki, doydum.
O kadar fazla para harcadı ki, parası kalmadı.
Siz bizi o kadar çok sevdiniz ki, bizi ziyarete
geldiniz.
Alışverişe o kadar ihtiyacımız oldu ki, dükkâna
gittik.
Onlar o kadar mutlu insanlardı ki, sokakta
şarkı söylediler.

exercise 3
Çok yedim. Böylece/sonuç olarak doydum.
O fazla para harcadı. Böylece/sonuç olarak
parası kalmadı.
Siz bizi çok sevdiniz. Böylece/sonuç olarak
bizi ziyarete geldiniz.
Alışverişe ihtiyacımız oldu. Böylece/sonuç
olarak dükkâna gittik.
Onlar mutlu insanlardı. Böylece/sonuç olarak
sokakta şarkı söylediler.

exercise 4

Yağmur dersini çoktan bitirdi. Ancak henüz/daha/hâlâ müzik dinlemeye başlamadı.

Biz sizi çoktan davet ettik. Ancak siz bizi henüz/daha/hâlâ görmeye gelmediniz.

Hasta çocuk çoktan bir çok ilaç içti. Ancak henüz/daha/hâlâ iyileşmedi.

Michelle sabahları koşar. Ama daha/hâlâ kilo alıyor.

Siz henüz/daha/hâlâ çok gezmediniz. Ama çoktan güzel yerler gördünüz.

Siz artık İstanbul'da daha güzel bir ev satın aldınız. Şimdi hemen taşınabilirsiniz. Artık bu evde kalmazsınız.

Unit 13

Dialogue 1
Answers: 1. No, he doesn't cough any longer., 2. No, he can't because he feels very weak.

Dialogue 2
Answers: 1. A nurse will measure his temperature and pulse. And the doctor wanted to see his blood and urine test results., 2. If he needs, the doctor will ask other tests including x-ray.

Dialogue 3
Answers: 1. According to him, the medicine will be helpful because it's very effective., 2. In case İbrahim won't take the medicine regularly, he may get worse.

exercise 2

Eğer açsan, yemek sipariş edeceğim.
Eğer yağmur yağarsa, ıslanırız.
Eğer paraları çok olursa, yeni bir araba alırlar.
Eğer isterseniz, başarırsınız.
Eğer gelirsem, sevinir misin?

exercise 3

Eğer açsan, yemek sipariş et.
Eğer yağmur yağarsa, evde kalın.
Eğer çok paranız olursa, yeni bir araba al.
Eğer başarmak isterseniz, çok çalışın.
Eğer gelirsem, sen de gel.
Eğer kar yağarsa, sakın / asla dışarı çıkmayın.
Eğer kilo almak istemezsen, sakın / asla fazla yeme.

exercise 4

zorunda, harfiyen, sağlıklı, acı

Unit 14

Dialogue 1
Answers: 1. He apologizes for staying in the hotel room because of his sickness., 2. She thinks staying in the hotel resting is a part of their vacation, too.

Dialogue 2
Answers: 1. According to Michelle, İbrahim is more polite than Lütfi because İbrahim is the kindest person in the world., 2. İbrahim thinks that he's the happiest person in the world because he's married to the most beautiful woman in the world.

Dialogue 3
Answers: 1. Yes, he still feels sorry., 2. Yes, they want to come to Türkiye in January. They also want to participate in Sema and Lütfi's wedding then.

exercise 1

kızıl, dul, hepsi, iltifat

exercise 2
Kâmuran bahçede. Sebzeleri suluyor olmalı.
Fahriye mutfakta. Yemek hazırlıyor olmalı.
Sema telefonda. Nişanlısıyla konuşuyor olmalı.
İbrahim eczanede. Hasta olmalı.
Michelle internette. Annesine mesaj yazıyor olmalı.

exercise 3
Kâmuran bahçede. Sebzeleri suluyor olabilir.
Fahriye mutfakta. Yemek hazırlıyor olabilir.
Sema telefonda. Nişanlısıyla konuşuyor olabilir.
İbrahim eczanede. Hasta olabilir.
Michelle internette. Annesine mesaj yazıyor olabilir.

exercise 4
Kâmuran bahçede. Belki de sebzeleri suluyordur.
Fahriye mutfakta. Belki de yemek hazırlıyordur.
Sema telefonda. Belki de nişanlısıyla konuşuyordur.
İbrahim eczanede. Belki de hastadır.
Michelle internette. Belki de annesine mesaj yazıyordur.

exercise 5

Kâmuran en çok sevdiğim amcamdır.
Fahriye bildiğim en iyi aşçıdır.
Sema telefonda en çok nişanlısıyla konuşur.
Bugün en soğuk gün.
Michelle en çok annesini özler.

exercise 6

İbrahim öğretmen. Kendisi, aynı zamanda, yorgun.
Serra akıllı. Kendisi, aynı zamanda, çalışkan.
Otel büyük. Kendisi, aynı zamanda, yeni.
Eymen yaramaz. Kendisi, aynı zamanda, başarılı.
Annem muhasebeci. Kendisi, aynı zamanda, ev hanımı.
Anıtkabir merkezî. Kendisi, aynı zamanda yakın.

Unit 15

Dialogue 1

Answers: 1. No, all the planes are full that day., 2. Either they can bring the tickets to the hotel or they can get on the plane with electronic tickets (without regular tickets).

Dialogue 2

Answers: 1. The identification and the passports., 2. No, they can only take hand baggages with them. The others should be given to the counter.

Dialogue 3

Answers: 1. Yes, Michelle thinks they match well., 2. Yes, they'll probably come to the wedding.

exercise 1

boş	dolu	yavaş	hızlı
önce	sonra	ince	kalın
geç	erken	kalabalık	sakin
sağlıklı	hasta, sağlıksız	ilk	son
evli	bekâr, dul	aç	tok
ıslak	kuru	sıcak	soğuk
uzun	kısa	iyi	kötü
üzgün	mutlu	az	çok
genç	yaşlı	dar	geniş
küçük	büyük	üst	alt
ağır	hafif	ileri	geri
acı	tatlı	birlikte	ayrı, yalnız
şekersiz	şekerli	sesli	sessiz
aynı	farklı	geçici	sürekli

exercise 2

binmek	inmek	hastalanmak	iyileşmek
gitmek	gelmek	çıkmak	inmek
satmak	(satın) almak	ayrılmak	birleşmek
uzanmak	kalkmak	uyumak	uyanmak
oturmak	yatmak	dinlemek	yorulmak
ateşi yükselmek	ateşi düşmek	yatmak	kalkmak

exercise 3

Kesinlikle bugün bizde kalamazsın.
Kesinlikle bizimle Türkçe konuşamazsın.
Kesinlikle işten bugün biraz erken çıkamazsın.
Kesinlikle bana bir şey söyleyemezsin.
Kesinlikle buraya biraz uzanamazsın.

exercise 4

Hayır, sakın bugün bize gelme.
Hayır, sakın bizimle bir şey konuşma.
Hayır, sakın bugün eve biraz erken gitme.
Hayır, sakın bana bir hediye alma.
Hayır, sakın buraya oturma.

exercise 5

Anahtar bulundu.	Ben anahtarı buldum.
Eşyalar taşınacak.	Ben eşyaları taşıyacağım.
Arkadaşımı davet ettim.	Arkadaşım davet edildi.
Yemek pişirilecek.	Ben yemeği pişireceğim.
Arabamı sattım.	Arabam satıldı.

Unit 16

Unit 16: Reading Text 1

Answers: 1. The police try to catch the members of a multinational gang., 2. Yes, the did.

Unit 17

Unit 17: Reading Text 1

Answers: 1. Yes, he absolutely regret his decision to leave the dorm., 2. Yes, he felt regret and loneliness.

Unit 18

Unit 18: Reading Text 1

Answers: 1. *No, their choices were opposite., 2. Both of them like the adventurous movies.*

Unit 19

Unit 19: Reading Text 1

Answers: 1. *No, the food wasn't enough for him., 2. No, he missed the first bus.*

Unit 20

Unit 20: Reading Text 1

Answers: 1. *Because he heard someone talking to him., 2. No he didn't see anyone.*

Glossaries

The words listed in the glossaries are given only with the meaning mentioned in this book. So, please note that all meanings and variations may not be included.

Türkçe – İngilizce

Turkish – English

abartmak	*exaggerate*	alışveriş arabası	*shopping cart*
abi	*elder brother*		
abla	*elder sister*	alışverişe çıkmak	*to go shopping*
abur cubur	*snack, junk food*		
acı	*pain*	almak	*to buy*
aç	*hungry*	almak	*to take*
aç karnına	*when hungry*	Alman	*German person*
açık	*open, light*	Almanca	*German language*
açıklamak	*to explain*	Almanya	*Germany*
adalet	*justice*	altı	*six*
adam	*man*	altıncı	*sixth*
âdet	*tradition*	altmış	*sixty*
âdeta	*almost*	ama	*but*
adres	*address*	amca	*uncle*
ağız	*mouth*	Amerikalı	*American*
ağrı	*pain*	amir	*chief*
ağrı kesici	*painkiller*	anahtar	*key*
ağrımak	*to ache*	Anıtkabir	*Atatürk's Mausoleum*
ak	*white*	anlaşmak	*to agree*
akıcı	*fluent*	anlayışlı	*considerate*
akıl	*mind*	anne	*mother*
akıllı	*clever*	araç	*vehicle*
aklına gelmek	*to come to the mind*	aralamak	*to open*
akraba	*relative*	aramak	*to try to find, to call*
aksi takdirde	*otherwise*	aranmak	*to be called*
aksiyon	*action*	Arap	*Arab*
akşam	*evening*	Arapça	*Arabic*
akşam yemeği	*dinner*	arasında	*between*
aktarma yapmak	*to transfer*	arka	*back*
		arkadaş canlısı	*friendly*
alan	*field, area*	armut	*pear*
alın	*forehead*	artı	*added to*
alınmak	*to be taken*	asılsız	*unfounded*
alışmak	*to get used to*	aslında	*in fact*
alışveriş	*shopping*	Asya	*Asia*

aşçı	*cook*	beden	*size*
aşçıbaşı	*chef*	beden numarası	*size number*
ateş	*fever*		
ateş düşürücü	*antipyretic*	bekâr	*single*
ateşi çıkmak	*to have a high fever*	beklemek	*to wait*
ateşi düşmek	*to (fever) fall*	beklenmek	*to be waited*
ateşi yükselmek	*to have a high fever*	bel	*waist*
		belgesel	*documentary*
atıştırmak	*to eat sneaks*	ben	*I*
atmak	*to throw*	bence	*in my opinion*
Avrupa	*Europe*	benim	*my*
ayırmak	*to split*	benzin	*gasoline*
aylık	*for a month, monthly*	berbat	*awful*
ayna	*mirror*	beslemek	*to feed*
aynı	*the same*	beş	*five*
ayrı kalmak	*to stay apart*	beşinci	*fifth*
ayrıca	*in addition*	bey	*Mr.*
ayrılmak	*to leave*	beyaz	*white*
az	*little, few*	beyaz peynir	*white cheese*
baba	*father*	beyefendi	*gentleman*
baca	*chimney*	bırakmak	*to leave, to stop*
bacak	*leg*	biber	*pepper*
bagaj	*luggage*	bilet	*ticket*
bahar	*spring*	bilgi	*information*
baharat	*spice*	bilgisayar	*computer*
bahçe	*garden*	bilinmek	*to be known*
bakakalmak	*to continue looking*	bilmek	*to know*
bakmak	*to look*	binmek	*to get on/in a vehicle*
balkon	*balcony*	bir	*a, one*
banyo	*bathroom*	bir an önce	*as soon as possible*
bardak	*glass, cup*	bir de	*and, too*
baskın	*raid*	bir şey	*something*
baş	*the beginning of, head*	bir şeyler	*something*
başarılı	*successful*	biraz	*a little, some*
başarısız	*unsuccessful*	biraz gezmek	*to take a short trip*
başı dönmek	*to feel dizzy*	birazdan	*soon*
başka	*other, else*	biri	*someone*
başlamak	*to start*	birinci	*first*
başlanmak	*to be started*	birleşmek	*to merge*
batı	*west*	birleştirmek	*to join*
bay	*Mr.*	birlikte	*to getter*
bayan	*Mrs., Ms.*	biz	*we*
bayat	*stale*	blok	*bloc*
bazen	*sometimes*	bluz	*blouse*
bazı	*some*	Boğaz	*the Bosphorus*

boğaz	*troath*	çıkmak	*to go up*
bomboş	*empty*	çift	*a couple*
boş	*empty, unoccupied*	çikolata	*chokolate*
boş zaman	*free time*	çilek	*strawberry*
boyunca	*during*	çimen	*grass*
bölü	*divided by*	Çin	*China*
böyle	*like this*	Çince	*Chinese language*
böylesi	*such*	Çinli	*Chinese person*
bu	*this (is)*	çirkin	*ugly*
bu arada	*in the meantime*	çocuk	*child, boy or girl*
bugün	*today*	çok	*very, a lot*
bulmak	*to find*	çorap	*socks*
bulunmak	*to be found*	çökertmek	*to smash*
buluşmak	*to meet*	çünkü	*because*
bulut	*cloud*	daha	*more than*
bulutlu	*cloudy*	dakikalarca	*for minutes*
burada	*here*	damat	*son-in-law*
burun	*nose*	dar	*narrow*
buzdolabı	*refrigerator*	davranmak	*to behave*
bütün	*whole*	de /da	*also, too*
büyük	*big*	değişim	*exchange*
büyük beden	*large size*	değişim yapmak	*to exchange*
cadde	*avenue*	değiştirmek	*to exchange, to change*
cam	*glass, window*	dehşet içerisinde	*in horror*
cevap	*answer*	demek	*to mean, to say*
cevap vermek	*to give an answer*	demlemek	*to brew*
cevaplamak	*to answer*	demlenmek	*to be brewed*
ciddî	*serious*	denemek	*to try*
civar	*vicinity*	deniz	*sea*
civarı	*around*	depo	*warehouse*
cüzdan	*wallet or purse*	ders	*lesson*
çaba	*effort*	ders ortamı	*lesson environment*
çağırmak	*to call*	desteklemek	*to support*
çalışkan	*studious / hardworking*	devamlı	*permanent*
çalmak	*to play*	dışında	*outside, out of, apart from*
çanta	*bag*	diğer	*other*
çare	*solution*	dikilmek	*to stand up*
çarpı	*multiplied by*	dikkat	*attention*
çatal	*fork*	dikkat etmek	*to pay attention*
çatı	*roof*	dilemek	*to wish*
çay	*tea*	dilim	*slice*
çerez	*nuts*	dilimlemek	*to slice*
çeşit	*kind*	dinî	*religious*
çete	*gang*		
çıkarmak	*to throw up*		

dinlemek	*to listen to*	düzenlemek	*to arrange*
dinlendirici	*relaxing*	eczacı	*pharmacist*
dinlenmek	*to rest*	eczane	*pharmacy*
dinmek	*to (wind, snow, or rain) stop*	eğlenceli	*entertaining*
		ekmek	*bread*
direnmek	*to resist*	eksi	*subtracted from*
diş fırçası	*tooth brush*	eksik	*missing, lacking*
diş macunu	*tooth paste*	el	*hand*
dizel	*diesel*	el çantası	*hand bag*
dizi	*tv series*	elbise	*dress*
doğa	*nature*	ele geçirmek	*to capture*
doğal gazlı kombi	*natural gas boiler*	elli	*fifty*
		elma	*apple*
doğramak	*to chop*	emekli	*retired*
doğru	*right, correct*	en azından	*at least*
doğrultmak	*to point at*	en son	*finally*
doğu	*east*	endişelenmek	*to worry*
doksan	*ninety*	enişte	*brother-in-law*
doktor	*doctor*	epey	*rather*
doktora görünmek	*to be seen by a doctor*	erik	*plum*
		erkek kardeş	*brother*
dokuz	*nine*	erkenci	*early*
dokuzuncu	*ninth*	eski	*old*
dolu	*full of*	esmer	*brunette*
domates	*tomatoes*	eşim	*my spouse*
dondurma	*ice cream*	eşya	*belonging*
dondurma	*ice cream*	eşya (mobilya)	*things, furniture*
dost	*friend*	et	*meat*
dönmek	*to return*	etek	*skirt*
dördüncü	*fourth*	etmek	*to do, to perform*
dört	*four*	etraf	*surrounding*
dudak	*lip*	ev hanımı	*housewife*
dul	*widow*	evet	*yes*
duymak	*to hear*	evli	*married*
duyulmak	*to be heard*	evvelsi gün	*the day before yesterday*
düğün	*wedding*	fakat	*but*
dükkân	*store, shop*	falan	*or else, etc.*
dün	*yesterday*	fark etmek	*to make a difference*
dünya	*world*	farklı	*different, various*
dürüm	*roll*	fasulye	*bean*
düşünce	*thought*	fayda	*advantage*
düşünceli	*thoughtful*	fayda sağlamak	*to gain advantage*
düşünmek	*to think*		
düz	*standart, straight*	fazla	*too many, too much*
düzenleme yapmak	*to make arrangements*	fena	*awful*

fevrî	*impulsive*
fırın	*stove*
fikir	*opinion*
fincan	*cup*
fiş	*receipt*
fiyat	*price*
folklorik	*folkloric*
fotoğraf	*photograph*
fotoğraf çekmek	*to take photographs*
Fransa	*France*
Fransız	*French person*
Fransızca	*French language*
futbol	*soccer*
garson	*waiter*
gayet	*rather, very*
gece	*night*
gece yarısı	*midnight*
geç	*late*
geç	*late*
geçerli	*valid*
geçici	*temporary*
geçirmek	*to spend time*
geçmek	*to pass, to go, to recover from an illness*
gelin	*daughter-in-law*
gelmek	*to come*
genç	*young, yougster*
geniş	*wide*
gerçek	*reality*
gerçekten	*really*
geri	*reverse*
geri dönmek	*to return*
getirmek	*to bring*
gezmek	*to take a trip*
gıcırtı	*creak*
gibi	*like*
gidiş geliş	*round trip*
girişmek	*to engage in*
gitar	*guitar*
gitmek	*to go*
gizlenmek	*to hide*
gömlek	*shirt*
göndermek	*to send*
görev	*task*
görkemli	*majestic*
görmek	*to see*
görmek	*to see*
görülmek	*to be seen*
göz	*eye*
göz atmak	*to take a glance*
göz gezdirmek	*to review*
gram	*gram*
gri	*grey*
güneş açmak	*to (sun) shine*
güneşli	*sunny*
güney	*south*
günlük	*for a day, daily*
günümüzde	*in these days, today*
gürültülü	*noisy*
güz	*fall*
güzel	*nice, beautiful, well*
güzün	*in the fall*
haber	*news*
hafif	*light*
hafif müzik	*soft music*
hafta	*week*
haftalık	*for a week, weekly*
haklı	*right*
halı	*carpet*
halsiz	*weak*
hangisi?	*which?*
hanım	*Mrs., Ms.*
hanımefendi	*lady*
hap	*tablet*
hareket etmek	*to move, to be active*
hareketlenmek	*to start moving*
hareketli	*with lots of activity*
hareketsiz	*still*
harfiyen	*exactly*
harika	*wonderful*
hasta olmak	*to be sick*
hastane	*hospital*
haşlamak	*to boil*
hata	*fault*
hatırlamak	*to remember*
hatırlanmak	*to be remembered*
hâttâ	*even*
hava	*weather*
havuç	*carrot*
hayır	*no*

haz almak	*to enjoy*	ilaç yazmak	*to write a prescription*
hazır	*ready*	ilaç yutmak	*to take medicine*
hazırlamak	*to prepare*	ilâve	*additional*
hazırlık	*preparation*	ile	*with*
hazırlık yapmak	*to make preparations*	ileri	*forward*
		ileride	*in the future*
hediye	*present*	ilgilenmek	*to be interested in*
hediyelik eşya	*souvenir shop*	ilginç	*interesting*
hem	*by this way, and*	ilk	*first*
hemen	*right away*	ilk bahar	*spring*
hemşire	*nurse*	ilkokulda	*in elementary school*
her ikisi de	*both*	iltifat	*compliment*
her yere	*to everywhere*	iltifat etmek	*to make a compliment*
herkes	*everyone*	ince kıyafet	*light clothes*
herşey	*everything*	indirim	*discount*
Hindistan	*India*	indirmek	*to discount*
Hintçe	*Indian language*	İngiliz	*English*
Hintli	*Indian person*	İngiliz	*English person*
hissetmek	*to feel*	İngilizce	*English language*
hobi	*hobby*	İngiltere	*England*
hostes	*hostess*	inmek	*to land, get off, to go down*
hoş	*cute*	internet sayfası	*internet page*
hoşlanmak	*to like*		
ılık	*warm*	internet üzerinden	*on the internet*
ısıtma	*heating*		
ısıtmak	*to heat*	irkilmek	*to startle*
ıslak	*wet*	İspanya	*Spain*
ısrar etmek	*to insist*	İspanyol	*Spanish person*
iade almak	*to (accept) refund*	İspanyolca	*Spanish language*
iade etmek	*to (apply for the) refund*	İspanyolca	*Spanish*
iç çamaşırı	*underwear*	istemek	*to want*
iç içe olmak	*to be intertwined*	istenmek	*to be wanted*
içecek	*drinks*	istifra etmek	*to throw up*
içeride	*inside*	istihbarat	*intelligence*
içilmek	*to be drunk*	iş	*job, work*
için	*for*	iş insanı	*businessman or businesswoman*
içmek	*to drink*		
idrar tahlili	*urine test*	işaret parmağı	*forefinger*
ihbar	*notice*	işitmek	*to hear*
ihtiyacını karşılamak	*to satisfy, to meet one's need*	İtalya	*Italy*
		İtalyan	*Italian person*
ihtiyaç	*need*	İtalyanca	*Italian language*
iki	*two*	iyi	*fine*
ikinci	*second*	iyi gelmek	*to do good*
ilaç almak	*to take medicine*	iyileşmek	*to get well*
		izlemek	*to watch*

Japon	*Japanese person*	kepçe	*ladle*
Japonca	*Japanese language*	kesilmek	*to (wind, snow, or rain) stop*
Japonya	*Japan*	kırk	*forty*
kabir	*tomb*	kırmızı	*red*
kadar	*until*	kısa	*short*
kadın	*woman*	kış	*winter*
kafa	*head*	kışın	*in the winter*
kahvaltı	*breakfast*	kışlık	*for winter*
kahvaltılık	*food for breakfast*	kıta	*continent*
kahve	*coffee*	kıvrılmak	*to turn*
kahverengi	*brown*	kıyafet	*cloth, clothing*
kalabalık	*crowded*	kıyafet dükkânı	*clothing store*
kalın kıyafet	*warm clothes*	kız	*daughter*
kalkmak	*to stand up*	kız kardeş	*sister*
kalmak	*to stay*	kızartmak	*to fry*
kalp atışı	*heart beat*	kızıl	*scarlet*
kalp atmak	*(for the heart) to beat*	Kızılay Meydanı	*the Kızılay Square*
kan tahlili	*blood test*	kibar	*kind*
Kanadalı	*Canadian*	kilo almak	*to gain weight*
kapkaranlık	*full darkness*	kimlik	*identification*
kar	*snow*	kimlik kartı	*identification card*
kar yağmak	*to snow*	kiralama	*renting*
kara	*black*	kiralamak	*to rent*
karakol	*police station*	kirli	*dirty*
karar	*decision*	kişilik	*for a person*
karar vermek	*to decide*	kişisel	*personal*
kararlı	*determined*	klima	*airconditioner*
kardeş	*brother or sister*	kol	*arm*
karın	*abdomen*	kolay	*easy*
karlı	*snowy*	kolayca	*easily*
karpuz	*watermelon*	koltuk	*sofa*
karşı	*opposite*	komedi filmi	*comedy movie*
karşıda	*at the opposite*	komşu	*neighbor*
kasap	*butcher*	konuşkan	*talkative*
kâse	*bowl*	korku filmi	*scary movie*
kaşık	*spoon*	kovmak	*to fire*
kaşımak	*to scratch*	kovulmak	*to get fired*
kat	*story, floor*	koymak	*to put*
kavşak	*intersection*	koyu	*dark*
kavun	*melon*	koyulmak	*to start doing something*
kayısı	*apricot*	köpek	*dog*
kedi	*cat*	köprü	*bridge*
keman	*violin*	köşe	*corner*
kenar sehpası	*end table*	kredi kartı	*credit card*
kenarda	*on the sideline*		

kulak	*ear*	meşhur	*famous*
kurmak	*to set up*	metro	*metro, subway*
kurtulmak	*to run away*	mevcut	*there is*
kuru	*dry*	mevsim	*season*
kusmak	*to throw up*	meyve	*fruit*
kutu	*box*	mide	*stomach*
kuyumcu	*jewelery store*	mide bulantısı	*nausea*
kuzen	*cousin*	milyon	*million*
kuzey	*north*	misafir odası	*guest room*
küçük	*little, small*	mobilya	*furniture*
küçük beden	*small size*	mobilyalı	*furnished*
kültürel	*cultural*	mobilyasız	*unfurnished*
lezzetli	*delicious*	mor	*purple*
lezzetsiz	*unsavory*	muayene etmek	*to examine*
lider	*leader*		
litre	*liter*	muhabbet	*a warm conversation*
lokanta	*restaurant*	muhabbet etmek	*to have a warm conversation*
lokum	*delight*		
Londra	*London*	muhasebeci	*accountant*
macera filmi	*adventure movie*	mutfak	*kitchen*
maç	*match*	mutlaka	*for sure*
mahalle	*neighborhood*	mutlu	*happy*
makine	*machine*	mutluluk	*happiness*
manav	*green grocer*	mutsuz	*sad*
mangal	*barbecue*	muz	*banana*
manzara	*view*	mühendis	*engineer*
marul	*lettuce*	mümkün	*possible*
masa	*table*	müsabaka	*competition*
masraf	*cost*	müsait	*available*
mavi	*blue*	müşteri	*customer*
maydanoz	*parsley*	müze	*museum*
mekân	*site*	müzik	*music*
melodram	*melodram*	nabız	*pulse*
menemen	*eggs cooked with with tomatoes and peppers*	nafile	*futile*
		namlu	*barrel*
menü	*menu*	nane	*mint*
merak	*curiosity*	nasıl?	*how?*
merak etmek	*to wonder*	navigasyon cihazı	*navigation device*
meraklı	*curious*		
merkez	*centre*	ne kadar?	*how long?, how many/much?*
merkezî	*central*		
mesafe	*distance*	ne?	*what?*
mesâi	*working shift*	neden?	*why?*
mesaj	*message*	neredeyse	*almost*
meselâ	*for instance*	neşeli	*joyful*
meslek	*profession*	nişanlı	*engaged, fiance or fiancee*

o	*he or she*	öğle arası	*lunch break*
o nedenle	*because of that*	öğle yemeği	*lunch*
o sebeple	*because of that*	öğleden önce	*before noon*
o yüzden	*since*	öğleden sonra	*afternoon*
ocak	*oven*	öğlen	*at noon*
oda	*room*	öğrenci	*student*
oda tutmak	*to stay in a hotel*	öğrenmek	*to figure out, to learn*
oğul	*son*	öğretmen	*teacher*
okul	*school*	öğün	*meal*
okumak	*to read*	öksürmek	*to cough*
okunmak	*to be read*	öksürük	*cough*
oldukça	*rather, very*	ölçmek	*to measure*
olmak	*to be*	ön	*ahead*
on	*ten*	önce	*before, first*
on altı	*sixteen*	önemli	*important*
on beş	*fifteen*	örneğin	*for instance*
on bir	*eleven*	örtü	*cover, cloth*
on dokuz	*nineteen*	özel	*special*
on dört	*fourteen*	özlemek	*to miss, long for*
on iki	*twelve*	özlenmek	*to be missed*
on sekiz	*eighteen*	özür dilemek	*to apologize*
on üç	*thirteen*	pantolon	*pants*
on yedi	*seventeen*	parça	*piece, part*
ondan dolayı	*because of that*	park etmek	*to park*
onlar	*they*	pasaport	*passport*
onun	*his/her*	patates	*patatoes*
onuncu	*tenth*	patlıcan	*eggplant*
orada	*there*	peçete	*paper towel, tissue*
orası	*there, that place*	pek	*rather, much, many, a lot*
orta	*with a little sugar*	pembe	*pink*
orta beden	*medium size*	pencere	*window*
orta parmak	*middle finger*	perde	*curtains*
orta sehpa	*coffee table*	peynir	*cheese*
ortada	*in the middle*	pilot	*pilot*
ortam	*environment*	piyano	*piano*
ortasında	*in the middle*	poğaça	*pastry*
otel	*hotel*	pop müzik	*pop music*
otel yöneticisi	*hotel manager*	porsiyon	*portion*
otobüs	*bus*	portakal	*orange*
otomatik	*automatic*	poşet	*bag*
oturma odası	*living room*	program	*program*
oturmak	*to live in a place, to sit*	pusu	*ambush*
oyuncu	*actor or actress*	raf	*shelf*
ödeme yapmak	*to make a payment*	rahatsız olmak	*to get irritated*
ödemek	*to pay*	randevu	*appointment*

reçel	*jam*
reçete	*prescription*
referans numarası	*reference number*
renk	*colour*
resim	*picture*
resim çizmek	*to draw pictures*
resmen	*officially*
röntgen	*x-ray*
Rus	*Russian person*
Rusça	*Russian language*
Rusya	*Russia*
rüzgâr	*wind*
rüzgâr esmek	*to (wind) blow*
rüzgârlı	*windy*
saat	*hour, clock*
saatlik	*for an hour, hourly*
sabah	*morning*
sabun	*soap*
saç	*hair*
sade	*without sugar and milk*
sadece	*only*
sağ	*right*
sağlık	*health*
sağlıklı	*healthy*
sahanda yumurta	*scrambled eggs*
sakin	*quiet, calm*
saklanmak	*to hide*
salam	*salami*
salata	*salad*
salatalık	*cucumber*
salon	*living room*
samimi	*sincere*
sandalye	*chair*
sarı	*yellow*
sarımsak	*garlic*
sarışın	*blond*
sarmak	*to wrap*
satıcı	*seller*
satılmak	*to be sold*
satmak	*to sell*
savaş	*war*
sayı	*number, quantity*
sebze	*vegetable*
seçenek	*choice*
seçmek	*to choose*
sedye	*stretcher*
sekiz	*eight*
sekizinci	*eighth*
sekreter	*secretary*
seksen	*eighty*
selâm söylemek	*to send best regards*
semaver	*samovar*
sen	*you*
sence	*in your opinion*
serin	*cool*
seslenmek	*to call*
sesli	*loud*
sessiz	*silent, quiet*
sevgili	*dear*
sevinmek	*to be happy*
sevk edilmek	*to be sent*
sevmek	*to love*
seyahat	*trip*
seyretmek	*to watch*
sıcak	*hot*
sıcak içecek	*hot drink*
sıcaklamak	*to get hot*
sıfır	*zero*
sıkılmak	*to get bored*
sırt	*back*
sigorta	*insurance*
sinirlenmek	*to get angry*
sipariş etmek	*to order food*
site	*site*
siyah	*black*
siyah zeytin	*black olive*
siz	*you (pl)*
sofra	*dining table*
soğan	*onion*
soğuk	*cold*
soğuk içecek	*cold drink*
soğutma	*cooling*
soğutmak	*to cool*
sohbet	*a warm conversation*
sohbet etmek	*to have a conversation*
sokak	*street*
sol	*left*

son	*end*
son bahar	*fall*
sonra	*later, after, later on*
sonuncu	*last*
sormak	*to ask*
soru	*question*
sorun etmek	*to trouble*
söylemek, anlatmak	*to say, tell*
su	*water*
sucuk	*sausage*
sulamak	*to water*
sulanmak	*to be watered*
Suudi Arabistan	*Saudi Arabia*
sürekli	*permanent*
süresinde	*during*
sürmek	*to drive*
süt	*milk*
sütlaç	*rice pudding*
şampuan	*shampoo*
şapka	*hat*
şarkı	*song*
şarkı söylemek	*to sing*
şarkıcı	*singer*
şef	*chef*
şeftali	*peach*
şeker	*sugar*
şekerli	*with sugar*
şekersiz	*wthout sugar*
şımartmak	*to spoil*
şiirsel	*poetic*
şikâyet	*complaint*
şimdilik	*for now*
şişe	*bottle*
şoför	*driver*
şöhret	*fame*
şöyle	*like this*
şu anda	*for the moment*
tabak	*plate*
tabanca	*pistol*
tabîat	*nature*
tam	*right at the, full or complete*
tamamen	*completely*
tamir etmek	*to repair*
tane	*each, piece*
tanımak	*to recognize*
tanınmak	*to be recognized*
tanışmak	*to meet, to introduce*
taraf	*side*
tarak	*comb*
tarih	*date*
tarihî	*historic*
taşımak	*to take, to move, to transport*
taşınmak	*to be moved*
tatil	*vacation*
tatlı	*dessert*
tavsiye	*advice*
tavuk	*chicken*
taze	*fresh*
tebrik etmek	*to congratulate*
tek sefer	*one way*
tek yön	*one way*
telefonla aramak	*to call on the phone*
tembel	*lazy*
temiz	*clean*
temizlik malzemeleri	*cleaning materials*
temizlikçi	*cleaner*
tepe	*hill*
ter	*sweat*
tercih etmek	*to prefer*
tereyağı	*butter*
terlemek	*to perspire*
terzi	*tailor*
tesirli	*effective*
teslim etmek	*to deliver, to give*
teyze	*aunt*
tezgâhtar	*cashier*
tırnak makası	*nail scissors*
titremek	*to tremble*
tok	*full*
tok karnına	*when full*
toplam	*total*
toplamak	*to collect*
toplu taşıma	*public transportation*
tören alanı	*parade ground*
traş malzemeleri	*shaving materials*

tuhaf	strange	üzerinde	on top of
turistik	touristic	üzerini çıkarmak	to uncover the upper body
turşu	pickle	üzgün	sad
turuncu	orange	üzülmek	to be sad
tutku	passion	üzüm	grape
tutmak	to rent, to support	vaha	oasis
tutuk	inarticulate	vapur	ferry
tutuklamak	to arrest	var	there is / are
tutuklanmak	to be arrested	vaz geçmek	to change mind
tuvalet	restroom	ve	and
tuvalet kâğıdı	toilet paper	vermek	to give
tuz	salt	viraj	curve
tüm gün boyunca	all daylong	vişne	sour cherry
tür	kind	vites	transmission
Türk	Turk	vücut	body
Türkçe	Turkish language	yabancı	foreign
Türkçe	Turkish language	yabancı dil	foreign language
Türkiye	Türkiye	yağmur	rain
türkü	folkloric song	yağmur yağmak	to rain
türkücü	singer (folkloric)	yağmurlu	rainy
ud	ud	yakın	close to
uğraşı	activity	yakında	close, near
ulus	nation	yakışıklı	handsome
ummak	to hope	yakışmak	to match with
uslu	docile	yakıt	fuel
utandırmak	to make someone feel ashamed	yakmak	to light
utanmak	to feel ashamed	yalnız	alone
uygun	available	yanaşmak	to approach
uymak	to obey	yanında	with this
uzak	far from	yani	in other words
uzakta	far	yanlış	wrong
uzanmak	lie down	yapayalnız	all alone
uzatmak	extend	yapmak	to do
uzman	specialist	yaramaz	naughty
uzun	long	yardımcı	helper
ücret	price	yarın	tomorrow
üç	three	yaşlı	old
üçüncü	third	yatak odası	sleeping room
üniversite	university	yatmak	to go to bed
ürün	product	yatmamak	to stay up
üstelik	moreover	yaygın	common, widespread
üstüne	over something	yaz	summer
üşümek	to get cold	yazın	in the summer
üye	member		

yazlık	*for summer*	yiyecek	*food*
yazmak	*to write*	yoğurt	*yogurt*
yedi	*seven*	yok	*there isn't / aren't*
yedinci	*seventh*	yol	*road*
yeğen	*nephew, niece*	yorgun	*tired*
yemek	*to eat*	yormak	*to make tired*
yemek	*food, meal*	yorulmak	*to get tired*
yemek odası	*dining room*	yönetici	*manager*
yemek tarifi	*recipe*	yumurta	*eggs*
yemekhane	*dining hall*	yurt	*dorm*
yemyeşil	*lush green*	yüklemek	*to load*
yenge	*sister-in-law*	yüksek	*high*
yeni	*new*	yüksek ateş	*high fever*
yenmek	*to be eaten*	yürüme mesafesi	*walking distance*
yer	*place, room*		
yer ayırmak	*to approve the reservation*	yüz	*a hundred, face*
yer ayırtmak	*to apply for a hotel reservation*	yüz ifadesi	*face expression*
		zamanı kalmak	*to have time left*
yerleşmek	*to settle*	zamanında	*on time*
yerleştirmek	*to put*	zevk	*pleasure*
yeşil	*green*	zeytin	*olives*
yeşil zeytin	*green olive*	zıt	*opposite*
yeşillik	*green*	ziyaret etmek	*to visit*
yeterli	*enough*	zor	*difficult, hard*
yetiştirmek	*to grow*	zorunda	*necessary*
yetmek	*to be enough*	zorunda kalmak	*to have to*
yetmiş	*seventy*		
yıllık	*for a year, yearly*		
yirmi	*twenty*		

İngilizce - Türkçe
English - Turkish

a	*bir*	at least	*en azından*
a couple	*çift*	at noon	*öğlen*
a hundred	*yüz*	at the hotel	*otelde*
a lot	*çok, pek*	at the opposite	*karşıda*
abdomen	*karın*	attention	*dikkat*
accountant	*muhasebeci*	aunt	*teyze*
action	*aksiyon*	automatic	*otomatik*
activity	*uğraşı*	available	*müsait, uygun*
actor or actress	*oyuncu*	avenue	*cadde*
added to	*artı*	awful	*berbat, fena*
additional	*ilâve*	back	*arka, sırt*
address	*adres*	bag	*çanta, poşet*
advantage	*fayda*	balcony	*balkon*
adventure movie	*macera filmi*	banana	*muz*
advice	*tavsiye*	barbecue	*mangal*
after	*sonra*	barrel	*namlu*
afternoon	*öğleden sonra*	bathroom	*banyo*
ahead	*ön*	bean	*fasulye*
airconditioner	*klima*	beautiful	*güzel*
all alone	*yapayalnız*	because	*çünkü*
all daylong	*tüm gün boyunca*	because of that	*o nedenle, o sebeple, ondan dolayı*
almost	*âdeta, neredeyse*	before	*önce*
alone	*yalnız*	before noon	*öğleden önce*
also	*de /da*	belonging	*eşya*
ambush	*pusu*	between	*arasında*
American	*Amerikalı*	big	*büyük*
and	*ve*	black	*kara, siyah*
answer	*cevap*	black olive	*siyah zeytin*
antipyretic	*ateş düşürücü*	bloc	*blok*
apart from	*dışında*	blond	*sarışın*
apple	*elma*	blood test	*kan tahlili*
appointment	*randevu*	blouse	*bluz*
apricot	*kayısı*	blue	*mavi*
Arab	*Arap*	body	*vücut*
Arabic	*Arapça*	both	*her ikisi de*
area	*alan*	bottle	*şişe*
arm	*kol*	bowl	*kâse*
around	*civarı*	box	*kutu*
as soon as possible	*bir an önce*	boy or girl	*çocuk*
		bread	*ekmek*
Asia	*Asya*	breakfast	*kahvaltı*

bridge	köprü	cloudy	bulutlu
brother	erkek kardeş	coffee	kahve
brother or sister	kardeş	coffee table	orta sehpa
brother-in-law	enişte	cold	soğuk
brown	kahverengi	cold drink	soğuk içecek
brunette	esmer	colour	renk
bus	otobüs	comb	tarak
businessman or businesswoman	iş insanı	comedy movie	komedi filmi
		common	yaygın
but	ama, fakat	competition	müsabaka
butcher	kasap	complaint	şikâyet
butter	tereyağı	complete	tam
by this way	hem	completely	tamamen
calm	sakin	compliment	iltifat
Canadian	Kanadalı	computer	bilgisayar
carpet	halı	considerate	anlayışlı
carrot	havuç	continent	kıta
cashier	tezgâhtar	conversation	muhabbet, sohbet
cat	kedi	cook	aşçı
central	merkezî	cool	serin
centre	merkez	cooling	soğutma
chair	sandalye	corner	köşe
cheese	peynir	correct	doğru
chef	aşçıbaşı, şef	cost	masraf
chicken	tavuk	cough	öksürük
chief	amir	cousin	kuzen
child	çocuk	cover	örtü
chimney	baca	creak	gıcırtı
China	Çin	credit card	kredi kartı
Chinese language	Çince	crowded	kalabalık
		cucumber	salatalık
Chinese person	Çinli	cultural	kültürel
choice	seçenek	cup	fincan
chokolate	çikolata	curiosity	merak
clean	temiz	curious	meraklı
cleaner	temizlikçi	curtains	perde
cleaning materials	temizlik malzemeleri	curve	viraj
		customer	müşteri
clever	akıllı	cute	hoş
clock	saat	daily	günlük
close	yakında	dark	koyu
close to	yakın	date	tarih
cloth	örtü	daughter	kız
cloth, clothing	kıyafet	daughter-in-law	gelin
clothing store	kıyafet dükkânı	dear	sevgili
cloud	bulut		

decision	*karar*	empty	*boş*
delicious	*lezzetli*	end	*son*
delight	*lokum*	end table	*kenar sehpası*
dessert	*tatlı*	engineer	*mühendis*
determined	*kararlı*	England	*İngiltere*
diesel	*dizel*	English	*İngiliz*
different	*farklı*	English language	*İngilizce*
difficult	*zor*		
dining hall	*yemekhane*	English person	*İngiliz*
dining room	*yemek odası*	enough	*yeterli*
dining table	*sofra*	entertaining	*eğlenceli*
dinner	*akşam yemeği*	environment	*ortam*
dirty	*kirli*	Europe	*Avrupa*
discount	*indirim*	even	*hâttâ*
distance	*mesafe*	evening	*akşam*
divided by	*bölü*	everyone	*herkes*
docile	*uslu*	everything	*herşey*
doctor	*doktor*	exactly	*harfiyen*
documentary	*belgesel*	exaggerate	*abartmak*
dog	*köpek*	exchange	*değişim*
dorm	*yurt*	extend	*uzatmak*
dress	*elbise*	eye	*göz*
drinks	*içecek*	face	*yüz*
driver	*şoför*	face expression	*yüz ifadesi*
dry	*kuru*	fall	*güz, son bahar*
during	*boyunca*	fame	*şöhret*
during	*süresinde*	famous	*meşhur*
each	*tane*	far	*uzakta*
ear	*kulak*	far from	*uzak*
early	*erkenci*	father	*baba*
easily	*kolayca*	fault	*hata*
east	*doğu*	ferry	*vapur*
easy	*kolay*	fever	*ateş*
effective	*tesirli*	fiance or fiancee	*nişanlı*
effort	*çaba*		
eggplant	*patlıcan*	field	*alan*
eggs	*yumurta*	fifteen	*on beş*
eight	*sekiz*	fifth	*beşinci*
eighteen	*on sekiz*	fifty	*elli*
eighth	*sekizinci*	finally	*en son*
eighty	*seksen*	fine	*iyi*
elder brother	*abi*	first	*birinci, ilk, önce*
elder sister	*abla*	five	*beş*
eleven	*on bir*	fluent	*akıcı*
else	*diğer, başka*	folkloric	*folklorik*

folkloric song	*türkü*	gentleman	*beyefendi*
food	*yemek, yiyecek*	German language	*Almanca*
food for breakfast	*kahvaltılık*	German person	*Alman*
for	*için*	Germany	*Almanya*
for a person	*kişilik*	girl or boy	*çocuk*
for instance	*meselâ*	glass	*bardak, cam*
for instance	*örneğin*	gram	*gram*
for minutes	*dakikalarca*	grape	*üzüm*
for now	*şimdilik*	grass	*çimen*
for summer	*yazlık*	green	*yeşil*
for sure	*mutlaka*	green	*yeşillik*
for the moment	*şu anda*	green grocer	*manav*
for winter	*kışlık*	green olive	*yeşil zeytin*
forefinger	*işaret parmağı*	grey	*gri*
forehead	*alın*	guest room	*misafir odası*
foreign	*yabancı*	guitar	*gitar*
foreign language	*yabancı dil*	hair	*saç*
fork	*çatal*	hand	*el*
forty	*kırk*	hand bag	*el çantası*
forward	*ileri*	handsome	*yakışıklı*
four	*dört*	happiness	*mutluluk*
fourteen	*on dört*	happy	*mutlu*
fourth	*dördüncü*	hard	*zor*
France	*Fransa*	hardworking	*çalışkan*
free time	*boş zaman*	hat	*şapka*
French language	*Fransızca*	he	*o*
French person	*Fransız*	head	*baş, kafa*
fresh	*taze*	health	*sağlık*
friend	*dost*	healthy	*sağlıklı*
friendly	*arkadaş canlısı*	heart beat	*kalp atışı*
from inside	*içinden*	heating	*ısıtma*
fruit	*meyve*	helper	*yardımcı*
fuel	*yakıt*	her	*onun*
full	*tam, tok*	here	*burada*
full darkness	*kapkaranlık*	high	*yüksek*
full of	*dolu*	high fever	*yüksek ateş*
furnished	*mobilyalı*	hill	*tepe*
furniture	*mobilya*	his	*onun*
futile	*nafile*	historic	*tarihî*
gang	*çete*	hobby	*hobi*
garden	*bahçe*	hospital	*hastane*
garlic	*sarımsak*	hostess	*hostes*
gasoline	*benzin*	hot	*sıcak*
		hot drink	*sıcak içecek*

hotel	*otel*	Italian person	*İtalyan*
hotel manager	*otel yöneticisi*	Italy	*İtalya*
hour	*saat*	jam	*reçel*
hourly	*saatlik*	Japan	*Japonya*
housewife	*ev hanımı*	Japanese language	*Japonca*
how long?	*ne kadar?*		
how many/much?	*ne kadar?*	Japanese person	*Japon*
how?	*nasıl?*	jewelery store	*kuyumcu*
hungry	*aç*	job	*iş*
I	*ben*	joyful	*neşeli*
I want	*isterim*	junk food	*abur cubur*
ice cream	*dondurma*	justice	*adalet*
identification	*kimlik*	key	*anahtar*
identification card	*kimlik kartı*	kind	*çeşit*
		kind	*kibar*
important	*önemli*	kind	*tür*
impulsive	*fevrî*	kitchen	*mutfak*
in addition	*ayrıca*	ladle	*kepçe*
in elementary school	*ilkokulda*	lady	*hanımefendi*
		large size	*büyük beden*
in fact	*aslında*	last	*sonuncu*
in horror	*dehşet içerisinde*	late	*geç*
In my opinion	*bence*	late	*geç*
in other words	*yani*	later, later on	*sonra*
in the fall	*güzün*	lazy	*tembel*
in the future	*ileride*	leader	*lider*
in the meantime	*bu arada*	left	*sol*
in the middle	*ortada, ortasında*	leg	*bacak*
in the summer	*yazın*	lesson	*ders*
in the winter	*kışın*	lettuce	*marul*
in these days, today	*günümüzde*	lie down	*uzanmak*
		light	*açık*
in your opinion	*sence*	light	*hafif*
inarticulate	*tutuk*	light clothes	*ince kıyafet*
India	*Hindistan*	like	*gibi*
Indian language	*Hintçe*	like this	*böyle*
Indian person	*Hintli*	like this	*şöyle*
information	*bilgi*	lip	*dudak*
inside	*içeride*	liter	*litre*
insurance	*sigorta*	little	*az*
intelligence	*istihbarat*	little	*az*
interesting	*ilginç*	little	*küçük*
internet page	*internet sayfası*	living room	*oturma odası*
intersection	*kavşak*	living room	*salon*
Italian language	*İtalyanca*		

London	*Londra*	narrow	*dar*
long	*uzun*	nation	*ulus*
loud	*sesli*	natural gas boiler	*doğal gazlı kombi*
luggage	*bagaj*		
lunch	*öğle yemeği*	nature	*doğa*
lunch break	*öğle arası*	nature	*tabîat*
lush green	*yemyeşil*	naughty	*yaramaz*
machine	*makine*	nausea	*mide bulantısı*
majestic	*görkemli*	navigation device	*navigasyon cihazı*
man	*adam*		
manager	*yönetici*	near	*yakında*
many	*pek*	necessary	*zorunda*
married	*evli*	need	*ihtiyaç*
match	*maç*	neighbor	*komşu*
meal	*öğün, yemek*	neighborhood	*mahalle*
meat	*et*	nephew	*yeğen*
medium size	*orta beden*	new	*yeni*
melon	*kavun*	news	*haber*
member	*üye*	nice	*güzel*
menu	*menü*	niece	*yeğen*
message	*mesaj*	night	*gece*
metro	*metro*	nine	*dokuz*
middle finger	*orta parmak*	nineteen	*on dokuz*
midnight	*gece yarısı*	ninety	*doksan*
milk	*süt*	ninth	*dokuzuncu*
million	*milyon*	no	*hayır*
mind	*akıl*	noisy	*gürültülü*
mint	*nane*	north	*kuzey*
mirror	*ayna*	nose	*burun*
missing, lacking	*eksik*	notice	*ihbar*
monthly	*aylık*	number	*sayı*
more than	*daha*	nurse	*hemşire*
moreover	*üstelik*	nuts	*çerez*
morning	*sabah*	oasis	*vaha*
mother	*anne*	officially	*resmen*
mouth	*ağız*	old	*eski, yaşlı*
Mr.	*bay, bey*	olives	*zeytin*
Mrs., Ms.	*hanım, bayan*	on the internet	*internet üzerinden*
much	*pek*	on the sideline	*kenarda*
multiplied by	*çarpı*	on time	*zamanında*
museum	*müze*	on top of	*üzerinde*
music	*müzik*	one	*bir*
my	*benim*	one way	*tek sefer, tek yön*
my spouse	*eşim*	onion	*soğan*
nail scissors	*tırnak makası*	only	*sadece*

open	*açık*	pop music	*pop müzik*
opinion	*fikir*	portion	*porsiyon*
opposite	*karşı, zıt*	possible	*mümkün*
or else, etc.	*falan*	preparation	*hazırlık*
orange	*portakal*	prescription	*reçete*
orange	*turuncu*	present	*hediye*
other	*diğer, başka*	price	*fiyat*
otherwise	*aksi takdirde*	price	*ücret*
out of	*dışında*	product	*ürün*
outside	*dışında*	profession	*meslek*
oven	*ocak*	program	*program*
over something	*üstüne*	public transportation	*toplu taşıma*
pain	*acı, ağrı*	pulse	*nabız*
painkiller	*ağrı kesici*	purple	*mor*
pants	*pantolon*	question	*soru*
paper towel, tissue	*peçete*	quiet	*sessiz, sakin*
parade ground	*tören alanı*	raid	*baskın*
parsley	*maydanoz*	rain	*yağmur*
part	*tane, parça*	rainy	*yağmurlu*
passion	*tutku*	rather	*epey, gayet, oldukça, pek*
passport	*pasaport*	ready	*hazır*
pastry	*poğaça*	reality	*gerçek*
patatoes	*patates*	really	*gerçekten*
pear	*armut*	receipt	*fiş*
peach	*şeftali*	recipe	*yemek tarifi*
pepper	*biber*	red	*kırmızı*
permanent	*devamlı, sürekli*	reference number	*referans numarası*
personal	*kişisel*	refrigerator	*buzdolabı*
pharmacist	*eczacı*	relative	*akraba*
pharmacy	*eczane*	relaxing	*dinlendirici*
photograph	*fotoğraf*	religious	*dini*
piano	*piyano*	renting	*kiralama*
pickle	*turşu*	restaurant	*lokanta*
picture	*resim*	restroom	*tuvalet*
piece	*tane, parça*	retired	*emekli*
pilot	*pilot*	reverse	*geri*
pink	*pembe*	rice pudding	*sütlaç*
pistol	*tabanca*	right	*doğru, haklı, sağ*
place	*yer*	right at the	*tam*
plate	*tabak*	right away	*hemen*
pleasure	*zevk*	road	*yol*
plum	*erik*	roll	*dürüm*
poetic	*şiirsel*	roof	*çatı*
police station	*karakol*		

room	oda, yer	sister or brother	kardeş
round trip	gidiş geliş	sister-in-law	yenge
Russia	Rusya	site	mekân
Russian language	Rusça	site	site
		six	altı
Russian person	Rus	sixteen	on altı
sad	mutsuz, üzgün	sixth	altıncı
salad	salata	sixty	altmış
salami	salam	size	beden
salt	tuz	size number	beden numarası
samovar	semaver	skirt	etek
Saudi Arabia	Suudi Arabistan	sleeping room	yatak odası
sausage	sucuk	slice	dilim
scarlet	kızıl	small	küçük
scary movie	korku filmi	small size	küçük beden
school	okul	snack	abur cubur
scrambled eggs	sahanda yumurta	snow	kar
sea	deniz	snowy	karlı
season	mevsim	soap	sabun
second	ikinci	soccer	futbol
secretary	sekreter	socks	çorap
seller	satıcı	sofa	koltuk
serious	ciddî	soft music	hafif müzik
seven	yedi	solution	çare
seventeen	on yedi	some	bazı, biraz
seventh	yedinci	someone	biri
seventy	yetmiş	something	bir şey, bir şeyler
shampoo	şampuan	sometimes	bazen
shaving materials	traş malzemeleri	son	oğul
		song	şarkı
she	o	son-in-law	damat
shelf	raf	soon	birazdan
shirt	gömlek	sour cherry	vişne
shop	dükkân	south	güney
shopping	alışveriş	souvenir shop	hediyelik eşya
shopping cart	alışveriş arabası	Spain	İspanya
short	kısa	Spanish	İspanyolca
side	taraf	Spanish language	İspanyolca
silent	sessiz		
since	o yüzden	Spanish person	İspanyol
sincere	samimi	special	özel
singer	şarkıcı	specialist	uzman
singer (folkloric)	türkücü	spice	baharat
		spoon	kaşık
single	bekâr	spring	bahar
sister	kız kardeş		

spring	*ilk bahar*	third	*üçüncü*
stale	*bayat*	thirteen	*on üç*
standart	*düz*	this (is)	*bu*
still	*hareketsiz*	thought	*düşünce*
stomach	*mide*	thoughtful	*düşünceli*
store	*dükkân*	three	*üç*
story, floor	*kat*	ticket	*bilet*
stove	*fırın*	tired	*yorgun*
straight	*düz*	to (accept) refund	*iade almak*
strange	*tuhaf*	to (apply for the) refund	*iade etmek*
strawberry	*çilek*		
street	*sokak*	to (fever) fall	*ateşi düşmek*
stretcher	*sedye*	to (for the heart) beat	*kalp atmak*
student	*öğrenci*		
studious	*çalışkan*	to (sun) shine	*güneş açmak*
subtracted from	*eksi*	to (wind) blow	*rüzgâr esmek*
successful	*başarılı*	to (wind, snow, or rain) stop	*dinmek*
such	*böylesi*		
sugar	*şeker*	to (wind, snow, or rain) stop	*kesilmek*
summer	*yaz*		
sunny	*güneşli*	to ache	*ağrımak*
surrounding	*etraf*	to agree	*anlaşmak*
sweat	*ter*	to answer	*cevaplamak*
table	*masa*	to apologize	*özür dilemek*
tablet	*hap*	to apply for a hotel reservation	*yer ayırtmak*
tailor	*terzi*		
talkative	*konuşkan*		
task	*görev*	to approach	*yanaşmak*
tea	*çay*	to approve the reservation	*yer ayırmak*
teacher	*öğretmen*		
temporary	*geçici*	to arrange	*düzenlemek*
ten	*on*	to arrest	*tutuklamak*
tenth	*onuncu*	to ask	*sormak*
the beginning of	*baş*	to be	*olmak*
the Bosphorus	*Boğaz*	to be arrested	*tutuklanmak*
the day before yesterday	*evvelsi gün*	to be brewed	*demlenmek*
		to be called	*aranmak*
the same	*aynı*	to be drunk	*içilmek*
there	*orada, orası*	to be eaten	*yenmek*
there is	*mevcut*	to be enough	*yetmek*
there Is / are	*var*	to be found	*bulunmak*
there isn't / aren't	*yok*	to be happy	*sevinmek*
		to be heard	*duyulmak*
they	*onlar*	to be interested in	*ilgilenmek*
things, furniture	*eşya (mobilya)*		
		to be	*iç içe olmak*

intertwined	
to be known	*bilinmek*
to be missed	*özlenmek*
to be moved	*taşınmak*
to be read	*okunmak*
to be recognized	*tanınmak*
to be remembered	*hatırlanmak*
to be sad	*üzülmek*
to be seen	*görülmek*
to be seen by a doctor	*doktora görünmek*
to be sent	*sevk edilmek*
to be sick	*hasta olmak*
to be sold	*satılmak*
to be started	*başlanmak*
to be taken	*alınmak*
to be waited	*beklenmek*
to be wanted	*istenmek*
to be watered	*sulanmak*
to behave	*davranmak*
to boil	*haşlamak*
to brew	*demlemek*
to bring	*getirmek*
to buy	*almak*
to call	*aramak, çağırmak, seslenmek*
to call on the phone	*telefonla aramak*
to capture	*ele geçirmek*
to change mind	*vaz geçmek*
to change, to exchange	*değiştirmek*
to choose	*seçmek*
to chop	*doğramak*
to collect	*toplamak*
to come	*gelmek*
to come to the mind	*aklına gelmek*
to congratulate	*tebrik etmek*
to cool	*soğutmak*
to cough	*öksürmek*
to decide	*karar vermek*
to deliver	*teslim etmek*
to discount	*indirmek*
to do	*etmek*

to do	*yapmak*
to do good	*iyi gelmek*
to draw pictures	*resim çizmek*
to drink	*içmek*
to drive	*sürmek*
to eat	*yemek*
to eat sneaks	*atıştırmak*
to engage in	*girişmek*
to enjoy	*haz almak*
to everywhere	*her yere*
to examine	*muayene etmek*
to exchange	*değişim yapmak*
to explain	*açıklamak*
to feed	*beslemek*
to feel	*hissetmek*
to feel ashamed	*utanmak*
to feel dizzy	*başı dönmek*
to find	*bulmak*
to fire	*kovmak*
to fry	*kızartmak*
to gain advantage	*fayda sağlamak*
to gain weight	*kilo almak*
to get angry	*sinirlenmek*
to get bored	*sıkılmak*
to get cold	*üşümek*
to get fired	*kovulmak*
to get hot	*sıcaklamak*
to get irritated	*rahatsız olmak*
to get off	*inmek*
to get on/in a vehicle	*binmek*
to get tired	*yorulmak*
to get used to	*alışmak*
to get well	*iyileşmek*
to getter	*birlikte*
to give	*teslim etmek, vermek*
to give an answer	*cevap vermek*
to go	*gitmek*
to go down	*inmek*
to go shopping	*alışverişe çıkmak*
to go to bed	*yatmak*
to go up	*çıkmak*
to grow	*yetiştirmek*
to have a	*sohbet etmek*

conversation	
to have a high fever	*ateşi çıkmak*
to have a high fever	*ateşi yükselmek*
to have a warm conversation	*muhabbet etmek*
to have time left	*zamanı kalmak*
to have to	*zorunda kalmak*
to hear	*duymak*
to hear	*işitmek*
to heat	*ısıtmak*
to hide	*gizlemek, saklamak, gizlenmek, saklanmak*
to hope	*ummak*
to insist	*ısrar etmek*
to introduce	*tanışmak*
to join	*birleştirmek*
to know	*bilmek*
to land	*inmek*
to learn	*öğrenmek*
to leave	*ayrılmak, bırakmak*
to light	*yakmak*
to like	*hoşlanmak*
to listen to	*dinlemek*
to live in a place	*oturmak*
to load	*yüklemek*
to look	*bakmak*
to love	*sevmek*
to make a compliment	*iltifat etmek*
to make a difference	*fark etmek*
to make a payment	*ödeme yapmak*
to make arrangements	*düzenleme yapmak*
to make preparations	*hazırlık yapmak*
to make someone feel ashamed	*utandırmak*
to make tired	*yormak*
to match with	*yakışmak*
to mean	*demek*
to measure	*ölçmek*
to meet	*buluşmak, tanışmak*

to meet one's need	*ihtiyacını karşılamak*
to merge	*birleşmek*
to miss, long for	*özlemek*
to move	*hareket etmek*
to move	*taşımak*
to obey	*uymak*
to open	*aralamak*
to order food	*sipariş etmek*
to park	*park etmek*
to pass	*geçmek*
to pay	*ödemek*
to pay attention	*dikkat etmek*
to perspire	*terlemek*
to play	*çalmak*
to point at	*doğrultmak*
to prefer	*tercih etmek*
to prepare	*hazırlamak*
to put	*koymak, yerleştirmek*
to rain	*yağmur yağmak*
to read	*okumak*
to recognize	*tanımak*
to recover from an illness	*geçmek*
to remember	*hatırlamak*
to rent	*kiralamak*
to repair	*tamir etmek*
to resist	*direnmek*
to rest	*dinlenmek*
to return	*dönmek*
to return	*geri dönmek*
to review	*göz gezdirmek*
to run away	*kurtulmak*
to satisfy	*ihtiyacını karşılamak*
to say, to tell	*demek, söylemek, anlatmak*
to scratch	*kaşımak*
to see	*görmek*
to sell	*satmak*
to send	*göndermek*
to send best regards	*selâm söylemek*
to set up	*kurmak*
to settle	*yerleşmek*
to sing	*şarkı söylemek*
to sit	*oturmak*

to slice	*dilimlemek*	to wish	*dilemek*
to smash	*çökertmek*	to wonder	*merak etmek*
to snow	*kar yağmak*	to worry	*endişelenmek*
to spend time	*geçirmek*	to wrap	*sarmak*
to split	*ayırmak*	to write	*yazmak*
to spoil	*şımartmak*	to write a prescription	*ilaç yazmak*
to stand up	*kalkmak*		
to stand up	*dikilmek*	today	*bugün*
to start	*başlamak*	toilet paper	*tuvalet kâğıdı*
to start doing something	*koyulmak*	tomatoes	*domates*
		tomb	*kabir*
to start moving	*hareketlenmek*	tomorrow	*yarın*
to startle	*irkilmek*	too	*de /da*
to stay	*kalmak*	too	*bir de*
to stay apart	*ayrı kalmak*	too many	*fazla*
to stay in a hotel	*oda tutmak*	too much	*fazla*
		tooth brush	*diş fırçası*
to stay up	*yatmamak*	tooth paste	*diş macunu*
to support	*desteklemek, tutmak*	total	*toplam*
to take	*almak, götürmek*	touristic	*turistik*
to take a glance	*göz atmak*	tradition	*âdet*
to take a short trip	*biraz gezmek*	transmission	*vites*
		trip	*seyahat*
to take a trip	*gezmek*	troath	*boğaz*
to take medicine	*ilaç almak, ilaç yutmak*	Turk	*Türk*
		Türkiye	*Türkiye*
to take photographs	*fotoğraf çekmek*	Turkish language	*Türkçe*
to think	*düşünmek*		
to throw	*atmak*	tv series	*dizi*
to throw up	*çıkarmak, istifra etmek, kusmak*	twelve	*on iki*
		twenty	*yirmi*
to transfer	*aktarma yapmak*	two	*iki*
to transport	*taşımak*	ud	*ud*
to tremble	*titremek*	ugly	*çirkin*
to trouble	*sorun etmek*	uncle	*amca*
to try	*denemek*	underwear	*iç çamaşırı*
to try to find	*aramak*	unfounded	*asılsız*
to turn	*kıvrılmak*	unfurnished	*mobilyasız*
to uncover the upper body	*üzerini çıkarmak*	university	*üniversite*
		unoccupied	*boş*
to visit	*ziyaret etmek*	unsavory	*lezzetsiz*
to wait	*beklemek*	unsuccessful	*başarısız*
to want	*istemek*	until	*kadar*
to watch	*izlemek, seyretmek*	urine test	*idrar tahlili*
to water	*sulamak*	vacation	*tatil*

valid	geçerli	whole	bütün
various	farklı	why?	neden?
vegetable	sebze	wide	geniş
vehicle	araç	widespread	yaygın
very	çok, gayet, oldukça	widow	dul
vicinity	civar	wind	rüzgâr
view	manzara	window	cam, pencere
violin	keman	windy	rüzgârlı
waist	bel	winter	kış
waiter	garson	with	ile
walking distance	yürüme mesafesi	with a little sugar	orta
wallet or purse	cüzdan	with sugar	şekerli
war	savaş	without sugar and milk	sade
warehouse	depo		
warm	ılık	woman	kadın
warm clothes	kalın kıyafet	wonderful	harika
water	su	work	iş
watermelon	karpuz	working shift	mesâi
we	biz	world	dünya
weak	halsiz	wrong	yanlış
weather	hava	wthout sugar	şekersiz
wedding	düğün	x-ray	röntgen
week	hafta	yearly	yıllık
weekly	haftalık	yellow	sarı
well	güzel	yes	evet
west	batı	yesterday	dün
wet	ıslak	yogurt	yoğurt
what?	ne?	you	sen
which?	hangisi?	you (pl)	siz
white	ak	young	genç
white	beyaz	youngster	genç
white cheese	beyaz peynir	zero	sıfır

Expressions

(Benim) Adım ...	*My name is ...*	**Çok şükür!**	*Thanks God!*
(Sen) Kimsin?	*Who are you?*	**Çok teşekkürler!**	*Thanks a lot!*
(Siz) Kimsiniz?	*Who are you (pl)?*	**çok uluslu**	*multinational*
Aaa!	*What!*	**dalga geçmek**	*to make fun of*
acaba	*I wonder*	**doğru dürüst**	*properly*
Açım.	*I'm hungry.*	**Doğru!**	*Right!, Correct!*
Aferin!	*Good job!*	**duyar duymaz**	*not later than*
Affedersiniz!	*Excuse me!*	**Eline sağlık!**	*Good job!, Bless your hands!*
avuç içi kadar	*as small as a palm (very few or little)*	**Eminim ki,**	*I'm sure that*
ayağa kalkmak	*to stand up*	**Erkenci miyiz?**	*Are we early?*
Aynen öyle!	*Just like that!*	**Eşim İngiliz.**	*My wife / husband is English.*
Aynı zamanda	*At the same time*	**fazla tepki vermek**	*to overreact*
Ayrıca	*In addition*		
Bak!	*Look!*	**Fiyatta da ayrıca bir kolaylık yaparız.**	*We'll make an extra discount on the price.*
baş köşe	*the best place in the room*		
baştan aşağı	*all over*	**Geç kaldık.**	*We're late?*
Ben de memnun oldum!	*Nice to meet you, too!*	**Geçmiş olsun.**	*Get well soon.*
		Gideriz.	*Let's go./We'll go.*
bence	*in my opinion*	**göz gözü görmemek**	*to be unable to see anything*
Benim ismim ...	*My name is ...*		
bir sebep yüzünden	*for a reason*	**gözlerinden yaşlar akmak**	*to have tears in the eyes*
bir şeyden olmak	*to lose something*	**gözünü kocaman açmak**	*to open the eyes wide (to get shocked)*
Biz yabancı mıyız?	*We're close to each other, not strangers.*		
		Güle güle oturun.	*Stay in good health.*
Bu kim?	*Who is he/she?*	**Günaydın!**	*Good morning!*
bugüne özel	*special for today*	**gururu incinmek**	*to feel his pride is hurt*
bununla kalmamak	*not to stop there*	**Hadi! / Haydi!**	*Come on!*
Buyur!	*Go on!*	**Haklısın.**	*You're right./ It's a good idea.*
Buyurun!	*Welcome!, Please!, Come in!, Tell me!, Go on, I'm up to you!, or After you!*	**Harika!**	*Excellent!*
		havaya girmek	*to get in the mood*
		Hepsi o kadar	*Is that all?*

mı?	
Herşey yolunda.	*Everything is fine.*
Hesabı alabilir miyim lütfen?	*Can I take the account/bill please?*
hızlı ve kesik nefes alıp vermek	*to breathe fast and shallow*
Hoş bulduk!	*Thank you! (In response to Hoş geldiniz!)*
Hoşçakalın!	*Goodbye!*
İşte garson da geliyor.	*Here comes the waiter.*
istiyorum	*I want*
İyi ki,	*Fortunately,*
İyiyim.	*I'm fine.*
kaça?	*how much?*
kaçacak bir gedik aramak	*to look for a place to hide*
kalbi yerinden fırlamak	*to get shocked*
Kapalıçarşı	*the Grand Bazaar*
Kesinlikle!	*Absolutely!*
Keşke	*I wish*
Kim arıyor?	*Who's calling?*
kimseye gözükmeden	*without being seen by anyone*
Korkacak bir şey yok.	*There's nothing to be afraid of.*
kramp girmek	*to have a cramp*
küfür etmek	*to swear, to curse*
Kullandıkça bizi hatırlayın.	*Remember us when using it.*
Kusura bakma.	*Excuse me.*
Kusura bakmayın!	*Excuse me!, Excuse us!*
Lütfen!	*Please!*
Malesef!	*Unfortunately!*
Memnun oldum!	*Nice to meet you!*

Merhaba!	*Hello!*
N'olur n'olmaz!	*Just in case!*
Nasıl olur?	*How come?*
Nasıl yani?	*How come?*
Nasılsın?	*How are you?*
Ne bakıyorsunuz?	*What do you want to take?*
Ne dersin?	*What do you think?*
Ne gerek vardı?	*You shouldn't have done it.*
Ne heyecanlı!	*How exciting!*
Ne iş yapıyorsun?	*What do you do (for a living)? (lit. What job do you do?)*
ne kadar olur?	*how much?*
Ne oldu ki?	*What happened?*
Ne olduğunu kestirmek	*to guess what's going on*
Ne olmuştu yani?	*So what happened?*
Ne olsun be?	*Everything is fine.*
ne olup bittiğini	*what's going on*
Ne yazık ki,	*Unfortunately,*
Ne zahmeti?	*It's not a big thing.*
Neden zahmet ettiniz?	*Why did you do that?*
nefesini tutmak	*to hold the breath*
nefretle yüzünü ekşitmek	*to make a wry face with hatred*
Nerede?	*Where?*
Neredensiniz?	*Where are you from?*
Nerelisin?	*Where are you from?*
of çekmek	*to heave a sigh*
olay çözmek	*to solve a case*
olayın çözülmesi	*solution of a case*
Önden buyur lütfen!	*After you!*
Onun adı ...	*His/her name is ...*

Onun adı ne?	*What's his/her name?*	**Tabii ki!**	*Sure!*
Osmanlı dönemi	*the Ottoman period*	**tam anlamıyla**	*literally*
Oteldenim.	*I'm from the hotel.*	**tam zamanında**	*just in time*
Pek değil!	*Not much!*	**Tamam!**	*Alright!, Okay!*
Pekâlâ!	*Well!*	**Tanıştığımıza memnun oldum!**	*Nice to meet you!*
Peki!	*Well, alright!*		
pür dikkat kesilmek	*to pay close attention*	**terk etmek**	*to leave a place*
		Tokum.	*I'm full.*
pusu kurmak	*to ambush*	**Türkiye'ye hoş geldiniz!**	*Welcome to Türkiye!*
saçma sapan	*nonesense*		
Sen?	*You? / What about you?*	**Üzgünüm!**	*I'm sorry*
		Üzgünüm.	*I'm sorry.*
Senin adın ne?	*What's your name?*	**utanç kaynağı**	*embarrassment*
Seninle aynı fikirdeyim.	*I agree with you.*	**Ya sen?**	*And you? / What about you?*
Size lâyık değil ama ...	*It's too little for you but ...*	**Ya!?**	*How exciting!*
		Ya?	*What about?*
Size nasıl yardımcı olabilirim?	*How can I help you?*	**Yani**	*So*
		yanlış anlamak	*to misunderstand*
soğuk soğuk terlemek	*to sweat cold (to be afraid of something)*	**Yeriz.**	*Let's eat./We'll eat.*
		yönünde olmak	*to point*
Sonuç olarak,	*As a result,*	**yürütülen çalışmalar**	*studies carried out*
Sorun değil!	*No problem!*		
Şöyle bir bakmak.	*to take a glance*	**yüzünü ekşitmek**	*to grimace*
		zihninden geçirmek	*to think*
Şükür Kavuşturana.	*Thanks God.*		

As a further reading material and an entertaining Turkish novel, I recommend my daughter's newly published book.

Osman iyice kendinden geçmeye başlamıştı. Sesi gittikçe yükseliyordu ve artık yağmurun ortasında bağırmaya başlamıştı.
- Kimsin sen? Kimsin? Konuş!
- Ben senim.
- Saçma sapan konuşma! Ben zaten benim. Sen kimsin, kim?!
- Ben senin içindeyim Osman. Hep içindeydim, hep içinde olacağım.
- Böyle bir şey olamaz. İmkânsız. Dalga geçme benimle.
- Peki, o zaman. Beni duyuyorsun değil mi? Ama beni göremiyorsun. Neredeyim ben? Hadi bul beni.
Osman etrafına öyle bakışlarla baktı ki burada kelimeler kifayetsiz. Uzun, dar, karanlık ve ıslak bir sokakta yapayalnızdı. Pencereden niçin bağırdığını merak edip ona bakan küçük bir çocuk ve yaşlı bir teyzeden başka kimseyi göremiyordu. Fakat Lütfi'nin sesi oradaydı."

Edindiği tek arkadaşından saçma bir yanlış anlaşılma nedeniyle ayrılmak zorunda kalan üniversite öğrencisi Osman'ın hayatı, bir tek kendisinin duyup görebildiği Lütfi ile tanışmasının ardından tahmin edilmesi güç maceralara sürüklenir.
İpin Ucunu Kaçıran İnsanlar, okumak için başka bir kente gelmiş içe dönük ve hayalperest bir gencin, birbirinden garip olasılıklara kapı aralayan yaşamını yer yer romantik ve kimi zaman da tüm sert gerçekliğiyle okuyucuya sunmaktadır.

The book was published in Türkiye in November, 2020. You can order the paperback from any bookseller in Türkiye. You can also obtain an e-book version of the book.

Other supporting material

In this book, you will find 29 short texts, the funny and witty anecdotes of Nasreddin Hodja, and develop your reading and understanding of Turkish. Nasreddin Hodja stories are fun to read, sometimes including double meanings, and at times pretty straightforward. But this is not all for these stories; these stories are cultural phenomenon. Every Turk is familiar with at least one anecdote of Hodja. Every Turk loves to use one of Hodja's witty jokes. These anecdotes find their way to our daily language and encounters. When used in conversation, Nasreddin Hodja anecdotes bring joy and prestige to the conversation. Many cultural elements present in the stories are still relevant to this day, making them a valuable source of getting to know the people and the culture of Türkiye.

This Learners' Dictionary is designed for Turkish learners at the intermediate and advanced levels only. So, it should be noted that all meanings and variations of the words may not be included.

This Learners' Dictionary is designed to avoid unnecessary subjects, words, or phrases. So that, you could save your precious time and get directly to the point.

Please check out other Turkish self -study books of the author.